ADAMS

Streetwise

Small Business Start-Up

Your comprehensive guide to starting and managing a business

by Bob Adams

ADAMS MEDIA CORPORATION
HOLBROOK, MASSACHUSETTS

ACKNOWLEDGMENTS

The author thanks the many people who have helped create, produce, and review the material in this book and related CD-ROM, including: John Adams, Javier Amador-Peña, Elise Bauman, Jim Beardsley, Larry Carleton, Chris Ciaschini, Chris Cruz, Howard Davis, Susan Tyrell Donelan, Jim Donnelly, Ewa Erdman, Tracy Fitzsimmons, Judi Hershman, Cheryl McKeary, Frank Micciche, Tom Nickel, Stefan Pagacik, Richard Perkett, Zick Rubin, Art Schnure, Elizabeth Seaman, Aryana Soebagjo, Peter Sylvan, Allan Tatel, Bill Thorpe, Betsy Tomlinson, Levin Waters V, Sarah White, and Greg Wyler. In addition, I thank all the employees of Adams Media Corporation for their invaluable help, support and devotion in building this successful business.

Published by Adams Media Corporation
260 Center Street, Holbrook, Massachusetts 02343

ISBN: 1-55850-581-4

Printed in the United States of America.

J   I   H   G   F   E   D   C

Library of Congress Cataloging-in-Publication Data
Adams, Bob, 1955–
Adams Streetwise small business start-up / by Bob Adams.
p.   cm.
Includes index.
ISBN 1-55850-581-4 (pb)
1. Small business—Management. 2. New business enterprises. I. Title.
HD62.7.A3   1995
658.02'2—dc20   95-53135
CIP

Adams Streetwise, Adams Streetwise Small Business Start-Up, and Adams Media Corporation are trademarks of Adams Media Corporation.
All other products and names mentioned are trademarks of their respective companies. PhotoDisc™ Images ©1996, PhotoDisc, Inc.

This publication is designed to provide accurate and authoritative information with regard to the subject matter covered.
It is sold with the understanding that the publisher is not engaged in rendering legal, accounting, or other professional advice. If legal advice or other expert assistance is required, the services of a competent professional person should be sought.
— From a *Declaration of Principles* jointly adopted by a Committee of the American Bar Association and a Committee of Publishers and Associations.

This book is available at quantity discounts for bulk purchases. For further information, call 1-800-872-5627 (in Massachusetts, call 617-767-8100). Multi-media versions of this text are available in CD-ROM form for Windows or Macintosh. Check your local retailer, or call 1-800-872-5627 (in Massachusetts, call 617-767-8100).

Visit our home page at http://www.adamsmedia.com

Book design by Amy C. Thompson
Front and rear cover photos by Bob Frangioso of Frangioso Studio.

Table of Contents

1 STRATEGY

- Adams' Rules for Small Business Success 3
- Ideas for New Businesses 5
- Buying a Business 12
- Franchising 16
- Company Strategy 20
- Business Plan 28
- Growth 51
- Selling a Business 56

2 MARKETING

- Positioning 67
- Marketing Plans 73
- Cheap Marketing Tricks 86
- Publicity 89
- Point of Sale 102
- Literature 103
- Trade Shows 104
- Competing with Giants 111

3 SALES

- Choices 121
- Face-to-Face Selling 123
- Telemarketing 128
- Independent Sales Representatives 136
- Internet Marketing 142
- Wholesalers, Distributors, and Importers ... 144
- Fax Marketing 148
- Exporting 149

4 ADVERTISING

- Choices 157
- Direct Mail 167
- Newspaper Advertising 176
- Magazine Advertising 181
- Yellow Pages Advertising 187
- Radio Advertising 193
- Television Advertising 199
- Outdoor and Transit Advertising 203

San Francisco

Table of Contents

5 PEOPLE

- Making Work Fun! 211
- Hiring 213
- Performance Reviews 228
- Compensation 237
- Problem Employees 245
- Firing 251
- Leadership 259
- Policies 262

6 MONEY

- Basic Accounting 269
- Pro Formas 281
- Credit 292
- Purchasing 300
- Taxes 305
- Getting Money! 310
- Cash Is King! 317
- Money Problems 322

7 LEGAL

- Sole Proprietorship 331
- Partnership 333
- Corporation 336
- Employment Issues 347
- Staying Out of Court 354
- Contracts 358
- Intellectual Property 361
- Fair Selling 363

8 OFFICE

- Home Office 367
- Commercial Office 373
- Equipment 378
- Getting Organized 383
- Successful Time Management 386
- Conducting Meetings 389
- Customer Service 392
- Tips on Negotiating 393
- Common and costly mistakes of small business owners 397
- Index 399

Starting a small business may be easier than you think. You don't necessarily need a lot of money, time, or experience, or even a great idea!

I started all of my eleven businesses with $2,000 or less. I seldom had any prior experience in any of the businesses I started, and some I successfully got up and running in the few weeks of my summer or winter vacation from college. They included two map businesses, a boat brokerage firm, a housepainting business, and a bicycle rental firm.

There are many excellent business opportunities available today that you can start part time without even quitting your full-time job. Even my current business—Adams Media Corporation, a $10 million dollar book/software publisher—is one that I started part time in my basement apartment with $2,000 and no related experience.

While some businesses require more expertise than others, there are plenty of businesses that you can start with minimal or even no skills and experience. Your ultimate success will probably have a lot more to do with your drive and will to succeed than with the knowledge you bring to your business.

You can always pick up the necessary knowledge along the way. Throughout this book, I'm going to give you every bit of advice that I can, including a lot of streetwise advice that I often learned the hard way . . . by making mistakes.

If you're considering starting a business but arc not sure, my advice is simple—go ahead, take a chance! You only live once!

> *Starting a new business doesn't always require a lot of time, money, or experience!*

Bob Adams
Founder and President
Adams Media Corporation

S·T·R·A·T·E·G·Y 1

Adams' Rules for Small Business Success ▶ **3**

Ideas for New Businesses ▶ **5**

Buying a Business ▶ **12**

Franchising ▶ **16**

Company Strategy ▶ **20**

Business Plans ▶ **28**

Growth ▶ **51**

Selling a Business ▶ **56**

Regardless of whether you manage a business by yourself from your basement or a global conglomerate, success is going to come a lot easier if you have a simple strategy backed up by a detailed plan that you update at least once a year.

Adams' Rules for Small Business Success

Have a clear-cut strategy!

1 A good strategy immediately distinguishes your business from those of your competitors, and gives your customers a solid reason for choosing to do business with you.

A good strategy should be developed after considering the market, customer needs, the competition, and your business's relative strengths and weaknesses. While the strengths of large, established competitors may seem overwhelming—such as deep financial resources and an established customer base—any new firm has built-in advantages too, such as more flexibility and the knowledge of how existing firms have already positioned themselves in the marketplace.

Many small businesses try to be all things to all people—which is really having no strategy at all! Even if you do everything else right . . . it will be much harder, if not impossible, to succeed in business if you don't have a decisive strategy!

Test your advertising!

2 Having bought advertising in every media from TV to subway cards, and having sold advertising for the newspapers, magazines, and phone books that I published, I have seen plenty of successful businesses built largely on the power of advertising. But creating successful advertising is a lot trickier than it may appear. Even the largest corporations and the most prestigious ad agencies find it difficult to create advertising that consistently works. So whether you're starting a company or managing an established one, don't spend a lot of money until you are sure that you have found a marketing mix that works for you!

With whatever advertising method you choose, you can greatly increase your chances of success with what I call "cheap marketing tricks," such as new customer specials, coupons, trial offers, events, exclusive offerings, giveaways, and more. Save the image advertising for big, rich corporations—small business advertising should focus completely on leading customers directly to action today!

Follow a plan and a budget!

3 Develop a plan before you start your business and update it at least once each year. A plan and a budget help you attain higher goals than if you just plugged away at your business one day at a time. If your company starts to go in the wrong direction, a plan and a budget will provide an early-warning system and help get you back on track.

You don't need accounting experience to set up a budget—but you do need to be very meticulous in projecting and recording each expense and every sale.

Guard your cash like King Midas!

4 As a small business owner, you are going to be fighting a constant battle to hold onto your cash. Overruns in start-up costs, lower-than-anticipated profit margins, and sales that grow slower than expected are among the most common cash drains on new businesses. Even established, highly profitable, fast-growing businesses often run out of cash because of the need to finance growing inventories and customer receivables.

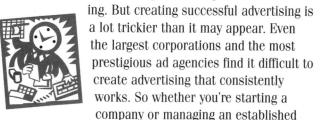

You will also find that well-meaning employees will constantly be suggesting new ways to spend or invest your precious cash. You are going to have to pull in the reins and say "NO. NO. NO." to the many different demands on your money. You need to learn to project cash flow with a fair degree of accuracy. If you don't become disciplined in controlling your cash, you can get into trouble very quickly.

Watch your profit margins!

Many small businesses focus too much on sales and not enough on profit margins. And many underprice their goods and services. Can you increase your prices? Even if you can, it's crucial to keep your costs down!

Let's say you have a profit margin of 5 percent. If you're able to lower your overall costs by just 5 percent, you can *double your profits*! But to raise profits the same amount by increasing sales you would have to increase sales by 100 percent! A small change in your cost structure can go a long way toward improving your profit margins.

Treat your people right!

Virtually all employees want to work hard to help your business succeed. Treat them right, show interest in them, and compliment their every success. You'll be much more likely to not only retain them, but to keep them motivated too! Otherwise a lot of money and time can be wasted hiring and training new hires.

Beware the friendly salesperson!

Once you open your small business, you are instantly going to be a prime target for every salesperson within calling range. New business owners often have a hard time saying "No," until they get burned buying something they don't need. Salespeople are not there to help you! They are there to separate you from your cash! Chances are that when you are starting or running a small business, you need your cash a lot more than you need what they are selling.

Worship your customers, but don't give away the store!

It is important to create good products and run an efficient business, but you also need to be responsive to the needs of customers—even when doing so may sometimes require changing the way you are currently doing business. Listen to your customers' comments, and do what you can to give them what they want. But don't give away the store! Be sure that at least over a period of time, you are realizing a good profit with every customer, no matter how much they spend!

Have fun!

Just because many other businesses are boring, stale, routine places to work doesn't mean that your business has to be too! Make work fun, exciting, and challenging for your employees, and you'll find that in addition to happier people you'll have less turnover and higher productivity. Besides—*you* just might have a little more fun too!

Ideas for New Businesses

Retail

Don't be tempted to start a retail store just because you find a cute, affordable space. Location means everything in retail and a good location usually costs a lot of money. In fact, a super location, good signage, and an attractive storefront may be all the marketing you need.

- Computers
- Office supplies
- Software
- Luggage
- Maps
- Rare books
- Flowers
- Candles
- Jewelry
- Pets
- Appliances
- Ice cream
- Wine
- Baked goods
- Auto parts
- Coffee and tea
- Children's clothes
- Paper goods
- Sporting goods
- Medical equipment

Secondhand stores

A secondhand store can provide a reasonable income with minimal investment and minimal risk. Buy used items cheap enough so you can mark them up at least 100 percent. If you are considering selling expensive items like cars, consider selling on consignment—never actually taking ownership of the items, but displaying and selling them for a hefty cut of the sales price.

- Cars
- Furniture
- Office equipment
- Computers
- Books
- Boats
- Antiques
- Industrial equipment
- Auto parts
- Formal dresses
- Baby clothes
- Medical equipment
- Televisions
- Musical instruments
- Electronic games
- Auto parts
- Phone systems
- Sports equipment
- CDs
- Lawn care equipment

Ideas for New Businesses

Services

Service businesses offer a lot of advantages, especially for start-ups. They tend to be local and you usually don't have to compete with as many heavily financed national or international corporations as you might in a retail, wholesale, or manufacturing business. Service businesses also require less capital. You don't need to finance a large inventory or work-in-progress, and customers can usually be asked to pay immediately upon completion of the work.

- Blade sharpening
- Manicuring
- Athletic recruiting
- Funeral home
- Mobile disc jockey
- Hot-air balloon rides
- Tour packaging
- Portrait photography
- Temporary employment
- Resume service
- Telemarketing
- Window washing
- Chimney sweeping
- Carpet cleaning
- Lawn care service
- Bungee jumping instruction
- Wake-up service
- Dance instruction
- Trophy engraving
- Monogramming service

Restaurants

Restaurants have a high failure rate. Steady, loyal patronage may take years to build up. Owners of successful restaurants usually have extensive restaurant experience, work endless hours, and either rely on their large, close-knit families for assistance or have a knack for attracting, retaining, and motivating good kitchen and service staff.

- Deli
- Food service
- Espresso bar
- Seafood
- Gourmet ice cream
- Family style
- Steak house
- Sushi
- Mexican
- Sports bar
- Chinese
- Vegetarian
- Bagel
- Indian
- Thai
- Greek
- Italian
- Catering
- Pizza
- Pushcart

Ideas for New Businesses

Consultancies

A consultancy is a great opportunity if you have many years of in-depth and specialized expertise that is in high demand. Those consultants who tend to be more successful are those who are in the later stages of their careers, have developed a rich network of contacts and references in their industry, and don't mind working alone.

- Meteorological
- Engineering
- Customs
- Noise control
- Government controls
- Disability
- Child development
- Wellness
- Gerontology
- Forensics
- Medical management
- Nutrition
- Food manufacturing
- Gardening
- College
- Relocation
- Marketing
- Small business
- Employee benefits
- Database

Rentals

Rentals are not as easy a way to make money as you might think. On the income side, the typically modest rental fees don't seem to amount to much. On the expense side, you've got marketing costs, repair and maintenance costs, expensive liability insurance, and theft costs. One positive note—periodic sales of rental items might net more than you paid for them new!

- Automobiles
- Televisions
- Furniture
- Office equipment
- Carpeting
- Lock boxes
- Storage facilities
- Party equipment
- Vacation homes
- Bicycles
- Musical instruments
- AV equipment
- Computers
- Videotapes
- Copy machines
- Outdoor furniture
- Tuxedos
- Limousines
- Carpet cleaners
- Arcade games

Ideas for New Businesses

Wholesale

If you're thinking about opening a wholesale business, think twice! While it's easy and quick to reach a high level of sales, you'll find it difficult to make money and keep afloat. Most wholesalers operate on very thin profit margins that are possible only because of highly sophisticated computer systems and extremely efficient warehouse and selling systems, tight credit and collections control, and most of all, a large volume of sales over which to spread overhead.

- Industrial supplies
- Textiles
- Retail equipment
- Food items
- Herbal products
- Restaurant equipment
- Footwear
- Luggage
- Sports equipment
- Vending machines
- Computers
- Appliances
- Educational software
- Coffee
- Carpets
- Clothing
- Office supplies
- Books
- Tapes
- Flowers

Advertising

Publishing a magazine, newspaper, or other vehicle to sell advertising space is very tempting because the profit margins can be very high. But, no matter how good your product, advertising never sells itself. Save up a lot of energy, and a lot of money for paying good salespeople.

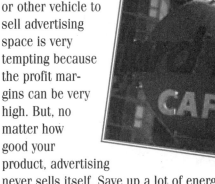

- Classified ads
- Handbills
- Magazines
- Videotext
- Drive-by broadcasting
- Hotel information systems
- Mall kiosks
- Taxis
- Public transportation
- Subway systems
- Radio
- Broadcast television
- Cable television
- Yellow pages
- Card decks
- Giveaways
- Billboards
- Trade show handouts
- Pens
- Stickers

Streetwise Advice on New Business Ideas

☞ **Competitive advantage**

Almost any business you start will have competition. When choosing a business, take into consideration what you will be able to offer customers that provides a significant advantage over your competition's offering. Stress this advantage in your sales and marketing strategy from day one—whether it's faster service, better selection, lower prices, better quality, or whatever else potential customers for your product or service may really care about.

☞ **The competition**

How tough is the competition in the market you are considering? Maybe the same concept would fare better in a nearby market or in another related product or service niche. Remember, the only time you can "choose" your competitors is *before* you start a business.

☞ **Market size**

You need to consider the size of your potential market, especially if you are considering a local, specialized business. Are there enough collectors in the vicinity to support a dollhouse collector's store? Is the local market large enough to support another full-service Mexican restaurant?

☞ **Hobbies often stay hobbies**

A lot of people may advise you to consider hobbies when looking at options for a business theme. Do this cautiously. While there certainly are exceptions to this rule, many hobby-based businesses fail to realize the sales or profitability that their founder-hobbyist anticipated. One reason for this is that many hobbies have very narrow and extremely segmented audiences. Another is that there are often an abundance of talented people in any hobbyist industry, people who are content to sacrifice a higher potential income in another field just to be able to work at something they truly enjoy. In other words, your competition may be stiff.

☞ **Economies of scale**

Unless you plan a major public offering on a public stock exchange, you will probably be starting a relatively small business. Avoid industries in which you would be competing directly with firms that have a significant market advantage in terms of their size alone.

☞ **Related field**

If you don't go into business in a field you know extremely well, you are going to be in for a long uphill struggle. Not only will you be facing a problem all start-up businesses face—established competition—but your competition will know the business a lot better than you do. If you really want to go into business in a field that is not directly related to your past experiences, education, or expertise, you should at least consider buying a franchise.

"If you don't go into business in a field you know extremely well, you are going to be in for a long uphill struggle."

Questions & Answers on New Business Ideas

I definitely want to start a business, but I have no idea what type of business I should choose.

Wait. Hold onto your job before you have firmly decided on a particular business and established a solid plan for starting your business. You will be investing a large amount of money, time, and energy in this business—so don't rush the process. Be sure that you are not going to say "I wish I had started a bowling alley instead," six weeks after you open a pizza parlor!

I want a nice income from my business, but not huge risks . . . any ideas?

Consider a service business. Generally service businesses require less investment than other kinds of businesses. Retail, wholesale, and manufacturing businesses require large investments in some combination of inventory, raw materials, finished goods, receivables, equipment, space leases, and/or leasehold improvements.

Service businesses are also less likely to get clobbered by powerful national firms. And profit margins can be sky-high, even with a relatively small level of sales.

With a service business you are less likely to become a billionaire, but you are also less likely to end up flipping hamburgers for someone else after your business fails!

I have a new business idea that is so great that I don't want to tell anyone about it. Should I keep it a secret?

First, let me assure you that there are literally millions of ideas for new businesses floating around and you can't be paranoid about people stealing your particular idea. It is unlikely that any people hearing of your idea will become so excited about it that they will junk their current work pursuits to pursue it.

Also, you should be asking for feedback on your ideas, preferably from potential customers, before you invest your life savings in a new business. And, you will need to be able to tell investors, lenders, employers, and suppliers about your idea or they will not be able to provide support, services, and/or backing for your business.

While it is conceivable that your idea is so strong that you may create the next Microsoft or Wal-Mart, chances are overwhelming that a company based on your idea is going to be a lot riskier than a company based on an existing business that you are trying to execute with a new twist.

How can I quickly learn more about a business I am considering starting?

There is no substitute for working in the business. Even if you work for a very short period of time in an entry-level capacity you are going to get a much better grasp of how that business works than you would through research or reading.

For example, I decided to start a newspaper while I was in college. Instead of waiting several years to work my way through each position on a newspaper staff, I worked for five days as a proofreader. Proofreading a newspaper is not much different or more fun than proofing a term paper, but it placed me in the middle of a working newspaper office. It allowed me the time to observe the more interesting and important work that everyone else was doing. I was able to start up my newspaper with a working knowledge base, as well as the help of some very motivated, but equally inexperienced friends.

An alternative approach, if you are buying a business, is to have the seller work with you for a short period of time to show you how things are run. Be sure to write any such understanding into the purchase and sales agreement, including holding back part of the payment until you have learned how to run the business.

You can also contact the trade association connected with your industry and see if it offers any seminars or has information packets about getting started in that particular business.

Should I keep my full-time job when I start a new business?

If you have a good job and are starting a relatively small and simple business, I would strongly suggest you keep your existing job while starting your business. In a fairly uncomplicated business, such as a lawn care service or local retail store, you can hire hourly workers to do the core work during business hours for less than you are earning in your full-time job. Then you can do the more critical work, such as quoting jobs or developing promotional schemes at night or on weekends. The cash flow of a new business invariably starts slowly and tends to be more erratic than most people anticipate. Holding onto a salaried job can really help you make it through the slow seasons typical of a new business.

My grandfather actually started his shoe factory, by no means a simple business, while retaining his full-time job as a sales manager for another shoe firm. He even got his boss to finance his new venture!

Is starting a business a good time to relocate?

Relocating a business can be very expensive in both terms of cash outlay and disruption to the operation of the business. It can also be psychologically and physically draining to relocate and start up a business at the same time. In addition, you won't have the time to develop new friendships, network, and create the community ties that are often so necessary to business success. I suggest that you relocate only if there are strong business reasons to do so.

In starting a business that serves the local market, you need to consider how you are going to successfully compete with existing firms. Remember that once you enter the marketplace, existing firms may very well react and copy all or part of your marketing strategy. So it may be wise to consider relocating to a less competitive marketplace.

If you are starting a firm that will serve a national market, you may want to relocate to a state that is hospitable to business in general. While taxes, utility rates, and bureaucratic red tape may not be a big factor as you start your business, they could become more significant as your business grows.

The advantage of buying a successful business in comparison to starting a new one can be overwhelming. Perhaps the biggest plus is that a huge amount of risk and uncertainty is eliminated. There are not only existing customers, but a track record of what is selling and what isn't. And, since the basic business infrastructure is already in place, you can focus on improving the existing business, rather than on reinventing the wheel.

Customers

The most important asset you may acquire in buying a business are the customers. Even with a great product or service, building clientele can take time. Be sure the customers are satisfied and that they will remain loyal to the business after the current owners have sold out.

Employees

Identify and assess the value of all key employees. Arrange to meet with them. Ask yourself: How critical are the current employees to the business? Do the salespeople have strong relationships with key customers? Would a particular engineer's or designer's talents be difficult to replace? How important is the role of the current owner? You might even consider offering incentives to certain employees to assure that they will remain with the business at least through the transition period.

Facilities

Leases are not an integral part of the balance sheet yet they can be a tremendous hidden liability. Find out if the current owner personally guaranteed the lease(s) and ascertain whether or not the landlords will insist you personally guarantee them as well.

There are important regulations to consider as well. Environmental legislation, in particular, places the burden of polluted property cleanup on current property owners and in some cases leaseholders. Find out if the property was ever owned or leased by a manufacturer involved in activities that created hazardous wastes that could have contaminated the soil. Find out whether or not any cleanup action has already been taken.

Financial statements

Don't take historical financial statements at face value, especially if they are not accompanied by a satisfactory audit letter from a CPA firm. Don't confuse a compilation (basically adding up the numbers provided by the client) or a review (a compilation with a few ratios figured out) with an audit. Only an audit requires that a CPA test financial information. If the seller offers you projections, don't even look at them!

Receivables

Chances are, if the business has receivables, their value is overstated. Carefully examine an aging of the receivables and determine what amount is outstanding past normal industry practices (nominal stated terms are often ignored). Then assume that an appropriate amount of receivables that are still current will also become bad debts.

Inventories

The market value of the inventory is almost certainly going to be a lot less than what was paid for it. While even larger businesses tend to have a fair amount of slower- moving items in inventory, many small businesses are even more hesitant to write down or sell off obsolete items.

Buying a Business

Competitors

Be sure that you are not walking into a competitive minefield! Is a price war beginning? Are your competitors slashing their margins to the bone? Did the current seller hear advance reports of a powerful international corporation entering their market niche?

Attorneys

Much more so than in buying a house, you need to consult with an attorney familiar with small businesses before signing an offer to buy. This is particularly important because of the many hidden liabilities you may be taking on, such as contracts, employment obligations, pending litigation, bills to vendors, leases, and more.

Confidentiality

You need to have a firm agreement with the current owner as to with whom, at what stage of the negotiations, and under what conditions you can discuss your interest in buying the business. Telling key customers that you are considering buying a business that is not yet publicly for sale can pose a risk to the business and expose you to potential litigation from the current owner.

Valuation

Start by carefully estimating the net positive cash flow for the next five years, after subtracting a good salary for your talents—one in line with your market value if you were employed in a similar management capacity elsewhere. Then determine the appropriate multiple of earnings to use to arrive at a fair valuation. The appropriate valuation should reflect the amount of risk inherent in the business and the importance of your efforts towards making the business succeed.

Simple Valuation Guidelines

1. An extremely well-established and steady business with a rock-solid market position, whose continued earnings will not be dependent upon a strong management team.
A multiple of eight to ten times current profits

2. An established business with a good market position, with some competitive pressures and some swings in earnings, requiring continual management attention.
A multiple of five to seven times current profits

3. An established business with no significant competitive advantages, stiff competition, few hard assets, and heavily dependent upon management's skills for success.
A multiple of two to four times current profits

4. A small personal service business where the new owner will be the only, or one of the only, professional service providers.
A multiple of one times current profits.

Streetwise Advice on Buying a Business

☞ Inspect all recent tax returns

Insist upon seeing tax returns from recent years. All too often, you will be told "well, of course we under-reported our sales ... doesn't everybody?" No, not everyone under-reports their income. Suspect any seller who gives you this line. Not only does he or she lie on the tax returns, despite the risk of severe penalties, but probably is less than truthful in other respects as well. Assume everything this person tells you, verbally or in writing, is a lie. Get independent verification. And, of course, this includes verifying that the sales were actually underreported!

☞ Hold on to key people

Unless you completely understand a business "cold," work strong financial incentives into your buy/sell agreement to keep key people in place during a significant transition period. This is particularly important for businesses for whom contact with major customers, such as through salaried salespeople, is a major means of selling products or services.

☞ Ignore pressure to close a deal

Sellers and business brokers love to pressure potential buyers by mentioning that other people are seriously looking at the business. A number of these "potential buyers" are probably just window shoppers. When I sold a six-month-old map business, with total sales under $15,000, I had almost fifty inquiries but only one serious offer. Even the smallest of businesses often take many months to sell.

☞ Dig into nonquantitative factors

Profits are realized, in part, because some nonquantitative aspect of the business appeals to a broad customer base—the service, the product, or the sales team, to name a few. Make an effort to pinpoint both the positive and negative nonquantitative aspects of the business you are considering purchasing.

At some point in the negotiation process you should get permission from the buyers to talk with their key customers. These people often have interesting insights into the business. Compare "your" products or services with those of the competition. And be sure to look into the overall market projections for "your" product or service. Will there be a market for the product or service tomorrow, five years from now ... always?

☞ Advantages to buying

Despite the many caveats to consider before buying a business, remember that buying an existing business is, generally, a much safer and faster route to profitability than starting from scratch.

☞ Get a non-compete agreement

Include a non-compete agreement as part of the buy/sell agreement to guarantee that you won't soon be competing with the seller.

"Buying an existing business is, generally, a much safer and faster route to profitability than starting from scratch."

Questions & Answers about Buying a Business

? *I was planning on buying a small mail-order business, but I don't like the idea of paying the three to five times earnings that the business will sell for. Wouldn't I be better off starting from scratch than giving away the first three to five years' profit?*

Probably not. An up-and-running business showing any profits means that you have established customers, marketing avenues, and sales momentum. If you put the energy and talent that it takes to start a new business into improving an existing business, you should be able to dramatically increase earnings and recoup your purchase price very quickly.

? *Can I assume that, like people selling a house, business sellers never expect to get the asking price, but something fairly close to it?*

Most people selling a business have a very inflated idea of what it is worth and this view is often reflected in the asking price. Few small businesses sell for anywhere near the asking price, and selling prices at half or even less

are quite common. This is especially true when hard assets such as real estate are not a major factor. Remember, a business is a much less liquid asset than a house. In other words, relatively few people are interested in buying a particular type, size, and location of business.

? *How much can I rely on information provided by a business broker?*

Basically—not at all! The broker makes money only if the sale goes through, and this is almost always in the form of a commission. So, the higher the price you pay, the more money the broker makes. And, more importantly, the broker's source of information is typically the seller!

? *I am close to making an offer on a profitable small service business. The business is only fourteen months old but the owner is selling because he is pursuing a terrific opportunity in an unrelated field. What do you think?*

Don't do it. Other than hard assets, when you purchase a business you are buying goodwill and forward momentum from an established pattern of doing business. Even if the business really is profitable, the owner couldn't have created much goodwill or developed an established

market position in such a short period of time. Furthermore, I'd always worry about the real reason the business is being sold so quickly—if the new opportunity looks terrific to the seller, then his current business, obviously, looks less terrific. In addition, with a service business, you need to ascertain how much of the business' success has been due to the personal characteristics or contacts of the proprietor.

? *I am negotiating to buy a packaging company. Should I be concerned that after the deal is consummated the seller may start a competing business?*

Absolutely! An aggressive person can regain market position overnight in a new business through personal contacts, industry reputation, and market knowledge. You should at least have the seller agree to sign a non-compete clause. If you are really concerned, you should also consider paying for the business in partial payments over a period of time.

After I negotiated to purchase a magazine from the Harvard Business School, a former licensee announced that it was going to compete with me despite a non-compete agreement. I persuaded Harvard Business School to pay the related legal fees and retain title during my first year of operation to ensure the validity of the non-compete agreement.

Pros and Cons of Franchising

dvantages

✚ Experience of the franchisor

A strong argument for buying a franchise is the experience of the franchisor. Franchises such as Burger King, MacDonald's, Midas Mufflers, and others have been in business for many years and you can take advantage of their consumer recognition and proven business formulas.

✚ Training

Any franchisor who has been successful for many years will, in all likelihood, provide excellent training with ample resources at the home office to get you started in your own franchise.

✚ Buying and advertising

One of the fastest ways to drain cash is to spend heavily on advertising. As a franchisee, you can take advantage of the public awareness of the franchisor's name and its national advertising budget. The franchisor will have volume purchasing power for supplies that may (or may not) be passed on to the franchisee.

✚ Research and development

The R&D budget for a franchisor will often be substantial, providing the franchisee with new products and services as well as advice on how to introduce the new product or service.

✚ Business synergy

When you buy a franchise, you are, in effect, buying into a family of other franchisees. You are all working toward the same goal and have adopted a similar mission on behalf of the franchisor. Some of the best ideas for the franchisor come from the "family"—you become part of a network of franchisees who regularly talk to the home office as well as other franchisees.

Disadvantages

▬ Added expenses

All franchisees are required to pay an up-front fee to the franchisor in order to use the franchisor's name and open shop. These fees can run into six figures. The franchisor will usually require ongoing fees as well.

▬ Uniformity

Individuals who have problems taking direction will find franchising a difficult business route to take. Franchisors achieve success through the development of conformity among all the franchisees from management style right down to supplies. If adhering to rules bothers you, you should look into some other form of business structure.

▬ False expectations

It is easy to fall into the trap of feeling that, just by buying into a popular franchise, you will be an instant success. Franchising is just like any other business. You must work hard and make sacrifices to achieve a measure of success.

▬ Cannibalization

If you live in a metropolitan area, the chances are good that you will see several like franchises within a ten-mile radius. The franchisor will, one way or the other, realize profits through this situation. But for you, the individual franchisee, this situation can be a competitive nightmare that might ultimately force you to close your doors.

▬ International vs. domestic

If the franchisor has headquarters in a foreign country, problems may arise if you require assistance or need to speak to a company representative in person. Make sure the franchisor has an office in your country or, at least, sends a representative to your country on a regular basis.

Franchising Success Story

Jim Donnelley has successfully operated a franchise business offering support services for several years. He offers advice on choosing the type of franchise to buy into, as well as weighing the benefits of franchise versus the cost.

Choose Carefully

66 The franchise might bring volume purchasing into the act; it might bring better discounts on office equipment. It brings name recognition. But will all that generate enough extra sales to pay the licensing and royalty fees that are required? If it will, you should go with it; if it won't, you shouldn't. It's a business decision. 99

Choose for Yourself

66 As you look, you've got to say to yourself, 'Am I going to get up every day and be happy going to work at a particular franchise?' You don't want to pick it just because you think it *might* be good. 99

Don't Buy Into Guarantees for Success

66 The franchisor cannot guarantee success. There's no way to do that, and you should walk away from any franchisor who promises that. But even though they can't provide guarantees, they can make it a much safer journey. 99

Streetwise Advice on Franchising

☞ To franchise or not to franchise

If you don't have a lot of solid business experience or don't have experience in the particular field you are planning on entering, you should definitely consider buying a franchise rather than an existing business or starting a business from scratch. True, even a successful franchise typically nets smaller profit margins than other types of businesses because of franchising fees and expenses, but the odds of surviving in business at all are much greater.

If you are entering a field with a very strong consumer name recognition factor, I would urge you even more stridently to consider doing so through a franchise. Whether you have experience in the field—fast foods, automotive, or whatever—without the name recognition advantage, you are going to have to work extremely hard to offset the huge benefits of your franchised competitors.

☞ Due diligence

Perhaps even more so than buying an existing business, you need to do a lot of homework before you purchase a business. You absolutely must have a lawyer review all documents and consider issues that may not be presented contractually. Find out if the franchisor has a history of dissatisfaction among its franchisees. Have lawsuits been brought by franchisees against the franchisor? Why? Who won? Do exhaustive searches of the business and trade media for articles on the franchise(s).

Don't take the word of a salesperson for the franchisor when looking for accurate information on the franchise. Get out and talk with as many current franchisee managers and/or owners as possible.

☞ Issues to consider

There are many issues to consider before purchasing a franchise. These are just a few.

- **Exclusivity.** Can another franchise be sold in your area? If so, what is the proximity regulation—two miles? one mile? next door?
- **Hidden costs.** Has every conceivable or possible cost been disclosed? Will the agreement between yourself and the franchisor protect you from hidden costs? How much will you have to contribute to either local, regional, or national advertising budgets?
- **Cost calculators.** Is the fee schedule subject to revision or escalation under any circumstances?
- **Revocation of franchise agreement.** Under what conditions could the franchise be revoked? What processes are involved in a revocation? Are any investment costs paid by you reimbursable?
- **Cash flow.** Carefully plan the cash flow of the business, especially prior to breakeven. The franchisor may place restrictions on your business that may restrict your ability to cut costs if you get into a cash-flow bind.

☞ Competing franchisors

There will most likely be several franchisors to choose from in your field. If you don't have a lot of experience in the industry, buy into one of the more recognizable or established franchises (despite the greater cost). But do comparison shop and research your particular market area before you decide. This is, after all, a major purchase!

Questions & Answers about Franchising

How does a franchisor make money?

Usually a franchisor sells the right to a franchise for a hefty fee over the actual out-of-pocket costs of setting up the business. Then the franchisor receives ongoing payments—usually a percentage of the sales, not the profits. Most franchisors also sell supplies and services to franchises.

In selecting a franchise, should I be more concerned with the initial fee or the ongoing franchise fees?

If you are buying into a successful franchise, you should be more concerned about the ongoing charges. These costs are paid yearly. And, since these fees are typically extracted from sales, not profits, they can cut your profits to shreds. For example, if your pre-tax profit margin is 10 percent, but your franchise fee is 5 percent, your profit is halved!

If you are buying a less established franchise, be leery of up-front costs. You could lose your investment altogether if the business fails.

In either case you should examine

all costs and contracts, and talk to current franchise owners before signing.

Is it worth it to pay a percentage of sales, even for a really good franchise?

This is the $64 million dollar question you must ask yourself. Many people who buy franchises think it is a great deal when they are able to turn an early profit—but in later years, with experience under their belts, they come to view the franchise fees as onerous.

You need to evaluate what you are getting by buying into a franchise and how valuable what you are buying will be to you in several years. If you are just using the franchise as a means of learning industry skills, then you might be better off working for someone else for a period of time instead. If, on the other hand, you already have industry skills and business expertise and want to apply them through an established brand-name business in a competitive market, the franchise route may be right for you.

Other than franchise fees, what other costs should I watch out for?

Often you will have to pay a percentage of local, regional, or national advertising costs as a separate fee over and above the franchise fees. You may also be required to purchase supplies and services directly from the franchisor.

What else should I watch out for in buying a franchise?

If you are relatively inexperienced in running a business, buying a franchise may be a much better option for you than starting a business from scratch. But do be aware that even a franchise isn't a foolproof expressway to business success.

In addition to issues that may be peculiar to the particular industry you are buying into, there are general issues that should be considered. Can you sell the franchise easily, and how? Can the franchise fees be increased for any reason? Are new competitors affecting market share? What level of applicable industry or business skills did the typical franchise owner possess before he or she bought into the franchise?

Get out and talk to as many current franchise owners as you can before making any commitments—this just can't be overemphasized.

Company Strategy

A company strategy is the unique formula for success that forms the foundation of a business plan as well as governing day-to-day operations. This strategy is not a business definition and summary of pertinent markets, but instead, it is an account of the one or two key factors that distinguish the firm from its competition and are most expected to contribute to the firm's long-term success.

To be most effective, a company's strategy should be no longer than one page, at most. For many businesses, a single sentence would be ideal. The strategy theme should be easily and frequently communicated to employees so that a cohesive business focus is always maintained.

Why develop a strategy?

All firms, from one-person start-ups to global conglomerates, should have a strategy. Following a good, distinctive strategy will ensure that a business builds, maintains, and continually strengthens a specific identity in the marketplace.

By serving as a jumping-off point for annual business planning, a strategy will become the nucleus around which an annual business plan is developed. It will also form a framework for helping to consider mid-term deviations from the plan. In addition it will help set a consistent direction for key functional areas. A good strategy should endure year after year, and hence will tie together one year's business plan to the next. This will enable the company to easily build upon the accomplishments of the previous year.

Without a clearly defined or closely followed strategy, companies of all sizes tend to lose sight of their direction when they run into temporary difficulties, or when management just gets bored operating "the same old business."

It is amazing to see so many very small businesses, after having had a few moderately successful years, adding completely unrelated product lines or services to their agendas that only muddy their identity. This tactic signals customers that the management has no clue as to what the nature of the business really is. What would you think if your favorite ice cream parlor began offering a full- service dinner menu literally overnight? Or if the local boat dealer suddenly decided to devote 50 percent of his floor space to lawn mowers? You'd think they were confused, right?

No one business type is immune from this appalling lack of strategic discipline—not "Mom and Pops," not large corporations. Large or small, the sales and profit results from unrelated business diversification are almost always disappointing.

Four Basic Factors to Consider
- Market
- Customer needs
- Competitors
- Your relative capabilities

Get client list from Bob ... Have Helen set up appointments for Tuesday and Wednesday of next week

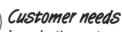

Factors

Before you create a strategy, you need to consider four basic factors:

Market

In evaluating a market, you need to consider the size of the current market as well as the potential market for new customers. Ask the following questions:

? Is the market fairly flat, growing, booming, or declining?

? Are technology, fashion, or other elements rapidly changing the market?

? Are there distinct market segments? For example, in the restaurant industry, the fast food segment is highly distinct from the fine dining segment. A fast food hamburger chain, however, is less distinct from a casual full-service restaurant serving hamburgers at a moderate price.

? Is the market local, regional, or national?

? How far will people travel to buy the product or service?

? Do business customers patronize distant competitors? Is the market consolidating, with the lion's share of the dollar volume going to larger national firms?

Customer needs

In evaluating customer needs you want to pay attention not only to what is, but to what could be. This isn't an easy task. However, if you can satisfy a customer need that exists but is not currently being met by a competing product or service, your business will be off to a great start.

Maybe you will find, for example, that while most people may currently buy fishing lures at their local stores, they are not happy with the depth of the selection or the pricing, and that they would rather buy from a mail-order catalog.

Or maybe you will find that, while local businesses currently hire separate firms to do landscaping, office cleaning, and snow removal, they would rather have one firm handle all maintenance activities.

One of the best ways to evaluate customer needs is to talk with people. Or you could drive to a nearby town with similar demographics and see how services such as the ones you plan to offer are met and received. These methods aren't foolproof, but they are a start.

Competition

Your analysis needs to extend beyond who the existing competitors are and encompass the nature of the competition. Advertising and company literature may reveal insights into how the competition is approaching the marketplace; in short, their marketing strategies. For example, do their ads emphasize prices or features? Images or substance? Does their literature make comparative claims such as "the only product that features . . ." or "the fastest way to . . ." or "the most dependable . . ."?

Remember that you *do not* necessarily have to compete against the same factors as your competitors. But you *do* need to be aware of what they are doing.

You also need to analyze who may become a competitor and whether or not a product substitute could replace your product in the future. For example, newspapers held a near-monopoly as an advertising vehicle until the advent of radio. Both newspapers and radio had to share their piece of the advertising pie with television when it hit the marketplace. Now cable television and the Internet are also vying for advertising dollars!

Capabilities

You need to do a realistic comparison of the strengths and weaknesses of your firm versus those of your competition. If your firm is smaller and newer than the competition, the weaknesses will probably be more easily identifiable. Lack of financial strength, minimal consumer awareness, and less purchasing power would be among some obvious weaknesses.

A newer, smaller firm will have its inherent strengths as well. You need to identify those. Lower overhead, for instance, may enable you to price your product very competitively. However, be sure you don't squander your advantages by choosing the wrong company strategy!

While the possible elements of a successful strategy are limitless, here are some of the most common ones. Many strategies will include several of these elements.

Price and quality

Price and quality are the most common strategic elements. The strategy may be to produce a superior quality product or service and charge an appropriate price, or to produce a lower-cost item and charge a lower price.

Scope of product line

A broad product or service line allows customers to do one-stop shopping, saving them time and effort. It may also allow economies of scale that can benefit customers. A narrower product line may allow more depth of product, perhaps including more alternatives for the same product type. It may be coupled with more in-depth expertise.

State-of-the-art products

Offering the most technically advanced products can form a powerful strategy if the firm truly has the capability to offer state-of-the-art products. Usually technically advanced products will cost more than less advanced ones.

What makes you so different?

High Quality and Price	Low Quality and Price
Narrow Product Line	Broad Product Line
High-Tech Products	Low-Tech Products
Trendy Products	Conservative Products
Brand-Name Products	Generic Products
Customized Products	Standard Products
Niche Market	General Market
High Service	Low Service

Trendy products

Fashionable products can earn premium prices, but they cost more to design and are riskier, necessitating higher prices.

Brand-name products

Products with established brand names command higher prices, but generic products are proving increasingly popular. Creating a memorable national brand requires an expensive, market saturating advertising campaign.

Customized products

One of the least risky strategies for smaller firms is to offer a high degree of customization, allowing them to differentiate their offerings from the typically more standard offerings of larger firms.

Niche market

Offering unique products or services serving obscure niche markets is another less risky strategy for smaller firms. Typically, the smaller volume requires higher operating costs, but the lessened competition more than makes up for it.

Service

Coupling product offerings with a high degree of service can often be used to differentiate a business from a competitor offering minimal or no service.

Sample Strategy Plans

*E*very business has several options for developing a successful strategy. The following are four alternative strategies for the same fictional business. They work even when you are facing tough competition.

The scenario

Central City Booksellers, for many years, was the largest bookstore in Central City, a large metropolitan area. But over the last five years Central City has been hit with tough competition from several different national bookstore chains including two nearby "superstores" that offer over 100,000 titles. This is five times as many as Central City Bookseller's 20,000 titles. These superstores have six times Central City Bookseller's 4,000 square feet of retail space and are offering 10 percent discounts on all hardcovers and national bestsellers.

Strategy option no. 1: Specialization

Because of its downtown business center location, Central City Booksellers could position itself as the bookstore for business people. Because the superstores already have a deep inventory of business books, Central City would have to do more than just increase its stock of business books. For example, it could move its business books to the front of the store, hold special in-store events for business people, focus its marketing efforts on business people, solicit bulk corporate orders from businesses, and build a mailing list of customers interested in business books. And, as long as Central City places an enormous emphasis on its specialized business book niche, it could continue to sell books in other categories.

Strategy option no. 2: Affiliations

Central City Booksellers could target its marketing efforts toward building relationships with local membership organizations. It could select and promote titles appropriate to those organizations by advertising them through club or association newsletters, mailing lists, or events. It could offer members special store discounts. And it could help the organizations find nationally recognized authors to speak at organization functions and workshops.

Strategy option no. 3: Super deep discounts/limited stock option

One of the best ways to develop an effective strategy is to adopt a strategy from a similar industry, in this case the software industry, where leading software stores stock many fewer titles than bookstores, display them all face out, work on a smaller mark-up, and turn their inventory over much more quickly. To follow this path Central City could cut its stock to the fastest selling 4,000 book titles, display them all face out; offer really deep discounts (such as 20 to 25 percent); and turn over its inventory faster.

Strategy option no. 4: Full-service restaurant

In contrast to the typical superstore limited-menu cafes, Central City could open a full-service restaurant. Such an offering should build store traffic and create a distinctive atmosphere. If the management of Central City is uncomfortable with restaurant management, they could lease out part of their store to a third party interested in opening a restaurant.

Streetwise Advice on Creating Strategy

☞ **Price**

In a service business, particularly in a situation where you are personally providing service, competing on price is a very common strategy. Until you have established your business, price competitiveness is often necessary. However, in a product business, especially one in which you are competing with larger firms, you shouldn't base your strategy on price competition. No matter how hard you try, you probably won't be able to achieve the cost efficiencies of a larger firm that are necessary to compete on price alone.

☞ **"To be the best"**

Utilizing a "best" or "highest quality" approach as a strategy is, generally, not the best marketing tactic. Think about it. What does this tactic say to a potential customer? Nothing. Everyone says their products or services are the best. Instead, develop a strategy that instantly sets you apart from the competition.

☞ **Changing strategy**

Chances are that, after being in business for a year or two, you may determine that it is necessary to modify your strategy to a greater or lesser degree. Fine. But avoid adopting a completely different approach. All of the goodwill and name recognition you have worked to achieve will be wasted.

☞ **Is it working?**

Do a survey of your customers and ask them if they can express, in one sentence, what makes your business different from the competition. If they can't, your strategy isn't working. And don't be surprised if you find that your business is viewed in a different light than you intended. In this case, take a look at how you are transmitting your strategy "message" to your customers. Don't hesitate to make adjustments in advertising, customer service, sales pitch, or other "message" channels necessary to effectively communicate your strategy.

☞ **Shout it every day!**

Don't keep your strategy a secret! Any competitor on the ball will see exactly what you are trying to do—whether you try to keep it a secret or not. Be absolutely sure that all of your employees know what the strategy is, and that through their work they communicate that message. And don't forget to reinforce your strategy—your competitive edge—in the minds of your customers on a continual basis as well.

"Develop a strategy that instantly sets you apart from the competition."

Questions & Answers about Creating Strategy

Why can't my strategy be based on being "the best"?

Aiming to be "the best" isn't a strategy. Everyone tries to be the best. Strategy is the means you choose to make your business the best option for existing and potential customers. For example, offering a more personalized service than that offered by your competitors would be a strategy.

Also, attempting to be the best in every aspect of your business is tantamount to setting yourself up for failure. It is unrealistic to try to achieve and sustain superior performance throughout all areas of your business operation. A wiser goal is to try to be good in all areas but select only those one or two areas that are crucial to distinguishing your business from the competition in which to strive for perfection.

I own a car wash business that has two direct competitors. What are some good choices for a company strategy?

You could use strategy to widen your gap of direct competition to boost your profit margins. For example, you could develop add-on premium services such as hand drying, high-luster waxing, detailing, or shampooing of car interiors. Not only should services like these offer higher dollar sales and higher profit margins, but they might also enable you to raise prices for your basic car wash service as well.

I don't ever seem to have the time to put together a strategy for my business. How important is it, really?

On a scale of one to ten—fifteen! If you don't have a strategy, it is quite possible that you could work eighty hours per week all year long and only break even or possibly even lose money. With a great strategy you might be able to work one day a week and make piles of money!

Football provides a good analogy. If a football team works very hard but initiates the wrong plays, it won't be going to the Super Bowl. If the team continually executes passing plays against rivals that are terrific at interceptions, it might as well have forfeited the game before it began!

Can a strategy work for any business, even personal service businesses such as consultants, lawyers, and accountants?

Absolutely. A common, yet good strategy in competitive personal service businesses is to specialize. The more you can be recognized as a specialist, the less competition you will have and the higher rates you can charge. Initially you may want to take any client that comes along. At the same time, however, you should start writing newspaper or trade magazine articles or giving seminars that focus on your particular area of expertise. As your ability to profit through higher-priced specialty work increases you can, proportionately, phase out your lower-priced less specialized work.

Strategy Success Story

Ruby Shoes Studio is a graphics communication firm with a unique strategy. They develop and maintain client relationships by making the overall work experience fun and interesting. Everything from the name of the company to the design of the office draws on one of the most popular movies ever made—The Wizard of Oz. **Susan Tyrell Donelan,** creative director, describes some of the ways Ruby Shoes Studio has implemented this creative strategy.

Consistency

66 It's really consistency. You figure out the strategy and are just consistent. You keep saying the message in as many ways as you can say it to many different people so that they all get the message. And the message has to be clear to begin with. 99

Make It Fun!

66 *The Wizard of Oz* plays on our hold button. I've had clients get upset because I've interrupted a favorite part. They are on hold, waiting for me, and I pick up the phone and they go 'Oh, the tin man was just about to get his heart.' Then I feel bad that I've interrupted! They like being on hold and they like hanging out in the studio. It's just a fun place. 99

By far the most common types of overall plans for small businesses are annual plans and business plans. Annual plans are assembled each year, primarily to help managers chart a course for the upcoming year. Business plans are typically used by a start-up business to attract investors.

Annual plans and business plans share many elements and are similar in many ways. But there are typically two crucial differences: the objective of the plan and the audience for the plan.

Annual plans

Annual plans are generally used by the managers of a business to help guide the business in specific directions over the course of the year. Because an annual plan is intended primarily for internal use, its form and scope can vary dramatically from one firm to the next. Adapt a format that works best for you.

Start with a brief summary of the overall company goals for the year. If they are not obvious, explain how these goals support the company's strategy and build on its competitive strengths. *Goals may be achievement-oriented,* such as raising profitability, decreasing costs, boosting market share, or producing new products. *Or they may be process-oriented,* such as reducing turnaround time on orders or improving employee morale.

Have each functional area prepare its own goals and detailed budget for the year, including what it is going

to do to support the overall company goals. You also need to create monthly profit and loss, cash flow, and balance sheet pro formas.

If your firm is experiencing trouble or if your market or industry is experiencing rapid change, consider producing a full-blown business plan as described later in this section. If you are preparing to launch a major new product, consider producing a marketing plan, as described in the marketing section, as part of your annual planning as well.

Business plans

Business plans are used primarily to attract capital. The primary focus of such a plan should be to interest investors or lenders.

If your plan is being used to borrow money, you need to write the plan in a manner that will attract lenders, as opposed to equity investors. *Lenders want to be assured that they are going to be paid back.* Projected profits mean nothing to lenders. They will not be sharing in your gains. In fact, lofty projections may make them nervous because, typically, very high potential returns are often accompanied by very high potential risks. *Equity investors, on the other hand, are looking for a much higher return than they could get by investing in a more established company.*

Whether your audience is venture capitalists, bank lenders, or your own management team, *a "spiral" approach will really deliver your message because it is conveyed in order from most important to least important.*

This approach is particularly effective when seeking the financial aid of outside investors such as venture capitalists, who review hundreds or even thousands of plans for every one they decide to invest in and generally give only a cursory look at most submissions. Get your primary message across immediately! Potential lenders and even members of your own management team will be able to discern the key elements of your plan easily as well.

There are two keys to the "spiral" approach. First, position a brief summary of the plan at the beginning. This allows the reader to discern the most important aspects of the plan up front without reading through the entire plan. Second, save your financial projections for the end of the plan. Potential investors or lenders are going to assume your numbers look great. They are more interested in the assumptions behind the numbers.

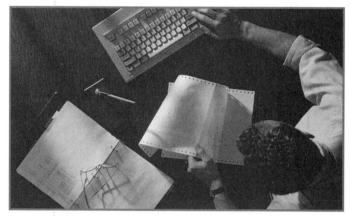

Developing a Business Plan

Objective

Throughout the process of creating a plan, you need to keep in mind the objective of the plan. Why are you writing the plan? Is it to manage the business? Or is it to raise money?

Annual plans are used to manage a business. Business plans are used to attract capital. But there are exceptions, and often the difference between annual plans and business plans becomes muddled. Banks and other lenders or investors may require a copy of each year's annual plan. And management may use the start-up business plan as a basis for operating the business.

Keeping a clear distinction between annual plans and business plans is not important. What is important is keeping the primary objective of and the primary audience for the plan clear. As a rule of thumb, if the plan will be used to attract investors or lenders, this is the primary objective and outsiders are the primary audience. If the plan will help manage the business, this is the primary objective and insiders are the primary audience.

Some or all of the following elements should be a part of your plan, depending upon your objective.

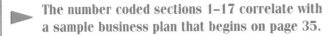 The number coded sections 1–17 correlate with a sample business plan that begins on page 35.

1 Summary

Summaries should be short and concise—one page is ideal. It should cover the following points:

- **Strategy overview.** Start with a brief overview of your business strategy. If your business will be based, at least initially, on a particular product or service, describe it in the introductory paragraph.
- **Strategy logic.** In the the next paragraph or two explain why your strategy makes sense or why your product or service has promise. Are you entering a fast-growing market or providing a unique product or service that distinguishes your business from existing businesses?

- **Business development.** Next, you should describe the stage your business is in.
  - ❓ Is it already generating sales?
  - ❓ Have you done test marketing?
  - ❓ Is a prototype developed?
  - ❓ Has market research been performed?
- **Business development.** Name the key people in your organization and describe, briefly, what special talents, expertise, or connections they will bring to the business.
- **Financial objectives.** If your plan is being developed to raise capital, be clear about the amount of capital you are seeking and how you plan to use investor or lender funding.
- **Business organization.** Describe the form of business organization you will take and where the company will be located.

Remember to keep your summary short and easy to understand. Avoid technical jargon and details. Don't try to summarize all of the different major elements of your plan. Just focus on the key elements that you think will be of most interest to your audience. Skip the pie-in-the-sky profit projections and outlook generalizations.

2 Concept

The concept is a clear explanation of your business strategy. It is not a definition of the business or a summary of its markets but, instead, a quick summary of the one or two key factors that set your business apart from the competition.

- **Product description.** New business strategies are often closely tied to a particular product or service. If this is your situation, include a clear and substantive description of your principal product or service. Follow this with a focused discussion of what will make your product or service stand out from any similar offerings in the marketplace. Focus, in depth, on just a few of the most competitive attributes of your product or service.

Developing a Business Plan

• **Impact factors.** You should also describe any other aspect of your business that is fundamental to your strategy. Areas that might have significant impact on your strategy are marketing, research and development, or strategic alliances with other firms. For example, if everyone else in your industry is selling their product through retail channels but you feel that you can develop a strong competitive advantage by selling via direct mail, then you should discuss this in the concept section.

Market conditions and the competition should be included as points of reference only when necessary. An in-depth analysis of these factors will be included later in the plan.

③ Current situation

This section is most appropriate for plans being used to seek financing. Within this section you will describe what stage of development your company is in and what the sought-after financing will be used for.

There are three basic reasons for seeking outside financing: start-up financing, expansion financing, and work-out financing.

• **Start-up financing.** If you are seeking start-up financing, you will need to list specific milestones that have been achieved and emphasize all positive developments without being misleading. You should anticipate the questions your lenders or investors may ask.

❓ Has the market research been done?
❓ Has a prototype product been developed?
❓ Have facilities been leased?
❓ Is the management team in place?
❓ Has manufacturing been contracted?
❓ Are marketing plans finalized?

Whether or not you receive financing and the terms of that financing will depend upon the stage of development your company is in. The more fully developed your company is, the better your financial arrangements will be.

• **Expansion financing.** If your business is already up and running and you are seeking expansion financing, you

need to give clear evidence that you are not, in reality, seeking financing as a way to solve existing problems, or to cover losses or extraordinary expenses such as might be experienced during a start-up.

• **Work-out financing.** Many investors and lenders do not like to offer work-out financing. Those who are willing to consider it will want to see a plan that clearly identifies the reasons for current or previous problems and provides a strong plan for corrective action.

No matter what type of financing you are seeking, financiers like to be apprised of the source and amount of any capital that has already been secured. They will expect key executives to have made substantial personal equity investments in the business. They will feel even more comfortable if they recognize any other investors who may have participated in earlier stages of the financing process.

④ The market

Later in this book, you will learn how to develop and write a marketing plan. You may want to refer to that section now. Aspects of that plan need to be addressed in your business plan.

❓ How large is the potential market?
❓ How many people or businesses are currently using a competitor's product that is the same or similar to the one you are offering or plan to offer?
❓ How many prospects potentially have any possible use for the product?
❓ Is the market growing, flattening, or shrinking?

⑤ Market segmentation

Almost every market has some major and distinctive segments. Even if it is not currently segmented, the probability that it could or will be is great. This is particularly true if the marketplace for your product or service is multi-regional or national. If this is the case, segmentation is almost necessary, especially for a small firm, if you hope to be competitive.

You will need to discuss segmentation within your business category and how you intend to cope with any positive or negative affects it may have on your particular business. Almost all markets are segmented by price and quality issues. Generally, however, price and quality do not provide the most clear or definitive market segmentation. Much stronger segmentation can usually be found through an evaluation of product or service uses and importance to various consumers.

6 Consumer analysis

In your business plan you will need to evaluate the typical consumers within the market segments you are targeting. There are countless variables to consider when analyzing consumer behavior. Try to focus on those behavioral possibilities that best determine how viable your product will be in your target markets. Look at

- Which features will most appeal to consumers?
- How are choices made between competing products?
- Which marketing promotions or media avenues seem to offer the best vehicles for reaching the consumer base?

And ask the following questions:

- How much disposable income do target consumers have to spend on this product?
- How do your target consumers reach purchasing decisions?
- Are consumers presold on a particular brand before they visit a store or do they buy on impulse?
- What characteristics influence the purchase of one product or service over a competing one?

7 Competition

Include an overview of those firms and their products and/or services that you will be in direct competition with. Identify the market leader and define what makes it successful. Emphasize those characteristics of the firm or offerings that are different than yours.

Don't dismiss this section just because you don't have any current competition. If there isn't a product or service similar to yours on the market, identity those firms that provide products or services that perform essentially the same function. You should also make an attempt to identify any firms that are likely to enter the market or are in the process of developing products or services that will be competitive with those you are offering.

8 Product features and benefits

You briefly described the key features of your product or service in the concept section of the plan. In this section you should explore features and benefits in depth. It is essential to be clear not only about the distinguishing features of your product or service but also to delineate any strong consumer benefits. What makes your product or service significantly better than competitive offerings?

9 Competitive analysis

In this section you need to do an in-depth analysis of the competitive advantages and weaknesses of your firm. When exploring weaknesses you should include information that will help allay any concerns that may arise as to their ability to significantly hinder your success.

This section is important, especially if your company is a start-up, because you will, typically, be competing with established companies that have inherent advantages such as financial strength, name recognition, and established distribution channels.

10 Positioning

Positioning can be thought of as a marketing strategy for your product or service. Positioning defines how you are going to portray your product to your targeted marketplace.

Your first step is deciding who your target market will be. It will consist of those potential customers toward whom you will direct most of your marketing efforts. Often this group will not be the sole or even the largest market for your product, but it will be the market that, based on competitive factors and product benefits, you feel you can most effectively reach.

Start-ups are more likely to be successful if they focus on a highly specific, very narrow target market. General markets are usually dominated by large, well-established firms.

Once you have determined who your target market is, you need to decide how you want consumers to perceive your product.

- ❓ Is it the premium quality leader?
- ❓ Is it a low-cost substitute?
- ❓ Is it a full-service alternative?

If you have a one-product or service company, your marketing strategy may coincide with your overall business strategy. This doesn't necessarily have to be the case, however, but, it is extremely important, in all cases, that your product strategy be in sync with your overall business strategy.

11 Advertising and promotion

Use this section to provide an overview of your general promotional plan. Give a break-out of what methods and media you intend to use and why. If you have developed an advertising slogan or unique selling proposition you may mention it, but it isn't strictly necessary. (A detailed explanation of unique selling propositions and their purpose can be found in Chapter 2, "Marketing".)

You should outline the proposed mix of your advertising media, use of publicity, and/or other promotional programs.

- Explain how your choice of marketing vehicles will allow you to reach your target market.
- Explain how they will enable you to best convey your product features and benefits.

Be sure that your advertising, publicity, and promotional programs sound realistic, based upon your proposed marketing budget. Effective advertising, generally, relies on message repetition in order to motivate consumers to

make a purchase. If you are on a limited budget, it is better to reach fewer, more likely prospects, more often, than too many people occasionally.

12 Sales

Your sales strategy needs to be in harmony with your business strategy, marketing strategy, and your company's strengths and weaknesses. For example, if your start-up company is planning on selling products to other businesses in a highly competitive marketplace, your market entry will be easier if you rely on wholesalers or commissioned sales representatives who already have an established presence and reputation in the marketplace. If your business will be selling high-tech products with a range of customized options, your sales force needs to be extremely knowledgeable and personable.

13 Research and development

A discussion of research and development is, obviously, not germane to all companies. If it applies, though, financiers are going to want to know that research and development projects are aimed at specific, realistic objectives. And they will want to be assured that an undue portion of the company's resources is not plowed into this area. Remember that banks generally lend money to businesses on a short-term basis, and venture capitalists and other first-round investors generally want to cash out in just a few years.

14 Operations

Operations is a catch-all term used to describe any important aspects of the business not described elsewhere. If the start-up is a manufacturing concern, discuss critical elements of the manufacturing process. For retail businesses, discuss store operations. Wholesalers should discuss warehouse operations.

In addition to discussing areas that are critical to operations, briefly summarize how major business functions will be carried out, and how certain functions may run

Developing a Business Plan

more effectively than those of your competitors. But, don't get into long descriptions of any business or operation practices that will not sell your business plan to financiers.

15 People

The focus here is key people and positions. Primary attention should be on key people who have already committed to joining the firm. Elaborate on their relevant past experience and successes and explain what areas of responsibility they will have in the new company. Resumes should be included here as part of an appendix or exhibits inclusion at the end of the plan.

If there are any important positions that have not been filled, describe position responsibilities and the type of employment/experience background necessary to the position.

If there is a board of directors, present each member, and summarize that person's background. If they will have an active role in running their business, elaborate that role here.

If consultants have been engaged for key responsibilities, include a description of their backgrounds and functions.

Fill as many of your key positions as possible before you seek funding. Many financiers reject plans if the management team is incomplete.

16 Payback and exit plan

Both debt and equity lenders will want to know how they can expect to receive their investment back and realize interest or profit from the company.

Most private investors and venture capitalists will want to be able to exercise a cash-out option within five years. They will be concerned that, even if the company becomes highly profitable, it may be difficult for them to sell out their share at an attractive price. This concern is particularly true in the case of minority stake holders. This is why you must provide an exit strategy for investors.

Ideally, investors hope a firm will be so successful that it will be able to go public within five years and their shares will become highly liquid investments, trading at a hefty multiple of earnings. But, often, a more realistic goal is to make the company large and successful enough to sell to a larger firm. State what your exit plan is and be sure it appears realistic.

17 Financials

In this section you need to show projected, or "pro forma," income statements, balance sheets, and cash flow. Existing businesses should also show historical financial statements. While how far into the future you need to project and the number of possible scenarios you can anticipate depends upon the complexity of the business, three to five years for financial projections and three scenarios are average.

Scenarios should be based on the most likely course your business will take, a weak scenario with sales coming in well under expectation, and a good scenario with projected sales well over expectation.

Pro-forma income statements should show sales, cost of operation, and profits on both a monthly and annual basis for each plan year. For all but the largest businesses, annual pro-forma balance sheets are all that are necessary. Cash flow pro formas should be presented in both monthly and annual form. And, if your business is already established, past annual balance sheets and income statements should also be included.

Include information that will assist potential lenders in understanding your projections. Lenders will give as much credence to the assumptions your projections are based on as they do the numbers themselves.

BUSINESS PLAN
for
INTERNET TOOL COMPANY, INC. (ITC)

1 Summary

Internet Tool Company, Inc. (ITC) has been formed to create Internet development tools. The market for Internet tools is growing very rapidly. ITC's first development tool, with a working name of "The Tool," provides a major technical breakthrough by virtue of its "intelligent agent" feature. The intelligent agent makes it very easy to create documents and at the same time offers great flexibility in changing documents and other graphic material.

ITC plans to position "The Tool" as a premium product. The product will be sold direct and via catalogs in a carefully targeted marketing campaign.

"The Tool" is now in final BETA testing.

A solid management team is in place, including James Smith, CEO, whose previous successes include the start-up firm, Internet Consultants, Inc.; his brother John Smith, Vice President of Engineering, who directed many successful new product development efforts at Hewlett Packard; Helen Jones, Vice President of Marketing, who has a long and successful record in marketing at IBM; and Fred Adams, Vice President of Finance, who was previously CFO of a fast-growing manufacturing firm, American Durables Corporation.

ITC was formed twelve months ago as a California Corporation, with its principal office in San Jose.

At this time the corporation seeks $400,000 to start up production (which will be contracted out) to begin marketing, and for short-term working capital needs.

Note: This sample plan is fictitious.

2 The Concept

Internet Tool Company, Inc., will focus on creating leading-edge Internet development tools. These tools will be designed for consumers (not businesses or professional users) who are willing to pay a premium for a higher-quality product. ITC will be a research- and development-driven company, and will continually work on upgrades or better products to serve its market.

The main distinctive feature of the company's first product, "The Tool," is its intelligent agent. The Tool "walks" users step by step through the process of creating a document. "The Tool" also makes it very easy to change documents after they are completed.

The company will use its leading-edge product strategy in marketing by aggressively seeking publicity coverage of new products, as well as upgrades.

The company will avoid the brutal competition for retail shelf space by selling its products direct or through catalogs.

3 Current Situation

"The Tool" is now in final BETA testing. An earlier BETA test with fifty participants over a period of six weeks revealed surprisingly few technical glitches, all of which have since been corrected.

Marketing research conducted by an independent research firm hired by ITC has indicated that there is strong consumer demand for the product. (See Exhibit A for a summary of the market research report.)

Initial capitalization was provided solely by the initial officers of the corporation: James Smith, John Smith, Helen Jones, and Fred Adams. (See Exhibit B for a break-out of stock ownership.)

At this time TIC seeks $400,000 in equity capital to take "The Tool" from prototype to market.

This money would be used to hire twelve additional employees, beyond the five officers currently on the payroll; lease warehouse space; provide funding for marketing efforts; pay for the first production run (to be contracted out); and provide working capital for the first year of sales. ITC plans to avoid any bank or other debt financing, at least for this first year after sales begins.

ITC believes that it can have "The Tool" in the marketplace within six to eight months after funding is completed.

④ The Market

Over thirty million people are currently using the Internet. Internet users are expected to grow in number by at least 25 percent each year for the next five years. The potential number of consumers for Internet development tools is at least twenty million now with the potential for thirty million in two or three years. Recent trends indicate that, while Fortune 500 businesses will continue to seek out the Internet, faster growth will be seen in the home and small business market.

⑤ Market Segmentation

The market is divided into three relatively distinct segments. They are the corporate/professional segment, the small business segment, and the consumer segment.

Corporate/Professional Segment
This market includes large corporations, institutions, government agencies, and professional developers. Internet development tools aimed at this market are expensive, costing upwards of $500; may take some time to master, even for seasoned technical developers; but do provide the maximum number of options and flexibility in site design.

Small Business Segment
Internet development tools aimed at this market are mid-priced, typically costing from $100 to $500; they are designed to be used by people without development experience, although ease of use is a secondary feature to the ability to create the broad range of functionality likely to be required by a small business.

Consumer Segment
This segment is driven by low price (under $100) and ease of use, with breadth of functionality typically being sacrificed.

ITC is positioning its product for the consumer segment.

⑥ Consumer Analysis

The target group of consumers for this product are heavy recreational computer users. They typically have used computers for three or more years. They have already used a commercial on-line service and have used at least several software packages extensively. They also tend to buy new software from time to time, if not regularly.

While the target group is increasingly buying software at retail outlets, many (especially those that tend to use their computers the most) buy their software through mail-order catalogs, and quite a few order at least some software direct from the publisher. Even when buying software in retail outlets, this group tends less to buy on impulse and often are more apt to be looking for a specific item that they are presold on. This group is most likely to be presold by editorial coverage in computer publications such as reviews and product announcements and by word of mouth. Because this audience is exposed to so much information about so many competing products, it is most likely to decide on a particular item as a result of multiple exposure to information about a product— often from different types of sources.

Members of the target group tend to live in suburban or urban areas. They are typically male, aged thirty to forty-five, college educated, have household incomes of $40,000–$100,000, are homeowners, and hold professional jobs. Many belong to computer clubs.

They typically read two or more computer publications, a major metro newspaper, and one or more consumer magazines. While they watch television several hours per week, their viewing tends to be less than average. They tend to listen to radio stations while they commute in their cars, tuning into a broad variety of formats.

7 Competition

While there are many firms selling Internet development tools and certainly many more are likely to emerge, there are two products that are currently competition for "The Tool."

International Development Systems, Inc., (IDS) is currently the market leader in development tools for the Internet for general consumers. With almost one hundred million dollars in sales, a strong name identity, and a strong retail presence, this firm advertises heavily and outsells its nearest competitor by four to one. Its product "IDS-Internet" has a street price of around $50. The product is stable and well proven, having been in use for almost two years, but it is tedious to use and offers almost no ability to change the design of a completed document.

Eastern Internet, Inc., introduced a product six months ago that is slowly gaining market share. Its product, called "Express," is the most similar to "The Tool." Express helps users place objects on a layout page by using "place-holders." However, Express does not give users the flexibility of moving objects about once they are in place. Express is sold primarily through retail stores, typically for about $75, but is not anywhere near as widely available as IDS-Internet. Eastern is a small start-up that appears to have limited resources and has engaged in limited advertising and promotion for its product.

8 Product's Features and Benefits

There are already several products in the marketplace selling in the $100 or under price range that offer similar functionality. These products offer powerful editing capability for text-only documents, as well as for graphics. They give users the capability of moving large amounts of text or graphics into a form translatable to a language understood by the Internet.

ITC's main distinctive feature is its intelligent agent. The benefit to consumers is that the product is easier to use and more flexible than competing products. The intelligent agent "walks" users step by step through the process of creating a document. The most similar competing product (Eastern's Express) offers more passive help by using "placeholders" where the user places objects on a layout page. While the placeholder approach gives users the ability to quickly assemble creative material, it does not give the user the flexibility of moving objects about.

9 Competitive Analysis

Strengths

Engineering: As shown by the features of its first product, ITC has a strong competitive edge in its engineering capabilities. The intelligent agent is a leap ahead of its competitors. This strength should help ITC keep ahead of its competition in the future as well.

Fast Development Cycle: Even with a product offering superior capabilities, ITC was able to create its first product from scratch in a very short period of time. This ability, coupled with superior engineering skills, should give ITC the ability to stay on the leading edge of product design over a sustained period of time.

Closeness to Market: Almost all key employees have a long experience of personal Internet use and keep in close touch with many industry people and people at many different computer clubs, who are also heavy Internet users. This gives ITC the ability to keep abreast of the marketplace and strong insight into the changing demands of its core customers.

Weaknesses

Financial: Even after raising the additional planned funding, the company will be substantially less well capitalized than some of its competitors. This would make it particularly difficult to finance a national advertising and promotion campaign, which would be important if the company were to try to obtain shelf space at nationwide computer retailers.

No market presence: The company currently has no other products in the market or due to hit the market soon. It has no relationship with any resellers. This contrasts with several competitors who are already selling product through many outlets, including retailers, and some competitors who have other offerings in their product line.

Weak marketing and sales staff: The company has one marketing manager and no sales staff. The marketing manager has several years of experience in selling hardware add-ons directly to major corporate customers, but no experience selling software and products to consumers.

10 Positioning

This product will be positioned as the premier Internet development tool for heavy computer users. ITC will target its marketing efforts narrowly at the core heavy user market. Because the product's ease of use is of less importance to highly experienced computer users, ITC will give more marketing emphasis to the product's other key benefit: flexibility.

ITC will completely avoid the retail store marketplace, where its lack of ability to fund expensive national and co-op advertising campaigns and its lack of presence in this marketplace would make it very difficult to compete anyway, or even gain entrance. Wholesalers and retailers are often more interested in the marketing support and name recognition that products enjoy, rather than functionality and features.

Instead, ITC will focus its marketing on selling direct. ITC will provide its product at the very high end of the consumer segment at $100 to further emphasize the product's superiority and to take advantage of the fact that consumers buying direct (versus those buying on impulse at retail stores) are less price-sensitive.

11 Advertising and Promotion

Because ITC's budget is very limited, it will keep its message very simple, emphasizing its product's flexibility first and secondarily its ease of use.

With the company's very limited budget, initial ads in direct-mail catalogs will be small—typically no larger than 1/8 page. Ad copy will contrast with competitive products that are shrink-wrapped and sold at lower prices to less experienced computer users.

Press releases will first emphasize the company's two key benefits. But they will also offer a lot of technical details that will appeal to the editors and publications most important to effectively reaching the core target market.

The company's top technical people will give talks at computer clubs, again to help position ITC on the leading edge.

Packaging will be subdued and professional-looking to further contrast ITC's product with the competitor's offerings.

12 Sales

ITC will sell the product via established direct-mail catalogs and through publicity and promotional efforts with computer clubs.

Direct-mail catalogs will be chosen on the basis of how closely catalogs' demographics match the demographics of ITC's target market of core users.

To help get consumers to order directly, ITC will accept orders on the Internet and via a toll-free 800 line.

13 Research and Development

ITC plans on focusing all of its research and development effort for at least the next two years on Internet development tools. While many of its competitors in this marketplace view Internet development tools as a secondary product line, ITC sees them as its only product line. Furthermore, ITC anticipates rapid growth in this area and, along with this growth, anticipates user demand for increasingly sophisticated development tools.

ITC plans on continually adding improved features to "The Tool," not only to improve the capability of the product, but also to garner more media attention.

14 Operations

Operations will be greatly simplified by contracting out as much work as possible. Reproduction of disks and production of packaging will be contracted out. Packaging design will be contracted out. Customer support will be contracted out.

Because direct sales will be so important, ITC will hire its own salespeople to take incoming phone and electronic orders. It will also maintain a small warehouse staff in order to maintain high quality and fast turnaround of shipping, in keeping with its premium product positioning.

People

(See the exhibits for resumes of key people):

President: James Smith
Mr. Smith founded three successful start-ups, including the highly recognized Internet Consultants, Inc. In addition to bringing a wealth of experience managing start-ups, Mr. Smith has a strong technical background and a long history of pioneering work on the Internet. Mr. Smith is highly recognized in the industry and has been profiled in several leading industry magazines.

Vice President of Engineering: Helen Jones
Ms. Jones has directed corporate marketing activities for different products at IBM for a number of years. Her sales programs have included direct sales, telemarketing, direct mail, and publicity campaigns.

Vice President of Finance: Fred Adams
Mr. Adams was, for the last two years, CFO of a small, but very fast-growing manufacturer of patio furniture, Beechtree Furniture Corporation. Beechtree raised private capital twice during Mr. Adams's tenure and placed a successful public offering six months ago.

Other Key People
The company is ready to hire two engineers, who have worked with John Smith in the past, once the funding is completed. Other key people the company is now conducting searches for are a Customer Service Manager, a Human Resources Manager, and an Operations Manager. Searches for all remaining positions will begin after funding is completed.

16 Payback and Exit Plan

Because the market for Internet tools is expected to continue its rapid growth for many years into the future, ITC anticipates not only rapid sales growth, but also rapid appreciation in the value of its stock. ITC believes these factors, coupled with its premium product strategy, will make the firm a strong takeover candidate by a large public corporation or even possibly a candidate for a broad public offering within five years.

17 Financials

See spreadsheets following.

17

PRO FORMA PROFIT AND LOSS STATEMENT FOR YEARS 1, 2, AND 3
for
INTERNET TOOL COMPANY, INC. (ITC)

	Year 1	Year 2	Year 3
SALES			
First-year unit sales projection	15,000 units	30,000 units	45,000 units
Retail price	$100	$100	$100
Net price	$80	$80	$80
Gross revenue	**$1,200,000**	**$2,400,000**	**$3,600,000**
COST OF GOODS			
Manufacturing costs per unit	$12	$12	$12
Total	$180,000	$360,000	$540,000
MARKETING			
Catalog ads	$100,000	$200,000	$300,000
Press packages and literature	$15,000	$20,000	$25,000
Travel	$18,000	$30,000	$40,000
Salary for marketing manager	$50,000	$70,000	$85,000
ENGINEERING			
Salaries	$170,000	$210,000	$250,000
Other engineering expenses	$12,000	$18,000	$22,000
GENERAL AND ADMINISTRATIVE			
Plant and equipment	$42,000	$50,000	$60,000
Salaries	$115,000	$150,000	$180,000
Telephone and postal services	$8,000	$12,000	$18,000
Other	$15,000	$20,000	$25,000
TOTAL COSTS	**$725,000**	**$1,140,000**	**$1,770,000**
PROFIT BEFORE TAXES	$475,000	$1,260,000	$1,830,000
TAXES	$190,000	$504,000	$732,000
PROFIT AFTER TAXES	**$285,000**	**$756,000**	**$1,098,000**

MONTHLY PRO FORMA PROFIT AND LOSS STATEMENT FOR YEAR 1
for
INTERNET TOOL COMPANY, INC. (ITC)

	JAN	FEB	MAR	APR	MAY	JUNE	JULY	AUG	SEPT	OCT	NOV	DEC	TOT
SALES													
First-year unit sales projection						1600	1800	2000	2200	2400	2500	2500	15000
Retail price						$100	$100	$100	$100	$100	$100	$100	$100
Net price						$80	$80	$80	$80	$80	$80	$80	$80
Gross revenue						$128000	$144000	$160000	$176000	$192000	$200000	$200000	$1200000
COST OF GOODS													
Manufacturing costs per unit						$12	$12	$12	$12	$12	$12	$12	$12
Total						$1200	$21600	$24000	$26400	$28800	$30000	$30000	$180000
MARKETING													
Catalog ads			$10000	$10000	$10000	$10000	$10000	$10000	$10000	$10000	$10000	$10000	$100000
Press packages and literature	$1000	$1000	$1000	$2000	$2000	$2000	$1000	$1000	$1000	$1000	$1000	$1000	$15000
Travel	$1500	$1500	$1500	$1500	$1500	$1500	$1500	$1500	$1500	$1500	$1500	$1500	$18000
Salary for marketing manager	$4167	$4167	$4167	$4167	$4167	$4167	$4167	$4167	$4167	$4167	$4167	$4167	$50004
ENGINEERING													
Salaries	$12000	$12000	$12000	$12000	$12000	$14000	$16000	$16000	$16000	$16000	$16000	$16000	$170000
Other engineering expenses	$1000	$1000	$1000	$1000	$1000	$1000	$1000	$1000	$1000	$1000	$1000	$1000	$12000
GENERAL AND ADMINISTRATIVE													
Plant and equipment	$3500	$3500	$3500	$3500	$3500	$3500	$3500	$3500	$3500	$3500	$3500	$3500	$42000
Salaries	$7000	$7000	$7000	$8000	$9000	$11000	$11000	$11000	$11000	$11000	$11000	$11000	$115000
Telephone and postal services	$667	$667	$667	$667	$667	$667	$667	$667	$667	$667	$667	$667	$8004
Other	$1250	$1250	$1250	$1250	$1250	$1250	$1250	$1250	$1250	$1250	$1250	$1250	$15000
TOTAL COSTS	$32084	$32084	$42084	$44084	$45084	$68284	$71684	$74084	$76484	$78884	$80084	$80084	$725008
PROFIT BEFORE TAXES	($32084)	($32084)	($42084)	($44084)	($45084)	$59716	$72316	$85916	$99516	$113116	$119916	$119916	$474992
TAXES (Estimated at 40%)	($12833.6)	($12833.6)	($16833.6)	($17633.6)	($18033.6)	$23886.4	$28926.4	$34366.4	$39806.4	$45246.4	$47966.4	$47966.4	$189996.8
PROFIT AFTER TAXES	($19250.4)	($19250.4)	($25250.4)	($26450.4)	($27050.4)	$35829.6	$43389.6	$51549.6	$59709.6	$67869.6	$71949.6	$71949.6	$284995.2

PRO FORMA BALANCE SHEETS FOR LIKELY SALES SCENARIOS
for
INTERNET TOOL COMPANY, INC. (ITC)

	Current	End of Year 1	End of Year 2	End of Year 3
ASSETS				
Current assets				
Cash	$415,000	$775,000	$1,507,000	$2,626,000
Inventory	0	$60,000	$60,000	$90,000
Total current assets	**$415,000**	**$835,000**	**$1,567,000**	**$2,716,000**
Fixed assets				
Equipment	$100,000	$100,000	$100,000	$100,000
Less accumulated depreciation	$15,600	$30,200	$45,800	$61,400
Total fixed assets	**$84,400**	**$69,800**	**$54,200**	**$38,600**
Total assets	**$499,400**	**$904,800**	**$1,621,200**	**$2,754,600**
LIABILITIES AND OWNER'S EQUITY				
Current liabilities				
Accounts payable	0	$30,000	$30,000	$45,000
Taxes payable	0	$90,000	$50,000	$70,000
Total current liabilities	**0**	**$70,000**	**$85,000**	**$115,000**
Owner's equity				
Common stock	$600,0000	$600,000	$600,000	$600,000
Retained earnings	($100,600)	$184,800	$941,200	$2,039,600
Total owner's equity	**$499,400**	**$904,800**	**$1,541,200**	**$2,639,600**
Total liabilities and owner's equity	**$499,400**	**$904,800**	**$1,621,200**	**$2,754,600**

A Sample Business Plan

MONTHLY PRO FORMA CASH FLOW FOR YEAR 1
for
INTERNET TOOL COMPANY, INC. (ITC)

	JAN	FEB	MAR	APR	MAY	JUNE	JULY	AUG	SEPT	OCT	NOV	DEC
STARTING CASH	$415000	$384216	$353432	$312648	$269864	$206880	$265496	$336712	$421528	$469944	$583160	$704376
CASH FROM SALES						$128000	$144000	$160000	$176000	$192000	$200000	$200000
CASH USES												
Cost of Goods					$19200	$21600	$24000	$26400	$28800	$30000	$30000	$30000
Marketing												
Catalog ads			$10000	$10000	$10000	$10000	$10000	$10000	$10000	$10000	$10000	$10000
Press packages and literature	$1000	$1000	$1000	$2000	$2000	$2000	$1000	$1000	$1000	$1000	$1000	$1000
Travel	$1500	$1500	$1500	$1500	$1500	$1500	$1500	$1500	$1500	$1500	$1500	$1500
Salary for marketing manager	$4167	$4167	$4167	$4167	$4167	$4167	$4167	$4167	$4167	$4167	$4167	$4167
Engineering												
Salaries	$12000	$12000	$12000	$12000	$12000	$14000	$16000	$16000	$16000	$16000	$16000	$16000
Other engineering expenses	$1000	$1000	$1000	$1000	$1000	$1000	$1000	$1000	$1000	$1000	$1000	$1000
General and Administrative												
Plant (less depreciation)	$3500	$3500	$3500	$3500	$3500	$3500	$3500	$3500	$3500	$3500	$3500	$3500
Salaries	$7000	$7000	$7000	$8000	$9000	$11000	$11000	$11000	$11000	$11000	$11000	$11000
Telephone and postal services	$667	$667	$667	$667	$667	$667	$667	$667	$667	$667	$667	$667
Other	$1250	$1250	$1250	$1250	$1250	$1250	$1250	$1250	$1250	$1250	$1250	$1250
Taxes									$50000			$50000
Total Cash Uses	$30784	$30784	$40784	$42784	$62984	$69384	$72784	$75184	$127584	$78784	$78784	$128784
NET CHANGE IN CASH	($30784)	($30784)	($40784)	($42784)	($62984)	$58616	$71216	$84816	$48416	$113216	$121216	$71216
ENDING CASH	$384216	$353432	$312648	$269864	$206880	$265496	$336712	$421528	$469944	$583160	$704376	$775592

NOTES ABOUT FINANCIAL STATEMENTS

- These financial statements are ficticious.
- They are simplified for easier understanding.
- To learn about financial statements, see Chapter 6.
- To learn how to prepare pro forma financial statements, see Chapter 6.
- Pro forma financial statements used to raise money should show at least three scenarios: most likely, weak, and strong cases.

ASSUMPTIONS ABOUT FINANCIAL STATEMENTS

- Starting position includes $400,000 expected to be raised in additional equity
- For simplicity, all sales are for cash, not credit
- For simplicity, assumes all purchases, except cost of goods sold, are paid for in cash
- Assumes a steady 60 days of inventory on hand, bought on 30-day terms
- Assumes product first ships from completion of funding

Streetwise Advice on Business Plans

☞ **People, people, people**

In seeking equity money from venture capitalists or other outside investors, you will increase your chances of success if you get someone committed to your management team who, if not known personally by a potential investor, at least will have a recognizable name. If you can't manage this, you should consider getting one or more people on your Board of Directors whom potential investors may be familiar with.

Alternately, you can include as exhibits to your plan any positive media clippings you can find, such as items from trade publications, about members of your management team. If you don't have any clippings, try contacting relevant publications to get media coverage—perhaps about your start-up business proposal.

☞ **Keep the tone of your business plan factual**

Don't use hyperbole or generalizations to describe the potential of your business plan. Investors and lenders don't want to hear phrases like "this business has incredible potential." They want to use the more factual information you present to reach their own conclusions.

☞ **Keep your plan succinct**

Whether creating a business plan to raise money or an annual plan to run your business, keep it succinct. People tend to use too much detail when creating plans. If a business plan is too long, it might be skimmed. If an annual plan is too long, focus on what is really important might be lost.

☞ **Involve everyone**

Both for business and annual plans, you need to have key employees create their area budgets. Then work with them until you are satisfied. Have key people get together to get the plan in sync and to get any disagreements out in the open. The more input people have in creating the plan, the more responsibility they will feel toward it.

☞ **Annual plans are not just budgets**

If an annual plan includes any financial projections, I find that almost everyone tends to focus on them almost exclusively, de-emphasizing the qualitative aspects of planning. While you do need to use numbers to run a business, numbers alone lead to a shallow plan. Companies run just by the numbers lose direction, drift from their strategy, and never realize their full potential. It is essential to the planning process to articulate clearly what the direction of the company will be for the coming year and what the role of each person will be in supporting the direction of the company overall.

☞ **Use the annual plan to improve performance**

In the real world nothing ever goes exactly according to plan but your annual plan gives you a way of measuring your company's actual performance against projected performance. Meet with key people at least once a month to review how the company is performing relative to the plan. The emphasis should not be on browbeating those managers whose areas are underperforming, but on how performance can be improved in the future.

Questions & Answers about Business Plans

What are the most common reasons venture capitalists pass on funding proposals?

They often aren't impressed by the management team. Ideally they want to see someone in the group who has already participated in a highly successful start-up. Lacking this, they want to see that people with solid and relevant experience are already committed for the key positions.

They are most likely to reject proposals that are still at the idea stage. The later the development stage the firm is in, the greater the chances for funding.

Venture capitalists aren't satisfied with a business that has only moderate profit potential. They are looking for companies that will not only be profitable but have the possibility of quickly developing into a huge business, returning to investors a large multiple on their initial investment.

If your business plan is not well thought out or well presented, venture capitalists aren't going to have confidence in your ability to run the business.

How much equity will I have to give up to equity investors?

This primarily depends on what development stage your firm is at and how much money you are seeking relative to how much capital you have already raised. If your firm is up and running and showing profitable sales, and you are looking for additional capital to finance your expansion, you will probably need to give up only a small portion of equity. On the other hand, if your firm is only at the idea stage and the outside investors are going to contribute over 90 percent of the funding, then you will probably have to give up at least half, if not more, of the equity.

Should I hire an expert to prepare the financials for my business plan?

It's better to prepare them yourself. A potential lender or equity investor wants to see not only that the numbers look good, but also that you understand them inside and out. If you can't answer highly detailed or thorny questions about how you arrived at your numbers, you aren't going to get your funding.

How far in advance should we start our annual planning process?

As a rule of thumb, I would suggest that you begin the annual planning process four to six months before the beginning of the next calendar year.

Many large corporations begin planning several years in advance, and this is why larger firms have a well-deserved reputation for moving as slow as dinosaurs. For a smaller, growing firm, it is a waste of time to do any detailed planning more than a year in advance; the company, your markets, and your competitor's plans will have changed too much to make such long-term planning valuable. The closer you are to the upcoming year when you plan, the more relevant your plans will be.

On the other hand, though, if you wait until the last minute to start annual planning, then you will have to rush through the process to get it done. The emphasis then will be on getting the plan done, not making it as good as possible. You and everyone working on a plan need to have enough time not only to get the plan done, but to do it well. You should also have time to weigh major alternatives and reconsider how well each function contributes to the overall plan after you've completed it.

Questions & Answers about Business Plans

❓ Should all parts of the annual plan be given equal attention?

No. If some parts of your business will change little during the next year, there is no reason to summarize these areas in great depth.

Remember that the role of the owner or CEO is to be sure that the planning efforts focus primarily on the areas that will really matter to the success of your business. Often planning can become focused on rivalries between different functions or lost in debates about factors that are relatively insignificant or not within your control. The CEO needs to see that plenty of attention is given to larger issues, such as

❓ How many new products should we launch next year?

❓ Why is our marketing budget so high as a percentage of sales?

❓ What are the risks of increasing prices on our core products or services?

❓ What level of detail should budgets contain?

Budgets in business plans to raise money should have little detail beyond breaking expenses out by departments or functions. You should, however, have supporting details available on request.

Similarly, when creating annual plans, even for a very small, one-person business, I suggest that you have two levels of detail. One should be a budget summary that has just one entry for projected sales of each major product or service line, and just one entry for projected costs in each functional area such as marketing, cost of goods sold, etc. A budget summary is very important in helping you get a handle on the cost structure of your business and its major trends.

Then have a separate, more detailed budget for each functional area. But don't get buried in detail. I would suggest a maximum of ten to twenty entries for projected expense categories if your business is small.

❓ How hard should I try to stay within budgeted expenses?

You should be more concerned in seeing that each function stays within its entire budget. For example, if the marketing department spends much more than projected on publicity, but makes up for it by spending that much less on advertising— that's fine.

Don't be terribly concerned about staying within budget if sales are above budget. But more than once I have let expenses soar above budget because sales were above budget. Then, later in the year, I discovered that expenses rose more quickly than sales. So if sales are increasing, make sure expenses increase only by a like percentage.

Questions & Answers about Business Plans

Is it worthwhile to completely redo the budget in the middle of the year?

Generally, no. It just takes too long and too much effort to make it worthwhile.

If your sales are running way above budget, try to be sure that expenses are not rising disproportionately. Watch out particularly for new, discretionary expenses that were not on the budget—they can always be added to the budget for the following year.

If your sales are running a little below budget, try to cut expenses in a few limited areas.

However, if your sales are running way below budget, I strongly recommend reworking the entire plan and carefully re-examining each and every item of the budget.

What should I watch out for in the annual planning process?

Most of all, you want to keep the emphasis on considering major alternatives and new initiatives and re-examining the ways the firm is currently doing its business. You want to be sure you and the other managers (if there are any) don't spend all of your time just making sales and expense projections—that's just forecasting the future, not managing the business. For example, if you are cur-rently shipping your product to local customers with your local delivery truck, you don't want to just project how much it will cost to run the truck next year. Instead you may want to consider selling the truck and contracting out the work to an outside delivery service.

Do salespeople tend to be overly optimistic in forecasting?

Yes. But there are some who try to be very conservative so they have less pressure during the year or so they can look better when they deliver sales that are way over budget. After you work with different people you will find how people in every functional area tend to approach the budgeting process, and you can work with each one to be as realistic as possible. Also, I'm a big believer in frank and open discussions about budgets, and I think that people from other functional areas can often offer constructive suggestions and serve as a reality check for one another.

Why do I need a budget? Can't I just try to be really frugal on every expense?

Believe me—I've tried this approach, and it never worked. Running a business of any size is too complex to do by the seat of your pants. I've found that even if I try to be cheap as dirt on every expense, without a concrete plan, costs can still mushroom out of control and wipe out profitability.

How can I tell what costs for different parts of my operation and net profit and goals should be?

You need to get data for firms in your industry—perhaps from an industry association. Sometimes trade maga-zines and newsletters publish statis-tics for their industries. Compare your numbers with firms of similar size in the same industry.

*ast growth in and of itself can help motivate employees and help project a very positive image to customers. So trumpet your successes continually to both employees and customers!

When setbacks occur, explain them to employees. But, certainly, depict them as small blips in your course to success. Everyone wants to feel like he or she is on the winning team or buying products or services from the winning team. Success does breed success.

Sustaining fast growth can be tricky, though. Preserving cash, keeping people motivated, and continually finding more office space are just a few of the issues that you will encounter. The farther in advance you can plan and prepare for such challenges, the more likely it is that you will be able to minimize any negative effects.

Following are a few of the growth issues you may have to contend with.

Hiring

A fast-growth business means lots of hiring. And it's very easy to underestimate the time and direct costs of hiring lots of new people—and the right people. You will need to spend considerable time developing job descriptions, posting help-wanted ads, sorting through resumes, conducting and arranging phone and in-person interviews, and checking references. Even if you are very busy with other issues, you can't afford to skimp on the amount of time required to conduct a careful hiring process. If you hire someone who can't perform the job satisfactorily, your business performance will most likely suffer. If you have to fire someone you will engender bad morale and run some legal risks. Or you may hire someone who can adequately perform the task, but has an attitude problem—the hiree might want to be doing something else or working at another firm. This type of person will not perform to his or her full potential and may quit. Either way, you will have to go through the entire time-consuming hiring process again.

Unless your company is large enough to have a human resources manager, this time will be spent by you or other managers. It is time taken from the management of ongoing business activities. It is difficult to predict how much time will be involved in filling positions, especially senior positions, because the response to help-wanted ads can fluctuate greatly from one week to the next and, even with a terrific response, it is difficult to gauge how interested any given candidate is in the job until you actually offer it.

Help-wanted advertising can be expensive. Many small businesses underestimate the out-of-pocket costs necessary to conduct a employee search. Because responses to help-wanted advertising can be erratic, firms often find themselves advertising over an extended period of time in order to attract qualified candidates—especially for more demanding positions. Be prepared for the cost!

People

While every business benefits greatly from having good people, the importance of having above-average people in a fast-growth business can't be overemphasized. Workloads will constantly be expanding and may not be predictable. New issues and problems will constantly pop up and innovative solutions will have to be implemented quickly. You need people who can think on their feet, adapt well to constant change, and put in the extra hours that will be needed to get you through the unusual pressures and surprises of managing a business in upward transition. You need people who can get excited about being a part of *your* growing business!

Stagnant managers

One of the thornier issues you are going to confront in a fast-growth business is that some people, even those who are committed to your business and work hard, won't be able to adjust to the changes brought about by growth. For example, the person who supervised two people in your warehouse well when you first started out may not be able to manage a team of forty. As the business grows you need to make hard and objective assessments of your key managers. Are they up to handling an increased or changing workload? Can a strong assistant, supplemental education, automation, or computerization bring a weaker manager up to speed? Do you need to bring in a more senior manager to oversee that person's work? Or do you

need to make the most difficult decision of all and replace them? Even one weak manager in a key position can really drag down the performance of an entire organization.

The impact of new people

Current employees often feel threatened by the influx of new personnel. Senior employees are likely to feel that their stature within the organization is being undermined, and less senior people may feel that they are being neglected.

Before you advertise for new positions you should work to retain the confidence of existing staff. Involve your employees in the process of structuring new positions. If a new position will cut into the responsibilities or authority of a current employee, meet with that employee privately to discuss the need for an added position and, if the employee's performance has always been satisfactory, say something positive about that performance or contributions to the company. Emphasize your confidence in his or her ability to continue being a positive asset to the company. Post all job openings internally at the same time, if not before, you place outside advertising.

When you are interviewing candidates for new positions, consider having all employees who may be threatened by the new position participate in the interviewing process. This will make them feel more confident about their position within the organization and less threatened by the new hire.

Money

Fast-growth businesses burn money! Even with good profits, there will almost certainly be times when a growing business will run tight on cash as expenditures occur before related sales are realized. Businesses with inventory or receivables will run into this situation particularly fast. But all fast-growth businesses are going to run into plenty of unforeseen costs.

Growth

Planning

The faster a business is growing or changing, the more difficult it will be to plan future expenditures or income. But you must! Careful planning and constant updating of plans, particularly cash flow projections, is of tantamount importance in a fast-growing business. While most businesses may do a major overhaul of their projections and business plan once a year, with minor updates monthly, a fast-growth business should consider completely revamping its plans, or at least its cash flow projections, several times during the year as significant deviations from what was projected occur in ongoing sales and/or expenditures.

Because fast-growth business expenses have a tendency to skyrocket faster than sales, you need to stay on top of the changes in projected cash flows. This will enable you to make timely cuts in expenses and, if necessary, slow growth so that you don't run out of money. Have in mind which areas can easily run on less cash or maintain momentum even with less growth.

Profits

In a fast-growth business it is very easy to become excited about rapidly rising sales and lose track of profits. This is especially true when an organization shifts from a very small entrepreneurial organization to a professional organization with many managers. Be aware that during the transitional phases overhead expenses can mount rapidly!

Profit margins

Fat profit margins are essential for growth. If you are trying to attract outside investors, banks, or other lenders, they will want to see good, healthy profit margins. More sophisticated lenders and investors will also pay a lot of attention to the trends in your profit margins. You will need fat profit margins even if you are trying to finance growth internally. A business with a 10 percent profit margin can financially sustain twice the growth rate of a similar business with only a 5 percent profit margin.

Fat profit margins leave more room for error. With thin profit margins even a small mistake or expense underestimation can plunge your firm into an unprofitable state.

Taxes

It is easy to underestimate the impact of taxes when planning for a growing business. Don't assume that taxes rise parallel to raises in sales. As your business becomes more profitable and grows, your tax bill will likely increase at a higher rate than anticipated because either you personally, or the company (if it is incorporated), will move into a higher tax bracket.

You should also remember that the size of your quarterly tax estimates will need to increase in order to cover the total yearly increase in taxes.

Facilities

A fast-growth business may need an increasing amount of space to house additional equipment and/or personnel. You could anticipate growth and lease an initial space that will accommodate plenty of future growth, but this commits you to a space larger than you need now and squanders money needlessly. Or you may find a landlord willing to rent space on a short-term basis—six months to a year—so that you can upgrade square footage with some immediacy. But moving can be disruptive to operations. What should you do then?

Compromise! Try to attach an option to your lease that allows you to continue renting for renewable twelve-month periods of time after an initial two- to three-year firm commitment. And look for a facility that has a small amount of growth space for your operations. If your space becomes crowded, explain to your employees that these conditions aren't forever and that you foresee moving to a more spacious facility soon. If the overcrowding is severe, consider renting a separate, nearby space for one group or department until such time as you can rent a space large enough to hold all of your staff.

☞ **Hire people in batches**

It is much more efficient to hire several people at once. Systematically evaluate hiring needs, write up job descriptions, place help-wanted ads, sort through candidates, conduct interviews, execute the hirings, and provide new employee orientation for a group of people at one time. This allows existing managers to expend energy on the hiring process for a limited amount of time. If this rule isn't followed, especially in a fast-growth business, hiring will become an endless procedure that seriously infringes on time better spent on running the business.

☞ **Establish credit lines that grow**

Whenever possible, try to establish credit lines that will grow along with the business. For example, in setting up a credit line with your bank, try to get a credit line based on a percentage of your receivables, rather than a constant, static amount. Chances are your credit line will be reviewed by your bank annually and will be sub-

ject to ceilings and restrictions, but try to build as much flexibility into your borrowing relationships as you can. This will leave you better equipped to finance fast growth. Also try to establish credit lines with your trade suppliers that grow along with your business as well.

☞ **Add systems and procedures**

As your business grows, you won't be able to spend as much time personally checking over details as you did initially. So, set up systems and procedures that will help you be sure that management and staff are continually making checks in the same manner you would have. Maybe, for example, you need to set specific product quality control standards. Or maybe you need to set up purchasing procedures. The more your day-to-day business operations rely on systems and procedures, the more growth you will be able to effectively achieve.

☞ **Watch nonfinancial limits**

Because money, or rather the lack of it, is such an overwhelming impediment to growth, it is easy to overlook other issues that may limit your ability to grow. You might feel that some people on your staff, your com-

puter system, your facilities, or some other component of your business is being overtaxed by continuous growth. If so, don't hesitate to slow down the pace of growth for a while until you feel that that component of your operations is running smoothly again. It takes a wise, disciplined manager to hold back on unbridled growth to ensure that the company can continue to deliver quality products in a professional manner.

☞ **Use ROI criteria to determine which investments to pursue**

Because a fast-growing business often has more profitable options to pursue than it has money, a decision must be made as to which options should be pursued. One way to determine which options offer the best opportunities for success is to select those with the highest return on investment (ROI). A simplified example is that of a store trying to decide which of two different product lines with equal profit margins to carry. Using ROI criteria, the store may decide to carry the product line that sells faster because its money or investment will be tied up for a shorter period of time, giving a higher return on the investment.

Questions & Answers about Growth

Is it easier to sustain fast growth in certain businesses?

Generally businesses with very standard products serving large national or international markets can sustain the demands of fast growth more easily than firms offering nonstandard or customized products that serve small markets. It is difficult to maintain a consistent level of quality and service for custom or special products when a company is experiencing rapid expansion. And, if the potential market is small, a firm will have to expand into additional markets to sustain high levels of growth.

On the other hand, high-growth companies that produce standard products for large domestic or international markets are more likely to attract well-financed national or international competitors.

When is fast growth too fast?

Sustainable fast growth must be "controlled" fast growth. No matter how fast you are growing, you need to have time to keep your business plan up to date. Your projected cash flow should allow for enough room in your credit line at the bank to allow for unforeseen or underestimated expenses. Your profit and loss projections should be sufficiently up to date so that it accurately represents your current and projected cost structure. You need to feel relatively comfortable about the ability of your key managers. You should also feel great about the quality of your product and service. And perhaps most of all, you should not feel "burned out."

Does a fast-growth business require a different type of bank?

Fast-growth businesses inherently involve more risk. Some small, local, or conservative banks may not see an upside opportunity in financing your growth. If your business hits its targets, your lending needs may outpace your bank's legal lending limits. When you approach a bank, find out what types of businesses it typically finances. If its clientele has been restricted to the local funeral parlor, barber, and corner grocery store, it won't be your best bet if you are seeking financing for a high-flying, international concern manufacturing a highly technical product.

What problems beset fast-growth firms?

Fast-growth firms are likely to encounter all of the problems less growth-oriented firms experience, but they tend to run deeper and happen more frequently and simultaneously. Loss of control is often at the root of these problems. Problems might strike companywide if a firm experiences a cash shortage because of poor cash forecasting. Or problems might be limited to one or two functional areas if a manager becomes overworked, is in over his or her head, or is unable to keep up the pace.

What should I do if I feel growth is "out of control"?

First, try to get cash flow under control, because without cash or credit, your options are severely limited. Project cash flow out carefully for a twelve-month period. Make sure your profit and loss projections for the next year or so are up to date. Compare your profit margins to competitors—are they in line? Evaluate the direction your business is headed in and discuss it with your managers. Is your direction in line with your business strategy? Is it in sync with your current strengths and weaknesses. Evaluate each functional area of your business and determine its ability to handle future growth. Fast growth will amplify any weaknesses in your company—make sure each component of your organization is as strong as it can possibly be.

Selling a Business

If you have a successful small business, sooner or later you'll consider selling it off along with all its worries and responsibilities. You'll fantasize about living the rest of your life in an exotic tropical paradise. Remember, though, that the degree of care and effort you put into the sales process could have a huge impact on the price you receive and how long it will take to complete that sale—and leave you free to pursue your pleasures!

It's probably going to take you a lot of time and effort to sell your business. Anyone who makes an offer is going to demand a tremendous amount of information regarding the business. You are going to have to determine how much you want to divulge prior to the sale. And you are going to have to spend an extensive amount of time with prospective buyers explaining the ins and outs of your particular business.

Selling a business for a price you deem fair and equitable isn't a sure thing. Many people place their businesses on the market and then decide not to sell because they either don't receive any offers or don't receive any offers they consider to be acceptable. Throughout the selling process you should be prepared for the possibility that an appropriate buyer may not come forward.

Remember that it will continue to be necessary for you to devote enough energy, time, and other resources to maintaining the business in good shape. And don't forget to carefully weigh the impact of announcing that the business is for sale to your employees, customers, vendors, bankers, and other people you do business with.

Selling a business also involves a lot of legal issues. You will need to consult an attorney before you prepare your prospectus which, typically, describes the business right up to the time the sale closes.

Business brokers

A business broker acts as an agent for an owner looking to sell a business. Some real estate agents broker businesses but most business brokers are, themselves, small local businesses representing area small businesses or larger businesses in a particular industry. They can be found through telephone listings or advertisements in local newspapers or trade magazines. They typically charge the owner 10 percent of the final sales price, which is payable at closing.

There are several advantages to using a business broker. The broker will allow you to maintain confidentiality if you don't want your intent to sell to be public knowledge. It saves you the time of talking to potential buyers, thus allowing you to focus on running your business Also, some prospects may be more comfortable, at least initially, talking to an intermediary about a business rather than talking directly to the owner. Also, a broker who specializes in a particular industry may have excellent contacts at larger corporations that might be interested in buying out your company at a higher price than an individual buyer might.

Nonetheless, a broker's fee is substantial and you will want to weigh the expense before you decide to list your business through a broker.

Partial sale

You may decide to sell part of the business, rather than all of it. If one segment of your operation is growing much more quickly than another, you may want to consider placing the less successful portion on the market. If you are able to sell it, you will have more money and time to invest in the remainder of your company.

In order to make a partial sale, you will have to break out the financial information and prepare a two-year profit and loss statement for the separate business segment you are selling. This may be tricky, and you might want to consider having an independent accountant perform the work or at least check yours out.

Financial statements

The basic financial information needed to sell most small businesses are profit and loss statements and balance sheets from the last five years of operation. If you are three or four months into a new fiscal year, you should also provide an interim financial statement.

One of the first questions a prospective buyer will ask is who prepared your financial statements. Even if you have prepared your own financial statements in the past, you should consider having an outside firm prepare or review them for the sale. This will increase the value of the business in the eyes of potential buyers and increase the likelihood of making the sale. If you decide against using an outside accounting firm to prepare your financial statements, offer to show copies of your corporate or, in the case of a sole proprietorship or partnership, personal tax returns to serious potential buyers. This will help to substantiate your businesses profitability.

Selling a Business

Management agreements

Often the prospective buyer will express an interest in having the current owner continue to run the business after the sale takes place. If you are interested in doing this, be sure to get any such agreement in writing. Working relationships between new owners and ex-owners are often highly subject to friction!

Will anyone buy my business?

The only way to find out for sure is to place your firm on the market. Generally, a small business that is relatively new, unprofitable, or has a sharply declining sales history will be difficult to sell. Reviewing the simple valuation guidelines will give you some indication of how marketable your business may be.

The higher the suggested multiple of earnings for your business, the more chances you have of finding a buyer.

Valuation

The *selling* prices of similar businesses in your area will provide an indication of what you can expect to receive for your business. Do note that we are talking selling price, not asking price. Typically, small businesses sell for significantly less than the asking price.

Sophisticated buyers might evaluate your business on the basis of projected cash flow for the next few years. They will then discount the value of that cash flow to reflect the amount of risk inherent in the business and the importance of their personal efforts in maintaining the success of the business. They will also consider what their money could be earning in a "risk free" investment such as a U.S. government Treasury bill.

Selling to larger corporations

Sometimes it is possible to sell your business to a larger corporation for more than it is worth to an individual buyer.

A larger corporation that is active in the same business area you are may be able to improve on your profit margins by folding your business into one of their business units. It might also be able to eliminate or reduce back-office expenses such as accounting or warehousing and sales expenses such as paying independent commission representatives by using their own staff and facilities.

Also, a larger corporation that is trying to grow quickly in a new strategic area may be willing to pay a fat premium to quickly acquire market share.

Any corporation with which you are currently engaged in any type of cooperative effort should be targeted as a potential buyer.

Simple Valuation Guidelines

1. An extremely well-established and steady business with a rock-solid market position, whose continued earnings will not be dependent upon a strong management team.
A multiple of eight to ten times current profits

2. An established business with a good market position, with some competitive pressures and some swings in earnings, requiring continual management attention.
A multiple of five to seven times current profits

3. An established business with no significant competitive advantages, stiff competition, few hard assets, and heavy dependency upon management's skills for success.
A multiple of two to four times current profits

4. A small personal service business where the new owner will be the only, or one of the only, professional service providers.
A multiple of one times current profits.

Attorneys

There are two areas where it is strongly suggested that you consult with an attorney when selling a business. The first instance is when you prepare a circular or prospectus summarizing your business for potential buyers, and the second is when you prepare a purchase and sales agreement.

While you may have operated your business successfully year after year, a new buyer without your particular skills, expertise, or personality may easily run into problems. If the business turns out to be less successful or easy to run than the buyer anticipated, he or she may assume that the business was fraudulently represented. One way to reduce the risk of litigation in this is to have an attorney review your circular or prospectus. The attorney will undoubtedly advise you to avoid projecting future sales or profits or at least be extremely careful when doing so.

Even if you are selling a very small business, you should have your attorney review, if not actually prepare, the purchase and sales agreement. Buying and selling businesses is often much more complex than, for example, making real estate transactions. There are more variables and much less standardization in the wording of business sales agreements.

Employees

Make sure that employees hear about a potential sale of the business from you and not a third party. Rumors breed nervousness. Some of your staff may decide to seek employment elsewhere and leave immediately.

If you decide to advertise the sale of your business openly, tell your employees before the advertisements run. Explain that the sale could take a long time to happen and, unless you plan to close down if no sale occurs, may not happen at all. If you expect to find a buyer who will keep all or most of your employees on the payroll, tell this to your staff. Remain truthful, but emphasize the positive.

If you decide to advertise the business confidentially, make a concerted effort to avoid any leaks to employees.

Consider using a business broker and have any interested buyers sign a nondisclosure agreement. Potential buyers should also visit your operation during off hours.

You may also decide that one or more of your employees is the best potential buyer for your business. Employees know the business better than outsiders and may be able to persuade investors or lending institutions to help them finance a leveraged buyout.

Qualifying buyers

During the course of selling a business you will get a lot of tire kickers. They won't really be interested in buying and can waste a lot of your time. You need to be able to quickly judge the seriousness of a prospect so that the energy you put into discussing the business isn't entirely fruitless. After all, you still need to concentrate on running your business.

Selling a Business

Here are a few questions that will assist you in qualifying potential buyers.

? Have you ever bought or owned your own business before?

A potential buyer who has owned a business before, and particularly has bought a business before, is much more likely to be a serious prospect.

? What is your time frame for buying a business?

A prospect that indicates anything less than an interest in being ready to buy the right business opportunity today is not a serious prospect.

? What other types of businesses are you looking at?

A potential buyer who is looking at a wide array of different types of businesses is less likely to be a serious prospect.

? Do you have adequate cash to buy this business?

If the prospect indicates anything less than a strong "yes," don't consider him or her seriously. Even if your prospect is a multimillion dollar business, ask to see proof of sufficient resources.

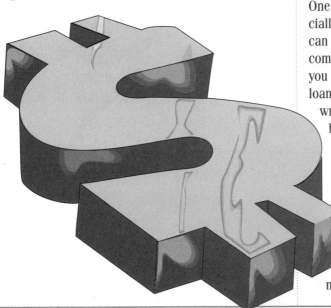

Seller financing

One of the biggest obstacles in selling a business, especially for the price you want, is finding a buyer who has or can borrow the cash to buy the business. Hence, it is very common for businesses to be sold with seller financing. If you do decide to provide financing, have the buyer sign a loan agreement with you and be sure to get an attorney to write up the documentation. Also, don't assume, just because you ran the business profitably, that the new owner will do so as well. Try to get as much solid collateral as you can in order to protect your loan.

If your business includes real estate, motor vehicles, machinery, or other hard assets, you may want to consider selling them separately or even leasing them to the new owner. This could increase the pool of qualified prospects, increase your chances of completing a sale, and decrease the need for seller financing.

Streetwise Advice on Selling a Business

☞ **Start with a reasonable asking price**

Many business owners put ridiculously high asking prices on their businesses. They are making a serious mistake. A high asking price scares away many potential buyers. It tells some people that you are not serious about selling your business, And, because it means your business will probably remain on the market for a long period of time, it will make other potential buyers wonder if there isn't some hidden problem with your business that has kept other prospects from negotiating a deal.

☞ **Determine what your bottom-line price is in advance**

While you never want to mention what your rock-bottom price is during preliminary negotiations, you will find that having set both a target and a minimum price in your mind will enable you to negotiate more decisively.

☞ **Be sure you are serious**

Deciding to sell your business is not a decision that should be taken lightly. Selling a business will take up a lot of your time and effort. It will probably cause some business disruption, especially when employees, customers, competitors, and vendors are aware that your business is for sale.

☞ **Prepare statements and other information in advance**

Be sure you have done your homework before you run the first advertisements announcing the sale of your business. Your first prospects may be your best prospects. Be sure you have prepared financial statements and literature promoting your business. Also, be sure to have an attorney review any material you will be using to corroborate the success or nature of the business you are offering for sale before you announce the sale publicly.

☞ **Selling a new business**

If your business is relatively new, such as younger than two years old, or is a small firm and has been consistently unprofitable, you are probably going to be better off not trying to sell. Your best bet would be to liquidate your assets and get on with your life. Selling a business for even a small amount of money can take up a lot of your time and energy. You just may be wasting your efforts trying to find a buyer.

☞ **Consider customers, suppliers, and vendors as potential buyers**

Firms in related businesses and firms that are familiar with your business are often great prospects and may pay premium prices. I once sold a very marginal map business to a large steamship line that had been selling some of the maps on their ships.

"Setting both a target and a minimum selling price in your mind will enable you to negotiate more decisively."

Questions & Answers about Selling a Business

How should I advertise my business?

For a small local business it is best to place an ad in the business opportunity section of the largest Sunday newspaper that circulates in your area. For a larger business, run an ad in an appropriate trade publication. You might consider running the ad "blind"—using the publication's address for inquiries—so that your entire industry does not become aware of your intention to sell.

Should I place a large display ad or a small classified ad?

Run a small classified ad. Anyone who is really serious about purchasing a business opportunity will be scanning small classified ads. Keep the copy brief and to the point. Rather than running a large ad, run the ad over a period of time. If you are using a newspaper as your advertising media, however, advertise only in the Sunday edition.

Are business brokers worth the commission?

Especially if you are selling a larger business, you may find it easier to find a qualified buyer using the resources of a business broker. For a very small local retail or service business, however, you might do just as well selling the business yourself.

If you are hesitant to use a business broker, make every effort to sell the business on your own for a reasonable amount of time. If you aren't successful, then consider giving your listing to a business broker.

Once you start advertising your business, you may find some business brokers willing to list your business on a nonexclusive basis. But wait until you can no longer afford either the time or effort required to sell the business yourself before you give over the listing to a business broker on an exclusive basis. Remember that a business broker will put much more effort into selling your concern when it is being listed exclusively through that agency.

If I provide seller financing, what interest rate should I charge?

If you must provide seller financing in order to complete the sale, you should charge an interest rate that is at least a couple of points higher than those currently being offered by commercial banks. You are almost certainly taking on considerably more risk than is involved in a typical bank loan. Also, you want to provide the buyer incentive to find his own financing through a bank, relatives, or any other source that may be available.

How long will it take to sell my business?

Assume it will take a lot longer than you think it will! While it varies greatly from one transaction to the next, the typical selling time for a very small business such as a retail or service business ranges from two to six months. For a larger business, a six- to twelve-month time frame is more common.

Common Strategic Mistakes

Following are the most common strategic mistakes made by small businesses.

They adopt a strategy that fails to differentiate them from their competitors

1 To cite an example, let's look at the bookstore that adopts customer service as its main strategy, emphasizing special ordering and suggesting titles to its customers. This isn't a strategy, since virtually every bookstore will special-order for customers, and to some degree every bookstore suggests some titles to their customers by virtue of bestseller displays and store signage.

They adopt some parts of many different strategies, but don't follow any one particular strategy aggressively

2 The problem with this approach is that in a competitive marketplace, the business with many strategies is not clearly differentiated from its competitors. Also, a small business, particularly a new one, lacks the resources to successfully execute many strategies at once. An example is the independent bookstore that has half as many titles as the largest nearby chain superstore; only half as great a discount on best sellers as a nearby warehouse store; half as many used books as competitors; half as many events as competitors; vending machines with candy and soft drinks instead of a full-service cafe; and a fraction of the sales per square foot as its competitors. The bookstore should focus on one or two types of services and try to do those extremely well.

They change their strategy too often

3 Changing strategy too often is a particular problem for small businesses struggling or facing better-heeled competitors. An example is the bookstore that initially refuses to discount its books when a national book discount chain moves into town. Then, when the small bookseller loses much of its market share, it will try to regain lost ground by instituting deep discounts. By this time, however, the national book discount chain has become known as the place to go for discounted books and the small bookseller is bound to be disappointed by its failure to increase sales. And, to compound matters, the small bookstore finally returns to a full-price strategy. This type of scenario, or any mixed message strategy, often leads to complete business failure.

M·A·R·K·E·T·I·N·G

Positioning ▶ 67

Marketing Plan ▶ 73

Cheap Marketing Tricks ▶ 86

Publicity ▶ 89

Point of Sale ▶ 102

Literature ▶ 103

Trade Shows ▶ 104

Competing with Giants ▶ 111

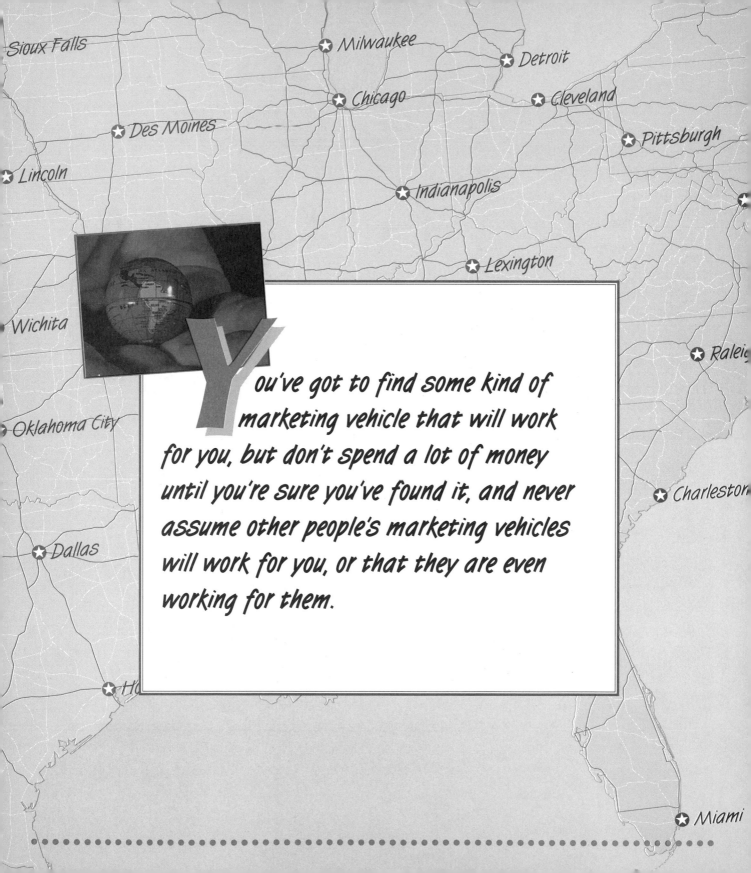

You've got to find some kind of marketing vehicle that will work for you, but don't spend a lot of money until you're sure you've found it, and never assume other people's marketing vehicles will work for you, or that they are even working for them.

Positioning

A unique selling proposition (USP) is a succinct, memorable message that identifies the unique benefits that are derived from using your product or service as opposed to a competitor's. A USP should be used as a strong and consistent part of an advertising campaign. It can be painted on the company's cars or trucks, printed on the letterhead, and used in the packaging copy. It becomes, essentially, a positioning statement—a declaration of your company's unique standing within the marketplace as defined by your product's benefits.

Often a USP is a quick and snappy condensation of the company's strategy. This is especially true when a company offers one type of product or service. But even more so than most strategies, USPs tend to focus on one or two of the most powerful and easily communicated benefits derived from using a product or service.

The USP might focus on price, quality, dependability, breadth or depth of the product or service line, technical edge, fashion, customization, specialization, or nature of service.

Why develop a USP?

Why can't a company simply describe its products, benefits, and features? Why must it be locked into a consistent image? Why can't the benefit focus change from one advertising or publicity campaign to the next?

Every day, each person is bombarded with literally thousands of advertising messages in newspapers and magazines, on television, on the radio, on the sides of buses, on billboards, and even through computer on-line services. Because advertisements are so inescapable, all of us tend to shut out a great deal of the messages they impart. Most ads also have a low recall rate—few people remember them for any length of time after having seen or experienced them.

To build long-term product recognition, an advertiser should focus on getting consumers to remember one succinct and consistent message regarding its product. To expect consumers to remember a continually changing or drawn-out message is a near-futile hope.

It is particularly important that a USP immediately convey one of the strongest competitive advantages of using your product. Otherwise you are simply engaging in trade association-type advertising or, in other words, promoting all products within your marketplace or industry.

Differentiation

Marketers should strive to create a significant perception of difference between their product and the offerings of competitors. This becomes particularly important, and of course a more difficult job, when competitive products or services have virtually identical features that offer like benefits. Developing a USP that accomplishes this task is called product differentiation.

For example, a perfume manufacturer could use the product name, packaging, and advertising to create a certain distinct mood or feeling about each of its product lines. It can carefully target each line to a specific audience.

Think of Shalimar—"The Gardens of Shalimar have inspired thousands of lovers. And one perfume." Or Liz Claiborne's Vivid—"A spirit that will not be denied."

Similarly, a cola bottler or brewer of beer may use a USP to identify its product with a fun and appealing lifestyle that creates a positive product differentiation.

Great examples of effective product differentiation include Wal-Mart's "Always the low price," FedEx's "Absolutely, positively overnight," UPS's "We run the tightest ship in the shipping business," Stouffer's "Nothing comes closer to home," or Midas Muffler's "Guaranteed for as long as you own your car."

" The Gardens of Shalimar have inspired thousand of lovers. "

— Shalimar
(perfume)

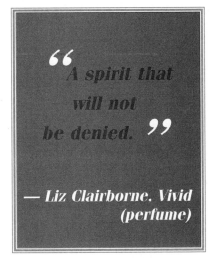

" A spirit that will not be denied. "

— Liz Clairborne. Vivid
(perfume)

" We run the tightest ship in the shipping business. "

— United Parcel Service (UPS)
(shipper)

Positioning Success Story

Silent Systems, Inc., manufactures computers that eliminate fan and and hard-drive noise. They compete against larger manufacturers of computers. *Greg Wyler,* President, shares his views on creating and protecting unique selling propositions.

Know Your Message

" It's important to know the message that you want other people to see. If you have three things to tell people, you tell it to them over and over and over again! "

Deliver It Quickly

" Consumers have only about 4 or 5 seconds in which to process your information. And if it doesn't ring a bell, if it doesn't stick to the back of their minds, then you've lost them. "

Protect Your USP

" If you see anything like your product, you have to jump on top of it and see whether it does or doesn't infringe. If it starts to, you've got to notify them. If it doesn't, then you've got to figure out how that affects your marketing position. If someone else came out with a silent PC, then we wouldn't be able to say we're the only one anymore. "

Streetwise Advice on Positioning

☞ **It's not strategy**

A quick way to differentiate a unique selling proposition from a strategy is that a USP works well in advertising copy. It should be catchy, cute, or snappy. Each product might have its own USP.

Since a USP is not your strategy, don't try to hit all of the key features of your products or even feel compelled to mention the most important. Instead try focusing on one benefit that is highly memorable. A good example is David Ogilvy's classic "At 60 miles an hour, the loudest noise in a Rolls-Royce is the sound of its clock." Clearly the strategy of Rolls-Royce is not to make the clock as loud as possible. Nor is the low level of interior noise the most important feature of a Rolls-Royce.

☞ **It's not easy**

It's not as easy as it may first look to come up with a unique selling proposition that is really powerful. This is one reason why major corporations spend tons of money on ad agencies in an often endless search for the "perfect" USP. Don't get frustrated if you don't come up with a great USP before you start your business. Chances are, your competitor doesn't have a very good one either.

But don't forget about a USP, or put off finding one forever, even if your competition is in the same boat as you. A good USP can be a powerful competitive edge. If you're stumped sitting at your desk trying to come up with a creative USP, try discussing it with your family or friends. Or just start jotting down all of your thoughts. Some of them may seem silly at first but may lead to something better in time.

☞ **Don't get bored with it**

Since you live, eat, and breathe your company every day of the year, you might quickly tire of a good USP. But don't drop it. Remember, your current customers, and more importantly, your potential customers, will not see your message every day and will not tire of it as easily as you might.

☞ **Do it yourself**

Yes, you could hire an advertising agency to come up with a USP. But I suggest that you do it yourself. For one, ad agencies are sometimes guilty of focusing a little too much on making USPs too cute, too clever, or too entertaining, and not on making them effective. And, more importantly, if you create your own USP, you will probably have more pride in it, be more committed to its meaning, and more apt to use it over a longer period of time. It will be a message you are more likely to use as a powerful marketing tool in presenting your business within the marketplace.

☞ **Don't misuse it**

Don't get straightjacketed by your USP, no matter how good it is. It should seldom be used as a headline in print ads or as the starting phrase in a radio or television spot. Instead you should consider placing it at the bottom of print ads or using it as the wrap-up line in radio or TV ads.

? I am having trouble creating a USP. How should I approach its development?

Focus on what is unique about your product or service. Is your product or service bigger, cheaper, more durable, faster, more personalized, more convenient, or easier to use than the competition's?

Then determine how that product or service feature that distinguishes you from the competition could be perceived as a benefit by the user. For example, if you are selling low-fat ice cream that tastes just as good as regular ice cream, your USP might be "Stay slim eating great ice cream."

? My consumer benefit doesn't sound convincing. What should I do?

In many businesses the principal consumer benefit sounds too similar to those of other firms and not particularly differentiating or convincing. For example, many product and service companies emphasize generic benefits such as high quality or low price. This works well as a strategy, but doesn't carry much punch as a USP.

A better approach is to give the reasons behind such generic benefits. For example, let's say you are running an accounting service for small businesses. A USP of "high-quality service" is not really unique. It won't sell your services and, frankly, would be a complete waste of your advertising expenditures. Instead, you may want to relate the reasons why your service is of such high quality. A common but effective method would be to state your years in business—"twenty-five years of experience."

Another approach would be to guarantee your benefit. For example, Midas Muffler emphasizes its quality with the USP of guaranteeing mufflers for "as long as you own your car."

In price-competitive markets, many retailers offer price guarantees. A typical guarantee is that the retailer will refund 100 percent of the difference in price if you find an identical product for sale at a lower price elsewhere within thirty days. Some firms take this approach one step further and offer 110 percent of the difference. One home office supply store actually offers 150 percent of the difference!

You may want to be creative in your attempts to stand out from the competitive crowd. Offer to refund the difference at 100 percent or better, plus promise a bonus—a bottle of champagne or perhaps tickets to a movie. Or, as one electronic store does, offer to monitor all competitor

ads for thirty days after the sale and promise to mail an automatic refund check if a lower price for the product sold is advertised within that period.

? Can my USP be the same as my strategy?

It can be, but doesn't have to be. However, your USP should be in harmony with your strategy.

For example, the basic strategy of warehouse club retailers is to offer very low prices by minimizing costs. Some of the ways these firms minimize cost is to offer larger-size packaging, fewer product choices, and less service in a less attractive environment than might be found in a department store or supermarket.

The USP of many warehouse clubs is usually similar to their core strategy—"low prices." The reasons behind their ability to offer low prices is, however, not emphasized because these reasons might be seen as drawbacks by some consumers.

There are exceptions. In the Boston area, for example, Boch Toyota has successfully used a USP that emphasizes both its lower pricing and the reasons behind its ability to offer such pricing. It holds no mortgages and pays cash for the cars it sells and is, therefore, able to pass on savings rather than financing costs to its customers

When should a USP be different than a strategy?

Two types of situations come to mind. One situation is where the customer will not be attracted to your business through knowledge of your strategy. For example, let's say your strategy is to rent furniture to lower-income people who cannot afford to purchase furniture. Your USP isn't going to be "Serving the lower-income populace, who can't even afford to own a chair." Instead you should focus on the benefit to the consumer. Something like "Great furniture you can afford today" would appeal without insulting.

Another situation would be when your basic strategy is similar to that of your competition. In this case, your USP needs to focus on a real or perceived difference to position your business against the competition effectively. An example of using a perceived difference is a bar and grill on Cape Cod that advertises "the coldest beer on the Cape."

Every business needs its own unique appeal to consumers, commonly called its "Unique Selling Proposition." Here are some factors to consider emphasizing in developing a unique selling proposition for your firm:

PRICE
QUALITY
DEPENDABILITY
BREADTH OR DEPTH
TECHNICAL EDGE
FASHION
CUSTOMIZATION
SPECIALIZATION
SERVICE

Marketing Plans

While usually referred to as a marketing plan, a thorough marketing plan should be thought of as a product plan. It should cover virtually all aspects of bringing a product to market.

Typically, marketing plans are used in product-oriented businesses, but have an importance to service companies as well. A separate plan should be devised at least once a year for each distinctive service or group of related services that the firm offers.

A marketing plan is not simply a list of advertising or other promotional activities. A good marketing plan should begin with an evaluation of the entire potential market for each product category and include an analysis of consumer behavior, the competition and its product, and the strengths and weaknesses of the company as a competitor. Then you need to detail your product positioning and product attributes, including its benefits and features. Planned sales and promotional activities also need to be addressed. Then you need to subject your spreadsheets to some heavy-duty numbers crunching and develop profit and loss pro formas (projections) for each product. The conclusion to a marketing plan predicts competitive reaction and a very brief consideration of possible longer-term product options.

Some steps in creating a market-ing plan that takes a serious, individual look at each product or service group will create analysis overlaps between other product or company-wide strate-gies. This is fine. It is extremely important to look at each product line and service separately. Doing your homework for each product may reveal very different product characteristics or competitive positioning requirements that may not have been considered otherwise.

Developing a Marketing Plan

❶ The market

The first step in any marketing plan should be evaluating the entire potential market for each product category. Ask

- How large is the potential market?
- How many people or businesses are currently using the product of any firm competing in this category?
- How many prospects have potential use for the product?
- Is the market growing, flattening, or shrinking?

Generally, a growing market is more desirable. Not only is there great sales potential, but it is usually easier to enter and build sales in a growing marketplace than it is to supplant competition in flattening or shrinking marketplaces.

For a very small firms, however, a large market can be a double-edged sword. On the positive side, of course, there is the potential for huge sales. Negatively, though, larger firms with established access to marketing channels and better financing may be tempted to enter such an attractive marketplace. Firms already involved in the particular industry may devote considerable resources to defending or increasing their current market share.

❷ Market segmentation

Almost all markets have some major and distinctive segments. Even if a market isn't currently segmented, it probably carries that potential. And, in the case of large national markets, it would be almost impossible for a small firm to be competitive unless the market were segmented.

Segmentation can come about in many ways. Often several types of segmentation are evident. Almost all markets can be segmented by price and quality points. So price and quality issues may not form the most clear and precise definition of segmentation within a marketplace. Reasons for strong segmentation are most often found through an examination of product use and the benefits consumers derive from product use.

For example, the personal automotive car market may be thought of as being divided into station wagons, sedans, pickup trucks, mini-vans, and sports cars. Each of these segmented categories may be further divided by price and quality. With the luxury sedan segment, for instance, a change in the pricing or quality of pickup trucks would have no competitive impact because the potential consumer for a luxury sedan isn't weighing a decision between purchasing a sedan or a pickup. However, if mid-price sedans are dramatically upgraded in quality, they may become competition for the luxury sedan market. This happened in the luxury car market in the early 1990s. Offerings from Infiniti and Lexus caught the attention of consumers who had previously only considered the more expensive cars manufactured by Mercedes, BMW, and Jaguar.

❸ Consumer analysis

You need to closely evaluate typical consumers in the market segments you are targeting. There are countless possible behavior patterns to consider. Try to focus on the patterns that are most likely to determine the viability of your product in the marketplace. Ask

- What type of product features most appeal to these consumers?
- How are choices made between competing products?
- How much disposable income do the target consumers have to spend on this product?
- How do these consumers reach decisions to purchase a particular product?
- Are these consumers typically presold on a brand before they visit a store, or are they impulse buyers?
- Which promotional vehicles are most often viewed by the consumer?
- How are the consumers geographically situated?
- What activities do these consumers most like to engage in during their leisure time?

▶ *The number coded sections 1–9 correlate with a sample marketing plan that begins on page 77.*

Developing a Marketing Plan

4 Product features and benefits

It is very important to make a clear distinction between the features of competing products and benefits to consumers of those features. Pay close attention to how strong the consumer benefit is from a particular feature.

A careful evaluation of the intended product benefits will help you and others ascertain the correctness of the product positioning. You should be able to determine whether or not individual features are worth the cost to manufacture and provide a foundation for building promotional and advertising programs.

5 Sales

Just because you have an existing sales force or an established method of selling products, do not assume current sales channels are appropriate for a new product.

For example, the positioning of your product within its market segment may affect how the product should be sold. Let's say you decided to position a new line of modular office systems as a premium product, complete with design consultation, targeted primarily to larger corporations. A highly trained, experienced, and knowledgeable sales staff, eager to visit customers' offices for face-to-face presentations, would be crucial. On the other hand, if your strategy was to sell economy office partitions to very small businesses at a low mark-up, then you could not afford an outside sales staff. While your inside sales group should be friendly and helpful, there would be little benefit in hiring higher-paid, design-oriented sales personnel.

If your positioning plan for a new product suggests the need for a new means of selling, you may want to reconsider the positioning plan. Ask yourself if you can afford the extra cost and energy required to sell a premium or specialized product.

6 Advertising and promotions

Your product positioning statement, along with an analysis of its strongest competitive features and consumer benefits, are basic starting points in developing advertising and other promotional plans.

For example, if you are starting the only all-business radio station in town, you may simply turn your basic positioning statement into your main advertising message: "WBUS: the only all-business radio station in town!" If your consumer analysis reveals that your targeted listeners are often driving in their cars, the same simple message might work well on outdoor billboard advertising. If your consumer analysis indicated that your intended audience commutes to work by train, subway, or bus, a transit ad campaign might be an appropriate way to impart your message effectively.

Alternately, you may learn that business people really like the current stations they tune into to receive news. In this case you may need to emphasize more specific features inherent in your broadcasting. You might want to play up the frequency of stock reports, investment advice, or business interviews that are a part of your format. To relay detailed information, it may be more appropriate to place print ads in the business section of the local newspaper or regional editions of national business publications.

You might find that business people aren't clear on what the benefits would be to them if they were to tune into your station. In this scenario, you might want to develop an ad campaign with a tag line such as "the station for the well-informed executive." You might run your ads during televised broadcasts of business programs. The ad might feature a business person getting praise at the office because he or she was able to disseminate timely news—news first heard on your station!

In short, there are important issues and endless alternatives to consider, from choosing advertising and promotional mediums to developing message themes to writing copy. You may want to refer to Chapter 4 on Advertising or the Publicity and Cheap Marketing Tricks of this chapter for helpful information and tips on putting together effective advertising and promotional campaigns.

7 Competitive reaction

If your marketing plans result in sharply declining market share for your competitors, you need to be prepared for their reaction. For example, if you introduce a new product or service with great fanfare at a lower price than offered by competitors, you may trigger a price war. This may culminate in the elimination of all but the strongest, most competitive, and best-financed firms. The victims may include you!

How can you avoid a competitive reaction that might backfire on you? Don't compete on price. Instead, try targeting a small niche within your marketplace that is not directly targeted by your competition. And, if you can, stay away from mature, stable markets with clearly defined competitors.

Try to think like your competition before you implement any marketing strategies. How would you react if you were an existing firm and a competitor came out with a new, improved, or lower-priced product that had the potential of chipping away at your consumer base and, ultimately, profitability? Decide whether or not it would be beneficial to the success of your business to alter your product, your pricing, or your unique selling proposition. Determine if you should go full speed ahead with your plans. If you do so, be at the ready for the expected competitive reaction.

8 The future

The perfect marketing plan is not complete without some focus on the longer term. If your plan succeeds
- Will it help you to realize the long-term strategic goals of your firm?
- Will you be able to build up long-term strengths in critical areas of your business operations?
- What effect will this particular product marketing plan have on other products and services offered by your company?

- Will there be logical related or follow-on products that can be developed and/or offered if this product release is successful?

9 Pro forma

No marketing plan is complete without a quantitative projection of profitability for each product. This is very different than your annual plan for the entire business. The marketing plan should, as much as possible, isolate every major expense relevant to a product, including an allocation of common expense items such as overhead.

You will, of course, need to carefully project a sales forecast. This forecast should realistically reflect, in numbers, all of the other factors detailed in this plan, including market size, sales of competing products, competitive factors, product features and benefits, and your promotional and advertising plans.

Sometimes it is discovered during the development of a sales forecast that the product's price is too low to clear a good profit. You will need to decide, at this point, whether the market would be receptive to a higher-priced product or a product with fewer features and benefits. Or, sometimes, the product makeup and price can remain the same and expense cuts can be made in the advertising or promotional budgets without affecting sales potential.

MARKETING PLAN
for
"THE TOOL"
offered by the
INTERNET TOOL COMPANY, INC. (ITC)

•

Summary

Internet Tool Company, Inc. (ITC) has been formed to create Internet development tools. The market for Internet tools is growing very rapidly. ITC's first development tool, "The Tool," provides a major technical breakthrough by virtue of its "intelligent agent" feature. The intelligent agent makes it very easy to create documents and at the same time offers great flexibility in changing documents and other graphic material.

"The Tool" will be positioned as the premier Internet development tool for heavy computer users. ITC will target its marketing efforts narrowly at the core heavy user market. Because the product's ease of use is of less importance to highly experienced computer users, ITC will give more marketing emphasis to the product's other key benefit: flexibility.

ITC will completely avoid the retail store marketplace, where its lack of ability to fund expensive national and co-op advertising campaigns and its lack of presence in this marketplace would make it very difficult to compete or even gain entrance. Wholesalers and retailers are often more interested in the marketing support and name recognition that products enjoy than the product's functionality and features. Instead, the product will be sold direct and via catalogs in a carefully targeted marketing campaign.

"The Tool" will be placed at the very high end of the consumer segment at $100 to further emphasize the product's superiority and take advantage of the fact that consumers buying direct are less price sensitive than retail buyers.

Note: This marketing plan is fictitious and intentionally covers much of the same ground as the complete business plan shown in the Strategy chapter.

A Sample Marketing Plan

1 The Market

Over 30 million people are currently using the Internet. Internet users are expected to grow in number by at least 25 percent each year for the next five years. The potential number of consumers for our Internet development tools is at least 20 million now with the potential for 30 million in two or three years. Recent trends indicate that, while Fortune 500 businesses will continue to seek out the Internet, faster growth will be seen in the home and small business market.

2 Market Segmentation

The market is divided into three relatively distinct segments: the corporate/professional segment, the small business segment, and the consumer segment.

Corporate/Professional Segment:
This market includes large corporations, institutions, government agencies, and professional developers. Internet development tools aimed at this market are expensive, costing upwards of $500; may take some time to master, even for seasoned technical developers; but provide the maximum number of options and flexibility in site design.

Small Business Segment:
Internet development tools aimed at this market are mid-priced, typically costing from $100 to $500. They are designed to be used by people without development experience, although ease of use is a secondary feature to the ability to create the broad range of functionality likely to be required by a small business.

Consumer Segment:
This segment is driven by low price (under $100) and ease of use, with breadth of functionality typically being sacrificed.

The consumer segment is the segment that ITC is positioning its product for.

A Sample Marketing Plan

③ Consumer Analysis

The target group of consumers for this product are heavy recreational computer users. They typically have used computers for three or more years. They have already used a commercial on-line service and have used at least several software packages extensively. They also tend to buy new software from time to time, if not regularly.

While the target group is increasingly buying software at retail outlets, many (especially those that tend to use their computers the most) buy their software through mail-order catalogs and quite a few order at least some software directly from the publisher. Even when buying software in retail outlets this group tends less to buy on impulse and are more apt to be looking for a specific item on which they are pre-sold. This group is most likely to be pre-sold by editorial coverage in computer publications such as reviews and product announcements and by word of mouth. Because this audience is exposed to so much information about so many competing products, it is most likely to decide on a particular item as a result of multiple exposure to information about a product—often from different types of sources.

Members of the target group tend to live in suburban or urban areas. They are typically male; aged thirty to forty-five; college educated; have a household income range between $40,000–$100,000; are homeowners; and hold professional jobs. Many belong to computer clubs.

They read two or more computer publications, a major metro newspaper, and one or more consumer magazines. While they watch television several hours per week their viewing tends to be less than average. They tend to listen to radio stations while they commute in their cars—tuning into a broad variety of formats.

④ Product Features and Benefits

Several products are already in the marketplace in the under $100 price range that offer similar functionality. These products offer powerful editing capability for text-only documents as well as for graphics. They give users the capability of moving large amounts of text or graphics into a form translatable into a language understood by the Internet.

ITC's main distinctive feature is its intelligent agent. The benefit to consumers is that the product is easier to use and more flexible than competing products. The intelligent agent "walks" users step by step through the process of creating a document. The most similar competing product offers more passive help by using "place-holders" where the user places objects on a layout page. While the placeholder approach also gives users the ability to quickly assemble creative material, it does not give the user the flexibility of moving objects about.

Strengths

Engineering: As shown by the features of its first product, ITC has a strong competitive edge in its engineering capabilities. The intelligent agent is a leap ahead of its competitors. This strength should help ITC keep ahead of its competition in the future as well.

Fast Development Cycle: Even with a product offering superior capabilities, ITC was able to create its first product from scratch in a very short period of time. This ability coupled with superior engineering skills, should give ITC the ability to stay on the leading edge of product design over a sustained period of time.

Closeness to Market: Almost all key employees have a long experience of personal Internet use and keep in close touch with many in the industry and at different computer clubs who are also heavy Internet users. This gives ITC the ability to keep abreast of the marketplace and strong insight into the changing demands of its core customers.

Weaknesses

Financial: Even after raising the additional planned funding, the company will be substantially less well capitalized than some of its competitors. This would make it particularly difficult to finance the national advertising and promotion campaign that would be important if the company were to try to obtain shelf space at computer retailers nationwide.

No Market Presence: The company currently has no other products in the market or coming to the market soon. It has no relationship with any resellers. This contrasts with several competitors, who are already selling product through many outlets, including retailers, and competitors who have other offerings in their product line.

Weak Marketing and Sales Staff: The company has one marketing manager and no sales staff. The marketing manager has several years of experience in selling hardware add-ons direct to major corporate customers but no experience selling software or selling products to consumers.

5 Sales

ITC will sell the product via established direct-mail catalogs and through promotional efforts with computer clubs.

Direct-mail catalogs will be chosen on the basis of how closely the demographics of the catalogs match the demographics of ITC's target market.

To prompt consumers to order direct, ITC will accept orders on the Internet and via a toll-free 800 line.

⑥ Advertising and Promotions

Because ITC's budget is very limited, it will keep its message simple, emphasizing its product's flexibility and ease of use.

With the company's very limited budget, initial ads in direct mail catalogs will be small—typically no larger than 1/8 page. Ad copy will contrast with competitive products that are shrink-wrapped and sold at lower prices to less experienced computer users.

Press releases will first emphasize the company's two key benefits. But they will also offer a lot of technical detail that will appeal to the editors and publications most important to effectively reaching the core target market.

The company's top technical people will give talks at computer clubs, again to help position ITC on the leading edge.

Packaging will be subdued and professional-looking to further contrast ITC's product with the competitor's offerings.

⑦ Competitive Reaction

By positioning ITC's product as the premier product at the top end of the price range, any price cutting by competitors will only help reinforce ITC's premium positioning. While deep pocketed competitors may trumpet their products with expensive, colorful magazine ads, these ads will be unlikely to have much impact on ITC's core audience of highly experienced computer users.

⑧ The Future

Because ITC has relatively weak marketing and financial strengths, it must rely upon continued product innovation to remain viable. Sooner or later competitors will mimic ITC's features. However, ITC's engineering and fast-to-market capabilities should allow it to stay one step ahead of competitors. And each new product feature will help ITC gain more publicity for its product.

⑨ Pro forma

See spreadsheet that follows.

9

PRO FORMA PROJECTIONS FOR YEAR 1
for
INTERNET TOOL COMPANY, INC. (ITC)

	Weak	Likely	Good
SALES			
First year unit sale projection	10,000 units	15,000 units	20,000 units
Retail price	$100	$100	$100
Net price after average 20% discount	$80	$80	$80
Gross revenue (units × average price)	**$800,000**	**$1,200,000**	**$1,600,000**
COST OF GOODS			
Manufacturing costs per unit	$12	$12	$12
Total (units x manufacturing cost per unit)	$120,000	$160,000	$240,000
MARKETING			
Catalog ads	$100,000	$120,000	$300,000
Press packages and literature	$15,000	$20,000	$25,000
Travel	$18,000	$30,000	$40,000
Salary for marketing manager	$50,000	$70,000	$85,000
ENGINEERING			
Salaries	$170,000	$170,000	$170,000
Other engineering expenses	$12,000	$12,000	$12,000
GENERAL and ADMINISTRATIVE			
Plant and equipment	$42,000	$42,000	$42,000
Salaries	$115,000	$115,000	$115,000
Telephone and postal services	$8,000	$8,000	$8,000
Other	$15,000	$15,000	$15,000
TOTAL COSTS	**$665,000**	**$725,000**	**$785,000**
PROFIT BEFORE TAXES	**$135,000**	**$475,000**	**$815,000**

Streetwise Advice on Marketing Plans

☞ **Consider abbreviated plans**

If you are in a business that is continually launching new services or products, you won't necessarily want to do a full-scale marketing plan during each planning phase of your year.

If you decide on a trimmed-down plan, the most important part to include is an overview with positioning statement. This, in reality, comprises the main strategy points for the particular product or service, and actually has more relevance than any budget numbers. You should also include a detailed look at any areas of the plan that are significantly different from your other product or service plans. Thirdly, include a projected sales, costs, and profitability statement.

☞ **Involve others**

When you have multiple products or services, you will be much more successful if you can assign primary responsibility for each product or service to a particular person. With all of your responsibilities you may not have adequate time to devote to managing each product or service line. Other people in your organization may not have as much experience as you, but that will usually be more than made up for by the extra focus they will be able to bring to developing and maintaining the goals of a marketing plan, or parts thereof, for their assigned product or service.

Remember, however, that in order to really give other people a sense of responsibility for a product or service, you must let them play a primary role in creating the marketing plan. Help them and encourage them, but give them space so they can really feel that the marketing plan is theirs, not yours.

☞ **Go/no go**

A marketing plan can be a terrific tool for evaluating whether or not you should launch a new product or service. If you are using a marketing plan for this purpose, keep the focus on the larger issues. Don't get carried away with such details as the frequency and size of advertising. Instead focus on broader issues such as market size, competitor implications, pricing, and projected sales.

Later, if you decide to go ahead with the proposed product or service, you can fill in the details for the highly specific marketing tactics you intend to implement.

☞ **What ifs**

People who are new to business often underprice their products and services. Luckily, one of the real blessings of computerized spreadsheets is the ability to quickly change key items such as price or sales projections. So don't be afraid to run different scenarios and get feedback from prospective customers on such issues as price or product features and benefits.

Be sure to work in a nice fat profit margin for yourself, even if you have to spend days thinking through different pricing and/or positioning alternatives to achieve this goal. A fat profit margin can prove to be a life saver if you need to cover the cost of any one of a multitude of possible oversights and mistakes that can be made in starting up and running a small business.

"A marketing plan can be a terrific tool for evaluating whether or not you should launch a new product or service."

How is a marketing plan different from the marketing part of the annual business plan?

If you have a simple one-product or service type business, the marketing plan may closely parallel the marketing segment of your annual business plan. However, a good marketing plan should reveal more depth regarding marketing elements and techniques than is customarily done in a general business plan. As shown in the sample marketing plan, an in-depth analysis of many factors, including the market, consumers, and competitors, as well as a detailed course of action, should be integral to the marketing plan.

If you have multiple products or services, you should create a separate, detailed marketing plan for each. Your annual business plan, on the other hand, should provide a summary of all anticipated combined marketing expenditures and a general overview of your marketing strategy. However, don't include individual marketing plans within the annual business plan.

When should a single-product business create multiple plans?

Even if your business has only one product or service, you should consider doing a detailed marketing plan each time you plan a significant change in your marketing approach or in the nature of your product or service. For example, a retailer may want to do a detailed marketing plan before launching a major off-price sale or for a seasonal promotional strategy. A service business may consider doing a detailed marketing plan before substantially changing prices or offering discounts.

Should a new marketing plan be created for each product or service?

If you produce multiple products or offer multiple services, you should prepare a separate marketing plan for each related product line, if not for each individual new product offering. If you are doing your analysis carefully, you might uncover some very important marketing differences between even closely related products. For example, competitive and marketplace studies may reveal that the low-end version of one of your products is similar to those made by several other firms. You may find that launching an expensive ad campaign for this product would be ineffective because there are no unique features or benefits to play up and the profit margins for the product can't support extensive promotional activities. On the other hand, careful analysis of the higher-end version of the same product may uncover a combination of insignificant competition and strong product features and benefits that fully warrant an all-out advertising campaign.

With multiple product offerings, won't we be creating marketing plans forever?

Yes, you might very well be creating marketing plans forever! But they are an essential competitive tool. They allow you to gain ground on your competitors and help you to channel the energies of your business in the right direction.

In our book publishing business, for example, we make a separate plan for not only every single book that we publish, but also for many we consider publishing but either decide not to or lose out to a competing publisher's offer. As a company we create about five to ten marketing plans every single week!

Questions & Answers about Marketing Plans

How often should marketing plans be updated or changed?

This depends upon the type of business you are in, as well as many other factors. However, most small businesses don't reevaluate their marketing plans as often as they should—or need to. Although a very small business offering a single service that is promoted through a limited advertising budget may continue to operate at or beyond expectation by subjecting its marketing plan to scrutiny on an annual basis, most businesses should plan a review at least quarterly, if not monthly.

If you aren't happy with the results of your marketing or think you have the potential to perform better, keep reevaluating. Subject your marketing plan to a review as often as is necessary to develop and maintain the business results you want.

If you can shift your marketing resources between different products and services, and the sales of your product or services are volatile, it might not be excessive to reevaluate your marketing plan weekly. Sometimes, especially if your product is trendsetting or timely, it is imperative to review marketing plans daily as new information on consumer preferences, sales projections, and/or distribution opportunities are brought to your attention.

At our book publishing company we review and often change several marketing plans every week. Sometimes, especially when we are launching a major new book, we will review and change marketing plans as often as every single day, after we receive new information on sales.

Who should be involved in creating marketing plans?

Unlike the annual business plan, one person should be assigned primary responsibility for developing a marketing plan for a particular product or service line. The most obvious choice for this task is the product manager or marketing manager for that product or service line. In smaller businesses, the owner or CEO will usually take on this role.

While one person is assigned primary responsibility for developing the marketing plan, he or she should seek input from everyone within the company as well as outsiders. Feedback from independent sales representatives and existing or potential customers can prove invaluable.

How do I determine prices?

Many small business people charge too little for their products or services and their profit margins suffer. Especially if you are selling a product that is at least a little different than other products, or selling just about any service, try not to sell on price points alone. As a rule of thumb, I would charge as much as the market will bear, raise prices aggressively each year, and make sure you make a healthy profit on each sale.

Cheap Marketing Tricks

mall start-up businesses don't usually have the resources to launch huge advertising blitzes in multiple media formats. In fact, even if you are already in business, chances are you don't have an extensive cash allocation earmarked for promotion, or you've tried many different advertising approaches and vehicles and haven't hit on a really successful campaign yet. You aren't alone!

Advertising is extremely expensive. Despite adequate funding, even large national companies often find it difficult to develop successful advertising campaigns. And, with an increasing number of companies advertising through every imaginable communication avenue, it is becoming increasingly hard to attract the attention of consumers.

However, there are non-advertising approaches to promotion. They generally require less money to implement and are often more effective. The only catch is that they require time and creativity to develop.

Coupons

You don't have to distribute coupons in print advertising or in big direct mail campaigns. You can hand them out on the street corner, at trade shows, or just about any-place else. You can send a few to your best customers, or you can include "next purchase" coupons in customer orders.

25% OFF
E·X·O·T·I·C
BOUQUETS

From Foreign Lands of Intrigue and Beauty... Birds-of-Paradise, Ginger, Fuji Mums, French Tulips, and Sprays of Heather

Surprise someone special ... or just delight yourself!

Coupons can be "quick and dirty" to design and print because their selling point is price, not image. To assure your chances of getting an additional sale or establishing an ongoing relationship with your customers, make your coupon offer exceedingly generous.

Contests

People love contests. They even love to see other people win! Just witness the phenomenal success of game shows on television. If you choose to develop a promotional contest, in-fuse it with fun, make it silly, and don't forget to really talk it up. If your contest is wacky and crazy enough, you should be able to get good media cover-age—and remember, this is essentially free advertising!

Gifts

People love to receive something for free, even if they have to pay a premium price for a more expensive item to get the freebie. Don't ask why! It may not make sense, but it doesn't have to, as long as you make money. While this technique has been used most successfully in the beauty and cosmetics industry, it can be used in almost any business endeavor. It isn't unheard of to see deals such as a free computer desktop with the purchase of a higher-priced notebook computer or, even a free subcompact car with the purchase of a full-price luxury sedan!

Frequent buyers

Frequent-buyer programs can be very powerful tools for building loyal clientele for both retail and service businesses. The more common approach is to give customers a card that is marked after each purchase and results in a free or reduced-price product or service offering after a specified number of regular-priced purchases. For example, ten haircuts may net one free haircut. Another approach is to give regular customers a discount on purchases upon presentation of their "Frequent Buyer" discount card.

Some businesses charge a small fee for their frequent-buyer cards. Others tie freebies or discount levels to purchase volume. For example, after spending $100 at a computer store you might receive a free subscription to their newsletter or 5 percent off your next purchase of $25 or more. After spending $250 you might receive a free storage disk or 10 percent off your next purchase of $25 or more.

Frequent buyer programs are also often implemented by independent retailers trying to survive the onslaught of superstores that offer their customers super-low prices.

Exclusive offerings

Offering exclusive purchases or previews of new merchandise to existing customers is a great way to inspire a feeling of excitement and loyalty. To enhance participation, you may wish to offer a discount. If the exclusive offering is in itself extremely attractive, the discount can be small.

Events

Hosting a special event in your business establishment, such as a celebrity appearance or a charity fundraiser, is a terrific way to introduce people to your business or maintain contact with existing customers. It also will create an aura of excitement and goodwill. You may even obtain media coverage!

RAY'S EASY CDs

Frequent Music Lovers Program

♥ ♥ ♥

Buy Ten Classical, Jazz, or New Age CDs and Get One Free

1 2 3 4 5 6 7 8 9 10

Cheap Marketing Tricks

Cross-promotions

You don't have to be a movie producer or own an international fast-food chain to cross-promote your product with another business. You might consider offering free tickets to the local theater with each purchase of a particular item or price level. Another great business-to-business cross-promotion might be to offer free tickets to a ball game to any business willing to invest fifteen minutes of time just to listen to your sales pitch.

Trades

Ever notice the ads for car washes on taxi roofs? Car washes don't pay cash for these advertisements! They get the exposure in exchange for cleaning the taxis periodically. If you are absolutely sold on developing an advertising campaign, remember that smaller media outfits will sometimes accept products in lieu of payment.

Giveaways

You're probably wondering how you can make money if you give away product! Well, it's a lot easier and less expensive than advertising. In fact, giveaways have their place in just about any type of business.

Selling business-to-business, you can generate goodwill with the people you choose—your best customers or a select roster of potential clientele—by occasionally giving them a small gift when you call on them. The giveaway should not be so expensive that a feeling of bribery is conveyed, but nice enough that it doesn't end up trashed the minute you leave.

For consumer service businesses, you may want to offer your product for free trial periods, or offer free estimates if you are in a service-oriented business.

Retail businesses may hand out balloons or other novelty items to build traffic or retain customer interest.

New customer offers

Attracting new customers is one of the most difficult marketing challenges to achieve even with powerful advertising or a dedicated sales force. That's why different businesses—national greeting card manufacturers to local oil delivery services—offer incentive pricing, freebies, or extra advertising allowances for new customers. Even lawyers customarily offer a free first consultation.

Publicity

Publicity is often overlooked as a primary marketing tool to gain attention and interest in a product, service, or company. Using publicity as a sales tool can be a more cost-effective method for generating sales than buying advertising.

No matter what business you are in, you can be your own publicist! If you want to act as your own PR firm, you can produce a simple press kit. This kit should include a "pitch" letter and a press release regarding your company, a new product, or a unique service. Once you have targeted and established appointments with print and broadcast media contacts, you can act as your own spokesperson to pitch your own image, product, or service. You will become the focus, the center of attention, as you create an awareness of your business that will turn into sales leads.

Publicity can take a variety of formats. You or someone connected with your business could appear on a local radio or TV talk show—your business

the topic of a particular segment. You could be the subject of an article in a local or national newspaper or magazine. You might become part of a broadcast business panel discussing issues that are pertinent to your product or service, or speak at trade association meetings, trade show seminars, or chamber of commerce gatherings. The creative publicist can find thousands of publicity opportunities available that allow for increasing image or product awareness.

The best part of publicity is that, for the most part, it is free! This is especially true if you manage your own publicity campaigns. However, if you do choose to hire an outside PR firm, the costs can still be a lot less than building the same amount of awareness via paid advertising.

How Publicity Works

1 Decide whether or not you want to do your own publicity

One advantage of being your own publicist is that you know your product or service better than anyone else. A great amount of time and effort can be expended apprising a PR firm or freelance publicist of your company and its products or services. Even so, no one will have the same enthusiasm for your company that you do. This sense of excitement will serve you well as you spread the word about your product or service and its consumer benefits.

It is a lot easier than you might think to create a "pitch" letter, develop a press release, find and approach media contacts, and make follow-up calls.

2 Create the hook

To create your own publicity, you need to communicate your story to those who access the public through the media—television, radio, newspapers, and/or magazines. You need to develop a "hook" or a compelling reason why someone should listen to your story. Media contacts must feel strongly that knowledge of your product or service would be of some value to their audience. Take time to build a cohesive "pitch" that really conveys the unique qualities and benefits of your product or service.

3 Make a list

Make a list of media contacts who you think would be interested in your product or service. Prioritize the list and decide what you want to tell each contact. This will give you a good idea of how much time you will need to spend compiling and sending press materials, as well as placing follow-up telephone calls.

4 Create a "mini" press kit

It isn't necessary to send an elaborate press kit to get a newspaper, magazine, or broadcast outlet to tell your story. If you are doing your own publicity, it is often just as effective to send a personalized "pitch" letter and a press release in a standard size business envelope to your media contacts.

5 Follow up with a phone call

Follow up your mailings with a phone call to each media contact. If you fail to get through the first time or if your media contact is too busy to talk to you, be persistent. When you do manage to get through, make an appointment to visit your contact.

6 Take extensive notes to the interview

If you sent your media contact a simple "pitch" letter and press release, you need to take additional material relating to your product or service to your media contact meeting. Product samples, testimonials, brochures, and a list of current vendors or consumers (with their permission) that use or carry your product or service will assist you in conveying an interesting and powerful story about your company.

7 Make a list of potential questions, and prepare answers

Prepare yourself for your media meeting by creating a list of possible questions the media representative might ask you. Be ready with answers!

Hiring a PR Firm

You should consider doing your own publicity first. You will make the best spokesperson for your product or service. However, if you are extremely busy or uneasy about certain aspects of handling your own PR, you can hire a freelance PR specialist or a PR firm.

PR firms typically charge either an hourly or monthly rate. And, they won't guarantee success no matter how many hours they bill you for! Some PR firms have extensive client lists, and if you aren't a top account, you won't be a priority account. Try to find out how important a client you will be. It could make or break the success of your publicity efforts.

Before you set up meetings to interview potential PR representatives, do a reference check. Ask individuals in your business community whom they recommend. Once you have made up a list of firms you are interested in, set up meetings so that the firm can "pitch your account." Remember that you have control over the meeting because the PR firm is bidding for *your* business. It is up to it to try to sell you on its ability to effectively deliver your message to the right people.

During the meeting you need to articulate your objectives in an up-front manner. Have a list of issues and questions prepared that focuses on your agenda. Listen carefully to their "pitch" and the answers they give to your questions. And include the following in your query:

- Who will be working on your account—a senior account executive, a junior account executive, or an entry-level trainee?
- How will you and the PR firm work together as a team?

Things to ask prospective PR firms
- *Who will be working on my account?*
- *How will we work together as a team?*
- *Who is responsible for copy?* — Need someone senior and very much on the ball!
- *Who is on their media list?*
- *What has been their most recent, effective media placement?*
- *Have they had any success creating publicity campaigns for companies in the same business as mine?* — Ask E.R. Webber about QSF campaign – looked great, any success?

- Who will be responsible for copy?
- Who is on the firm's media contact list?
- What have been their most effective recent media placements?
- What success have they had in creating publicity campaigns for businesses such as yours?

Don't leave the meeting until you feel that all of your questions and concerns have been answered.

If you do decide to hire a PR firm, you must stay on top of it and keep a proactive relationship in motion. This will ensure that your PR needs are fulfilled to your satisfaction.

Elements of a Standard Press Kit

The "pitch" letter

1 The first piece of information that an editor should see in your press kit is your "pitch" letter. This letter needs to immediately grab the editor's attention. It should be typed or printed on a letter-quality computer printer in black and on standard-sized 8.5" × 11" stationery. Ideally, it will be printed on your company letterhead. It should be personalized because editors typically disregard "blind" or "cold" letters.

Press release

2 The next piece an editor will look for is your press release. This piece should describe your product or service in detail and should provide the editor with enough newsworthy material to enable him or her to write a story about your product or service directly from the release. The press release should also be typed or printed on a letter-quality computer printer in black on your letterhead stationery.

Business card

3 Include your business card. Your business card should contain your name and title, company name, address, phone, fax, and/or any other communication avenue open to you—e-mail or other. You should staple it to the top left-hand corner of the "pitch" letter, or at the top left-hand corner of the press release, if you have decided against enclosing a "pitch" letter.

Company background

4 A company background gives a short history of your company. It often includes profiles of key players within your organization. Again, it should be printed on your letterhead in the same manner as the "pitch" letter and the press release. Include the name of your company as a header or title, in larger type, at the top of the page. Indicate that this is the company background.

Photos

5 Photos or slides of products can support the press release and create a more compelling story for your product. Use color photos if possible.

Testimonials

6 The testimonial sheet should be a one-page collection of quotes from anyone who has used your product and is willing to publicly support it. Again, use your letterhead for the testimonials.

Data sheet

7 The data sheet should contain all of the important statistics about your product including, if applicable, size, weight, pricing, components, materials used in manufacturing, as well as a part number. Print it on letterhead with "Data Sheet" centered in bold at the top of the sheet.

Folder

8 The folder, which will hold all of your press materials, should be simple in design—perhaps your logo in two-color. The folder size should be 9" × 12" with an insert on the right- or left-hand side for your business card.

If you are reluctant to spend the money to have a custom folder designed and printed, many office supply stores carry folders in a variety of styles and colors.

Eddie's Incredible Toys
151 NW Northwest • Bellingham • Washington 98225 • 206-555-5555 • 206-555-5550 fax

PRESS RELEASE
For Immediate Publication

Eddie's Incredible Toys
151 NW Northwest • Bellingham • Washington 98225 • 206-555-5555 • 206-555-5550 fax

October 12, 1995

Seattle Post-Intelligencer
Ms. Rita East
Home and Gift Editor
101 Elliott Avenue, W
Seattle, Washington 98119

Dear Ms. East,

With the Christmas season fast upon us I'd like to share with you and your
readers the magic that can be found — and brought to a good child's or
adult's smil.................................the handmade creations avail.................................ginal designs fashioned with ....*Photo*...........btle colorings. They
are truly a ....

..........................s 64
..........................r mind,
..........................th an

..........................zzle
..........................in
..........................t

Eddie's Incredible Toys
Edward K. Munchwerken
Designer • Founder
151 NW Northwest • Bellingham • Washington 98225
206-555-5555 • 206-555-5551 fax

Eddie's Incredible Toys
151 NW Northwest • Bellingham • Washington 98225 • 206-555-5555 • 206-555-5550 fax

DATA SHEET

Eddie's Incredible Toys
151 NW Northwest • Bellingham • Washington 98225 • 206-555-5555 • 206-555-5550 fax

TESTIMONIALS

Eddie's Incredible Toys
151 NW Northwest • Bellingham • Washington 98225 • 206-555-5555 • 206-555-5550 fax

COMPANY BACKGROUND

Mini Press Kit
A mini press kit may be used
to conserve costs and can be
as effective as a full-blown
press kit. It should include:
- A personalized "pitch" letter
- A press release
- A business card
- A #10 business envelope

Typical standard press kit components

Item	Specifications
Personalized "pitch" letter	20# bond stationery, 8.5" × 11", black ink
Press release	20# bond stationery, 8.5" × 11", black ink
Company backgrounder	20# bond stationery, 8.5 × 11, black ink
Business card	
Photos or slides of product	(exclusive of photographer)
Testimonial sheet	20# bond stationery, 8.5" × 11", black ink
Data sheet	20# bond stationery, 8.5" × 11", black ink
Folder	cover stock, 9' × 12', two-color
Jiffy bag mailing envelope	
Postage	

Eddie's Incredible Toys

151 NW Northwest • Bellingham • Washington 98225 • 206-555-5555 • 206-555-5550 fax

PRESS RELEASE

For additional information, please contact:
Edward, K. Munchwerken at
Eddie's Puzzle Toys
151 NW Northwest
Bellingham, Washington 98225
206-555-5555.

"Winter Solstice Star" Puzzle Promises to Become a Treasured Puzzle

Bellingham, Washington, October, 12, 1995 — Eddie's Incredible Toys has designed and fabricated a new and very special puzzle, the "Winter Solstice Star." This 64-piece puzzler resolves itself, if you have that special "puzzle" mind, into a beautiful three-dimensional star decorated with an old-fashioned nineteenth century winter skating scene. This enchanting puzzle has been hand-painted and finished in a gold leaf and lacquer technique that replicates the beauty of an antique.

The "Winter Solstice Star" puzzle is handcrafted in natural maple and finished using paints and lacquers that are child-safe. Finished size is 8" in diameter. The puzzle is shrink-wrapped complete and gift-boxed with a set of assembly instructions—that may or may not be consulted! The "Winter Solstice Star" puzzle is recommended for ages 6 and up.

It is so difficult to find true treasures to give as Christmas presents—something one can be amused by now and cherish through a lifetime. For those who are looking for new avenues to explore in gift giving, a visit to the wonderful world of toys at Eddie's Incredible Toys provides just that! You'll be among good company. The owner of Coffeebean Burst is a frequent shopper and "plans to give small tokens of appreciation from Eddie's to favored customers during the holiday season."

Edward K. Munchwerken, founder of Eddie's Incredible Toys, has been designing unique toys and puzzles for over thirty years. He has won several prestigious toy design awards. Eddie's Incredible Toys was established in 1992 and is located at 151 NW Northwest in Bellingham, Washington. Phone orders or requests for additional information are welcomed: 206-555-5555.

— 30 —

Note: This example is fictitious.

①
②
③
④
⑤
⑥
⑦
⑧
⑨

Creating a Press Release

1. Letterhead

The letterhead should include the company name, address, phone number, and fax number on a standard 8.5" × 11" piece of stationery and be printed in black or two-color ink.

2. Press release

Write "Press Release" in the top left-hand corner in black ink with a bold typeface.

3. Contact names

Contact names and phone numbers should appear in the top left-hand corner underneath "Press Release."

4. Headline

The headline should be in bold type and should articulate your story angle.

5. First paragraph

The first paragraph should tell a brief story so that if nothing else is published, it will highlight your main reason for sending the release. Include who, what, where, why, and when as may be applicable for the news you are conveying.

6. Body

The body of the release should give the editor or producer exhaustive details on your product or service. You want to be able to answer all questions about how the product or service was developed, who the market is for the product or service, how the market will benefit from using the product or service, and where it is available for purchase.

7. Testimonials

These are quotes from influential individuals who have used your product or service and are people that readers will respect.

8. Concluding paragraph

This paragraph should describe how to get product samples, literature, or more information about your company, product, or service.

9. Notation

The number "— 30 —" is used to signal the conclusion of the story. Any information following this notation are either notes to the editor or typesetter and are not intended for printing.

Eddie's Incredible Toys

151 NW Northwest • Bellingham • Washington 98225 • 206-555-5555 • 206-555 5550 Fax

October 12, 1995

Seattle Post-Intelligencer
Ms. Rita East
Home and Gift Editor
101 Elliott Avenue, W
Seattle, Washington 98119

Dear Ms. East,

With the Christmas season fast upon us, I'd like to share with you and your readers the magic that can be found—and brought to a good child's or adult's smile—at Eddie's Incredible Toys. All of the handmade creations available from Eddie's Incredible Toys are original designs fashioned with old-world charm in natural woods and subtle colors. They are truly a delight!

One very special puzzle is our "Winter Solstice Star." This 64-piece puzzle can be made into a beautiful three-dimensional star decorated with an old fashioned nineteenth century winter skating scene. It has been hand-painted and finished in a gold leaf and lacquer technique that replicates the beauty of an antique.

It is so difficult to find true treasures to give as Christmas presents—something one can be amused by now and cherish for a lifetime. The "Winter Solstice Star," and all of our toys, are truly perfect for special gift giving. I'd like to invite all of your readers to visit to the wonderful world of Eddie's Incredible Toys this Christmas buying season!

I will contact you early next week. I'd like to meet with you and share the "Winter Solstice Star" and a selection of other wonderful toys. We could even take a trip through Eddie's Incredible Toys' workshop and store via our portfolio. I'm sure that together, we can bring an awareness of a unique gift-giving opportunity to your readers.

Thank you for your time.

Sincerely,

Edward K. Munchwerken

Edward K. Munchwerken

Calling the Media

*D*ecide on the points you want to make and what you hope to achieve by the end of the phone conversation. Then find out the names of the proper contacts by asking the receptionist at the various print and broadcast media outlets. Get as much information as you can about radio and TV programs that have the demographic profile you seek for your product or service.

Write out what you want to say and practice a few times before making the call. Make your mistakes on someone other than the editor or producer. When you reach them, get right to the point.

 May
(receptionist)
Daily Telegraph. How may I direct your call?

 Ms. Jones
Good morning. Jack Woods, please?

 May
Hold, please.

 Mr. Woods
This is Jack Woods.

 Ms. Jones
Mr. Woods, this is Cynthia Jones from the Athabasca Restaurant on Middle Street. How are you this morning?

 Mr. Woods
Fine, thanks.

 Ms. Jones
My restaurant is about to begin serving Cajun-style cooking. This is a departure from the cuisine we have been offering. I feel that this will satisfy the requests of my current customers and attract new ones.

 Mr. Woods
OK, well what can I do for you?

 Ms. Jones
To celebrate, I am planning to have a three-night Cajun festival featuring T. J. Smith, a local country-and western singer who has made several albums. I would like to invite you to attend this event, as well as a pre-opening tour and dinner in two weeks.

 Mr. Woods
I can't attend the festival, but I can attend the pre-opening.

Publicity Success Story

Ewa Erdman, Vice President and Marketing Director, is one of the founders of **Take Two Photocraft**, a business that specializes in digital photo retouching. Most of their work is restorative, but they can also remove undesirable backgrounds (or people) from prints. Ewa has had great success with publicity by playing off some of the more interesting "retouching" the firm is capable of—like removing ex-spouses from photographs!

Serendipity

66 I sent out a sample of our work and a short press release and it appeared just three months after we opened. It was a huge boost to our business. But what made it even better was they wrote copy to go with the example I sent. The first line of the story was "Take out the no-good bum you divorced." Monday morning we had a line of divorced people at our door waiting for us to get "the jerk" out of their photos! 99

Follow up

66 In that particular case I did not have to follow up. But in every subsequent case, I've had to be a bulldog about it. 99

Streetwise Advice on Publicity

☞ **Before advertising**

If you can get publicity for your business, do it! It can be much less expensive than advertising and much more powerful. With a good press release and a couple of days of follow-up phone calls, you may be able to generate significant media coverage for your product or service.

☞ **Better than advertising**

Consumers tend to pay a lot more attention to feature coverage in newspapers, television, and radio than they do to advertising. A full-page feature article on your business in your local newspaper may generate several times the amount of inquiries or sales as a full-page advertisement.

For example, many years ago the *New York Post* ran a small feature article in their business section about one of our books, *The New York Job-Bank*, headlined "Here's the book for your job hunt!" Even though the story was only about three column inches, hundreds of books were sold as a result. Over the next few weeks I ran an exact copy of the article, several times in the same newspaper as an advertisement. The only qualification to printing the article as an ad was a small "disclaimer" at the top of the piece reading "Advertisement." No sales could be traced to the advertisement even though it was virtually identical to the highly successful feature story.

☞ **In advertising**

Publicity can also be used to make your advertising copy more effective. For example, movie reviews almost always contain quotes from reviewers. Even if you are not selling movies you can use favorable quotes from print, radio, and/or television interviews in your advertising copy. You may even want to reproduce the entire interview, frame it, and place it in your place of business. And definitely consider sending copies to your customers.

Keep in mind, though, if you are reproducing all or part of an interview, you should contact the publication or media outlet where the story appeared to get "reprint" permission. Even though the interview is about your business, the publication or media outlet has copyrighted the material and effectively owns it. Very few publications or media outlets refuse "reprint" permission or levy a charge for reprinting. There are exceptions, however. *Consumer Reports*, for instance, is concerned about maintaining the fairness of its image and completely prohibits the reprinting of any information from that publication.

☞ **Like selling**

Getting publicity is like selling in many ways. You usually need to make a lot of phone calls to get publicity. You need to make a presentation, overcome any objections, and close the sale. In making publicity calls you will get a lot of voice mail or be stalled at the receptionist's or assistant's desk. You will certainly experience a lot of rejection.

But if you can succeed in getting publicity for your company, it can go a long way toward making your business succeed.

"Consumers tend to pay a lot more attention to feature coverage in newspapers, television, and radio than they do to advertising."

Which media should I target?

Unlike advertising space, you are not directly paying for publicity coverage. So target every media vehicle imaginable! But give primary focus to the media avenues most relevant to your customers and those that you are most likely to get a story aired on or published in.

If you have a small local service business and an equal number of people in your town read either the local newspaper, the nearest metropolitan newspaper, or view broadcasting from a particular television station, then it would be wisest to concentrate on the local newspaper as a suitable venue for disseminating your story. Even though each vehicle reaches an equal number of readers or viewers, realistically, your chances of being published by the local newspaper are far greater.

However, once you scope out the local media and either succeed or fail in your attempt to receive publicity, begin calling on the less obvious media choices. You never know! The more stories you can get published, the more company awareness you create—the more sales potential you build.

Does publicity work consistently?

Not at all. The results of publicity are highly erratic and dependent upon many factors. The reach of the medium is very important. So, of course, is the viewpoint of the media. Did the media like your product or hate it? Did the product receive enough attention to actually motivate people to "drop everything" and run out to purchase your product? Or will they just be more likely to check it out the next time they are in a store that carries your product?

There are many other factors that affect the results of publicity. These factors can range from "Was it a sunny or rainy day when the publicity ran?" to "What other products were being featured by the same paper?"

Often even the most experienced public relations professionals can't figure out why a particular publicity piece worked or didn't work. So, because media results are difficult to predict, get as much different media coverage as you possibly can.

Should I plug my product aggressively in radio or television interviews?

The ideal situation in a radio or television interview, naturally, is for the host to recommend your product—not you. A radio or television host who sees that you are blatantly plugging your own product isn't going to do it for you. Wait a moment at the beginning of the interview to see if the host is going to name your product or service and recommend it to the audience. If the host doesn't do this, you need to kick into gear. But do it with finesse. Don't sound like an advertising pitchman, but work your product or service name in with subtlety. For example, "Any good house painter typically spends as much time on preparation as on the actual painting. At Central City Painter's we've determined that we spend an average of 4 man days on prep time—although that can vary from house to house." You've mentioned your company's name and service without being overbearing, and you've even given the impression that you have significant experience in and knowledge of your field.

Questions & Answers about Publicity

What's the big difference between radio and television interviews?

Generally, it is a lot easier to obtain radio features for your product or service than television features. In either case, you need to find a feature show that is appropriate for your product. If you are in the home repair business, try a handyman show; if you are in the landscaping business, try a lawn and garden show; or if you are in the catering business, try a cooking show. Maybe you can come up with a good reason why you should be interviewed on a public service show. Or you can try to tie your story into a recent news event. Just remember, television, except for local cable stations, generally offers fewer opportunities for local guests, the competition for interviews is high, and your likelihood of obtaining publicity through this venue isn't as high as it will be through radio.

During a radio interview, you need to focus on repeating the name of your company and product or service more often than you would on television. People who listen to radio are typically in their cars channel surfing or listening with only half an ear while negotiating traffic. Television viewers, on the other hand, are generally captive to the programs they are watching.

Radio hosts, on the whole, tend to choose interview topics that are of personal interest to them or are, in their opinion, of value to their listeners. Prepare carefully for a radio interview so that you can maintain the attention of your host. Television hosts, however, are driven by audience ratings—how they are perceived as personalities—and their chances of moving up in the world of television hosting. They will not be as concerned with the intricacies of your particular product or service. But it is always wise to be well prepared.

How should I handle newspaper interviews?

Newspaper writers like to feel that they are making a discovery for their readers, not promoting your business. Most newspaper writers hate to write puff pieces on business products or services. Some, but by no means all, think of themselves as soon-to-be-discovered "Pulitzer Prize" winners.

So don't plug your product or engage in any hyperbole with a newspaper journalist. Stick to the facts and let them "discover" and develop the story. Let them ask their questions first. Then, after they are done, try to add a summation. Mention a few important points about your business or product that they may have overlooked.

Do I have to sound like a polished pro on radio or TV?

Not at all. I've done hundreds of radio and TV shows, including a weekly feature on a major Boston radio station, and I don't have a perfect broadcasting voice or smooth intonations. But you don't have to be an actor or a radio announcer—just being an expert in *your* business is what is important.

I'm nervous about being on the radio or on TV. What can I do?

Do lots of shows—then any nervousness will fade away. I was especially nervous when I did my first television show locally, and when I first went on national television. But after you've done a bunch of shows they become old hat. I actually began to really enjoy interacting with media people. One nationally syndicated radio host even introduced me to his daughter, whom I dated for several years.

Point-of-Sale Displays

One of the best investments of your marketing dollars that you can make is in point-of-sale displays. These displays allow you to dramatically increase the impact of your product at the moment it counts most—at purchase time. Of course, such displays are most effective for impulse items or items for which consumers do not have brand loyalty.

Sales increases

Large displays set up in prominent locations in high-traffic supermarkets have been shown to increase the rate of sales by as much as 64-fold over the same items sold from their regular shelf locations. My experience, however, shows that more common sales increases are from one-and-a-half to threefold—still huge increases.

Set-up

The biggest difficulty in point-of-sale displays is getting retailers to actually use them. Most national retail chains are very selective in deciding which products to accept displays for. They often expect the manufacturer to offer cash incentives for the privilege of allowing you to set up a display in their stores. Some store managers of national retail chains will make their own decisions as to what displays they will accommodate on their floors, even if you have an agreement with the national office that is backed by cash incentives and guarantees a full chain display program. And even if you do manage to get display exposure, merchants prefer to keep displays up for short periods of time in order to keep the impression of their merchandise mix fresh and appealing to their consumers.

Dumps

Floor displays, commonly referred to as dumps, are most effective if placed at the front of the store. This location guarantees viewing by the maximum number of visiting consumers. This arrangement is the most powerful of all point-of-sale display options.

This type of display is often fabricated out of card stock. But it can be very expensive to manufacture. Typically merchants reserve the display of dumps for their top brands and fastest selling promotions.

Counter displays

Counter displays are sometimes called prepacks when the display also serves double duty as a counter item. Merchants generally use counter displays for low-priced items that a consumer might decide to purchase on impulse while they are waiting for sales assistance or standing at the cash register. Small novelty items are ideal for counter displays.

Counter displays need to be attractive, cute, and even whimsical. They also need to be conservative in space requirements and height so as not to obstruct the line of vision between the sales clerk and the customer.

Posters

Posters are the least inspiring point-of-sale display vehicle when used to attract consumers to products they were not previously aware of. But they can be very effective in pulling in customers to purchase a product they have some knowledge of—perhaps through an extensive advertising or publicity campaign.

Shelf talkers

Shelf talkers are signs that appear alongside a given item on the shelf. They can be very effective and, best of all, cost relatively little to produce. They require short, brief copy that can really grab a consumer's attention.

*O*ne of the easiest ways to project a great image is through your literature. You don't need to spend a lot of money on an expensive, full-color brochure designed by a world-renowned graphic artist. What matters, really, is consistency. You need to develop a logo and a particular look. You need to display that logo, maintain that look, throughout all of your printed materials. Use your logo and look on absolutely everything, from business cards to stationary to fax cover sheets to packaging.

The logo

A logo doesn't have to involve a graphic to be effective. Merely selecting an attractive typeface can help create a great logo with a strong impact. Of course, having an interesting name for your business will make an incredible difference. For example, if the name of your business is "Joe's Used Cars, Inc." it would be nearly impossible to offset the downscale image of your name, regardless of graphics. Remember, it's never too late to change the name of your business. After fifteen years as Bob Adams, Inc., we changed our name to Adams Media Corporation. Which name sounds better to you?

The designer

You could hire a graphic designer or a specialized image consultant to design your logo. This can be an expensive proposition, though. It's actually more fun if you do it yourself! Spend time browsing through magazines, checking clothing labels, or observing product packaging to get an idea of what appeals to you in terms of design, color schemes, and layout. Don't copy anyone's work, but use these ideas as inspirations for your own logo—one that appropriately expresses the nature of your business.

Trade Shows

There are many compelling reasons for attending trade shows. Don't view them as just an opportunity to write orders for your product. In fact, in many industries, few orders are taken on the trade show floor. The real reason for trade show attendance is company and product awareness and promotion.

Trade shows are a proven method for successfully introducing new product lines or unveiling seasonal offerings to consumers or distributors. They can even be terrific venues for launching a completely new business.

Another important role of the trade show is as a means to presell your product line. At some postshow date, when a sales representative or telemarketer calls on a prospective customer or when a direct mail piece is received by a potential client, the prospects are more likely to respond. This is because they have prior knowledge of your company and your product.

All in all, trade shows open the doors and pave the road to building strong future relationships with current and new customers, sales representatives, distributors, media people, and other influential players in your marketplace.

Before attending a trade show, however, carefully outline your objectives. Why are you participating? Then plan a strategy that seeks to meet your goals.

Special offers

It is common practice to offer "show specials" at a slightly higher than usual discount or with better terms such as free shipping as an incentive to purchase on the trade show floor. You may want to prepromote your "show special" by sending a preannouncement to attendees.Contact the convention organizers to see if you can purchase the preregistered attendance list. Often such lists are available preprinted on mailing labels. Don't forget to include your current and known potential customers in your mailing. You may want to offer this group of consumers the "show special" even if they don't plan on attending. Extend the offer for some limited period of time and specify how they can place an order.

Opening new accounts

Many companies offer "new account specials" at trade shows. Consider offering a slightly better discount on the opening order or, perhaps, a free gift or merchandise item of limited value. You may want to offer a freebie to get prospective consumers to drop by your booth. Anything that will attract attendees to your booth, obviously, will increase your sales opportunities.

You may do better at opening new accounts by calling show attendees right after the show closes. Or you can pass on the names of those people who visited your booth to your sales representatives for follow-up. Try setting up a "Prize Bowl" to collect business cards for a grand giveaway drawing. This can be a great way to amass leads! If you really want to attract new accounts, consider waiving credit checks or prepayments on first orders under a certain value. Be sure to inform such clients, however, that further credit orders will be contingent upon a favorable credit report.

Building relationships with current customers

No amount of dazzle in your booth is likely to do as much for building positive relationships with customers as taking the time to sit down and talk. The more senior the employees you have "working" the booth, the better. This shows that you take your trade show attendance seriously. Take care that your representatives are well-groomed, wear smiles, and possess a strong handshake. These seemingly small touches can go a long way toward building and maintaining customer relationships through trade shows.

Trade show attendees, even if current customers, can become frustrated if no one is available to talk to them. This is especially true at large-company booths with heavy traffic. The concern at smaller booths may be the absence of the one attending company representative. Make sure you have adequate personnel in your booth at all times.

Launching a new product line

To launch a new product line at a trade show, be prepared to offer potential customers as much specific information about the new product line as possible. It is always ideal to have a working sample of the product, but that isn't always possible. If this is the case, try to represent the new product as accurately as possible with prototypes, photographs, product specification sheets, or any other type of substantive material that will best display the salient features of the new product.

To create excitement about your new offerings and increase the number of visitors to your booth, many companies display life-size posters or even three-dimensional representations of their new products.

Emphasizing the firm's unique attributes

In the circus-like atmosphere of many trade shows, it is difficult to convey the subtle or numerous differences between your firm and product and that of your competition. The most effective way to set yourself apart from the noise is to focus on one major delineating feature of your product by highlighting it in a spectacular way. For example, you may choose to display a large sign reading "The Firm That Offers Free Freight All The Time," or "Product Support Is Our #1 Concern," or "Leading-Edge Products."

Portraying the firm as a major player in the industry

To portray your firm as a major player in the industry at a major trade show is going to cost a great deal of money. So, before you take this tack, you need to carefully consider the image ramifications of portraying yourself as a major player. You may have the best product on the market, but if you don't have significant market share or a broad product line, you will look foolish trying to palm yourself off as an industry leader.

If you can swing the image, you will have to do more than just rent the largest floor space. What you do with that space will make a more significant impression on customers. A professional, polished, display is absolutely essential. If you need to economize, give heavy emphasis to displaying your firm's name at the price of deemphasizing product displays.

Seeking publicity in trade publications

Send press releases and call the editors of trade publications well before convention time. Be sure to have information available on special offers, promotions, or giveaways during the shows and, of course, information on new products. These are your best bets for getting press attention. Remember, trade publications are also read by key prospects who are unable to attend the show.

Seeking independent sales representatives

Independent sales representatives are most likely to respond to a professional booth display. They cruise show floors and size up a companies at a glance. If your booth looks great, they will think you have a saleable product. You may wish to display a small, neat sign reading "Sales representatives needed for some territories." Even if you don't want to be as blatant in your representative search as a sign indicates, trade shows can be a terrific proving ground for lining up new sales representatives.

Seeking overseas distributors

Foreign distributors tend to avoid the smaller, least effective trade show booths. But even if your budget is tight, make sure your products are represented accurately. Given a choice, foreign distributors prefer seeing good production models of products over fancy booth displays. And unlike current domestic distributors, foreign distributors will be as interested in your existing product line as they will be in new offerings.

The best place to find overseas distributors is at large international shows. But large national shows will draw some foreign candidates as well.

Trade Shows

Seeking large distributors

Many key employees from large firms will be wandering the trade show floor looking for new ideas and products from small companies that would add to their distribution line. To attract a large distributor or distribution firm, place your product or product representation at the forefront of your booth. Have your company representatives make eye contact and conversation with personnel from large distribution houses that pass by the booth.

Meeting with key accounts

If you hope to have meaningful meetings with key accounts, you need to make arrangements in advance. If you have the luxury of leaving your booth periodically, the ideal situation is to meet your key accounts off the trade show floor. If this isn't possible, set up an area in your booth that is private, outfitted with chairs and a table, and relatively quiet in which to conduct your meetings. Instruct booth representatives to keep interruptions to a minimum while you are in the meeting.

Convention meetings are tricky. Everyone wants to get the attention of key buyers. It isn't unusual to have appointments changed or cancelled. You might even be stood up entirely. Don't be surprised.

In-depth demonstrations

If you need the full attention of current or prospective customers to demonstrate your product or service, you may wish to divide your booth into an area for displays and an area for demonstrations. Consider roping off the rear section of your booth for a seating or meeting area that will offer a comfortable atmosphere for viewing demonstrations. Remember, though, to encourage customers to stay at your booth for more than a cursory overview. During a busy trade show you'll need a really hot product or an incredibly exciting presentation.

Solving problems for customers

While trade show exhibitors often enter into the venture very excited about publicly presenting their new products, what your customers may hope to accomplish through trade show attendance may, surprisingly for you, not even include viewing your new products. They may hope to resolve vendor, delivery, quality, billing, or other significant issues. Always be prepared to spend time restoring good relationships with some of your customers.

Checking out competitors' products

Virtually all exhibitors at trade shows budget time for surveying their competitor's wares and latest offerings. Keep in mind, however, that while you are doing this—and it may be important—you aren't in your booth selling to and meeting customers. If you need to go on a competitor scouting expedition, just make sure your booth will be adequately and professionally staffed in your absence.

Seeking new products or services to distribute or buy

Trade shows afford a fast way to peruse other firm's products or services that you may wish to distribute or buy. Be cautious. It is easy to make hasty and premature decisions during the excitement of a trade show. If you have any hesitation at all about coming to an agreement at a trade show, back off until you get home and have a chance to think it through. Or, at the very least, wait until the end of the show, when you have had a chance to evaluate all of the potential products or services that may enhance your ability to meet your own customer's needs.

Keeping up contacts

Keep careful track of every contact you meet during a trade show. Even a direct competitor can be a source of important information in the future. Make a point of asking for business cards and handing out yours. And keep notes for future reference.

Streetwise Advice on Trade Shows

☞ **Beware the trade show dragon**

If you don't keep a careful lid on trade show costs, they can easily skyrocket out of control. Two of the easiest ways to be shocked by your trade show expenses is to participate in one without a formal budget, or to go nuts and make big booth-related purchases just before the show. Know what you can afford to spend, and stick to your budget.

☞ **Emphasize class, not mass**

A small, well-done trade show booth can look more attractive and inviting than a larger one that looks less professional. Keep in mind that it is a lot easier and takes a lot less money to make a small booth look attractive than a larger one.

"If you don't keep a lid on trade show costs, they can easily skyrocket out of control."

☞ **Portable exhibits make a lot of sense**

Most small companies that attend trade shows are best off buying a small portable exhibit. They are offered in a range of styles, from table-top versions that cost a few hundred dollars, to full-height exhibits. Professional-looking logos can be added to the top of the display and large full-color product photos can dress up the panels. Presto—a great little exhibit!

Portable exhibits are lightweight and fold down into compact shippable units. Custom-designed shipping containers are usually a purchase option and will help minimize shipping damage. Shipping costs, themselves, will be substantially reduced.

Portable exhibits are, in addition, extremely easy to assemble and seldom require the services of unionized booth assembly labor.

Ads for portable trade show exhibit companies can be found in business and airline in-flight magazines. Many of these companies have representatives around the country who would be happy to visit your office to present a demonstration.

☞ **What's a good booth location?**

As a new exhibitor you probably won't have much choice in booth selection. However, booth location can make a big difference in your floor traffic. Do whatever you can to get the best space possible. Get your application in early and be sure to request the best space available.

The best space is a high-traffic location. A corner booth should be your goal because these are the most visible from all possible approach angles. The front of the hall is terrific; the center of the hall is good. Spaces near major aisle intersections, food vendors, or restrooms also see a lot of activity.

Streetwise Advice on Trade Shows

☞ **Whom to send**

Even in a small company, the matter of who will attend a trade show can quickly become a political game. If the trade show is out of town and you pay the way for everyone who wants to attend, you'll bury your company in travel and accommodation debt. Make personnel choices and announce them early in order to minimize last-minute disappointments. If you attend several trade shows, try rotating the teams of booth representatives to give all of your key people a chance to attend a show. Remember, airfare and hotel accommodations are just the beginning of the expenses you will incur for each attendee.

When choosing booth staff, keep in mind personalities. Someone who interacts well with strangers, has a high energy level, is articulate, outgoing, and knows how to dress and act professionally is going to benefit your company's image. Send your best "people people," not your best engineers or product managers. While anyone staffing your booth should have adequate knowledge of your product, knowledge is of little value if your representatives won't take the initiative and talk to visitors. The bottom line is that dress and professional appearance in your booth staffers will outshine the physical appearance of your booth any day.

If you really want to give everyone on your staff an opportunity to attend a trade show, participate in a local one.

☞ **Share goals**

Even if you have only one or two people attending a trade show, be sure to clarify your objectives. Let your representatives know why you are exhibiting—are you seeking new accounts, new distributors, or new representatives? Inform them of any "show specials" that you are offering. Do each of your representative have specific responsibilities—talking to foreign distributors, booth set-up and dismantling, or entertaining customers? Do you need to keep certain product details from falling into the hands of the competition?

☞ **Establish an order target**

Writing orders is usually not the most important goal for attending a trade show. But if it happens to be one of your goals, it will certainly be easy to measure your success. A good target for sales goals is to at least meet the fee paid for the space in the exhibit hall.

Even if sales is not your major trade show goal, order totals can be used as a measure for gauging the success rate of one show versus another.

☞ **Follow-up makes the difference**

In the age of e-mail and fax machines, the trend continues to move away from on-the-spot order writing on trade show floors. Pay more attention to closing sales after the convention. Take business cards from every possible prospect, and note their particular interests and concerns. Make follow-up calls and/or mail requested information as soon after the convention as possible.

Do I have to go to trade shows to succeed in my industry?

No. There are plenty of businesses in all industries and sizes that don't participate in trade shows. Many are, nonetheless, very successful. Don't choose trade shows as a vehicle for promoting your company, products, and services simply because other firms you know are planning to exhibit.

Decide for yourself whether or not the exposure is worth the expense. If it is, set a budget and stick to it. Remember, awards from attending a trade show are generally intangible. Don't expect a big pile of orders from new customers.

Should I advertise in trade show publications?

Be prepared. You will get calls from media representatives offering ad space in their show publications. They might play on your fear that no one will visit your booth because they won't know you are there unless you advertise. This is nonsense! You will be much better off spending money on upgrading your booth presentation than you would be by advertising in a trade show publication.

What if I do decide to advertise in a trade show publication?

If you do decide to place trade show advertisements, advertise in a regular trade publication, in the preshow issue that features trade show news. Many of these trade publications also issue a special show guide that buyers often use in planning booth visits. Typically, advertisers are listed in these guides. Sometimes these publications also offer additional circulation of their trade show issue to trade show attendees, often at no additional cost, in addition to their usual circulation. Ultimately you will be much better off advertising in a regular trade publication that has a preshow issue than in any publication that is distributed solely at the show. You will reach show attendees as well as those buyers who don't attend the show.

Should I have giveaways?

In some industries everyone has some giveaways at a trade show. In other industries only the larger firms do. Play it by ear. And, unless you are restrictive about who gets your giveaways, you may very well give more of your products or gifts to the competition than you do to buyers!

How much work can I do without hiring union labor?

Each exposition hall (not each trade show) has its own rules. If your indus-

try's trade show is held in a different city each year, then the rules will vary each year. Rules at major convention centers tend to be very restrictive because they are usually built with public money and politicians are sensitive to the needs of labor unions.

At most larger convention centers you can't carry anything into the hall yourself that you can't carry in your hands. That means no two-wheelers or dollies. You can't hire labor that isn't union, and you can't use your own tools to set up your own booth. You can't even use your own ladder. So, if you can hand-carry your booth into the convention center and set it up without the benefit of tools, you are all set. Otherwise you will have to contract labor to do the delivery of your exhibit to the booth space and, at the very least, assist in booth assembly.

In setting up a multi-booth exhibit in Las Vegas the union steward complained to me about my lack of union help in setting up part of my display. I persuaded him not to push the issue because I had had a vertical sign set up earlier in the day which had required a lift truck and a three-man union crew.

To avoid any unpleasant ramifications that may result from the use of unauthorized or unacceptable labor, use the show's recommended labor vendors, decorators, electrical contractors, and other services.

Strategies for Competing with Giants

1. Study!
2. Block!
3. Tackle!

Study, but don't necessarily copy your competitor's moves. Visit their businesses, watch their ads, figure out their strategies, and find their Achilles heels! Always watch them like a hawk!

You may not be able to keep up with your competitor's strategy move by move. You should, however, be ready and able to blunt or block the impact of their moves. Then, later, you can make

your own offensive move at your own pace and in your own ball court.

For example, let's say you are selling a product on a national basis through retail outlets. You discover that your competitor is about to launch a gigantic, multi-million dollar advertising campaign. You don't have the time or money to create a competing campaign. What you may be able to do, though, is offer a special one-time deal to the trade—something like buy five items, get one free—for a limited period of time. This way, you can stock up the trade and limit the shelf space that is available to your competition. The added consumer traffic attributable to your competitor's advertising efforts will largely benefit your product since it is the available product. At a later point in time you can launch your own marketing effort or product introduction—perhaps during a typically slow period for your competitor.

Niches

A very powerful strategy, especially in larger market areas, is to focus your entire business on one specific niche. For example, let's say you own a local lumberyard and a national lumberyard chain moves into your sales region. You may be better off focusing your attention on serving local contractors.

If the market niche or niches you are considering are very small markets, you may want to retain some products and services that appeal to a wider range of customers, but have exceptional product depth in a few niche areas. For example, a local ski shop faced with competition from a national chain might decide to focus its primary effort on racing skis, while still retaining some selection for all levels of skiers.

The off-price option

It may be common wisdom that you can't compete against national businesses on price. But it's not a fact!

For example, many local retailers feel they can't compete with national discounters because national discounters are selling at prices far less than they can even purchase the merchandise for. This is defeatist thinking!

You can turn the tables on nationally based competitors. For example, there is a very powerful local chain of general merchandise discount stores in the Boston area called Building #19. They don't appear to be losing sales to Wal-Mart or the burgeoning crowd of warehouse clubs. And it's no wonder: Building #19 typically sells goods for a little as one quarter the price that tough national competitors can buy them for! How's that? Building #19 buys odd lots, closeouts, and damaged goods. And the beauty in this strategy is that their selection changes continually, giving shoppers more reasons to visit their stores on a regular basis.

You can adopt Building #19's strategy for just part of your business by devoting a portion of your retail space to off-price products. Many local businesses have traveled that road with great success.

Loss leaders

A local business or service can use "loss leaders" to sell against a tough national competitor in almost any category, be it retail, wholesale, service, product, etc.

Many national business often use complex pricing strategies to powerful competitive advantage. For example, grocery stores may sell milk at a smaller markup than

most other goods because they feel that consumers are particularly conscious of the price they pay for milk. Similarly, a discount department store typically sells name-brand health and beauty aids at a smaller markup than other goods. Airlines offer special prices on travel over Saturday night to lure more price-conscious nonbusiness travelers. For a time McDonald's sold its hamburgers for a mere 15¢ while marking up sodas significantly to realize an overall profit.

If you don't have a cost advantage over a competing larger national firm, offer very low prices on a limited quantity of heavily branded items that consumers are most likely to have noted competitor's pricing on. Also consider running very deep discounts for short periods of time, and change at least some of the items receiving the deepest discounts.

While a small business won't generally run into legal problems by selling goods below cost to stay in business, it is illegal to sell items below cost for the explicit purpose of driving a competitor out of business.

Strategies for Competing with Giants

Creative aerial dogfights

Even when you are going to go head to head against a large national firm, you can deploy creative competitive strategies.

For example, some years ago, a relatively new airline, Southwest, decided to carve out a major market share of the Houston-to-Dallas airline route. This strategy involved competing against an entrenched national airline. Southwest struck at its competition with a dramatically lower airfare offer. The national airline quickly matched the lower fares. Southwest went lower. The national airline went still lower. Fares finally bottomed at $19, and both airlines were losing money hand over fist. Then Southwest noted that most of the travelers were corporate executives who handled their own flight arrangements but didn't get involved in paying for them. Price wasn't the main selling factor and therefore wasn't the strongest point to compete on. So, Southwest changed its tactics, and jacked up its fares, but offered each adult passenger a complimentary bottle of Chivas Regal. Southwest soon dominated the market even with a higher ticket price!

Frequent customers

A powerful tool for holding onto your best customers is to give them specific rewards. One common strategy is the frequent-buyer program used by many retailers and service businesses. Witness the popularity of the frequent-flyer programs offered by airlines, wherein you earn discounted or free travel for specified levels of air mileage achieved.

Customers get incredibly attached to the frequent-buyer programs they have enrolled in. They often continue to patronize a store or use a product or service even if the competitor's prices are lower. People just enjoy receiving special treatment!

Service

One of the most common suggestions you will get from others on how to survive against major national competitors is to provide great service. While I want you to know that this is common advice, I want to tell you that I think you will generally be making a big mistake to bank on great service alone for your survival. Frankly, I think a lot of small stores retreat to the service option because it is the cheapest option and one of the hardest to measure. Also, more and more larger national businesses are doing an increasingly good job of offering good service.

☞ Learn from survivors

Learn from companies that have already successfully survived the onslaught of the giants in their market area. For example, if you are running a local hardware store and a major discount hardware store moves in across the street, get on your bicycle and pedal as fast as you can to other towns where this scenario has been played and where local businesses have survived against the same giant. Many small business owners who thought they were doomed found salvation in copying the survival ideas used by firms caught in similar situations in other markets.

You should also check with your trade association. They sometimes offer seminars and/or have reading materials and audiotapes on competing with giants.

☞ Ask your customers

Go ahead and ask your customers what they really want from your business. Ask them how they think your business compares with other businesses—even the giant.

Of course, what you really should do is ask people who patronize the competition what it is your competition is offering that appeals to them. Just don't conduct your survey on their premises!

And, remember, in responding to surveys, people's answers often reflect what they think the interviewer wants to hear. Judge responses carefully. Ask the same question in several different ways.

"Learn from companies that have already successfully survived the onslaught of the giants in their market area."

☞ Avoid the common failure route

One of the most common routes to failure typically taken by a small retailer battling a superstore begins with panic. Then the retailer briefly consoles itself with the notion that customer service and loyalty will keep its clientele from defecting to the large, discount competitor. Then, as customers dwindle, the retailer wakes up from this false security and lowers a few prices here and there as a token cost-cutting incentive. As worries about lost profit margins set in, it then begins to reduce inventories to maintain cash flow.

The small retailer is then left with huge price gaps and huge differences in inventory sizes. Business really begins to plummet, and it slashes prices to the bone in a desparate attempt to attract consumers and ultimately revive its business. But by this time, it is often too late.

Don't go down this road! Make your first move bold and decisive!

Streetwise Advice about Competing with Giants

☞ **When to change**

Completely and carefully reevaluate your strategy as soon as you hear a superstore is coming—or better yet, reevaluate your strategy today, because chances are that sooner or later you will face superstore competition.

Many small businesses that have been crushed by national firms simply waited too long to change their competitive strategies. Change your strategy, creatively and without panic, as soon as possible to adjust to competitive forces.

☞ **Don't panic**

Some small businesses change their strategy too often when faced with national competition. Don't panic! Come up with a sound strategy and don't switch your tactics at the first sign of problems. You need to retain a clear identity throughout the competitor crisis and instill a clear competitive advantage in your customer's minds.

You can change aspects of your identity now and then if you put a lot of effort into your image change and if the tone of your identity is clear and simple—something that can be easily communicated to your clientele without confusing them. Just don't continually switch the message you are conveying. Consumers need to be comfortable with where they stand with you. You need to appear reliable.

☞ **Strategies and plans**

All firms can benefit from a solid competitive strategy, a unique selling proposition, annual planning, and market planning. But it is imperative for a David-sized firm facing a Goliath-sized competitor to use these tools. It can spell the difference between survival and extinction.

Even if you had a good strategy and plan in place before the giant competitor arrived, you need to reevaluate it once the giant arrives on the scene. Despite the reputation that large national firms have for being slow to make major structural changes, some have an unending slew of new marketing plans waiting in the wings. You had better be able to anticipate such moves and be able to deflect attention from the marketing strategies with winners of your own. And, most of all, you need to find a means of distinguishing your business from the competitor's in a very positive and meaningful way.

"Don't panic! Come up with a sound strategy and don't switch your tactics at the first sign of problems."

Questions & Answers on Competing with Giants

Can I take legal action?

Don't bother taking legal action against a larger competitor even if it is selling goods below cost in your market. The chances that you can prove that it is intentionally deploying tactics specifically designed to drive you out of business are remote. And even if the court system finds in your favor, the legal costs could run into thousands of dollars, your time could be tied up for years, and the result just may be a pledge from the giant to stop practicing the specific activities that were found illegal. It won't prevent the giant from attacking you in any other manner.

But if you really want to pursue the matter, consult an attorney first. Find out what, if any, legal basis you might have for filing a complaint with the U.S. Federal Trade Commission or other appropriate state or foreign agency. Then see whether or not the government wants to spend their time and money on the case. Or see if your trade association wants to become involved in the matter.

There are many small communities where residents, including local business people, have banded together to prohibit large national super-stores from opening in their town. However, be leery of putting too much value on such movements. The superstore will simple open up one or two towns over and still pose a threat to you. And some superstores have been known to pay towns considerable sums of money to quell or avoid such opposition.

Should I consider selling my business?

If you sell your business knowing that a giant national competitor is opening in your area, and you don't provide this information to your buyer, not only is it unethical but you risk being sued for fraud. So if you do sell your business, have the purchase and sales agreement include a clause that spells out the specifics of any impending competitive threats.

Better yet, stick around for long enough to show that your company can realize a profit despite the competition. Then, when you sell your business, you may even get a bit closer to your asking price, considering that the company has been able to hold its own against a giant national competitor.

You could even consider selling your business to the competition if it is interested in it. But try to hold off from this "surrender the ship before the battle begins" alternative.

Can I join forces with other small firms to compete with the giant?

No. Amazingly, the giant firm, like any other company, is protected by law from attempts by a group of firms under different ownership that join forces specifically for the purpose of posing a competitive threat. You should certainly consult with an attorney before grouping with any other company or companies to create a competitive bloc.

The penalties for unlawful joint conduct are stiff, including triple damages and payment of the injured party's legal fees. There may even be harsh criminal penalties.

Even trade associations are restricted from targeting some types of action against specific firms, although they will often pursue targeted actions by stating that they are simply trying to maintain an environment of equal competition.

Questions & Answers on Competing with Giants

How can I work with other small firms to compete?

The key is that you can engage in normal business activities with other firms that don't specifically target one competitor, large or small. So for example, you could team up with another firm in the same line of business to share a warehouse or sales force in an effort to cut costs.

One interesting arrangement conceived by two retailers was to share workload. Each retailer felt it was spending too much time buying product and not enough time with customers. So, they divided their product lines into two parts and each retailer bought half of the product type that was sold in each of the stores.

Shouldn't I cut expenses to save cash for a rainy day, such as when a giant competitor emerges?

Unfortunately, this is exactly what many firms do—at their peril. By cutting important expenses such as inventory or marketing, they become more vulnerable to competition and hasten their own decline. Don't start cutting expenses until you work through a carefully detailed strategy.

How could I work with larger firms to compete with a giant?

The possibilities are endless. Here are a few examples.

- Small retailers can work with powerful wholesalers. Wholesalers are offering ever-faster shipping by allowing retailers to use wholesalers as if they were private warehouses. Many wholesalers are also offering the benefits of computerized inventory and ordering systems to retailers, and have developed customized retail marketing plans for their use.

- Small product firms often create successful alliances with larger firms to market or even manufacture their product. In a more limited alliance, the larger firm may sell the smaller firm's product under the smaller firm's name for a small percentage of the revenue. In a closer partnership, the smaller firm may even license its product to the larger firm, which completes all of the manufacturing and may even sell the product under its own name.

- Small service companies sometimes team up with larger national firms to sell their services. For example, some national firms selling home products offer to arrange for an independent local service company to provide installation services.

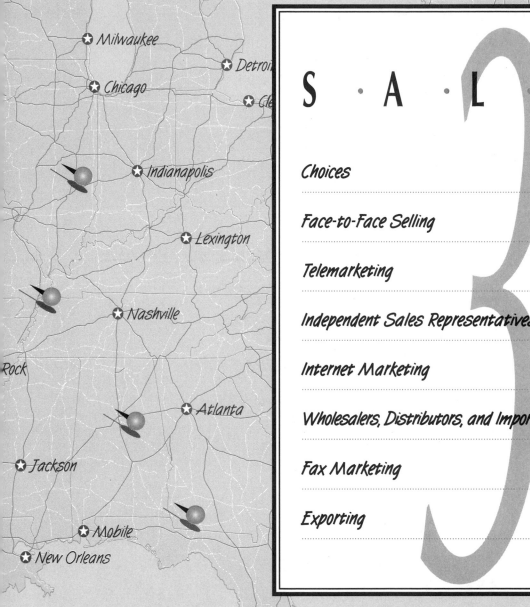

S · A · L · E · S

3

Choices .... ➤ 121

Face-to-Face Selling .... ➤ 123

Telemarketing .... ➤ 128

Independent Sales Representatives .... ➤ 136

Internet Marketing .... ➤ 142

Wholesalers, Distributors, and Importers ... ➤ 144

Fax Marketing .... ➤ 148

Exporting .... ➤ 149

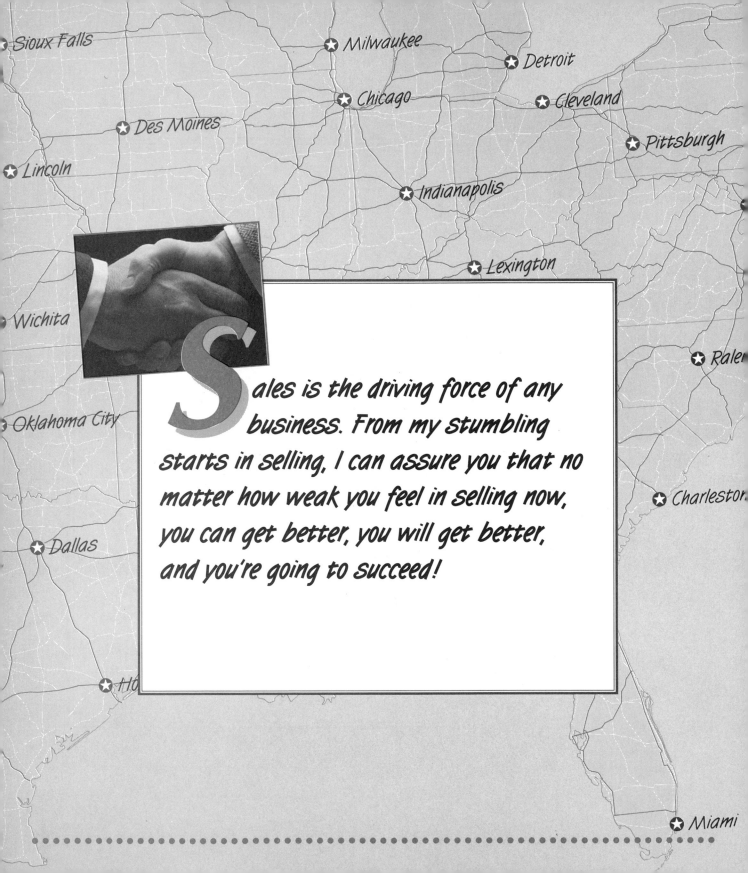

Sales is the driving force of any business. From my stumbling starts in selling, I can assure you that no matter how weak you feel in selling now, you can get better, you will get better, and you're going to succeed!

Choices

Your basic choices for selling products or services to the business-to-business trade or directly to consumers are through telemarketing or face-to-face selling. To help you make a decision regarding the sales method that is appropriate for your company, take a careful look at what other companies are doing. And don't just look at firms selling products or services similar to yours. Be more creative. Look at firms selling products and services with the same characteristics as yours in similar marketplaces.

Ultimately, however, deciding which sales process to use is more of an art than a science. Weigh all of the factors you think will be important contributors to making the sale of your product or service successful. Then make your decision—but don't be afraid to change your mind later on if your strategy isn't working or could be improved upon.

Choices

Face-to-face or telemarketing: Factors to consider when making the choice

- **Price**

  For a relatively low-priced item, telemarketing is a good bet. In choosing this option, though, make sure, in addition to the costs of manufacturing your product or offering your service, you can cover the cost of the telemarketer and the cost of the call and still make money.

  As the product or service becomes more expensive, the effectiveness of telemarketing decreases rapidly. High-priced items are simply impossible to sell over the phone. Just imagine a telemarketer attempting to sell a tractor trailer truck or executive Lear jet over the phone!

  Face-to-face selling is an effective way to sell any product or service. However, it is an expensive proposition. Not only do you have to pay your salesperson, but you need to cover his or her travel costs.

  In business-to-business sales, there is typically more time involved in face-to-face selling. In order to sell a product or service to another business, an appointment with the sales prospect is required. Just setting up an appointment often takes as much, if not more, time than actually selling a simple impulse item via telemarketing.

- **Customization**

  The more customized the product, the less effective telemarketing will be as a sales tool. The clear choice for selling highly specialized products or services is face to face.

- **Service**

  If the product you are selling requires servicing, face-to-face sales is the best way to sell the product.

- **Personal**

  Personal use products that a customer would require detailed information on in order to make a purchasing decision such as health insurance for individuals, should be sold face to face.

- **Product line**

  The broader the product line or the larger the number of services being sold, the less effective telemarketing will be. Even for simple, low-priced items, potential customers will not feel comfortable buying several different items of merchandise over the phone.

Face-to-Face Selling

Face-to-face selling can require a lot of time, energy, and expense, but the payoff can be tremendous. Despite all of the new high-tech alternatives, an in-person sales presentation is the single most powerful marketing tool in use today. National television advertising, telemarketing, e-mail, or print advertising have nowhere near the ability to motivate a particular customer to actually place an order as does face-to-face selling.

And despite any fancy slide or computer show or other dog-and-pony show you might use, your most effective selling tool will be your verbal presentation and interaction with the prospective buyer. In almost every case, the owner of a small business will be able to make the most effective sales presentation, even more so than someone with more extensive sales experience.

When you are starting out small, you are probably going to have to do a lot of selling yourself in order to jump-start your business. Your effectiveness as a salesperson will be an absolutely critical factor in the success of your business. Later, as your business grows and prospers, you may be able to delegate more and more of the selling process to your employees.

The majority of products and services being sold business to business, as well as many sold to consumers, require a personal sales call.

A Face-to-Face Dialogue

The following dialogue is an example of face-to-face selling techniques. The sales representative, June West, is selling advertising space in *Free Paper*, a free distribution advertiser, to the owner of a local furniture store, Hal Smith. Take note of how June continues to sell even when Hal expresses disinterest. Notice that June relies heavily on testimonials as she does this. And notice how she responds to an unspoken objection from Hal regarding his suspicions about *Free Paper's* circulation. Also note how June makes it easy for Hal to place an ad by offering to run the same ad Hal has already developed and is running in the *City Paper.*

 Hal

It is a pleasure to meet you. Please, won't you have a seat?

 June

It is a pleasure to meet you, Mr. Smith.

 Hal

I've been thinking about this *Free Paper* idea and I've decided it's just not the place for us to advertise. I'm sorry to have taken up so much of your time.

 June

Well, just yesterday City Furniture told me it was so pleased with the response to its ad that it wants to sign up for an annual contract.

 Hal

I'm sure it can work for some firms—but I'm just not sure that it's for us.

 June

And Mammoth Furniture told me it got more customers from the full-page ad it ran with us than it's gotten from any other media. Now, I've noticed that you advertise a lot in the daily paper and I was just wondering—do you have customers from all over the metropolitan area or are they mostly concentrated around your store?

 Hal Well, most of our customers are from adjacent towns.

 June The *Free Paper's* circulation is concentrated in the towns near you. And since we mail it free to every house, it reaches everyone the *City Paper* gets, plus many more.

 Hal I've had poor experiences with the alternative papers before.

 June Well, our figures are audited by Business Publication Audit International. So, you can be assured that you're getting 100% saturation coverage.

 Hal Our next sale starts in four days and I don't have time to put an ad together.

 June I can run the same ad you've been running in the *City Paper* and the rate would be less than half of what you're paying for the ad in the *City Paper*.

 Hal OK, I'll try it once.

☞ **Doing it yourself**

You might be wondering whether or not you should hire an experienced salesperson. The most important key to sales success isn't sales talent or experience. It's enthusiasm for your product or service. No one will have more interest in your product than you, and no one will be able to sell your product or service better than you. So practice your sales skills and get ready to hit the road!

☞ **"But I can't sell!"**

A lot of people hate the idea of "being a salesperson" or are scared of it. But you need to give it a try. With practice, you'll get better; with improvement, you'll gain confidence; and with a sale, you'll be flying!

☞ **Rejection**

The hardest part of selling is handling rejection. The rejection cycle begins when you start to set up appointments, continues through the presentation cycle, and will occur even when you think you're just about to close a sale.

If you can't close a sale, don't take it personally. No one closes every sale. A certain percentage of your prospects are not going to buy your product or service no matter how wonderful your presentation is or how great a salesperson you are. Accept this. On average, you are going to get rejected a certain number of times for each sale you make. Next time around, think of the failed sales call as being one step closer to a successful one!

☞ **Voice mail**

Voice mail is proving to be more pervasive and difficult to get by than receptionists and secretaries used to be.

The best approach is to avoid using voice mail. Call repeatedly in an attempt to catch your prospect "in person."

It seems that many people always leave their voice mail on. Keep trying. Call your prospects five times a day, every day, until you reach him or her.

If it turns out that the prospect's voice mail really is on all the time, there are alternatives. You can leave a message that provides enough information to the prospect to develop interest, but leaves enough out to pique the person's curiosity. For example, "We've saved three of your major competitors a lot of money in this area" without mentioning the competitor's names or what you did for them. Or, try pitching the prospect's assistant in order to persuade that person to arrange an appointment for you. Or, network your way to the prospect through mutual industry acquaintances.

☞ **Hiring others**

Hiring a sales staff may be the road to fast growth for your small business, but hiring even one person is a big step.

You will need to provide your salespeople with solid knowledge of your products, the competitor's products, and the market. You will also need to monitor their progress.

While it is a challenge to keep any sales force motivated, it is even more so when you have only one or two salespeople. Celebrate victories and provide encouragement after a defeat. And keep after them!

Good salespeople expect good pay. Provide a good base salary and a generous commission or bonus plan. Provide first-class sales materials and travel/entertainment allowances. Be sure you can afford all of this before you take the hiring plunge!

Questions & Answers about Face-to-Face Selling

What should I wear for sales calls?

Dress your best! Even in these days of increasingly casual corporate dress, salespeople are usually expected to look sharp. A man should wear a tie and a jacket. A woman should dress similarly and conservatively. They should wear minimal jewelry and keep their makeup simple. If the prospect the salesperson is calling on will be wearing a suit, the salesperson should as well.

When should I arrive?

Arrive five minutes before your scheduled appointment. If you arrive any earlier, sit and read in your car or go to a coffee shop to kill time. Arriving too early makes you seem overeager, puts pressure on the prospect to see you before the appointed time, and is unprofessional.

Should I invite the prospect out to lunch?

If your appointment is before lunch and you are building a good rapport with the prospect, inviting them to lunch is often a good way to improve the relationship.

But if rapport is developing slowly, a lunch invitation will seem awkward and may further weaken your standing with the prospect.

Should I stick to business on the first visit?

On an in-person sales visit, try to talk at least briefly about a nonbusiness topic. This tactic will usually make everyone feel more at ease and may even relax the prospective client into being more open-minded about your product or service offerings. Try discussing a noncontroversial trend in the industry or a personal hobby. But don't force conversation in this direction if the prospect doesn't seem interested. And don't let nonbusiness conversations detract from your sales presentation.

When should I try to close the sale?

Your best chance for closing a sale will occur after you have established a good rapport with the prospect and presented your product or service as carefully as possible. Determine in advance how much time you will have with the prospect. Ask the prospect or the assistant when you are scheduling the appointment what your time allotment will be. Then try to time your first attempt at closing the sale about three-quarters of the way through your appointment. This will

maximize your time for making the presentation while allowing you plenty of time to discuss any objections the prospect may raise.

How hard should I push?

Unless the prospect has committed to a series of meetings with you or someone else from your firm, the face-to-face meeting will provide the best opportunity for closing a deal. Push as hard as you can to make a sale during your meeting without completely alienating your prospect.

The great advantage of face-to-face meetings is that you can read the body language of the prospect. Is he or she listening to your arguments? Which points does he or she seem to pay the most attention to? Focus your arguments and try hard for a sale.

If you feel that a sale isn't forthcoming, try for another goal—a trial, a quote, a proposal, or even a commitment for another meeting.

Remember, it is much easier to close a sale in person than it is over the phone.

Telemarketing

*T*elemarketing gives small business owners a quick and cost-effective method of identifying and contacting, via phone, a specific large market of consumers for the purpose of selling a product or service. With an effective script and enthusiastic telemarketers, small business owners can generate sales without having to spend large amounts of money on traditional marketing vehicles.

Inbound vs. outbound

There are two types of telemarketing.

Inbound telemarketing involves sending out a flyer or a reply card to a target list of consumers inviting the consumer to call your company to purchase a product or service. When the consumer calls, your telemarketers will provide information on the product or service, but their primary function is to take orders rather than proactively sell the product or service to the consumer.

Outbound telemarketing, on the other hand, involves a proactive sales approach wherein your telemarketers make calls from your company to a target group of consumers to sell them your product or service.

Costs

The cost of a telemarketing program depends upon a variety of factors. These include how many phone lines you decide to install, the number of telemarketers you employ, the number of hours they spend calling prospective customers, the number of calls they make per hour, and the number of leads generated per telemarketer.

Making the call

When you are making outbound calls, you must attract the customer's interest in the first ten to fifteen seconds of the phone call. Engage the customer in a friendly conversation so that you can build trust and establish polite inquiry as to the person's state of mind. Open with something casual like "How are you today?" Do not attempt to launch into the sales pitch until you get the customer talking and feeling positive about your intentions.

When the customer first picks up the phone, speak slowly and clearly. Sound upbeat without losing your focus. Remember, too, that the customer's natural tendency, right off the bat, will be to say "no, thanks." You need to get past this response quickly and pique the customer's interest before he or she hangs up. Once you have the attention of a target customer, you can follow the telemarketing script for the product or service you are selling.

The Telemarketing Call

Opening

1 Confirm that you are speaking to the target customer. If the response is "no," ask if the individual is at home. If the individual is not at home, ask for an appropriate time to call back when he or she will be available to speak. If you are speaking to your target customer, begin "reading" your script, which should begin to introduce the product or service you are selling

Positive response

2 If, during your opening, the prospect indicates that he or she cannot or will not use your product or service, the conversation has ended and you should simply thank the person for their time. If the prospect seems receptive, continue with the script, which should contain questions that will help you determine whether or not this is a candidate for your product or service. Remember that at any juncture during the conversation he or she may object or ask questions such as "Are you trying to sell me something?" or "I'm sorry, we are right in the middle of dinner." You need to be prepared to handle these objections.

Qualifying and getting information

3 Before you can fully make your pitch, you need to find out more about the prospect's needs and if he or she is someone who would be a prime candidate for your product or service. As early as possible, you want to smoothly qualify this individual as a prospect without causing him or her to hang up. You must remember that the prospect is thinking "I don't want this" and your job is to reverse this thinking.

Presentation

4 By the time you are ready to make your presentation, you should have developed a good rapport with the prospect, gained his or her trust and confidence, and fully qualified the person as a potential candidate for your service or product. You are then ready to really begin the sales pitch.

Clearly articulate the strong points of your service. Find out how your product or service would complement your prospective customer's needs and lifestyle. Work toward making him or her feel totally at home with your product or service.

Give the consumer a strong and compelling reason to buy the product or service from you as opposed to someone else.

Trial close

5 Once you have fulfilled the above presale steps, you are now in a position to start to close in on the sale. During this third phase of the telemarketing call, you will make the buying decision easy for the consumer. He or she should be able to buy the product or service from you, right now, over the phone—not after he or she has thought about it for a few days. If the prospect asks you for time to consider your proposal, you have not given him or her enough information.

You have emphasized why the service has strong benefits for the prospect. You must now convince the prospect that it is easy to sign up for your service or purchase your product. Give a reason why it is important to sign up immediately. The prospect should be the last one to speak at this juncture. Prospects may have questions at this point and it is important that you answer each one and listen carefully to their answers.

Overcoming objections

6 During the course of any telemarketing call, expect that the prospect will have at least one or two objections and, in all likelihood, a list of reasons why not to buy your product or service. This should not discourage you as this is his or her way of asking for more information. How you handle these objections will go a long way toward determining whether or not you make the sale. Remember, the prospect's natural reaction is to say "no, thanks." Have convincing responses ready to counter the most common objections you can expect to encounter.

Final close

7 You now want to give a short summary of why the product or service you are offering is very attractive. Emphasize those points you feel struck a positive chord with the prospect. Finalize the sale and confirm this in language that the prospect understands. Confirm any information that is needed in order to close the sale. The prospect should completely realize at this time that he or she is now purchasing a product or a service. Avoid phrases such as "So do we have an agreement then?" or "Does this sound right to you?"

A Telemarketing Dialogue

Walker Oil Company offers maintenance service for oil heating units and home or business delivery of oil. They have chosen to broaden their customer base by implementing a telemarketing program. The following is an interaction between a Walker Oil Company telemarketer, Jenny, who is using a script, and a prospective customer, Mr. Adams, whom she has contacted. The phone rings...

Jenny   Hello, may I speak to Mr. Adams?

Mr. Adams   This is Mr. Adams.

Jenny   Hi, Mr. Adams. My name is Jenny Shields and I am calling from Walker's Oil Service. How are you today?

Mr. Adams   I'm fine, thanks.

Jenny   As you may or may not know, Walker Oil is one of the oldest and best-known oil companies in Massachusetts, with a reputation for high-quality oil, excellent maintenance service, and timely delivery. Mr. Adams, could you tell me if you use oil, gas, or electric heat?

Mr. Adams   We use oil heat.

Jenny   That's great! While oil burners are fuel-efficient and are workhorses, they do need regular maintenance to prevent costly fuel bills. Could you please tell me if you have had your burner inspected or cleaned in the last six months?

Mr. Adams   I don't really recall the last time we had the burner checked. Maybe last year.

A Telemarketing Dialogue

 Jenny I would like one of our service people to stop by so that you can take advantage of our free inspection and cleaning. Is Wednesday afternoon at 2:00 p.m. a convenient time for you?

 Mr. Adams You know, my wife and I are on a fixed income and we really can't afford to explore trial offers at this time.

 Jenny I completely understand, Mr. Adams. Walker Oil is known for delivering efficient and affordable solutions for home heating. In addition, you will also save a lot of money each year on your fuel bills with our free annual cleaning and inspection service.

 Mr. Adams My burner seems to be working just fine.

 Jenny Mr. Adams, do you remember how cold it was last winter? Fuel prices skyrocketed and many people had burners that broke down during the coldest weeks of the year. With our free annual inspections, you never have to worry about breakdowns during those fierce cold spells.

 Mr. Adams Okay, well, I suppose I could see you Wednesday.

 Jenny Mr. Adams, this offer will allow you to have peace of mind this winter knowing that you took the time to have your burner inspected and cleaned, thus reducing your overall fuel costs. Plus you get a free oil fill-up when you sign up for our regular oil delivery service. Mr. Adams, I have you down for Wednesday afternoon at 2:00 p.m. We look forward to seeing you on Wednesday. Have a pleasant evening.

Streetwise Advice on Telemarketing

☞ **Have a script**

Because prospects have much less patience over the phone than in person, you need to have a script for telemarketing. Every telemarketer needs specific instructions on how to begin, conduct, and end each call. Try different scripts. Measure which script works best, then make sure that the telemarketers stick to it.

☞ **Get to the point**

The most important part of the call is the beginning. You need to create some interest in the prospect's mind and assure him or her that you are not going to take up a lot of time. You also need to qualify your prospect and determine whether or not he or she is someone you should spend time with. This is why it is so important to have a script and to carefully evaluate its effectiveness.

☞ **Keep it sounding natural**

Ironically, while it is important to have a script, it is just as important for callers to sound like they aren't reading from one. Prospects are less likely to have patience or engage in conversations with callers that sound as though they are delivering "canned" presentations.

Keys to making a script sound natural are

- Don't read too fast
- Use natural and appropriate emphasis on key words
- Avoid speaking in a monotone
- Pause slightly at the end of each sentence
- Sound genuinely interested in the prospect's questions, concerns, or objections

☞ **Make lots of calls**

Even more so than in-person selling, telemarketing is a numbers game. No matter how good you are on each call, you're not going to sell to everyone. How many calls you make will make a big difference in your success. A super-aggressive telemarketer may reach as many as 150 decision makers in a single day. A less aggressive telemarketer may only reach 20. Which one do you think will make more sales?

☞ **Keep it short**

While you should encourage your telemarketers to build a rapport with their targets, this shouldn't take all day. Track the phone calls your telemarketers make to determine what length of time per phone call, on average, is ideal for qualifying, presenting, and closing a sale with a customer. Have your telemarketers try to stick to this "ideal" time frame.

"The most important part of the call is the beginning. You need to create some interest in the prospect's mind and assure him or her that you are not going to take up a lot of time."

Should I send a letter before calling prospects?

It depends upon the product or service you are selling, its price range, and the type of customer you are calling.

Generally, for business-to-business telemarketing, it is recommended that you send a simple letter, a flyer, and perhaps even a product sample before you place a sales call.

If you are selling a relatively expensive product or service to consumers you should also send a letter or flyer before calling. If you are selling a less expensive product or service to consumers you may want to experiment. Test your sales results with a pretelemarketing direct mail letter versus cold calling.

Sending announcements prior to phoning is least important when you are selling a brand-name product or a product or service that is easily described over the phone. It is also less important if the product or service that you are selling is relatively inexpensive.

Where can I get lists of good prospects?

For local businesses, an obvious place to start is with the phone book. You might also consider approaching local trade or special-interest groups to see if they make their lists available for sales use. They may require that you offer their members a special discount.

Other sources are the mailing lists of magazine subscribers or business lists compiled by mailing-list brokers. Most mailing lists are available in very small quantities and may be ordered with special selections—by state, zip code, or business size, for instance. There are also all types of business and manufacturing directories available through your local library that would enable you to compile your own appropriate list of contacts.

If I'm making my own calls, how can I motivate myself to place the calls?

Everyone has some degree of difficulty staying motivated to make many calls. Consider trying to call a certain number of prospects first thing each day. Or you might set aside an hour or two to make as many calls as you can.

More so than face-to-face selling, telemarketing can quickly get repetitive and boring. Try to call for shorter periods of time over a number of days.

How can I prevent my neck from hurting?

After even a couple of hours on the phone, you can develop a sore neck if you tend to cradle the phone between your shoulder and your head. The best solution is to get a headphone from your local electronics store. There are also pads that attach to the phone and decrease the angle you maintain between your head and shoulder to prevent the phone from dropping. This is a cheap solution, but also less effective.

Questions & Answers about Telemarketing

When is the best time to call people?

Try calling at different times of the day to determine what works best for you and your product.

With the increase in two-income families and individuals working more than one job, it can be difficult to find prospects at home. If you reach your prospects just after they have come home, they are less inclined to want to bother with a sales call. If you call late, they may feel you are intruding on their privacy. It's tough. Keep trying for the right balance.

When calling business-to-business, calling during business hours obviously makes sense. But try to avoid Mondays. Monday is usually a very busy day. The best day to call seems to be Friday. People tend to be in better moods as they look forward to their weekends.

Should I wait for prospects to call me back?

Prospects who offer to call you back if they are interested in your product are telling you one of two things. They might be politely informing you that they have absolutely no interest in your product. Or they might want to consider the product without any pressure. Unfortunately, it is often difficult for a telemarketer to determine which tack the prospect is taking and whether or not there is any potential for a future sale.

If you believe the prospect is showing some interest in your product, but you are certain that you can't close the sale during this particular call, offer to make a follow-up call yourself. End the conversation with "Tell you what—I'll call you back in a week. That will give you some time to think about it." Otherwise, even if the prospect really does have some interest in your product, chances are that he or she won't call back.

When should I make a follow-up call?

If the prospect is interested, but you can't close the sale on the first call, the timing of the second call can be crucial to completing a sale. Generally, call back four to seven days later unless the prospect has specifically asked that you call at a particular time.

Independent Sales Representatives

Most commonly, an independent sales representative or manufacturer's representative sells the products of several different companies on a business-to-business basis. They may represent and sell to retailers, wholesalers, or other types of businesses. Some representatives, however, represent only one firm and sell only a few products or services.

There are independent representatives who sell products to consumers, such as cosmetics, but the nature of consumer selling through independent representatives is quite different than that of business-to-business selling.

The good news about independent representatives, for small businesses, is that they require no money and little effort up front. They are generally paid on a commission basis, typically 5 percent to 15 percent of net sales. However, in some businesses independent representatives are paid on a "ledger" basis, which means that they can earn a commission on every sale made in their territory, even if a customer contacts the manufacturer directly.

In some fields independent representative firms are common. A representative firm acts like an independent representative in that you only pay commissions, but you pay the commissions to the group. These firms are often owned by an extremely seasoned and successful salesperson. The owner or partners in such a firm may pay their sales employees by salary, commission, or some combination of the two, such as a small base salary plus a bonus.

Finding representatives

Representative groups often comb trade shows looking for new lines to carry. But you might do better by finding out who other manufacturers use. Try to determine which representatives are looking for new product lines—like yours.

Independent Sales Representatives

Advantages

No sales force maintenance expenses

The travel expenses of a salesperson can be as high as his or her salary. Even phone expenses can be staggering. Therefore, the most obvious advantage to employing independent sales representatives to sell your products or services is that you won't be incurring the expense of maintaining a sales force. There are, however, other advantages that are just as compelling.

Longevity

A well-established representative will be around forever. They aren't likely to disappear after a few hard months on the road, like so many entry-level salespeople do.

Experience

Independent sales representatives tend to be experienced and successful. They also tend to net better sales results than a in-house sales force might. Why? Because they usually have long and successful career backgrounds that include sales experience with large, national firms.

Less management time

Independent sales representatives are usually more experienced than in-house representatives and need less management and direction. If you hire them, you will be less likely to need to hire a sales manager, and they will probably take much less of your time than in-house representatives.

Sales expenses rise and fall with your sales

This is a big plus for a growing business that doesn't have lots of cash in its early days, and also helps during downturns.

Disadvantages

No control

You can't control an independent representative. They will only push those products they feel have the best chance of selling and making them money. They will tend to put their best effort into selling the best products from their most established lines.

No commitment

As a new manufacturer you are an easy target for the "first time out of the bag syndrome." The representative will be looking to place orders for your product very quickly after he or she first introduces it. If that doesn't happen, your product might well not be presented again. Of course, unless you have an agreement to the contrary, which would be unusual in this business, the independent representative you are using may very well be selling your competitor's products, too!

You should keep in mind that even if you have an established, long-term relationship with a representative, you must constantly "sell" them on the potential of both your existing and new products or services.

Competing products

Unless you have an agreement to the contrary, an independent sales representative may take on a competing line or a line that competes with your products.

Representatives are focused on sales, not service

Commission representatives usually are very narrowly focused on making the sale and directly generating commissions. They will not usually provide the service and support that in-house representatives provide.

Sales Success Story

Jim Beardsley is an independent sales rep in the book publishing industry. Here, he discusses what characteristics to look for in a sales rep for your company.

Follow Through

" You've got to have somebody who is conscientious, somebody who is thorough, who will do a complete job. Here is another phrase that comes to mind: follow through. You, the sales rep, sell somebody a book or books. There's a problem in shipping. The bookstore owner only knows you. She doesn't know anybody in the accounting department or in customer service, or she doesn't feel comfortable calling somebody she doesn't know, but she knows you, so you're going to get the call. You may get it at ten o'clock at night; you may get home at the end of the week to discover you have twenty-nine messages on your answering machine. That does indeed happen in my case. It is up to you to solve problems. "

Praise Your Reps

" If you've got a good sales rep and you like that person, then for heaven sakes praise him. Tell him he's good, pat him on the back and don't ever stop doing it. "

A super solution

While there are certainly some disadvantages to working with independent representatives, overall, independent representatives are a great panacea for small or even medium-sized businesses. Even if you can afford to hire a sales force, you may be better off selling through independent representatives. They will have established contacts that you may not have, which can work to your advantage. They don't require the direction of a sales manager, nor will they eat up as much of your time as a sales force would. They are typically more stable. If your product sells, you can count on their services over a long period of time. And they are generally extremely talented salespeople.

Sell them

You must be sure that your independent representatives are convinced that your product or service is super. Let them know that your product is a winner and that it sells. Tell them successful sales stories. They will be much more impressed by sales results than they will be by any press coverage or awards that your products or services have garnered. Tell them how your other representatives are doing saleswise. Keep them updated on any important sales statistics via fax, phone, or letter when appropriate. But don't harass them. Don't imply that they might not be pushing your product hard enough. Be encouraging. Provide positive feedback whenever you can.

The best time to introduce an independent representative to your product or service is at a sales conference.

Political campaigns

Motivating sales representatives is like motivating people during political campaigns. Having a strong candidate is just the beginning of waging a successful sales effort. You need to constantly build momentum. Representatives always talk to one another even if their territories are geographically distant. If one representative likes your product and your company, his or her good word will encourage representatives in other regions to "push" it to their clientele.

Sales materials

Great products and great representatives still need great sales materials. Provide your reps with polished samples, literature, catalogs, and/or specification sheets—whatever seems most acceptable for your industry.

Avoid the biggest

In every territory and in every industry there are one or more independent representatives or representative groups who have been around forever. They "rep" the best and strongest lines, have the highest visibility, and, in the case of representative groups, have a large base of sales personnel. Sounds great—but avoid the best like the plague!

Unless your product line is one of the top lines in its field, it will probably just become lost in the array of "terrific" products already represented by a top representative. There won't be any incentive to push your product. And, more importantly, customers won't have the time, interest, or energy to hear about your product during the same sales presentation when they are already hearing about lots of other, stronger products.

Streetwise Advice about Independent Representatives

Instead, choose a representative who carries one or two lines that are strong enough to ensure being seen by most prospective customers but not so many lines that your product is unlikely to make it out of the bag. All too often, the customer will have had enough and say "Okay, that's enough for today. Leave me the literature on your smaller lines." This is the kiss of death. No presentation means no sale.

Be sure the independent representative or representative firm you choose is aggressive and hungry. Make sure the representative really wants to sell your line and sell it hard.

☞ Pay them first

Independent sales representatives are very sensitive to the timing of their paychecks. They may not call you and complain if your checks are irregular or late, but they just aren't going to sell your products as hard if you don't pay them promptly. Stretch payments to your suppliers, not to your representatives.

☞ Changes

It is especially important to monitor the sales efforts of your independent representative right from the start. If he or she doesn't measure up to your expectations quickly, it is better to "change horses" immediately. Once an independent representative or representative group views your entire line as nearly impossible to sell, it is easier to switch representatives than to adjust the negative attitude of your current representative toward your product or service line.

In evaluating a representative's ability to sell your product or service, look at both the number of orders the independent representative is writing for you and the volume of sales. The number of orders is generally the best indicator of the representative's interest in selling the line, while the volume of each order is more indicative of the customer's overall interest in your individual products or services.

If you are more established within your industry, you need to be careful about changing your independent representation. Competing representatives talk to one another and if you drop a representative who was bringing in relatively good sales, other representatives may feel the risk isn't worth the energy they will need to expend in order to represent you.

More importantly, many customers develop strong relationships with their independent representatives over the years. In the customers' minds, the independent representative is an integral part of the product line they are purchasing. To change your representation may provoke a loss of goodwill among your client base.

"It is especially important to monitor the sales efforts of your independent representative right from the start. If he or she doesn't measure up to your expectations quickly, it is better to 'change horses' immediately."

Questions & Answers on Independent Representatives

Do I have to pay independent representatives commissions on sales to wholesalers?

Independent representatives are traditionally paid a commission on every sale in their territory. In some industries, commissions on wholesale accounts may be less than those on retail accounts. They can be as much as half the retail rate.

Can I keep the established accounts for myself?

No! Especially with a relatively new or small firm, an independent representative will almost always insist on having the opportunity to make commissions on and making the presentations to all of the accounts in his or her territory.

How can I best use a limited budget to support my representatives?

The first thing you should spend money on is product samples, a very simple flyer, and an order form. Then fly standby, hitchhike, walk, or crawl to one sales meeting each year in order to make a personal presentation. If the independent representatives in your industry each have sales meetings in different cities at different times of the year, then try to gather them all together during a national convention or trade show for a presentation.

What should I say at the sales meeting?

Tell your reps how much you like them and briefly recap recent sales success stories. Make a presentation of the strongest new and current products or services you are offering.

Most importantly, develop for and give your independent representatives a one-sentence sell line, a "sales handle," that will help them interest clients in your product. It should be something simple that features the benefits of your product or service— "the lightest and most portable . . ." or "warrantied to be trouble-free . . ." Remember, the representatives only have a few minutes to present your line to their customers. Give them a sales pitch they can really use . . . not a long-winded product history!

When should I switch to salaried representatives?

I'd be very hesitant about switching to salaried representatives. Don't just switch because your sales have grown to the point where commissions equal what you would pay in salaries to salaried representatives. There are big hidden costs, such as your time, or the salary of a sales manager to manage an in-house sales force, as well as travel expenses, turnover, and the cost of potentially lost sales when one or more territories are left unstaffed, as often happens with newly established sales forces.

Internet Marketing

The Internet, commonly referred to as the Information Superhighway, is an interconnected group of computers linking businesses, government, and academia. Although a precise count of subscribers to the Internet is impossible to calculate, a good guess would place the number at approximately 30 million, and growing daily.

Marketing your product on the "Net" is relatively easy and inexpensive. A graphical user interface, such as Mosaic, allows potential customers to access the World Wide Web. The "Web" is a part of the Internet. One click can take a potential customer to a screen that has been created by your business. This type of screen is called a Home Page.

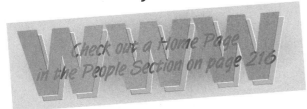

Check out a Home Page in the People Section on page 216

Marketing through a Home Page

A Home Page resides at a particular place on the Internet that has a specific address. You can use a Home Page to promote your business with text, graphics, sound, and video. You can provide pointers as well.

Pointers highlight text and act as navigational tools. Clicking on a pointer will take your potential client to additional information within your Web site that might provide important product and ordering details, for instance.

To set up a Home Page for your business, you can hire an outside consultant who specializes in assisting small businesses in creating Home Pages for the World Wide Web. Contact your local computer user group or local Internet service provider for the names and numbers of qualified consultants.

Designing your Home Page

Your Home Page should provide specific information about your product or service. It should be fun for your potential clients to view and use. Include interesting photos and/or entertaining videos that will gain and hold a potential customers attention. Try to create a Home Page that allows the consumer to make a purchasing decision while they are on the Internet.

If you anticipate that the typical consumer will have questions or would like to receive information about your company and its products or services through the mail, you can supply a pointer that takes him or her to your electronic mailbox. Through the mailbox consumers can leave a message for your response. Your consumers should also be able to order your products or services while on the Internet. You should provide ordering information including instructions for credit card use.

Walk before you run

A lot of companies have invested huge amounts of money into building elaborate Web sites and have been nevertheless disappointed with the resulting sales. Other firms have spent little money, built simple sites, and generated strong sales. So be sure to test a simple Web site before you "bet your business" on this tricky area.

Streetwise Advice on Internet Marketing

☞ **Don't expect to make money**

There are a lot of people making lots of money from marketing on the World Wide Web. But very, very few of these people are making money from their Web sites. So far, the big money is being made by the quick-buck artists and even some sizable corporations who are touting seminars, newsletters, and magazines on how you can get rich quick from a World Wide Web site! The second largest amount of money is being made by technical consultants who are contracted to design and build World Wide Web sites.

As a group, the companies and individuals who have footed the bill for building Web sites have spent huge amounts of money with very little sales to show for it, let alone any profits.

There are a few exceptions. For example, I know a person who sells his consulting services exclusively on the World Wide Web part-time while also holding a full-time job. He's not getting rich, but he's making a little money—not losing it on his Web site. So maybe you too can make a little money on your Web site—if you keep your costs down—but don't count on it. Do not count on any revenue from your Web site until you see it flowing in.

☞ **A lot of traffic doesn't usually translate into sales**

Even Web sites that have thousands of visitors each day have trouble generating any sales revenue at this time. For example, our employment Web site listing thousands of job listings (which we currently allow companies to run for no charge) and lots of career information is much busier than the typical site run by a small business, with over 20,000 "hits" per day. But even on a "good" day we may only sell one $15 book or one $40 software package. At the same time, we are spending between $200,000 to $300,000 per year on this site. Our experience is not atypical; there are plenty of other corporations spending even more money and generating even less revenue.

☞ **It doesn't have to be expensive**

You can create your own home page on the World Wide Web very inexpensively. With some of the off-the-shelf software options available today, you could build your own site without learning how to program. Even if you want to hire a consultant to do all the work and make the decisions, you can keep your costs down if you create a very simple Web site. The hundreds of thousands of dollars spent on a Web site like mine include the cost of developing and continually changing thousands of pages of material; maintaining a full-time

staff; and having dedicated high-speed phone lines, full-time customer support, sophisticated databases, a lot of marketing effort, and many other expenses you may be able to avoid.

☞ **Set a realistic objective for your Web site**

To date, the biggest success for Web sites has been in nonsales activities, such as providing service support for current customers and information for new customers. There are many other ways in which Web sites can and have been successful, including providing a communication link between employees and business associates who are located or traveling across the globe. Decide in advance what the goal of your Web site is going to be.

☞ **Set a budget and stay with it**

It's really easy to find excuses to break your budget on your Web site. Sites can be fun and colorful and a great thing to boast about with work and professional associates. But don't drain money out of potentially more lucrative parts of your business to fund a Web site that is not showing a quick payback. A small business needs to focus a lot more on short-term results than a larger corporation that has access to a lot more capital.

Wholesalers, Distributors, and Importers

There is a lot of confusion about the distinction between jobbers, wholesalers, distributors, and importers, and their role in the marketplace. Part of this confusion is even caused by experienced business people who use these terms incorrectly. And part of the confusion is caused by the unrealistic expectations of inexperienced newcomers.

To add to the confusion, many larger wholesalers are beginning to offer more selling services than is traditional within their sphere. And some are even creating separate distribution subsidiaries.

Don't let the terminology bother you. And don't assume that anyone else is using terms properly. When dealing with a firm, clarify its role. Be particularly clear about the selling services that will be provided.

Wholesalers and Jobbers

A wholesaler, or jobber, is a firm that typically buys goods from manufacturers and resells them to retailers. A wholesaler stocks goods from many different manufacturers in one or more warehouses and ships those goods as one combined order under one invoice.

Because wholesalers stock items from many different manufacturers, they have no particular incentive to push your product to their accounts, versus your competitor's products.

In highly competitive industries, such as those selling consumer products through retailers, several wholesalers might stock identical merchandise, putting a lot of pressure on profit margins. As a result, wholesalers are unlikely to offer ancillary services to you, such as advertising or sales solicitation and service unless someone, typically you, pay for these services in addition to the basic wholesaling charges.

So, selling your product to a wholesaler doesn't necessarily mean your merchandise will automatically end up on a store shelf. You and your sales force and/or independent representatives will have to take on the responsibility of creating order demand.

So, why wholesale? Retailers hesitate to buy direct from new, small vendors and just feel safer purchasing from established wholesalers. Even if you offer a very deep discount, retailers won't be anxious to buy from you direct. They won't see any value in processing the paperwork associated with establishing and doing business with a small account.

It may be essential for you to have your goods stocked at a wholesaler in order to conduct business with retailers. And you may still have to solicit the orders yourself.

With the worldwide trend in retail merchandise management moving towards Electronic Data Interchange (EDI) and just-in-time inventory practices, retailers are, more and more, relying heavily on wholesalers.

Distributors

Distributors typically serve a multipurpose role. They will perform in a manner similar to that of an independent representative in that they will solicit orders from the retailer for your products. They also act as wholesalers in that they stock your merchandise, too. Distributors may provide other services as well, such as catalog creation, trade advertising, and trade-show representation. Usually distributors represent manufacturers on an exclusive basis only within their territory.

In many industries a distributor will also sell to wholesalers in addition to retailers. In this case, the distributor is called a master distributor.

Because a distributor acts as your "salesperson" and often sells to both wholesalers and retailers, it will require a deeper discount rate when purchasing your merchandise than would be the rule with a wholesaler.

Most manufacturers don't use distributors. They prefer to sell direct to wholesalers, retailers, consumers, or some combination of all three themselves. However, a good distributor can be an excellent way for a small firm to instantly establish credibility and a presence within either their industry's domestic or foreign marketplaces.

Importers

The term importer means different things to different people. Often it is used to describe a firm that serves as an exclusive distributor to an overseas territory and provides sales solicitation, warehousing, and invoicing services.

Sometimes it refers to a firm that arranges to buy merchandise from a foreign manufacturer and resells the merchandise to one or more distributors who then handle the actual domestic sales functions. Typically, the importer will arrange to have the merchandise cleared through customs, and may also arrange for shipment from the country of origin.

☞ A great solution

When a very small firm or a larger firm is branching out into ancillary markets, such as a secondary domestic market or a foreign market, distributors can provide a great way to successfully traffic merchandise. For example, a publisher of golf books may do better to sell the books to book wholesalers and retailers through its own sales representatives, but find a distributor to sell the books to sports stores. The high discount required by the sports store distributor may seem prohibitive at first glance, but when the costs of funding a new in-house distribution effort are totaled, the distributor will probably prove to be quite a bargain!

☞ Clarify roles

Be sure that all parties understand who is responsible for what territory—in both geographic and market terms. Get it in writing! And be sure that you won't need to give much notice if you decide to cancel an exclusive agreement, in the event that sales are disappointing.

☞ Wholesaler promotions

Most wholesalers work on extremely tight margins and are constantly under price pressure. The are not only being challenged by their competitors, but their own clients often threaten to buy direct from the manufacturer if certain prices can't be met! As a result, many astute wholesalers have turned their ancillary services into important profit centers.

Many wholesalers will require that you spend a certain level of advertising money, generally expressed as a percentage of net purchases, on their promotional programs. If you don't comply, they won't stock your product. And, unfortunately, these advertising programs aren't always worth the money they cost.

Small firms, particularly, are reluctant to participate in these advertising programs. However, if you feel this way and make a fuss, you are being short-sighted. The ill will generated could very well result in the wholesaler refusing to stock your merchandise. While the advertising program may seem to be a scam, the wholesaler is, after all, selling your product at very, very thin profit margins and deserves to make some money. So, just participate with a smile. Ultimately, it's worth it!

If you carefully choose which advertising program you want to participate in and write your own copy, you might find that the promotion actually does you some good. Despite popular wisdom to the contrary, I have found that wholesalers' co-op programs can pull in a lot of sales.

☞ Sales reps

Even if you have your products stocked at every wholesaler in the country and are utilizing all of the advertising programs these wholesalers offer, you will still need the services of a sales representative to call on your accounts.

If your line is very simple, consisting of only one or two products, you may get away with telemarketing. But if your line comprises half a dozen products, you need an in-person sales representative to get initial orders, at the very least, into the wholesaler's hands.

> "Be sure that all parties understand who is responsible for what territory— in both geographic and marketing terms."

Why should I give a distributor an exclusive?

First of all, it probably won't take you on if you won't. Why should it have its sales representatives go around to wholesalers and retailers promoting your product if it is constantly risking orders for your products going to another source?

Do I need more than one wholesaler?

Many industries have one or more wholesalers who tend to dominate their industry, each selling to almost all retailers; as well as second- and third-tier wholesalers who may only sell to a portion of the retailers.

There are several advantages to having your product at more than one wholesaler. A few retailers may buy little product from some wholesalers or may even have an exclusive buying arrangement with only one wholesaler. Also, if one wholesaler is suddenly out of stock on one of your products for any reason, then there is the possibility that another wholesaler may still be in stock.

There are disadvantages to working with more than one wholesaler, particularly for very small firms. For example, you may not be able to sustain the minimum volume required by more than one wholesaler. Also, you may be required to carry more inventory to stock two wholesalers, especially if each has multiple warehouses. And you will probably have to partake of some of each wholesalers' promotional programs and make sales calls to each account. Also, some wholesalers may push your product more aggressively (acting to some degree like a distributor) if they know they are the only wholesaler selling your product.

One wholesaler I approached insisted on a deeper discount. What should I do?

It is bad business practice, and at least in the United States violates fair trade laws, to give one wholesaler better terms than another unless there is a solid economic reason for doing so. And, as well, many wholesalers insist that you sign a contract stating that you are offering them your best terms. Bottom line—in general, you are best off treating all wholesalers (and retailers) equally.

Should I sell on consignment?

Consignment basically means that you have not sold the goods until your wholesaler or distributor has sold the goods. On a practical level this means that you won't get paid until after the ultimate consumer has the goods—if then. I would, in general, avoid selling on consignment, especially to wholesalers, and certainly to retailers.

However, if you have an exclusive distributor arrangment, where the distributor really goes out and solicits orders for your product, consignment selling might make sense. This would be particularly true if the distributor acts as your personal sales force, warehouse, and credit and collections department.

Fax Marketing

A fax machine offers you a fast and inexpensive way to alert potential customers to new or service product offerings or special promotions. And, it provides an easy way for customers to send you orders. For an option to purchasing or leasing traditional fax machines, many personal computers being sold today include a fax/modem, which enable customers to send and receive faxes from the desktop as well.

Legal ramifications

You can send faxes to existing customers announcing a special offer on a new product. As of December 1992, however, the Telephone Consumer Protection Act has made it illegal to send unsolicited, commercial faxes.

Fax-back service

You can offer your customers fax-back service. A fax-back service allows a customer to call a business, listen to a prerecorded menu of options, select an option, and then request that the appropriate information be sent to a fax number. An automated fax-back system can print out a listing of how many customers called and where the information was sent.

Broadcast faxing

Broadcast faxing is a great way to reach a large target audience. If you have a generic fax to send to many locations at a specific time, you can set many fax machines and most computer fax programs to dial multiple numbers. If your customers rely on you for updates and product changes, then broadcast faxing is a terrific way to communicate that information.

Exporting

*D*oing business overseas may be a lot easier than you think! The key is lining up a good local distributor.

Initially, employ the services of an exclusive distributor for each country you plan to sell your product in. Sell your product to these distributors as cheaply as you can so that they can price it competitively and still make a good profit.

You will want your distributor to market your product as well. For some products, this will be as simple as having the distributor include your product in its catalog and present it at trade shows. For other products, it may involve the development of large advertising and promotional campaigns.

You will want a distributor who will clear your product through customs and stock it. And you will also want that distributor to buy product from you in bulk, on a nonreturnable basis, and resell it to their customers, thus assuming all of the credit risk.

Of course, you will need to carefully check out the credit references of any potential distributor.

Finding a distributor

The best way to find a distributor is to get a recommendation from another firm in your industry that is already successfully using that distributor. If you can't get this sort of information, or if no one else in your industry exports, you can seek foreign distributors at trade shows, through trade publications, and through international industry directories. In any event, be sure to get good references on both credit and sales before you ink a deal.

Exporting by Region

General

You need to decide which countries to focus your marketing efforts on and how much energy to expend. You also need to thoroughly examine the potential of each marketplace. The following examination of markets, organized by country, will offer you a broad overview. The actual market potential for you will may vary significantly depending upon the industry you are in and the types of products or services you will be offering.

United States

The United States is a primary market for any type of product manufacturer or service industry to consider. Because of the highly competitive nature of this rich market, however, products that launched easily and successfully elsewhere in the world may get off to a slow launch or may net less success in the United States.

Canada

All too often, Canada is thought of as merely an extension of the U.S. market. This isn't the case, and Canadians will resent any marketing approach used in their country that smacks of this attitude.

Canada is a relatively easy market for U.S. manufacturers to enter. Canadian consumers and businesses do, however, prefer to buy Canadian products and services if the choice is available. U.S. and other foreign manufacturers should line up a Canadian distributor for their products as opposed to handling the Canadian market from their home offices. Using a Canadian distributor will assist in making your products more acceptable in this independent-minded marketplace.

Western Europe

Western Europe is an extremely rich marketplace, with consumers and businesses quite open to making foreign product and service purchases. The only region that may be somewhat of an exception to this is France.

The biggest issue to consider here is the implementation of the European Common Market. As this organization becomes more and more of a marketing reality, distributors from one country may expect to have exclusive distribution rights for your product throughout all of Western Europe. Their coverage, however, may only have strength within their own national marketplace.

Eastern Europe

The spirit of capitalism is taking hold in Eastern Europe. You will find it very easy to line up distributors here who will be enthusiastic about representing your product.

Eastern European economies are still weak, though, and there is significant financial risk involved in participating in these markets. Get yourself well established in richer, more established marketplaces before tackling Eastern Europe.

When you are ready to enter this marketplace, you will find that many distributors are unseasoned. Extend credit slowly, and watch it rigorously.

The upside of all this is that eventually the Eastern European marketplace will stabilize and prosper. If you are already established in this marketplace, you will be in good position to reap the rewards.

Russia

The former Soviet Union occupies a large percentage of the globe, but it represents a very small piece of the world's economy. Occasionally, a foreign entrepreneurial venture takes hold here and makes bold newspaper headlines. But these companies are the exception to the rule. Don't even venture into this arena unless you are well established elsewhere in the world. Try Eastern Europe before you try your marketing hand in Russia.

Exporting by Region

Africa

This highly populated continent unfortunately, has little hard currency.

South Africa is the notable exception. This country does a tremendous amount of trading with Europe, has great wealth, and is a very developed marketplace. My company started doing business in South Africa before establishing ties in the United Kingdom, for instance.

Another African country to considering trading with is Nigeria. Nigeria is, however, a distant second choice. Hundreds, if not thousands, of small and not-so-small businesses around the world have been duped by offers from Nigerian "distributors" who simply disappeared with the merchandise and fees they collected. It also is an extremely dangerous country. Foreigner businesspeople are often victims of a wide range of serious crimes.

Japan

Japan is, by many standards, the most expensive country in the world. It also boasts the world's richest marketplace. But don't rush to trade here. Despite rhetoric to the contrary, the Japanese have done just about everything possible to make it difficult for foreigners to do business within its borders. The Japanese want to sell to the world, not buy from it!

Even if you cut through the bureaucratic red tape and manage to find distributors in Japan, the Japanese are very nationalistic and resist buying foreign products if there is a suitable local alternative. Only put your marketing energy into this marketplace once you are a well-established marketer everywhere else—from Singapore to Somalia.

Australia and New Zealand

The economies here aren't huge, but the markets are terrific. These two countries are used to importing and their customers don't possess that "not made here" syndrome.

Southeast Asia

Southeast Asia is a hotbed of activity for importers. Even in Vietnam, there is a surge in capitalism, and both foreigners and their products can expect a positive reception.

Some areas of the region are very sophisticated, such as Hong Kong, Singapore, and Malaysia. Other regions have incredibly low labor costs and very high work ethics. Combined with an excitement about capitalism, this marketplace is set to explode in growth.

Because there are so many small countries dotting this region, small businesses should consider using one distributor to cover the entire Pacific rim. Check Hong Kong, Singapore, or Kuala Lumpur, Malaysia for representation.

China

I know what you're thinking . . . if each of those Chinese people would buy just one of your products . . . Well, suddenly the Chinese market is starting to come alive and there is some hard currency there. A small business is probably best off getting into this marketplace through a distributor in Taiwan or Hong Kong.

India

Indians love foreign goods, but they can't pay a lot for them. This is, however, a fairly easy country to establish yourself in. Just do everything you can to minimize the cost of your goods.

Middle East

The Middle East is a highly diffuse marketplace. Businesses from most developed countries will find it easiest to establish a distributor for Israel. But the Israeli currency is weak and the market small.

For other parts of the Middle East, you should consider a single distributor. But don't make this region the first overseas initiative you take.

Mexico

At press time, the Mexican currency and economy was in terrible turmoil.

The size of the Mexican marketplace and its proximity to the United States does tend to make it more tempting to enter than it should be. It is, actually, a difficult marketplace for most products and is even in the best of times an unstable marketplace. It is large enough so that if you do a lot of exporting you certainly don't want to overlook Mexico, but don't make entering this market a high priority.

South America

While the issues vary from country to country, South American markets are generally rather difficult to penetrate. Red tape, moderate to weak currencies, and quickly fluctuating economies make it a risky venture. On the plus side, this continent has a long history of trading, especially with European countries.

Once you do decide to venture into this marketplace, try to find a distributor with experience throughout the region. If he or she has connections in Central America, Mexico, and the Caribbean, so much the better.

Ten common and costly sales mistakes of small business owners

1 Believing the myth that the world will beat down the door of whoever builds a better mousetrap

2 Believing the myth of the natural-born salesperson

3 Not trying to improve their own selling skills

4 Not viewing every customer inquiry as a sales prospect that should be carefully wooed and aggressively followed up on

5 Emphasizing their product features rather than their customers' needs

6 Not building a rapport with a customer before diving into their sales presentation

7 Not making lots and lots of cold calls to prospective customers

8 Not pressing the customer for more information after first hearing "I'm not interested"

9 Not aggressively following up on prospects who express some interest

10 Not setting up a highly lucrative bonus or commission structure for talented salespeople

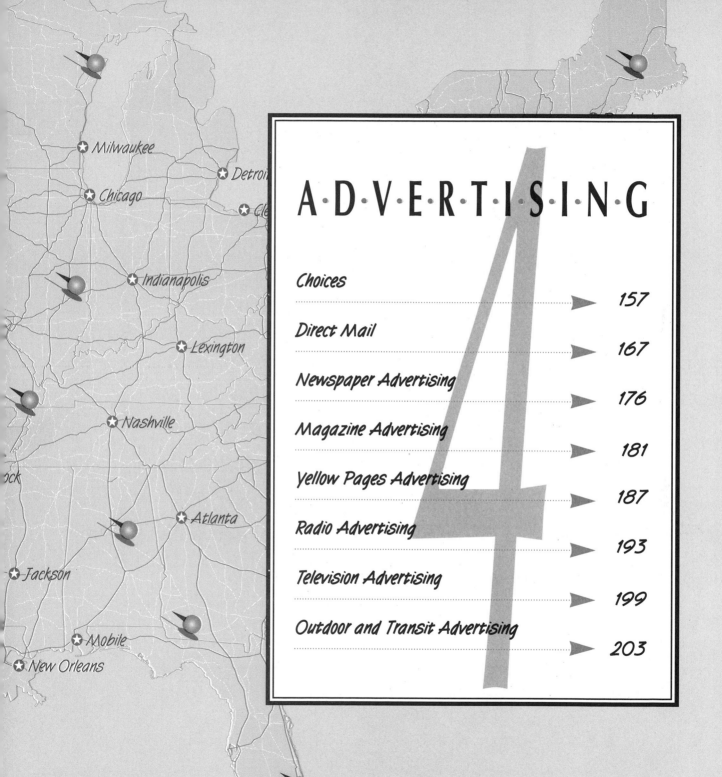

A·D·V·E·R·T·I·S·I·N·G

Choices .... ► *157*

Direct Mail .... ► *167*

Newspaper Advertising .... ► *176*

Magazine Advertising .... ► *181*

Yellow Pages Advertising .... ► *187*

Radio Advertising .... ► *193*

Television Advertising .... ► *199*

Outdoor and Transit Advertising .... ► *203*

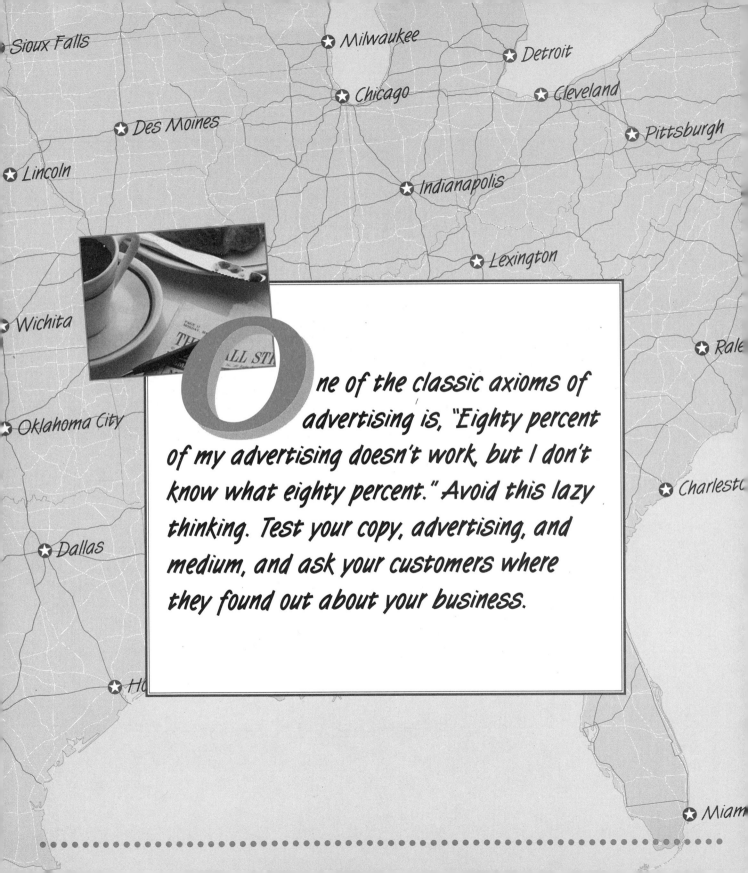

One of the classic axioms of advertising is, "Eighty percent of my advertising doesn't work, but I don't know what eighty percent." Avoid this lazy thinking. Test your copy, advertising, and medium, and ask your customers where they found out about your business.

Choices: Advertising Mediums

If money were no object, it would be easy to decide which advertising medium to go with. All of them! Unfortunately, the reality is that even with a hefty advertising budget, it is a challenge to create memorable advertising.

So unless you have truckloads of money to spend, you should try one medium at a time. What works for one product or service may not work for the next. There are so many different variables that can affect the results of an advertising campaign—from ad copy to the weather. You will simply have to test the effectiveness of your message in each medium to find the best vehicle for promoting your product. Advertising is an art, not a science!

Choices: Advertising Mediums

Relative impact of different advertising media

Relative Impact of Different Advertising Media	
Medium	Most (1) to least effective (6)
Direct Mail	1
Television	2
Radio	3
Outdoor and Transit	4
Magazines	5
Newspapers	6
Yellow Pages	—

- **Direct mail** has the highest impact of any medium. Your message reaches each recipient in a personalized way and at a moment they have chosen to consider your message. The cost of reaching an individual through direct mail can be even greater than television, making it the most expensive advertising medium per person reached.

- **Television** also offers the advertiser an opportunity to speak to a captive audience. In fact, television viewers are even more apt to fully "tune into" an advertisement. The cost, though, of purchasing a television spot is even greater than that of radio.

- **Radio** offers a dramatic improvement over "print" advertisements. The "listener" is captive to the message unless they switch stations or turn the radio off. The cost to reach the same amount of people that a print ad would reach, however, is significantly higher.

- **Outdoor and transit** advertisements are hard to avoid viewing. But, despite the high visibility factor, no one spends any great amount of time reading them. They are appropriate for very simple messages.

- **Magazines** offer a slightly better opportunity to catch the reader's attention. Readers tend to peruse magazines more carefully than they do newspapers, and because magazine ads are placed fewer per page, the competition for the reader's eye is reduced. But magazine ads cost more than newspaper ads.

- **Newspapers** are generally the cheapest way to reach a mass audience. However, newspapers carry many ads. It is easy for all but the largest display ads to get lost in the visual clutter. In any case, remember that newspapers are typically scanned by the reader. If an ad is seen at all, the headline will be glimpsed and the copy largely ignored.

> "Direct mail is the best bet, generally, for a small business that is trying to quickly boost sales today."

Choices: Advertising Mediums

Price advertising

Effectiveness of Price Advertising in Different Advertising Media

Medium	Most (1) to least effective (6)
Newspapers	1
Radio	2
Television	3
Direct Mail	4
Magazines	5
Outdoor and Transit	6
Yellow Pages	Not applicable

Price advertising is used when a benefit is being offered to potential customers that is based on price points such as special sales or everyday discount rates.

- *Newspapers* are the best bet if you are trying to inform a mass audience about a short-term sale or special price offer for a product or service. Newspaper readers are used to looking through the paper for specials. In some papers certain days are dedicated to certain categories. Wednesday is typically "food" day, for instance. Saturday is "automobile" day, and Sunday is "furniture" day. Advertising a category item on a category day will optimize the number of readers you reach even though your competition from other manufacturers or suppliers in your industry will be increased. Just make sure you have a great headline and a super-great special to offer.

- *Radio* is a reasonable second best bet for price advertising. The effectiveness will be increased if your product or service has consumer recognition in your market. Radio advertising costs more than newspaper advertising, however, and it is more difficult to convey price information in this format without overwhelming the listener.

- *Television* is too expensive for price advertising. Unless you are mixing a price advertising message with an image-building ad, don't consider this medium.

- *Direct mail* is a real wild card. In order to make this advertising medium cost effective for a "price" announcement, you will need to narrow your target audience. If you have access to a highly responsive small mailing list—of your own customers perhaps— this may be a very viable advertising option.

- *Magazines* don't offer immediate access to an audience. This may undermine the legitimacy of a special pricing offer, especially if the sale is for a very limited period of time. Consumers don't expect price advertising in magazines and are less likely to respond to such ads than if they saw them in a newspaper.

- *Outdoor and transit* displays aren't good for price advertising. Many of the objections that can be raised for using magazines as announcement vehicles for product or service sales can be applied here as well.

> "Newspapers should be your first choice if you are trying to spur people to action through a special price offer."

Choices: Advertising Mediums

Image advertising

Effectiveness of Image Advertising in Different Advertising Media	
Medium	Most (1) to least effective (6)
Television	1
Magazines	2
Outdoor and Transit	3
Radio	4
Newspapers	5
Direct Mail	6
Yellow Pages	Not applicable

Image advertising is used when the primary advertising goal is to create company, brand, or product awareness among a group of consumers so that they may be predisposed to making a purchase from you when they are in the market for the type of products or services you sell.

- **Television** is a terrific medium for image advertising. The visual action and audio allow viewers to feel involved with television. The per person cost to reach viewers through television, which is typically national in its reach, is very expensive. The emergence of local cable stations, however, is opening up this advertising avenue to many businesses who otherwise would not have been able to afford it. If you are targeting a small, local marketplace, check out the advertising programs offered by your local cable station.

- **Magazines** are not as effective as television as a medium through which to wage an image advertising campaign. They are a strong contender, though. The quality of magazine printing offers a nice venue for conveying exciting imagery. The use of color photography is especially effective in magazine print advertising.

- **Outdoor and transit** displays also rely on powerful photographs for message conveyance. They can be effective for simple image advertising messages, and especially to reinforce messages already being presented in other media.

- **Radio** is significantly less effective than magazines and television when used for image advertising. Radio can't effect the strong photographic impact of print advertising or the drama of television, and is, as such, a much more challenging medium through which to place a strong and lasting image in the listener's mind.

- **Newspapers** are not always an effective medium for carrying an effective image ad. The graphic reproduction is poor and the consumer has been conditioned to look at newspaper ads for price announcements, not image messages. If you do use newspapers as vehicles for running image advertising, make sure your ad space is large, perhaps as much as an entire page.

- **Direct mail** is a very tricky medium to use for image advertising. A "junk mail" label is the trap you risk here. But it can be effective. The most successful examples are the lavish four-color catalogs that many companies send out. If your budget is tight, be creative. For example, send an announcement piece that looks like an invitation to a society party.

" *Television is unmatched in its ability to build a company or product image.* "

Choices: Advertising Mediums

Local service advertising

Effectiveness of Local Service Advertising in Different Advertising Media

Medium	Most (1) to least effective (6)
✔ Yellow Pages	1
✔ Newspapers	2
✔ Direct Mail	3
✔ Television	4
✔ Radio	5
✔ Outdoor and Transit	6
✔ Magazines	Not applicable

Local service advertising is used when a service is being offered to consumers within a specific locale or small regional area.

- **Yellow Pages** or phone book advertising is the most cost-effective local service advertising medium for many area-specific service businesses. Advertising in the Yellow Pages requires a firm commitment for one year. If you are just starting out in business, don't go hog wild when you purchase ad space. Wait until you see what kind of results you net over the year. In this medium, your ad can be smaller than your competitors' because you are appealing to consumers who are already seeking your type of service.

- **Newspapers** can offer a highly effective format for advertising locally available services. Localized papers often run a directory of area tradespeople that readers automatically turn to in search of services. Metropolitan newspapers may group related services, such as educational or computer related services, together on an editorially related page on a specific day each week.

  Like Yellow Pages advertising, the fact that your ad will be placed alongside a competitor's isn't necessarily a negative. Also, the size of the ad can be relatively small and still have impact. Interested readers are already looking for you!

- **Direct mail** can be a highly effective medium for developing local service trade. The expense involved in implementing a direct mail campaign, however, may render this medium cost ineffective.

- **Television** certainly has impact, but this will be far outweighed by its expense. Unless your company has an image that must be communicated in order to attract clientele, such as a dating service might, this isn't a great option. However, local cable stations may be an avenue worth exploring if you are trying to zero in on a particular town where you expect response to your advertising will be high.

- **Radio** spots are a poor bet for local service business advertising. Use it as a last resort if other mediums haven't panned out for you. Try to find a station that covers the town or region you serve and is cost effective.

- **Outdoor and transit** ads are best left to image ads.

"Yellow page ads can work terrifically for local service advertising."

Business-to-business advertising

Effectiveness of Business-to-Business Advertising in Different Advertising Media	
Medium	Most (1) to least effective (7)
Direct Mail	1
Magazines	2
Radio	3
Yellow Pages	4
Newspapers	5
Television	6
Outdoor and Transit	7

While business-to-business marketing efforts should be centered on sales or telemarketing programs, advertising can play an important role in a successful sales effort. It can help you develop leads that you can follow up on with a phone call, and it can increase the chances that your salespeople will have their phone calls accepted or returned.

- *Direct mail* allows you to target an audience comprised of those businesses most likely to respond favorably to your products or services. Your product or service may have a practical application in many industries, but try to limit your mailings to those with the most probable buying potential. Consider placing geographical and industry size qualifications on your list, too.

  Always track your responses. Keep refining your lists as you gain more experience in direct mail results.

- *Magazine* advertising in trade-specific publications that cater to your industry can be effective. But don't rush out and buy full-page ad space in a general business national publication! There are hundreds of trade publications that will allow you to target your customer base more narrowly and at a much lower cost.

- *Radio* is a distant third choice for business-to-business advertising. It can be effective, however, if you find a business-only station or, as a second bet, a station, such as an all-news station, with a heavy concentration of listeners who are business people.

  This medium will work best if your product or service is unique but has an appeal to a broad business audience.

- *Yellow Pages* can be a wonderful venue, and even the best choice, for a few business-to-business companies in the service sector, but is totally inappropriate for most others especially product-based businesses.

- *Newspapers* aren't generally considered high-impact vehicles for business-to-business advertising. One obvious place to advertise in newspapers is in the business sections of both local and national general and business newspapers. However, most small business won't have much luck attracting responses through these fairly general mediums.

- *Television* may work fine for huge national business-to-business advertisers like airlines, but is unlikely to work for smaller businesses.

- *Outdoor and transit* displays have scant applicability in business-to-business advertising.

> " *Direct mail is the most effective advertising vehicle for selling to other businesses.* "

Choices: Advertising Mediums

Direct response advertising

Effectiveness of Direct Response Advertising in Different Advertising Media

Medium	Most (1) to least effective (5)
Direct Mail	1
Television	2
Magazines	3
Newspapers	4
Radio	5
Yellow Pages	Not applicable
Billboards	Not applicable

Direct response advertising is used when you want to prompt an immediate response from potential customers. In other words, you want them to make an on-the-spot decision to purchase your product or service directly from you and not through a retailer or dealer.

- *Direct mail* is a good first choice if you are trying to sell a product directly to consumers that is not available through retail outlets. It is expensive, but by limiting your target audience to those most likely to place an order, it can be much more effective than using another medium that may create interest but not an overwhelming desire to buy.

- *Television* is a very remote second choice. Television is, of course, a high-impact medium, but it is very expensive. It is no coincidence that most direct response ads you view on television run on weaker networks or local access channels during nonpeak viewing hours. This occurs because most direct response television advertisers negotiate below-rate-card deals in order to afford the exposure, sometimes even paying for their advertising with a percentage of the revenue from sales generated.

- *Magazines* work well if your industry has a specialty publication that allows you to target a specific audience, such as dollhouse collectors or sailboat racing enthusiasts. It would be very tough to make a direct response ad work in a general magazine.

- *Newspapers* aren't particularly effective venues for direct response advertisers. You do find these types of ads in national magazine supplements to Sunday papers. But don't be fooled into thinking this tack can work for you. Very few of these ads would gross enough to cover the advertising costs if rate card prices were paid. Some direct response advertisers who chose the newspaper medium purchase ad space at remnant prices, when the publication has odd ad spaces to fill in at the last moment. Still others negotiate deals to buy ads at further reduced rates when the publication can't even find advertisers to place at remnant rates. Who knows when you might get an appropriate space in either of these instances!

- *Radio* can be used, but isn't recommended. Very few listeners are likely to copy down product or ordering information.

"Direct mail is the obvious choice for direct response advertising."

Choices: Advertising Frequency

*I*t is very difficult to get potential customers to notice your ads, let alone respond to them. So, because advertising is so expensive, you should use some strategy to concentrate your advertising impact in the most effective manner for your business. The only exception to this advertising strategy might be for nonseasonal service businesses that advertise through the Yellow Pages or local newspaper service directories.

● *Peak season blowout*

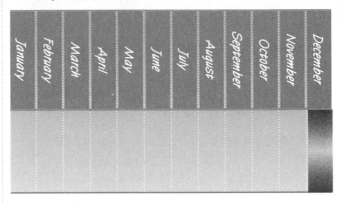

Employing a peak season blowout strategy involves saving all of your advertising money for one big campaign. This makes sense for businesses whose products or services are typically required during a particular season—for example, a snowplow service. In this case, the business might place its advertising in the month preceding the usual beginning of snowfall in their area. Another example would be a retailer who is particularly dependent on the Christmas trade, advertising heavily throughout December.

Choices: Advertising Frequency

• Quarterly blitz

Quarterly blitz advertising campaigns are quite common. They allow you to concentrate your ad dollars heavily during specific times, while also affording you a better chance of maintaining a place in your audience's minds throughout the year.

• See-saw approach

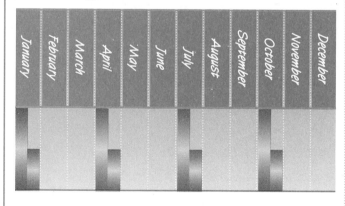

• Continuous advertising

All too many small businesses completely dribble away their advertising money throughout the year by placing a continuous stream of small ads. This approach never creates enough impact to net results. If you operate this way, stop it. Drop all advertising for a while and see if your business falls off. It probably won't, and you can then feel confident in adopting a new advertising schedule.

◄ The "see-saw approach," for lack of a formerly coined name for this strategy, is a campaign in which impact is created by running a big print ad or heavy radio/television schedule for one week, followed by smaller ad or lighter radio/television schedule in the succeeding week or weeks to reinforce the earlier impact at a lower cost.

Choices: Advertising Agencies

Even if you have the money to hire an advertising agency, try creating your advertising campaign first. You don't necessarily need to design your own ads. You can hire a freelancer to assist you in this effort. But do the development work and the copywriting yourself. No matter how difficult you might find this task, keep in mind that it isn't a cinch for agencies to put together great advertising strategies and write fabulous, attention-getting copy either! Plus, unless you are the biggest business game in town, an agency isn't going to assign its best people to, or put its best effort into servicing your account.

Another pitfall you can get trapped in through agency use is great-looking, great-sounding ads. Ads that win awards are nice, but the purpose of advertising is to attract sales. Great ads might, but don't guarantee, an increase in trade.

Creating ads takes time, but is a crucial part of your business. It is just too important a task to leave entirely up to the experts. You need to study your competitors' ads, get fresh ideas from other firms in other industries, test small inexpensive ads first, and keep tinkering with your graphics, message, and placement until you find the combination that works for you.

Direct Mail

Direct mail allows you to target a specific market better than any other advertising medium. You decide who gets your message, when they get it, and where they get it.

A direct-mail piece can be as simple as a postcard or as elaborate as a catalog. Direct mail is a terrific medium for creating action. Sending a direct-mail piece is much more likely to elicit an immediate response than television, radio, or newspaper advertising.

Direct mail usually costs more per person reached than any other advertising medium. The advantage of direct mail lies in its ability to target a specific consumer group. It allows you to concentrate your advertising budget on those people most likely to purchase your product or service.

You can budget as little or as much as you like to launch a direct mail campaign. How much you spend will be affected by decisions such as two- versus four-color printing, how many pages will be in your brochure or catalog, how many pieces will be in your direct mail package, paper size, and, most importantly, the number of pieces you want to mail.

How It Works

Why

Direct mail campaigns are good for targeting specific markets. They allow you to mail product information, coupons, or other advertising messages to specific groups of consumers.

Who

Direct mail should be targeted to those segments of the market in your sales territory that would most likely be interested in your product. If you are marketing a stain-resistant treatment for new carpeting, you should target your mailing to home and business consumers who have purchased carpeting within the last year and live or work in your sales area.

If you don't have a list of people or businesses in your targeted market group, contact a mailing list broker. It will be able to compile a list according to your demographic needs and supply mailing labels for your direct mail materials.

When

Send your direct mail to your targeted consumers when it would be most likely to catch their attention and fulfill an upcoming need. For example, in the case of the carpet treatment product, "spring cleaning season" might be a good time. Mail in February so that potential clients can call for appointments during March or April and coordinate this service with their other spring cleaning tasks.

Where

You should send your direct mail to the business or residence address of your targeted potential consumer—whichever is more appropriate or likely to catch their attention.

How

You can collate, stuff, and label your direct mail materials yourself. If your mailing is large, mailing list houses usually offer a full range of mailing services.

What

Direct mail materials should include all of the information a potential consumer needs in order to understand your product, become interested in purchasing your product, and act on a decision to place an order for the product.

Direct-Mail Piece

Direct mail packages vary from simple postcards to fat envelopes stuffed with full-color flyers and, typically, consist of the following:

Sales letter

The first thing you usually see when you open a direct mail package is a sales letter. This is an important piece, because the letter must quickly grab the prospect's attention or the rest of the package will be trashed. It is often printed in black ink on standard letter-size paper. It might be personalized with your prospect's name, or it could be a form letter addressed to Dear Sir or Madam.

Mail piece

The next piece one typically sees is a brochure or flyer. This piece is designed to reinforce the sales letter and set an image for the company and product. It is typically 11" × 17", folded to letter size, This brochure might be printed in one or two colors or feature four-color printing.

Business reply card

A postage-paid business reply card allows the customer to reply to the mailing easily. Or a postage-paid business reply envelope may be used so that the customer is able to mail a check back.

No. 10 business envelope

Direct mail is usually sent in standard business size (No. 10) envelopes. Sometimes a "teaser" is printed on the envelope to entice a customer to open it. The post office has kits that provide setup information for designing envelope "teasers" and placing important mailing information to ensure fast delivery.

Writing a Direct Mail Letter

1

SPRINGFIELD BANK

775 Ranchero Parkway ▲ Texastown ▲ TX 76010

(800) 555-5555

January 6, 1996

Ms. Jane Doe
123 Park Lane
Texasville, TX 75237

2

Dear Ms. Doe:

3

How would you like to save 20 percent on your computer purchases?

The Springfield Bank/Starlight Computer credit card saves you money on your computer purchases.

4

"My small business purchases were made with the Springfield Bank/Starlight Computer credit card and I built up enough credits to save 20 percent on my computer equipment."
– *Ken Turman, President, Truman Consulting, Springfield, Texas*

5

This credit card works just like every other credit card with one big exception: **it saves you money.** Every time you use the Springfield Bank/Starlight Computer credit card, you earn credits toward your next purchase of Starlight Computer equipment.

6

Call (800) 555-5555 now to receive your Springfield Bank/Starlight Computer credit card. An operator will take your information and process your application within 48 hours. Then you can start earning credits that will **save you money!**

7

Sincerely,

Hal Walker

Harold Walker
Vice President of Marketing

P.S. If you sign up before December 31, you will receive a free gift from Springfield Bank!

8

Note: This example is fictitious.

Writing a Direct Mail Letter

1 Letterhead

A sales letter should include your company logo, name, and address. You can have a printer print your letter on your existing letterhead stock, print the letter in combination with your standard letterhead design, or print a letterhead that has been specifically designed for your direct mail piece.

2 Addressee

Many direct mail pieces, particularly those mailed by local businesses, do not personalize each letter. Instead the letter begins with a generic introduction, such as Dear Sir or Dear Madam. If you are using a generic introduction, do try to personalize as much as possible with greetings, such as Dear Boston Resident or Dear Computer User. It is preferable to address the letter to a specific person, but it will add to the cost and the complexity of the mailing. If you are buying your mailing list from a large mailing list company, they can provide you with names and addresses on a computer disk. Most mailing houses will be able to print personalized letters using this disk for an additional charge.

3 Attention-grabber

Grab the reader's attention in the first sentence. This is the most important part of the letter. Unless your first sentence is highly compelling, most readers will not continue reading the letter.

4 Focus on benefits

You want to focus on the benefits of your product in the body of the letter. Your product has many features that your customers will ask about, but it is the benefits that will sell them. A feature is anything inherent to your product. A benefit is what your customer derives from the product.

5 Testimonial

A testimonial can be used to add credibility to your company and your product or service. The most important aspect of the testimonial is the person who offers it. Make sure the person is someone the reader will respect.

6 Highlight key phrases

Keep the reader's attention. Some readers will skim through your letter and could miss the most important points. Highlight key phrases that stress benefits to keep the reader interested in your product.

7 Call to action

Call your readers to action. They need to feel like they should act quickly or they will lose the offer. Make it easy for the readers to act, by listing a toll-free order number or including a postage-paid reply card.

8 Add a postscript

Add a postscript at the end of the letter. Many readers skip to the end of the letter for the "bottom line." A grabber "P.S." statement will ensure that your message isn't lost.

Producing a Direct Mail Piece

A direct mail piece should be carefully planned and executed. If you don't have advertising or marketing experience, enlist the assistance of a creative service to assist you in strategizing your unique selling proposition —your unbeatable selling point. Once you have developed your "message strategy," contract for various execution and distribution services.

Mailing list broker

If you don't have a mailing list, contact a mailing list broker. Ask the mailing list broker where their lists are sourced from—specialized industrial or membership directories, telephone books, and/or magazine subscription lists. Inquire about the availability of lists that have been used to sell products similar to yours. Narrow your list focus to match the demographics of your potential customer.

Copywriter

A professional copywriter will know how to phrase your unique selling point(s) to create a pitch that will grab the attention of your prospective customers. I recommend that you first try developing the copy yourself.

Graphic designer

For a "professional look," hire a graphic designer to create your direct mailer. He or she will know how to present the elements of your piece—type, photographs, illustrations— to command attention. The designer will also provide you with the camera-ready art.

Illustrator

If you need eye-catching illustrations of the product, how to use the product, or other information, hire an illustrator.

Photographer

A photograph is the best way to depict and sell your product. If you can, hire a photographer to do product shots. If you want to "dress" up your piece with photo illustrations, you can purchase the rights to use stock photographs available through stock photo houses. For royalty-free photographs, check with your suppliers or end users.

Printer

Choose a printer that specializes in printing pieces similar in quantity, size, and configuration to yours. Don't pay a four-color printer to print a one-color job or expect a quick printer to do professional four-color printing. Request samples and get quotes. Once you have chosen your printer, find out what its press and camera-ready art requirements are. Relay that information to your designer.

Mail house

For large mailings, contract the services of a mail house to fold, collate, stuff, label, and/or prepare your mailing according to postal regulations.

Post office

The post office publishes guides that outline formats and rules for designing and organizing advertising mail that will flow through the postal system quickly and efficiently. Ask!

WHAT CAN YOU AFFORD TO PRODUCE?

To determine your breakeven point calculate:

Average selling price per unit	$ _____
− Average cost of goods sold	$) _____
= Net revenue	$ _____
÷ Total cost to produce direct mailer	$ _____
by Net revenue	= X _____

X is the number of responses needed to break even. For a mailing of 10,000 pieces advertising a product with a Net Revenue of $60 per Unit at a Total Cost to Produce of $5960, 99 responses (or 1%) would be required to break even. It is wise get quotes from all of your prospective development vendors before you begin producing your piece!

Direct Mail Success Story

Datel Communications provides telephone service and systems to businesses. *Howard Davis*, president, has tried various methods of advertising over the years. Direct mail has proven effective, but it took a while to perfect the delivery! Here's how Howard chose direct mail as one of his advertising mediums and how he made it work for Datel Communications.

Experiment

66 We found that several different mediums work well and others don't. In our case, television and radio don't work. And direct mail, while postage and printing are very expensive, seems to be the most cost-effective way to get a customer to actually respond and say, 'I want to buy the product that you're selling.' 99

Keep It Simple

66 One mailing piece that we used was a very simple piece . . . very easy to read. The second one that was tried was a very elaborate piece. Again, we were thinking that being more elaborate was going to get us better results. But what more elaborate did was to make it more confusing to the people receiving the mail pieces, and most of them ended up in the trash. 99

Streetwise Advice on Direct Mail

☞ **Don't expect to make money on your first mailing**
Direct mail marketing is effective for many small and large businesses, but it can be hard to find the direct mail package that works best for you. Don't get discouraged if your first mailing doesn't incease sales. Keep trying!

☞ **Know your break-even point**
Successful direct mail campaigns typically get a response rate of 1 to 3 percent. Know how many responses you need to break even.

☞ **Test small mailings**
Test small, inexpensive mailings until you find the formula that works. Let's say you need two responses per hundred to break even on your mailing costs. If you do a two hundred-batch mailing, you need four responses to break even. If you get one response or no responses on your two hundred-batch mailing, it is not working. Chances are, it won't work no matter how many you mail.

☞ **Choosing the right list is critical**
Choosing the right mailing list will make a much faster improvement in your response rate than changing the package. Choose your list very carefully.

☞ **Your best list is usually your customer list**
Your best list is a list of people who have previously bought a product or service from you. Keep a good list of current and past customers.

☞ **Work your best lists hard**
Use your best mailing lists frequently. Mail to these lists again and again, until response dwindles off. Focus on using your best lists repeatedly, as opposed to testing a wide variety of new lists.

☞ **Focus your message**
Be specific. Direct mail is good at targeting a specific audience. Be sure to develop copy and a layout that are appropriate to your audience.

☞ **Call them to action**
Direct mail is great for calling customers to action. Don't forget to put a call to action in your piece.

☞ **Use coupons and redemption offers**
Give prospects a reason to act soon. Coupons with redemption dates give the offer urgency.

☞ **Make it easy to respond**
Always think ahead to what you want the recipients to do. Make it easy for them to take action. If you want them to return a reply card, make it postage-paid. If you want them to call you, include a toll-free number.

☞ **Test and refine**
Don't give up after one shot. You could have a wonderful design, great copy, and a solid offer, but be mailing at the wrong time. In the end, you have to test until you see what works for your situation. Test variations on design and timing to find out what works.

Questions & Answers about Direct Mail

Should I send my mailing first class or bulk rate?

Generally, you should use bulk rate. But personalize your mailing as much as postal regulations permit. Your envelope doesn't have to have "bulk mail rate" stamped across it, nor do you have to use a preprinted block in the top corner that says bulk rate. Instead, you may want to consider having the mail stamped in a meter with the abbreviation "blk. rate" in small type running vertically beside the correct rate. Ask the mail house about this option.

Bulk mail moves slower and less predictably than first-class mail since it is not given priority. But only a very small percentage of bulk mail is actually lost, and using it can save you a lot of money.

Is a phone response or mail back response better?

Both response mechanisms are effective. Some people prefer to phone in their response to direct mail offers, others prefer to respond by mail. So offer both options if possible.

Do I need a toll-free number for phone responses?

If you are doing local mailings and calling your number's a local call, you don't. Otherwise, you do, especially for consumer mailings. Consumers expect toll-free numbers when placing orders. While it can be a nice touch to offer business people a toll-free number, the lack of a toll-free number is not going to stop business people from calling you.

How much do credit cards help?

Accepting credit cards is essential for selling by mail. For one, credit cards allow you to get paid without having to take the risk of billing people. Also, consumers are more likely to respond to credit card offers. Many people find it less convenient to pull out a check than to use their credit card. Also, you can't use a check when ordering by phone. Using credit cards makes some customers more assured that you are offering a legitimate product or service, and that you are more likely to stand behind your product or service if they are not completely satisfied.

How much do credit card firms charge me?

Fees vary with each credit card company, depending on whether you process payments electronically or manually, your sales volume, average sale size, and sometimes your negotiating skill. A small firm will pay about 3 to 5 percent of their gross credit card sales. It's a worthwhile investment, considering the potential for additional sales and the fact that the credit card company advances you cash almost immediately and assumes virtually all of the credit risk.

Why do many direct-mail pieces include dated offers?

Dated offers generate more sales by pushing people to respond by a certain deadline. Especially if you are using bulk mail, be sure to give people plenty of time to respond. If you really aren't confident about when your mailing will arrive, you may want to make a special offer contingent upon "responding within ten days of receipt" for example, as opposed to by a specific date. I would recommend that you give people between ten and twenty-one days to respond to a direct mail solicitation from the time they receive the offer.

Newspaper Advertising

Newspaper advertising is often a double-edged sword. It can provide you with exposure and leads, but your response rate will probably be less than overwhelming in comparison to other advertising mediums such as direct mail or broadcast advertising.

Advertising in regional and national newspapers can be expensive. Advertising in local or community newspapers is less so and may provide a more focused advertising approach. If your business trade is localized, it certainly makes more sense to focus on the community or local papers that your customers are more likely to read.

Running ads in major metropolitan newspapers can be effective if your product or service offering is strong enough or unique enough to pull in customers from throughout the readership or circulation area.

Chances are that your competitors will be spending money on newspaper advertising, too. Remember that this will reduce the effectiveness of your newspaper advertising campaign, because you will be competing for your customer's attention and "mind share."

Newspaper advertising is sold by the column inch. Different advertising classifications may have different rates. For instance, a service directory advertisement may be less expensive per column inch than a small ad placed on a regular editorial page. Virtually all newspapers offer discounts for contract advertisers, depending upon the volume of space they commit to over the course of a contract year.

It's a Sweetheart Deal

She may forgive you if you forget to brighten her life with the promise of spring flowers on Groundhog Day. She may forgive you if you forget to shower her with silly balloons on April Fool's Day. But she'll forget you if you don't remember to bedazzle her with diamonds on Valentine's Day. At **BEDAZZLE**, we have a **PERFECT SELECTION** of **PERFECT DIAMONDS** — one just perfect for your budget, your love life, and the love of your life. And on **FEBRUARY 13TH** all of our diamonds will be offered at **HALF PRICE**, with credit terms so liberal you can just about write your own ticket!

BeDazzle

54 South Magnolia Boulevard ♥ Marietta, GA 30060

(706) 555-5553 ♥ Store Credit, MasterCard, Visa, American Express

Note: This sample is fictitious.

❶ Headline

Get the reader's attention with a headline or eye-catching phrase. Keep it short and simple, and avoid the use of controversial phrases or slang.

❷ Copy length

Use a copy length that supports your message. Long copy looks informative and is good for technical or business products. Short copy leaves room for graphics. This combination is appropriate for an image ad selling fashion, home decor, and other lifestyle products.

❸ Comparison

Use comparative advertising phrases such as "You've tried the others. Now try us!" only if your product or service has an obvious advantage over the offerings of your competitors.

❹ Benefits

The body of the ad should list benefits or reasons why the customers should buy your product or service now. Emphasize the customer by using the word "you" instead of the word "we." Use bulleted text to highlight key points.

❺ Closing

The closing copy should make the sale possible by including any contact, telephone, address, or other ordering information necessary for the consumer to act on his or her purchasing decision.

Streetwise Advice on Newspaper Ads

☞ The biggest waste

A huge percentage of newspaper advertising is a complete waste of money. Newspaper advertising *can* be profitable, but all too often, it isn't. This is especially true for small businesses.

Many small businesses feel they have to advertise, and without much thought or research toss ads into the local paper. Typically the only reason they have chosen newspaper advertising as their communication vehicle is because the newspaper ad salesperson was the first person to call on them!

Why don't newspaper ads always work for small businesses? The most common reason is that they get lost in the paper. Small businesses tend to run small ads with mediocre copy and no illustrative materials, such as photographs or art. And small business people often don't take the time to measure ad results. Without measuring results, they have no sound basis for improving their creativity, their copy, their offers, or even their choice of media.

☞ Product ad dilemma

It is extremely hard to make product ads work. For instance, we placed eighth- to quarter-page ads for different books that we publish in the national edition of the *New York Times* and regional editions of the *Wall Street Journal* in cooperation with various book store chains. These chains stock our books in hundreds of their stores, and we are able to track sales through their computer inventory systems and determine whether or not advertising can be linked to a sales increase on any given book. We found that an ad costing in the $2,000 to $10,000 range, not including production costs, typically generates less than ten additional book sales. These product ads, in effect, caused a 95% to 99% net loss in profitability.

The only "winning" ad that we placed for one of our books, for instance, ran under an extremely clever headline and offered a terrific discount. Still, it covered costs but did not net a profit!

☞ Product ad tips

Concentrate your product ad dollars in large ads rather than in frequent ones. Develop a punchy headline and include snappy illustrations or photos. Include sell copy for the serious potential buyer. And don't forget to tell prospects where they can purchase your product.

☞ Service ad tips

Run service ads where prospective customers will typically see them. The service directory of the local newspaper is usually an appropriate spot. Service ads need to clearly state the nature of the service offered. A great headline isn't necessary because the prospect is generally already interested in obtaining the type of service you are offering. But you do need to convey a powerful competitive message through your ad. This advantage can take the form of a free trial, new customer offer, special bonus, or free estimate. If your competitors advertise on any particularly strong points that have great consumer appeal, match those points. And highlight a unique reason for clients to call on you first. Some service seekers call every service provider for quotes, some call two or three, and some call one.

Streetwise Advice on Newspaper Ads

Make sure yours is the first call made.

And also remember, despite what an advertising salesperson may tell you, the most compelling, not necessarily the largest, ads tend to generate more "first calls."

☞ Generous offers

People expect to see "sale" and "specials" advertised in newspapers.

Whether you are advertising products or services, try to offer a special price or bonus to your customers. Make the offer generous. Ten percent off the regular price, especially in this age of national discount retailers and competitive pricing, just won't cut it.

It costs a lot of money to run ads and response is often iffy, so offer deep discounts on a limited range of products or services. This is a tactic that lures the customers in and, ideally, while they are browsing, they will purchase other nondiscounted items that have a higher margin. In a best-case scenario, they will become regular customers.

☞ Special rates

Large metropolitan newspapers and many small local or regional newspapers offer a lower ad rate called the "local" or "retail" rate to local or retail businesses. If you are selling a product through local retailers, you will save money if you get the retailer to place the ad even if you reimburse it for all costs involved. In some industries, however, the retailer typically shares some portion of the ad space with the manufacturer or supplier.

Newspapers also offer volume discounts if you guarantee to place a certain number of ads over the course of a year. Read the fine print regarding penalties for nonfulfillment on any contract you sign that involves a "frequency" rate. Generally, however, the penalty for failing to meet your placement obligations is payment of the "non frequency" rate for those ads you did place.

Still, it can be painful to reimburse the publication for the higher ad rate.

☞ Negotiating rates

Generally, you can negotiate rates off the rate card with smaller papers or papers that don't have the readership edge in their marketplace. And if your ads are particularly clever, you can sometimes negotiate a better rate deal with a larger newspaper.

Several years ago I wanted to run several full-page ads in a newspaper owned by a large U.S. media company. This company was notorious for adhering to their rate card. But I was determined to negotiate a discount. I called my advertising representative's boss and politely explained to her that I needed to negotiate a lower rate or I wasn't going to place an ad at all. This creative individual, wanting to keep my business but unable to go against a strict company policy on rates, established a new rate category just for me! I ran my ads for 30 percent less than any other advertiser in the publication!

"If you don't measure results, you won't have a sound basis for improving creativity, copy, offers, or even your choice of media."

Questions & Answers about Newspaper Ads

Should I take the newspaper up on its offer to design an ad for me for free?

Never! While the newspaper's ad rep may tell you that its art department can produce a great ad for free, don't believe it! The ads that staff newspaper production departments product are typically terrible. You would be better off hiring a freelancer, even a graphic arts student, and working closely with that person to put together an ad you are really pleased with.

Should I run the same ad repeatedly?

You should run the same basic ad design or format repeatedly. This will build a company identity for you and create awareness among consumers. It is also easier to come up with one terrific design concept and modify it periodically to meet the requirements of a new product offering or a special sale—say a new headline, a different copy slant, or a different photo—than to continually reinvent the ad.

Do I need a photograph or artwork to attract attention?

Many newspaper ads work well without photographs or artwork. This is especially true in the case of service ads. But whether you are running straight copy or an elaborate multiphoto advertisement, your ad must look professional.

What is the best day to run my ad?

This depends on the product or service category you fall into. For example, Wednesday is "food" day in most newspapers. If you are offering a food product or service, Wednesday would provide you with the optimum opportunity for reaching your target audience—people interested in food-related purchases. For more general products or services, one day of the week is as good as the next.

How important is position within the newspaper?

People look for ads for certain types of products or services in certain sections of the newspaper, such as auto products in the auto section. If you are offering a "category" product or service, be sure to run your ad in the appropriate section. If your ad does not fall into a natural category, then its positioning won't make much of a difference.

Should I run an ad in my local town newspaper or the metropolitan city newspaper?

You want to target your prospective market as directly as possible. If, for example, you are unlikely to lure customers out of the city to your small town for auto repairs, don't advertise in the metropolitan newspaper.

What about advertisers or free newspapers?

Advertisers and free newspapers are garnering a larger share of total ad expenditures. They do work and are less expensive per thousand readers than paid publications. Also, the percentage of households purchasing a newspaper has been in a steady decline. Free papers provide full saturation penetration because they are sent directly to the consumer's home without request or purchase. This is an attractive proposition for advertisers—so much so, in fact, that many traditional papers have created their own free circulation publications!

If you offer downscale products or low-cost services, consider giving a free newspaper your first advertising shot. If you offer more upscale offerings, stick with the paid publications.

Start out modestly with any advertising campaign, and test your results. This will provide you with a reasonable scale of effectiveness before you commit a lot of ad dollars recklessly.

Magazine Advertising

You've heard the phrase before. "I just bought the magazine to look at the pictures." There is a kernel of truth to that statement. Consumers are naturally drawn to the unusual graphics and pictures often used in magazines. It follows that magazine consumers are more likely to read those magazine ads that carry compelling images.

As with newspaper advertising, there will be intense competition for the "mind share" of the consumer. The option of using two- or four-color printing in magazine advertising gives the advertiser an opportunity to create a lasting image of his or her product that has no equal in any other print advertising vehicle save direct mail. To further entice the reader's desire for your product, some magazines even offer advertisers an opportunity to include product samples with their ads. For example, witness the proliferation of "scratch and sniff" perfume ads.

Naturally, all of these wonderful ad enhancements come at a premium. The cost of placing a full-page ad with all of the options in a magazine can be staggering. After all, the advertiser is actually paying for the production costs associated with printing a glossy, four-color publication.

Costs for placing magazine ads will vary from publication to publication. They will also depend upon the size of the ad placed and the positioning of the ad. Magazine ads are sold by the page or page increment—full page, half page, quarter page, etc. Rates also depend upon the frequency with which an advertiser places ads over the period of a year. Typically, advertisers offer one-time, three-time, six-time, and twelve-time rates. Twelve-time rates are usually significantly lower than one-time rates. But, of course, you are paying that rate times twelve ads.

Writing Magazine Copy

① Get the consumer's attention

You need to take the consumer by storm by focusing on creating an eye-catching headline or phrase. Include a graphic or logo to establish the tone of the message.

Avoid controversial headlines and pictures. Humor should be used judiciously. It's hard to come up with a humorous tone that is universally appealing. In addition, certain tones could actually be viewed as offensive by some members of your target audience. A clever phrase or impressive graphic will attract the attention of, and be appreciated by, almost everyone.

② Use color whenever possible

Magazines offer the opportunity to use four-color photos and artwork to enhance the meaning and impact of your message. Use this powerful tool. Give your ad color if you can afford it.

Four-color ads traditionally have the highest response rate from readers. The response rate typically decreases as use of color is eliminated—from four color to spot color to black and white. If you can't afford four color, but have a budget that will allow some "enhancement" over purchasing a basic black and white ad space, spot color is a good alternative. Most magazines offer standard spot colors—red, blue, green. orange, or yellow—at one rate, and specialized "matched colors" at a slightly higher rate. Matched colors are generally chosen from the Pantone Professional Color System and are commonly referred to as PMS colors. These colors are available in a wide assortment of hues and variations. Your printer or graphic designer should be able to show you the selection of colors available.

③ Make your pitch concise and simple

List the benefits and reasons why the consumer should buy your product or service. Keep it short and simple. Reader's aren't going to treat your ad like a novel and sit down for a long read. You have only ten to fifteen seconds to get your reader's attention and appraise him or her of the unique value of your product or service. So avoid long phrases or cute dialogue. Be precise and to the point.

④ Make it easy for the customer to reach you and order from you

In order to make it easy for potential customers to purchase your product or service, don't forget to include your phone number (toll-free if possible), fax number, and mailing address at the bottom of the ad. If other special ordering information is needed, include that as well.

Tread Ever So Softly

①

②

The WhisperWear VAGABOND Boot
The only thing they will hear is the personality of your shoe shining through. *Nothing is as beautiful, except you.*

- Patented WhisperSoul® soles
- Handstiched in a soft, natural, waterproof leather
- Available in chic noir, basic bone, and au courant cassis

③

WhisperWear of Wisconsin • Spooner, Wisconsin • Call 1·800·555·5559 for a retailer near you.

④

Note: This example is fictitious.

Streetwise Advice on Magazine Ads

☞ **Not appropriate**

Magazine ads won't work for most small, local businesses. Magazine advertising space costs significantly more than newspaper advertising space. You really need to have a good reason to justify this expenditure. If your business is upscale, it might be an appropriate choice. A classy restaurant with a menu that puts mom to shame and caters to a trendy crowd might want to pay for magazine advertising, perhaps to show off a four-color photo of diners feasting on a sumptuous meal in their chic establishment. An upscale women's boutique might want to advertise in magazines to show off to full effect the one-of-a-kind fashionable apparel they sell.

You should also consider how closely a local magazine parallels your core market. Most local businesses find their trade in their home or immediately adjacent towns. Many local magazines are distributed over a wide region—say, from fifty to one hundred towns. Carefully calculate what, if any, return you will get from advertising to a geographic base that is much broader than your typical trade reaches.

☞ **Specialty magazines**

While the cost per thousand readers reached may be high for specialty magazines, they may offer the lowest cost per thousand qualified prospects. More readers of a specialty magazine are potential purchasers of your applicable specialized product or service than would be true of a general readership publication.

Specialty magazines tend to be thoroughly read, not scanned, and smaller ads often work well in these vehicles. Mail-order products, especially in narrow fields in which products are not readily available at the retail level, tend to net good results from specialty magazine advertising.

But there is a much less expensive, sometimes even free, advertising alternative. Find a mail-order company that is willing to purchase your product at discount and feature it in its catalog. Some of these outfits don't charge you for space in their catalogs, and some do. Often, those catalog companies that do charge for "ad" space will allow you to pay for this space with free product at the wholesaler price instead of with cash.

☞ **Trade magazines**

Like specialty magazines, trade magazines allow you to zero in on your target audience. Trade magazines tend to have smaller circulations and even lower advertising rates than specialty magazines.

You should run full-page ads in trade publications, however. Do this even if it means you need to reduce your ad frequency to meet your advertising budget, and even if can only afford one full-page ad per year. Readers of trade magazines don't usually bother checking less than full-page ads even if they get caught up in carefully reading the editorial content. These readers know that only small start-up companies tend to buy small ad space and they aren't interested in any risks involved in purchasing from a less than well-established firm. In fact, some companies even purchase double truck, or facing full pages, multiple page, cover gatefolds, or special insert ads that they have printed themselves in order to really impress the publication's readers with their image and reputation.

☞ Quality

No matter what magazine you decide to advertise in, readers expect magazine ads to be much slicker and more attractive than newspaper ads. And they expect the copy to read just as cleverly as a radio spot.

While you need to ensure that your ad is effective, it also must be visually appealing. Here is a suggestion that will help you judge what works and what doesn't. Develop more than one ad design idea or concept. Place mock-ups of these ad concepts in an old copy of the magazine you plan to advertise in. What do you think? How do they compare as you flip through the publication? Which one really captures your attention? And, since you might not be the most impartial judge, it is important to ask other people what their opinion is.

☞ Be leery of "bingo card" responses

Measure sales generated by your magazine ads, not inquiries. Many new magazine advertisers are impressed when they get hundreds or even thousands of inquiries from magazine readers who have circled the company's name on readers' service cards. While you should follow up on these inquiries, my experience has been that very, very few of these inquiries add up to sales. Readers often circle dozens of names on readers' service cards when they actually have very little interest in the products.

> "No matter what magazine you decide to advertise in, readers expect magazine ads to be much slicker and more attractive than newspaper ads."

Questions & Answers about Magazine Ads

? Should I run magazine ads without photographs or artwork?

No. Generally this would be a waste of money. Even in limited circulation publications, small ads will appear substandard if they don't incorporate appealing graphics.

? Should I put color in my ad?

David Olgilvy, one of the all-time gurus of advertising, said that color is a bargain. It may cost about 50% more, but it delivers twice the response of a comparable black and white ad. Olgilvy's comment is right on the money.

However, when he talks about color adding approximately 50% more to the cost of an ad, he is only referring to the ad space costs. He does not take into consideration the appreciably greater cost involved in preparing a color ad for publication. (The production costs are a much smaller factor for huge national advertisers, like those Ogilvy used to service.)

One extra cost to consider is the creation of the four-color film, as opposed to one-color film for black and white

ads, necessary to print such an ad. For a small ad in a limited circulation publication, the cost of producing the ad may be more than the cost of placing the ad! But if you run the ad as frequently or run it repeatedly with black film text changes only, the productions costs become a smaller component of your total costs.

Black and white ads can be effective, but as a rule color ads are more likely to pay off.

? Do I need to advertise repeatedly to get results?

Advertising salespeople will try to talk you into running ads in their publication on as high a frequency schedule as they can. They will do this even if your ad didn't pull a response the first time it ran.

Unlike radio or television, one magazine ad should produce results. If it doesn't, you aren't going to improve your chances of making an impression on the readership no matter how many times you repeat the same message through the same venue.

When appraising the results of a magazine ad, keep in mind, however, that magazines provide a medium that works best for image advertising. The periodic nature of the format doesn't lend itself to inciting immediate action from a potential consumer.

? Why do so many trade magazine ads run without important company information such as a phone number?

The purpose of many trade magazine ads is image building—creating excitement for and awareness of a company's products or services in the mind's of potential consumers. They aren't designed to generate sales or even inquiries.

Large companies rely on their sales forces and/or distributors to make sales actually happen. Small companies may rely more heavily on telemarketers, independent representatives, direct mail, or trade show participation to effect actual sales.

The benefit of an image ad lies in its ability to "prep" potential consumers for making a purchase. Then, when they are personally contacted by a salesperson or telemarketer they already know who the company is and what the product is about. Just because they have heard of you, they are simply more likely to buy from you!

So while it may not hurt to include a phone number in a trade publication ad, don't be disappointed if it doesn't net a flurry of inquires. I have run six-page spreads that carry a toll-free phone number in national publications and have received zero direct inquiry phone calls! But that's not to say that the ad didn't reach the marketplace or, in one fashion or another, produce sales results.

Yellow Pages Advertising

*T*he Yellow Pages are the one constant in print advertising. If you need to find out who does what in a particular product or service category, the Yellow Pages provides a listing and phone number for those companies that offer that product or service.

Unlike other forms of print advertising, Yellow Pages advertising is sold on an annual basis. A basic one-line listing comes with your business telephone service. You can upgrade that listing and purchase a variety of ad sizes, ranging from just setting your listing in boldface type to a large full-page advertisement. You might add a second color to emphasize a logo, graphic, or line of type.

The cost for advertising in the Yellow Pages, obviously, depends upon the type of listing or advertising space you contract for as well as the circulation size of the book you will be listed in. A large metropolitan Yellow Pages book commands a much higher rate per ad than does a small-town book, for instance.

When considering Yellow Pages advertising and the type of listing or ad you want to have, remember that the competition will be brutal between some types of popular businesses—beauty salons, for instance.

You can support your Yellow Pages listing or ad with other types of advertising mediums. One small telecommunications firm, for example, supported its one-line Yellow Pages listing with image advertising. The basic premise to their strategy was that it was OK if people threw away their direct mail flyers without ordering a product or service. What counted was name recognition. When the time did come and the consumer was looking through the Yellow Pages for a telecommunications company they would, at least, remember their name. The awareness factor would give them an edge against the competition.

1 Headline

Identify your company and the area you serve. This should be in bold type or type that is at least a point size or two larger than your body copy.

2 Business type

Underneath the name of your business, state clearly and in as few words as possible what your business is all about. When developing this copy, include any unique product or service benefits or features that you can offer that your competitors cannot. Try to include any special information that would entice a consumer to call you as opposed to any other business listed under your heading.

3 Incentives

List any special incentives that your business offers, such as free estimates, free maintenance checks, or what have you. You might also consider offering a money-back guarantee to entice potential customers to call you.

CUTLER & SONS TRANSMISSIONS

1

"Serving the Upper Peninsula"

Rebuilt and New Transmissions Since 1961

"No job too big or too small for our transmission specialists"

2

- Foreign and domestic automobile transmission repairs
- Trucks including pre-1970 models
- Front and four-wheel-drive vehicles

FREE TOWING — FREE ESTIMATES

Ask about our money-back guarantee

All major credit cards accepted
MasterCard • Visa • Discover • American Express

3

189 Mt. Arvon North
Ishpeming

555-3555
In State Toll Free: 800-555-555

4

Note: This sample is fictitious.

---

4 Contact information

List your address and phone number as well as any credit cards that you accept. You may also want to list your hours of operation if they are part of

your service or product availability benefits—a twenty-four-hour hotline or twenty-four-hour beeper service, for instance.

Yellow Pages Success Story

Wordsmith is a desktop publishing company that generates a major portion of its business from Yellow Pages advertising. *Douglas Wilcox*, president of the firm, discusses the informal client surveys he uses to test the ads and the return his business realizes on the investment.

Ask "Where Did They Hear about You?"

66 On occasion, we do client surveys for a few months. When people come in, we say 'How did you hear about us? Was it through the Yellow Pages? If so, what section and edition?' We change our advertising every year. 99

Category and Cost Are Major Factors

66 There are some questions that are important to us. One is 'What category should we advertise in?' Another is 'How much should we spend on advertising?' It does tend to get very expensive. 99

Great Investment

66 Half our business started with Yellow Pages advertising. That initial $4,000 investment translates into $40,000, $50,000, maybe even $60,000 a year in income. 99

☞ Going broke

One cold winter day, while selling newspaper advertising, I called on a service business. The owner told me he was going out of business because he couldn't afford to pay the monthly bill for his Yellow Pages advertising. If he didn't pay his bill soon, the phone company was going to disconnect his phone.

This may be an extreme case. But many small business people buy larger Yellow Pages ad space than they should. Yellow Pages advertising salespeople are among the best in the industry and among the best paid. Usually a large portion of their pay package is incentive-based; the larger the ad they sell you, the more money they pocket.

Be aware of the common misleading pitch Yellow Pages salespeople make. They quote you the cost of your ad space in terms of x dollars per week, month, or day. "Think of the ad not as $12,000 per year, but only $32 per day." The problem is that you can't cancel your Yellow Pages ad in the middle of the year if it isn't working, if

business has fallen off for the season, or if you run into a cash flow problem. No matter how you are billed, you have purchased the ad space for one year. Think of it this way: your ad is permanently in the book for a period of one year, and it can't be removed mid-year!

Another common ploy Yellow Pages advertising people use is to offer to "assist you with the ad design." Oddly, the design concepts they recommend work best in the larger-size ads! And sometimes they even suggest that you place an ad under each of the several different categories your product or service relates to. Don't fall for this ploy!

Place one small ad under the single most promising category and test your results over the first year. Only if your results are good should you consider increasing your Yellow Pages exposure in future years.

☞ Testimonials

If you have a local service business, you may want to get feedback from noncompeting Yellow Pages advertisers in your category. You want to find out how their Yellow Pages advertising has worked out for them. You can do this by contacting advertisers that are not in your service area. If you don't have the numbers for such people, contact your trade association or ask one of your vendors. Don't ask a Yellow Pages sales representative for a referral.

You might also want to call each of the advertisers listed in your area book under your category. If more than a very small percentage of the phone numbers you try have been disconnected, think twice about placing an expensive ad in your Yellow Pages.

Streetwise Advice on Yellow Pages Ads

☞ **Test**

Advertising should be tested before you make a big commitment to a campaign or a large-size ad. Go light on your Yellow Pages advertising for the first year. If it really works for you, then consider placing a larger ad or expanding into ad spaces under multiple categories.

☞ **Other advertiser's ads**

Which Yellow Pages ads are working? You can't know for sure, but there is one way to be fairly confident.

Call up every advertiser in the category you are considering placing an ad in. See which firms quickly ask you how you heard about their business or where you saw their ad. Presto! This means the company is currently testing all of their advertising—and chances are this test procedure is an on-going policy and they tested last year as well.

Next, pull out your old phone books and see what type of ad they placed in that book. If their ad in last year's Yellow Pages is similar to this year's ad, then that ad is working for them. If this year's ad is larger, then the Yellow Pages have worked out terrifically for

them. If this year's is smaller, then they probably weren't pleased with the response.

☞ **Ad copy**

If you are having difficulty determining what ad copy to run in your Yellow Pages ad, follow one guideline. Be less experimental than you might be in other types of media ads. Remember, if the ad doesn't work, you can't change it until the following year.

Especially if you operate a service business, don't hesitate to run an ad that is similar to those being run by your successful competitors. Just don't copy their wording or ad format exactly! Keep in mind that a big ad is not necessarily indicative of a company's success or the success of their Yellow Pages advertising.

☞ **Buy advertising in one phone book first**

Unless you've got a ton of money to burn, try one Yellow Pages directory first, and measure results before advertising in additional directories. Service-based businesses especially should start with one directory first.

☞ **Keep it simple**

Don't cram too much information into a Yellow Pages ad or it won't attract people's attention. Have a strong headline that quickly gets your main selling point across.

"Advertising should be tested before you make a big commitment to a campaign or a large-size ad."

What is the best bet in Yellow Pages ads?

Before you spend a lot of money on large display ads in the Yellow Pages, start out by purchasing a small box in the basic listings column. Large display ads are very expensive and it would be foolish to commit to such an expenditure if you haven't tested the Yellow Pages medium before.

Small display ads tend to get lost. But a boxed listing in the basic listings column, believe it or not, is much less likely to be overlooked.

Should I pay extra for color?

While some Yellow Pages directories are now offering spot or even full process color, don't pay a nickel extra for it. Because the Yellow Pages are printed on yellow paper, the additional color doesn't give the same boost to an ad as it would on white stock. Even process color ads printed on glossy stock seem out of place in this utilitarian medium.

Yellow Pages ads seem expensive. How can I maximize the results?

You pay for the Yellow Pages every minute of the day, every day of the year, all year long. You will lose a lot of calls if you are only open during regular business hours—especially if you are in a service business. To counter this, and offset your ad expenses, set up a professional answering service during your off hours.

A good answering service will answer your phone in your name, sound professional, and allow you to pull in customers even when you are closed for business. You may want to have the answering service call you at home or beep you if the call is particularly important—an emergency towing request or emergency lock-out situation, for instance.

If you are feeling really, really cheap, just get an answering machine. But expect a lot of hang-ups that a good answering service might have converted into a sales opportunity.

Since the largest ads are placed first, isn't it important to take out a large ad?

No. If you haven't done a lot of Yellow Pages advertising you should be more concerned with staying in business and making money. Get some Yellow Pages experience under your belt before you go hog wild.

The first ads in any classification aren't the only ones that get results. A lot of individual as well as business consumers avoid calling companies that are advertised through large ad spaces because they feel that the products or services being offered are priced higher—perhaps to support higher advertising expenditures!

How can I be sure that my phone line won't be busy, without using call waiting or getting an expensive switchboard?

The phone company can provide you additional phone lines that do what is called "hunting." This means that you advertise only one phone number, but if that line is already in use the second incoming call will be automatically switched over to your unlisted phone line or lines.

Radio Advertising

Radio advertising offers you the opportunity to deliver a simple yet powerful message to a targeted group of consumers that may be interested in your product or service. You can write and produce the ad yourself with minimal effort and then identify those stations that best serve your market. If you are lucky, you might even find a popular radio DJ with a large following to take a personal interest in your product or service and deliver the message on air during his or her show. This will give an extra "endorsement" boost to your radio spot.

The cost of a fifteen-, thirty-, or sixty-second radio commercial will depend upon the frequency of the ad broadcast and the time of day that the announcement runs. Morning and evening drive times are usually more expensive than middle-of-the-day or late-night spots because the radio audience tends to peak during commuting hours.

The type of station you choose to advertise on should be determined by your target market. If you are looking to appeal to men between the ages of eighteen and thirty, for instance, you might want to consider advertising on an all-sports station or an FM rock station.

There are production costs to consider in addition to the spot expenditure. These will be determined by your need for music backgrounds, sound effects, and use of professional or amateur actors, such as yourself, to read your copy.

In general, since you know your product or service better than anyone else, you should write the copy yourself. Make sure you communicate the benefits of your product or service in such a way that listeners will immediately identify with your product.

Script for Radio Announcer

"I've been looking at some photographs that were touched up. And 'touched up' seems like such an inadequate term for what the folks at Take Two Photocrafts do with photographs. Let me give you a dramatic example. A family sits together for a portrait near the ocean. Unfortunately, when the picture was taken, two tourists ended up in the shot. When I looked at the picture after the folks at Take Two had dealt with it, the tourists were gone and only the family remained.

Now this family very much wanted a family portrait and this was the only time they were all together to take one. But the picture was spoiled because of the tourists. Take Two took them out. It's, well, I'd say it's magic but I happen to know it's technology, not magic. This business is amazing.

If you've got photographs that need touching up, that need someone added or someone taken out, if you've got photographs that are incomplete, cracked, or faded, you need to see the folks at Take Two.

Take Two Photocrafts at 202 Massachusetts Avenue in Arlington. Give them a call at 555-1274."

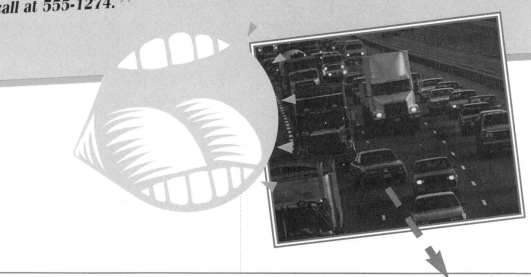

Radio Ad Success Story

Ewa Erdman, Vice President and Marketing Director, is one of the founders of *Take Two Photocraft*, a business that specializes in digital photo retouching and restoration. In the following excerpts she talks about a campaign her firm ran on a radio talk show.

The Announcer Is Key

66 We did a radio campaign. We found a host named Gene Burns, who I knew to be very interested in photography, and asked him to do commercials for us. We paid for sixty-second commercials, but he was so taken with the subject that the commercials usually ended up running for a minute and a half or even two minutes. All we did was to supply him with a photograph and its story—'This is my uncle Henry who came from Norway in 1917—this is what we did with the photo'—and he would just expound on it forever. 99

Repetition Is Important

66 Repetition over a period of time is important. Do a week, skip a week, do it again next week—but get both of those weeks in. Don't limit your advertising to one week. 99

👉 Critical mass

Radio is referred to by some advertising people as the "Cinderella medium." It can be spectacularly successful if everything clicks—the right offer, the right message, the right copy, the right stations. Or radio spots can fall on deaf ears.

Radio ads require repetition to work. A minimum run of at least fifteen ads on one station during a one-week period is recommended. Furthermore, if your entire advertising run on a particular station will be less than sixty spots during a month, try to keep the ads within a particular time slot. This way you will reach the same listening audience during each spot or often enough to create an awareness and ideally a desire to buy or inquire about your product or service. If your spots run on an erratic schedule, you might reach the full listenership of the station but you won't be reaching any one group of individuals often enough to motivate them to take action.

A great way to zero in on the same people and have added impact is to buy a sponsorship of a daily feature, such as a news or sports broadcast. A sponsorship guarantees your ad will run at a particular time and typically affords you a brief "sponsored by" message in addition to your ad spot.

👉 Errors and rip-offs

New advertisers are often suspicious as to whether or not their ads have run correctly or even run at all. Advertising salespeople respond by saying "No need to worry, our ads are recorded in our operating log as required by the FCC. To not run an ad would violate the law."

Don't believe the salespeople for a minute. One of the very largest Boston radio shows was subject to a major scandal a few years back because they were skipping clients' ads on a regular basis, logging the spots and billing the clients as if all of their spots had run as per contract.

While skipped ads are fairly uncommon, they can happen—and happen to you. What is a lot more common, however, is an unsatisfactory ad presentation. This is most likely to occur if all or part of the ad is read by on-air talent.

For example, in running a series of ads that included changing short live taglines on six major radio stations, I discovered that only one station read the ad correctly. Most made significant errors in the live taglines. Some actually skipped the tagline altogether. Some ran the wrong ad on the wrong day. One station even ran half of the recorded version of an ad, abruptly cutting it off midway through the spot.

You need to monitor your ads to assure that you are getting your money's worth of exposure. And don't hesitate to demand free spots, called make-goods, for significant goofs.

👉 Roadblocks

If your audience is fairly general and you have successfully tested radio ads on one station, you may want to consider running ads on many stations at the same time. The practice of airing television or radio ads on several stations simultaneously is called a roadblock. The advantages of this strategy are that you get multiple exposure, reach those people who frequently switch stations, and are more likely to benefit from word-of-mouth or viewers talking you up after the ads have run.

Streetwise Advice on Radio Ads

I once did roadblock advertising in the Boston marketplace and saw newsstand sales of a local magazine I was publishing almost double during a two-week period. I also saw the sales slide back toward their former level about a month after the ads stopped running.

As the results of my campaign show, radio ads tend to work best for advertisers who can concentrate a lot of money in one marketplace, with heavy concentration over an extended period of time.

☞ ## Let's make a deal

The real fun in radio advertising is negotiating rates. Try to wait until a slow season, then call every station that meets your demographics. Tell them either how much money you are considering spending on their station or how many spots you intend to place. Also tell them nicely, but firmly, that you are only going to run ads on the station or stations that give you the best rate deals. Get one or more of them to show you their ratings book, ideally from Arbitron, and compare how many people in your target audience they will be reaching.

Get all of the bids from each station. Then call each station back and say you still haven't decided which station to choose, and can't they do any better?

If you choose a slow time of year and are persistent but pleasant with people, you should be able to negotiate rates that are even lower than the those paid by large national advertisers that buy huge blocks of advertising time.

You will be amazed to see how much less than the published rate card price you can buy radio time for. You will also note that, from radio station to radio station, there is an enormous difference in the station's willingness to negotiate.

For example, a Boston station, which normally sold morning drive ad spots at $150 per second, sold me a package deal costing only $10 per spot. What you should typically expect through negotiating, however, is half the published rate. If you can do this, you are doing great!

"Radio is referred to by some advertising people as the 'Cinderella medium.' It can be spectacularly successful if everything clicks—the right offer, the right message, the right copy, the right stations. Or radio spots can fall on deaf ears."

Questions & Answers about Radio Ads

Should I let the radio station create my ads?

No. You are better off writing the ads yourself, even if you have never listened to the radio. You know your product or service best, and, more im-portantly, you know why people buy it.

Can I run an ad I create on only one station or can I run the same ad on many?

Most radio stations will allow you to run an ad that you have created in the studios of other stations. But you should get permission to do so in advance. Preferably, you should get this permission when you are still negotiating your deal with the radio station for advertising rates.

I need last-minute tips for writing my own ad.

Take one or two key selling features of your product or service and blast them repeatedly during the ad spot. Restate them slightly each time. You don't need a fancy advertising jingle. Also, stay away from humorous copy. It is extremely difficult to get humor to work in an ad.

Should I go live or use prerecorded spots?

If your audience really likes the on-air talent and the on-air talent especially likes your product or service, you may want to consider using live spots. Otherwise, don't. Radio stations have enough trouble airing prerecorded spots correctly, let alone live ones.

Should I be concerned if a broadcaster makes fun of my ad?

Amazingly, many on-air people do make fun of the advertising they present or run during their shows, even though this very same advertising provides their living. Oddly, however, the effect of their sarcastic, ironic, or otherwise deprecating remarks is often positive. It tends to make the ad more memorable.

However, there is often the occasion when you may feel that a negative impact has been created. Swallow your pride and try to weigh the impact rationally. Ask other people for their opinion of the "funny" comments. If you still feel that the comments really hurt the ad, then ask the station for a "make-good" or free advertising space.

Television Advertising

*T*elevision advertising provides a very powerful vehicle for delivering a message about your product or service to the widest audience possible. The visual impact of video simply has a great ability to capture and hold the audience—more so than the more static mediums of print or audio media.

Although it may seem like a daunting task, you can write and produce your own commercial at a television studio, or at a local college or high school that has an audio-visual department. The costs of producing a fifteen-, thirty-, or sixty-second television spot will vary depending upon the sets, special effects, talent, equipment, and crew necessary to pull off your concept.

The cost for placing a television ad depends upon the type of station, the time of day your ad airs, and the ad run frequency. Station types, in order of expense, include UHF, VHF, and local cable access. When determining which time slot to place your ads in, consider any documentaries, features, or sporting events with local content that cater specifically to an audience that would be interested in your product or service.

Remember that the frequency of your ads is as important as the time of day they air. Running your commercial once or twice a week, for example, is unlikely to generate any response at all.

Sample Television Ad

Float in and unwind at The Blue Cloud Cafe. Located in the downtown atrium, The Blue Cloud is the perfect spot for lunch or dinner—whether you've spent a pleasant day browsing the shops or have just been let loose from a very intense strategy session.

Our own Paula Merlot is an award-winning Cordon Bleu chef. The delectable menu she has designed for the Blue Cloud Cafe ranges from our tropical Lime Isle Chicken Stew to our celestial Star Fruit Sorbet with Blue Curaçao sauce. Or consider trying one of our daily specials featuring local produce. And don't forget to sample a selection from our extensive wine list.

Savor the flavors at The Blue Cloud Cafe today.

The Blue Cloud Cafe
The Atrium, 1st Floor
Boise
555-3969

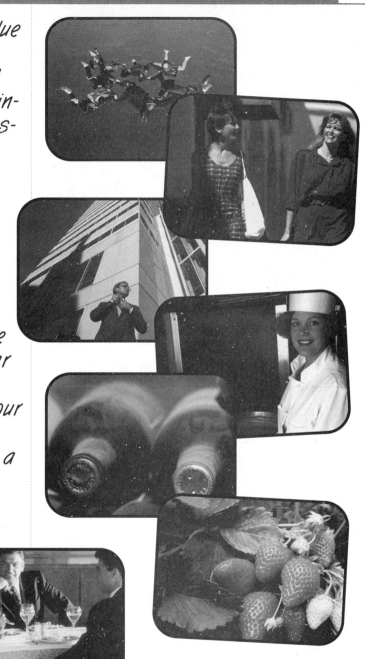

Note: This sample is fictitious.

☞ Too expensive?

I remember reading a quote from a senior executive at McGraw-Hill, a multibillion dollar media firm, saying that "television advertising is too rich for our blood." Well, television is too rich for just about anyone's blood. The cost of television advertising is usually much higher than radio and newspapers, and if you are going to spring for television, you need a product and message that really requires the drama only the medium of television can impart.

Remember too, that a good television ad can be very expensive to produce. Of course you can do your own talking-head ad and be your own star, but these "home-grown" ads are often laughed at by viewers. The quality of the presentation will contrast sharply, and negatively, against the slick nationals spots produced by Madison Avenue agencies.

Most of us have a secret desire to be television stars. If you decide to be the main attraction in your own commercial, make sure you are doing it for a rational, not an emotional rea-son. I once decided to do my own television advertisements. I believed that I was being rational, but on closer review, I wonder if my decision had anything to do with the fact that my fifth-year business school reunion was happening at the same time! The spots proved ineffective in comparison to the radio spots I later ran.

☞ The role of television

Remember, television is generally better than most other mediums for image advertising. It isn't a particularly great venue for price advertising. It is just not as well suited to directly leading people to buy or inquire about your product or service as other mediums such as newspapers or direct mail.

National advertisers, for example, generally use television for image advertising. They sometimes combine a television awareness-building campaign with local price advertising in other media. Typically, local dealers and distributors will place the price advertisements in local papers, but the financing will be provided by the national concern. For instance, an automobile manufacturer may run a heavy national television advertising schedule promoting features of a new luxury car without divulging its cost. At the same time, local dealerships may be running newspaper ads that feature a reduced-price offer on the same luxury car.

For a local business, television may be a good add-on medium if used to enhance the impact of price advertising in other mediums. But most of your advertising budget should be expended on newspaper, radio, or direct mail exposure. Small-budget advertisers should skip television altogether.

☞ Frequency

Television has more impact than radio, so fewer spots will still suffice in this medium. A minimum of five spots on one station during a week's period of time is recommended. If possible, air fifteen spots on a less popular and expensive program—this will ensure that you are making a solid impact on your audience.

☞ Local cable

For local businesses, local cable may be a viable option. The costs are still low in this television venue. And you can really zero in on a specific town or group of towns. Plus, cable subscribers typically have more disposable cash than nonsubscribers.

Can I save money by using short ad spots such as ten- or twenty-second airings?

No. You shouldn't run less than thirty-second spots. Otherwise, it will be very difficult to have an impact. Short spots are best used for conveying simple messages such as promoting name recognition for a heavily advertised national brand of detergent.

What about longer ad spots, such as sixty-second ones?

Conventional wisdom holds that you are better off with standard thirty-second spots. Your money will disappear a lot quicker with sixty-second spots. However, if you are trying to sell a product, not a service, and are airing a direct response number for immediate action, sixty-second spots may work out better for you. In fact, many direct response television advertisers purchase large chunks of viewing time—sometimes a half hour or more—in which to pitch their products.

Can talking heads be effective?

Yes. Just watching a person on television can work. But this is not necessarily a good use of television. If this is your approach, mix in some video of your product being used or video of consumers shopping at your place of business. Otherwise you may be wasting the medium, and might just as effectively convey your message through radio or print advertising.

Is the cost of television time as negotiable as that of radio time?

Pricing for advertising time on local, major market, or national television networks can be negotiated. But there is less price flexibility than is found in radio—especially in national network and major market television.

Television generally sells fewer ad slots than radio. And major market television stations carry a lot of network advertising, as well as advertising purchased directly in specific markets for national advertisers. Also, there are fewer major broadcast television stations in major markets than there are radio stations.

However, you will find a lot of room for negotiating ad rates with cable television networks. This is particularly true if the station has a lot of "excess inventory" or unsold spots.

Outdoor and Transit Advertising

Outdoor advertising, such as billboards, transit ads, or taxi tops are probably not a great advertising choice for small local businesses.

While outdoor ads are seen by huge numbers of people, these people are less likely to lead people to take immediate action. If you are trying to motivate a purchase in a relatively quick time frame, you should use radio, newspaper, or direct mail advertising.

Outdoor advertising is used by larger companies as one component among the many that comprise their multimedia national advertising campaigns.

However, outdoor ads may work for some local businesses in certain situations. For example, many new car dealers reinforce or announce their presence in an area marketplace by advertising on billboards that are located near their place of business.

Streetwise Advice on Outdoor Ads

☞ Support

Despite what the sales representatives for outdoor and transit ads may say, the strongest role of this medium is as a reinforcement for an already heavily advertised message. Conceptually, outdoor and transit advertising seems very strong. The cost per viewer would seem to be very low. Especially in the case of mass transit ads, in which a rider may have nothing better to do but stare at your advertisement for an hour, it would seem like the perfect venue for guaranteeing maximum impact for your message.

However, transit advertising for my local Boston magazine didn't work at all. And it doesn't appear to work well for other product and service advertisers either—unless they are advertising outdoors in conjunction with running the same campaign message in other media.

☞ Target the subconscious

While people see many transit and outside ads, sometimes for extended periods of time, many do everything imaginable to avoid focusing on these types of ads. Think about it. Have you ever seen anyone writing down a phone number from an ad displayed in a subway car? Have you ever seen anyone pull over to study a highway billboard?

So, if you are using this venue, keep the message short and simple and reinforce it through print, radio, direct mail, or television advertising. Use outdoor and transit ads to cement brand awareness in the viewer's subconscious mind. A chewing gum or a soft drink, for instance, could profit from these mediums.

☞ Short and sweet

If you do decide to run outdoor or transit ads, keep the message very, very short. Keep it catchy or cute to make it memorable. Remember, these ads work best when they are working on the subconscious.

☞ Check them

No matter how busy you may be, go out and check on your outdoor and transit advertising.

In running subway ads I became suspicious when, due to lack of any results, that my placards might not be riding the train, as paid for, along with tens of thousands of commuters every day. I took myself down to a station and hopped on and off arriving subway cars for the better part of two hours. In this brief period of time I made an educated guess that only half of my ads had been placed. I complained to the transit advertising sales firm which held an exclusive contract with the transit authority, Not surprisingly, they informed me that my determination had to be inaccurate and that this situation had no precedent. My answer—maybe no one else had counted their signs before! Finally, the transit advertising sales firm installed additional placards for me and doubled the time period of my exposure at no additional charge.

"The best advertising is free advertising."

Freebies

The best advertising is free advertising. If you choose a slow period of the year, your outdoor or transit ads may be left up for an additional period of time if the space has not been sold. Don't hesitate to ask or negotiate for a double run at a single rate cost if you are advertising in an off-sales period.

It doesn't cost outdoor and transit advertising firms anything extra to leave your advertising up over an extended period time if the space is unsold. The labor costs are a one-shot deal. So, pricing for these types of ads tends to be highly negotiable. Give it your best shot!

Repetition

For outdoor ads, repetition is important. You are generally better off buying lots of coverage for short periods of time, rather than fewer boards for longer periods of time. But as always, try to test, test, test, first!

"If you do decide to run outdoor or transit ads, keep the message very, very short. Keep it catchy or cute to make it memorable. Remember, these ads work best when they are working on the subconscious."

PROTECT YOUR WEALTH.
BUY OUR HEALTH.

HealthShield Medical Care Programs
(800) 555-5555

Note: This sample is fictitious.

Question & Answers about Outdoor Ads

For what time segments do advertisers typically buy transit or outdoor ad spaces?

Transit ads often run for periods as short as one week. They can run two weeks, one month, or longer. Keep in mind that after a period of time the effect of a transit ad wears off. Successful transit advertisers typically skip periods of time between ads.

Outdoor billboard space is generally sold by the month, although some particularly desirable, and often expensive, locations are sold by the week.

Should I produce my own transit or outdoor ad?

You should develop the concept and work up a scaled-down version with a freelance designer or your usual ad agency. Then locate a firm that specializes in producing outdoor and transit ads to handle the final ad construction.

When I ran transit ads, I designed and typeset the ad at reduced scale. I took the artwork to a transit ad production house and they enlarged my artwork and produced the signage using silk screening.

Can I put up my own billboard?

This can be a great idea. If you don't have suitable property, negotiate to place a billboard with someone who does. This is what billboard companies do. They certainly don't own the land or buildings on which they display.

Putting up your own billboard will require a fair bit of effort, however. Make sure the savings warrant any losses that might occur as a result of time spent away from running your business.

And, remember, even though you may have permission from a property owner to place your outdoor display, chances are you also need approval from the local zoning board.

What small businesses will billboards work best for?

Roadside service businesses such as restaurants and motels will benefit from the use of billboards. If travel-related services are your business, billboards may even be the only advertising vehicle that you need to use. If you are a lodging provider, however, temper your sales expectations of walk-in trade. Today, most travelers reserve rooms in advance at national chains and are not susceptible to billboards they may see in transit.

What kind of sales can I expect from a billboard ad?

Except for some specialized businesses that have immediate appeal to motorists, you can expect to attribute between very little and zero sales to a billboard ad. Billboards function best for image advertising or as reinforcement for messages being carried in other media. Don't expect billboards to be sales generators.

Ten common and costly advertising mistakes of small business owners

1 Not tracking results

2 Not continually testing new ad media, new ad copy, and new ad offers

3 Advertising evenly throughout the year rather than concentrating the effort for more impact

4 Not choosing the ad media that is most effective for the target market and product or service being offered

5 Not continually emphasizing the business' "unique selling proposition"

6 Failing to create a distinctive and consistent "look and feel" for their advertising

7 Failing to develop exciting promotions or events to maximize advertising impact

8 Not promoting separately and aggressively to current and past customers

9 Listening to advertising salespeople

10 Emphasizing product features instead of benefits to the customer

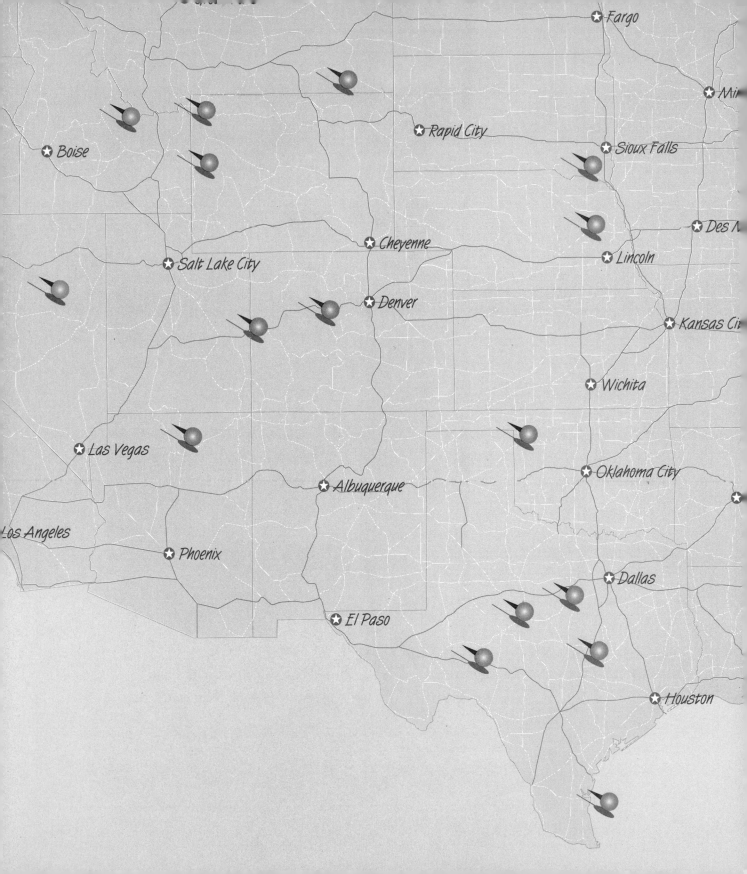

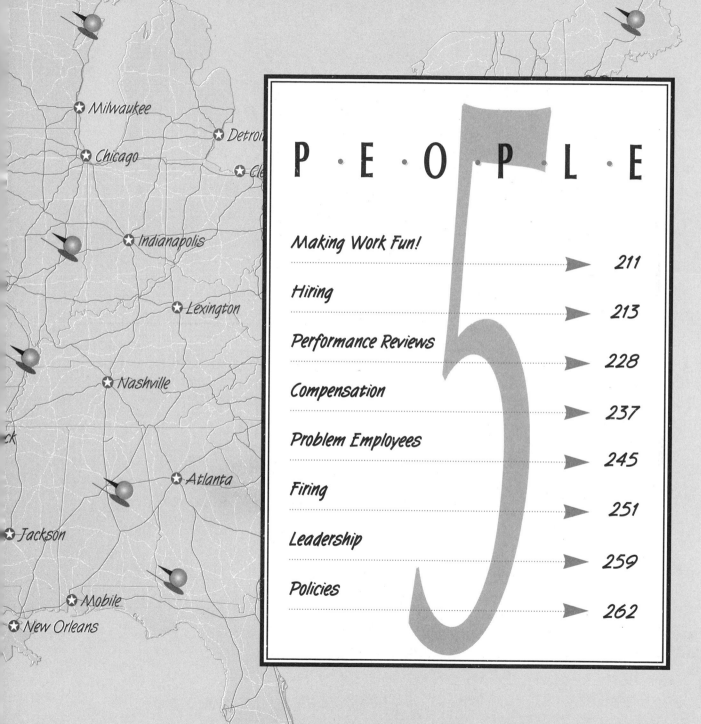

P·E·O·P·L·E

Making Work Fun! ▶ 211

Hiring ▶ 213

Performance Reviews ▶ 228

Compensation ▶ 237

Problem Employees ▶ 245

Firing ▶ 251

Leadership ▶ 259

Policies ▶ 262

5

Milwaukee

Detroit

Chicago

Cleveland

Indianapolis

Lexington

Nashville

Atlanta

Jackson

Mobile

New Orleans

Miami

*J*ust because other businesses are boring, stale, routine places to work doesn't mean that your business has to be too. Make work fun, exciting, and challenging for your employees. You'll find you have less turnover, happier people, and more productivity, and you might have more fun, too!

Making Work Fun!

Fair and consistent

1 Make sure that every employee in the company is treated equally. Supervisors in particular should see to it that employees know where they stand at all times, and how things are going with the company as a whole.

Challenge people

2 Try not to create jobs that consist of constant repetition with few variations. In every job definition include responsibilities in which the employee is likely to encounter situations in which he or she will have to tackle new problems or device new solutions for his or her tasks almost every day.

Give people input

3 Really listen to everyone's ideas. If your employees know that either you or their supervisors are taking them seriously, they are more likely to make contributions to your company—from simple good work habits to the development of new products or procedures.

Company outings

4 Organize regularly scheduled company lunches at local restaurants. And don't spend this "lunch hour" discussing business!

Celebrate victories

5 After a big sale, landing a new client, or the wrap-up of a successful project, gather everyone together for a celebration that marks the event as special.

Serve refreshments and use the opportunity to create an atmosphere of upbeat morale among your employees. Make sure everyone is aware of what is being celebrated!

Make the workplace interesting

6 Try a noontime concert series. Invite local musicians to perform outdoors during the summer or in a large conference room during the winter months. Keep using your "social" imagination to promote a team feeling among your employees.

Team sports

7 Organize an ongoing program of informal athletic competition. Play softball in the spring or summer, and sponsor indoor activities like bowling or basketball in the winter.

Praise people frequently

Showing appreciation for your employees is the best way to instill goodwill and a sense of fun among your employees. When it is time to be critical, don't pull any punches. But when the opportunity presents itself to tell someone what a terrific job he or she is doing—don't pass it up!

Hiring

The caliber of people who work for your company will arguably have more impact on the success of your company than any other factor. The easiest way to create a terrific work force is to hire terrific people in the first place. While you may never seem to have the time to hire people carefully, I suggest you do whatever it takes, even if you skimp on time spent on other pressing chores, to make sure you give hiring the effort it deserves.

1 Receiving resumes

You should start the screening process with a good quantity of candidates. Ideally you should have at least twelve applicants that meet the basic qualifications. Often, when conducting a thorough search for an important position, you may examine several hundred resumes. The more resumes you start your hiring process with, the better the chance you will have of finding the right candidate for the job.

At this point the hiring process may be thought of as the base of the pyramid because you have more potential candidates now than you will at any other time during the hiring process.

2 First resume sort

You should begin sorting through resumes immediately. Sort them from weakest potential to strongest. Your first pass at sorting resumes should be effective but shouldn't take up an inordinate amount of your time.

To successfully proceed through the pyramid hiring process you need to spend minimal time eliminating weaker candidates and invest more time weighing the subtle differences between stronger candidates.

Completing the first resume sort places you higher on the pyramid and closer to offering the position to a qualified applicant.

3 Second resume sort

Take a second look at your candidates from the first sort. Again, quickly eliminate the weak candidates and focus on developing a list of strong candidates.

4 Phoners

When you call the candidates from your second resume sort, conduct a brief phone interview in order to determine whether or not to arrange an in-person interview.

Phone interviews are great timesavers. You don't have to tell the candidate how long the phone interview will last. If you decide two minutes into the interview that the person isn't suitable for the position there isn't any need to pretend an interest for some promised time.

Go to the heart of the matter quickly. Even if a salary range was clearly stated in any position advertisements, confirm with the candidate that the pay scale is acceptable to him or her. If it isn't, say thank you and goodbye. Neither your time nor the time of the potential candidate has been wasted.

The "pyramid" hiring process

The next set of questions might revolve around any concerns you have about the candidate's qualifications based on his or her resume. If the interview goes well, you could possibly spend an hour or more on the phone with the candidate. If it goes unusually well, invite the candidate in for an interview. If it goes only pretty well, wait until you finish conducting all of your phone interviews before deciding whether or not to see the candidate in person.

5 In-person interviews

In-person interviews are invariably time consuming. Be cautious about how many candidates you invite in even for first interviews. Three to six candidates is generally a good number. If the position isn't very demanding or doesn't require extensive skills or vast experience, you may be able to select the candidate you will offer the position to from your first in-person interviews. If not, narrow the field down to those few people you'd like to invite in for a second interview.

6 Additional interviews

For most professional positions you will conduct two rounds of interviews. Be even more selective about who gets invited back for a second interview than you were in choosing the candidates for the first in-person interviews. Usually two people make it to the second interview stage. Sometimes only one person is invited for a second interview—the person the job is generally offered to.

Usually it is during the second interviewing round that additional people are called to interview the candidate or candidates. These are often people who would most likely interact closely with the applicant, should he or she be hired.

Final word

Remember that you want to spend as little time possible eliminating the weakest candidates. More time should be expended on discerning the subtle differences between your strong candidates—looking for those special experiences or skill sets that can make one qualified candidate really stand out from another qualified candidate.

"You want to spend minimal time screening out the weakest candidates and maximum time comparing the more subtle differences between the strongest candidates."

Attracting Quality Candidates

As someone who must manage every aspect of your business, you have precious little time to waste in finding quality employees. However, you can find top-notch talent by doing some work up front. Pick two or three critical areas of expertise that you absolutely require in the successful candidate. When you do your first and second resume sorts, look for candidates that possess good qualifications in those areas. Set aside all others.

Still, it can be a real chore to sort through a pile of resumes. Your selection process will go much quicker if you avoid being swayed by great layouts, fancy type styles, or glorious job titles. Look for concrete accomplishments and proven ability that matches your needs.

In today's job market it isn't hard to find a pool of qualified applicants for any type of position—entry level to senior management—in almost every field. In fact, you can save yourself time and money by utilizing old and new methods of locating applicants.

Help-wanted advertising

Help-wanted advertising is the most effective way to reach job seekers. Even people who may not be actively engaged in a job search but who would change jobs for the right opportunity can be found through the job classifieds.

Internal referrals

If you have already been successful at attracting top-caliber talent, ask these employees for referrals. Chances are, they know someone currently seeking employment who may be a good fit for your company and for the open position. As an added incentive, offer bonuses to your employees if one of their referrals is hired.

Employment agencies

Employment agencies usually work on a fee-per-placement basis, and are more interested in moving bodies than finding the most qualified candidate for your opening. They are cheaper than search firms but don't provide the same in-depth level of recruiting or interviewing capability.

College placement offices

College placement offices help alumni with job placement and provide a free listing service to employers seeking job applicants. They are also great places to check if you are looking for temporary or summer help.

Trade associations

You can usually post job openings with the trade association that represents your industry. Trade association members are more likely to possess the job experience you are looking for, and some candidates may even have knowledge of your particular company.

Executive search firms

Executive search firms typically cater to Fortune 500 companies seeking six-figure-salary executives. Some search firms will take a small business client if the company has a recognizable need for a senior-level manager. Remember, however, that search firms charge exorbitant fees. Unless you have a pressing need to attract a high-powered executive, stick with other methods of finding job candidates.

Internet/World Wide Web

More and more companies of all sizes are hiring for professional positions through ads on the World Wide Web, such as on Adams JobBank Online. In fact, at this time, Adams JobBank Online allows hiring companies to place up to 200 professional job openings on its Web site for free. For more information, call (617) 767-8100. (Adams JobBank Online is a division of Adams Media Corporation.)

Creating a Classified Job Advertisement

① Job title is important

A job title alone can produce responses. Choose one that reflects the most important overall responsibility of the position.

② Be specific

Avoid generalizations when you create classified job advertisements, or you may attract resumes that don't match your hiring needs.

③ Key job requirements

Focus on two or three key responsibilities and summarize them in one short sentence.

④ Concise background

Knowledge, skill, and experience requirements should be carefully thought out and conveyed precisely to discourage unqualified applicants from applying.

⑤ Use bullets

If you have a sizable list of responsibilities or background requirements, use bullets to make your job description easier to read. Bullets can also make your classified ad more noticeable.

⑥ Use words sparingly

Be concise. Ads can cost a lot of money. They should contain no more than three short sentences, including the company name, address, and fax number.

OFFICE MANAGER ①

Consulting Firm seeks Office Manager to manage accounting, inventory, and purchasing support. ③ Good salary and potential in rapidly growing company. Send resume to: HSS, 289 Spring Road, First Floor, Parkton, MD 44925

DESKTOP PUBLISHING

Moonscape Design, Inc. has a full-time opening in their Graphic Communications Department. ② Experience required in

- Windows & DOS
- QuarkXpress
- Ventura Publisher ⑤
- Corel Draw
- F3 ProDesigner
- Business forms
- Complex paste-ups

Great benefits. Send resume and salary requirements to RS34 Lemon Lane, Fogtown, VT 02222

MANUFACTURING ENGINEER

CaveTronics has an opening for a hands-on, methodical individual to design and modify manufacturing processes and tooling for sub-sea-level shop. Two to four years manufacturing engineering and electronics experience required. ④ Mail resume to CaveTronics, 101 Underhill Way, Thornrock, NM 12345

Note: These ads are fictitious.

Ten Good, Basic Interview Questions

Tell me about yourself

1 As a hiring manager, you are looking for the applicant to go beyond his or her resume and share some background that will give you an indication of whether or not the person can handle the job. How organized is the applicant's thought process? What does the applicant value about himself or herself? You should not be looking for a programmed response—just something that will give you a sign that the candidate is focused and can articulate his or her strengths in a concise manner.

Describe your ideal job

2 You should be on the alert if the "dream job" the candidate is describing is not in sync with past positions. There must be a close tie-in between what candidates did in their last jobs and what they want to do in their next jobs. There must also be some logical progression which indicates that the candidate has thought out what he or she wants to do based on the skills and abilities he or she has to offer.

Tell me about a measurable outcome that resulted from one of your efforts

3 Ask the candidate to give you an answer that provides details in terms of numbers and/or specific accomplishments that have some measurement value attached to it. The candidate should be able to cite examples such as reducing costs by 47 percent or increasing revenues by 60 percent. You, as the hiring manager, must probe to find out exactly how the candidate actually accomplished these feats within his or her job.

What are your strengths?

4 Is the candidate honest with himself or herself and with the people that he or she deals with? This is a measurable area because you are looking for specific tools the candidate possesses in order to do a particular job. You are looking at how the candidate applies his or her skills to their job. Also, does the candidate have a realistic view of what he or she can offer you in terms of effectively fulfilling the responsibilities of the position you are offering?

Where do you want to be in five years?

5 There is no way anyone can predict accurately where he or she is going to be in five years. But you, as the hiring manager, want the candidate to give some strong evidence of having thought out where he or she would like to be within your industry during the next five years. Job titles aren't necessarily important. What is important is having some reasonable expectations for the maintenance of or increase in duties and responsibilities in respect to their current career path. The answer to this question will provide a strong indicator of whether or not the candidate really wants to be in your industry or on the same career path he or she is currently on.

Ten Good, Basic Interview Questions

6. What is the most creative or innovative thing you have done?

Does the candidate have creative flair? Will this person's style work well in your environment? As a hiring manager, you must determine how the candidate goes about creating output and how his or her style is similar to or different from the way your company approaches the creative process.

7. What sets you apart from the crowd?

Ask the candidates to enumerate skills that make them unique and attractive. If a company had a large pool of talent from which to choose, what qualities would make that candidate appealing? Does he or she have intangible abilities that may not tie directly into the job being offered, but that could be attractive to you and your company or department at some future time? If the candidate can cite only the standard abilities that would enable someone to satisfactorily handle current needs, consider whether or not this would have a flat or negative impact on your company's' future.

8. What are your weaknesses?

Is the candidate realistic in terms of what he or she cannot offer you in the way of basic skills and abilities? Where does the candidate fall down on the job? Is the weakness legitimate or a canned response used to avoid dealing with an actual weakness? Are these weaknesses serious enough to hamper your company's or department's effectiveness?

9. Why are you ready to leave your current job?

As the hiring manager, you should try to find out early on why the candidate wants to leave their present position. Has the candidate been difficult to work with? Is there a productivity or attitude problem? Is the candidate unsure of his or her career choice? Although it is becoming common for workers to change jobs frequently, it is doubly important to determine why any candidate is seeking to leave a current employer if he or she has held the position only for a relatively short period of time. In all cases, you must be convinced that the candidate has a legitimate reason for wanting to leave the present job. You must feel fairly certain that the candidate will not pull out of your company in the same manner should you decide to hire him or her.

10. What are your salary goals and expectations?

Ideally, you want to qualify a salary or remuneration range before you bring candidates in for formal interviews. Make sure that the candidate has realistic expectations of what the job pays. Do not deviate from your salary range unless the candidate is truly exceptional. Determine not only what the candidate's expectations regarding salary are now but what they will be in the future. Are these expectations in keeping with your ideas on what to offer for this position and in the future?

Keeping Hiring Legal

In the United States federal law prohibits employers from discriminating among job candidates on the basis of race, color, national origin, religion, sex, physical handicap, or age. In some states or localities additional characteristics, such as sexual orientation, may also be prohibited from entering into the hiring equation.

While the actual law seems straightforward, court interpretations have more narrowly defined what constitutes discriminatory hiring practices. Even questions that negatively affect a protected class of applicants may be, and often have been, deemed illegal.

As a rule of thumb, job interview questions should focus specifically on the applicant's ability to successfully perform those tasks required in order to effectively carry out the duties inherent to the position being applied for.

Help-wanted ads

Advertising for job openings must be clearly nondiscriminatory. For example, an ad reading "Strong warehouseman able to lift 100-pound boxes all day long" is blatantly discriminatory against women who may be able to carry out the warehousing function described. An ad that reads "College students sought for summer house painting work" is illegal because there is no reason why a person needs to be a college student to paint a house.

Keeping records

You must kccp applications from all position inquiries on file for a period of one year if you have solicited those applications. You should also keep records of the criteria you used to select candidates and the reason why rejected candidates were not offered the position.

Remember

As a business owner you are responsible for all of the hiring practices of all of your managers. You need to make sure that they

- understand the law
- are careful to write nondiscriminatory help-wanted ads
- don't ask illegal questions during the interview
- and give full and fair consideration to all candidates.

Just Don't Ask

*T*he illegal questions that follow may not be asked in any form—not in person, not on an application form. These do not constitute all of the possible illegal questions that could be asked by an employer, but they are the more common illegal questions that are posed.

Just don't ask ...

Some Illegal Questions	Whom These Questions Primarily Discriminate Against
• Are you married?	Women
• Do you have children?	Women
• How old are you?	People 40 years of age and over. You may ask the applicant if they are less than eighteen years of age in order to maintain compliance with federal, state, or local child labor laws.
• Did you graduate from high school or college?	Minorities with minimal educational opportunities. An educational degree should not be a job requirement unless successful performance requires a specific level of education.
• Have you ever been arrested?	Minorities whose ethnic group, as a whole, has a higher-than-average crime rate. You are well advised to avoid questions regarding infractions of the law, even felonies, unless a conviction would be unusually relevant to the position being applied for.
• How much do you weigh?	Women and minorities, or anyone who is overweight.
• What country are you from, are you a U.S. citizen, or what is your native language?	People of different national origins, or people who lack. citizenship but are legally qualified to work in the United States.
• Are you physically challenged?	The physically challenged. Employers are required to make an effort to accommodate the needs of physically challenged employees.

WESTFORT CORPORATION

354 Sidewinder Place • Boise • Idaho 87554 • 208-555-5555 • 208-555-5550 Fax

August 26, 1996 ◄ **1**

Mr. John Smith
123 Mountain View Lane ◄ **2**
Boise, Idaho 87554

Dear Mr Smith, ◄ **3**

We hereby extend to you an offer of full-time employment as a Senior Project
Manager here at Westfort Corporation. Your first date of employment will be ◄ **4**
September 16, 1996.

Your compensation will be $2,543.67, payable every two weeks in arrears. ◄ **5**
Paychecks are distributed on alternate Thursdays for the two-week period
ending on the preceding Sunday.

Your first salary review will take place on September 10, 1997. Pay increases ◄ **6**
are based on merit as well as the financial situation of the company at the
time of the performance review.

The first ninety days of your employment will be regarded as an initial ◄ **7**
employment period. After successful completion of this period, you will be eligible for sick days, which accrue at the rate of 1/2 day per month.

The company offers medical insurance, group life insurance, and short- and
long-term disability as well as two weeks paid vacation per year. You will be
eligible for the company's 401K plan and bonus plan after you complete your
initial period of employment.

Please sign and return this agreement. This offer will remain in force for a ◄ **8**
period not to exceed fourteen days.

_____
John Smith

_____
Jane Jones
Human Resources Manager

Job Offer Letter

① Date
This should be the date you wrote and mailed the offer letter to the candidate you have chosen to hire. It is the first typewritten information to appear below the printed letterhead.

② Addressee
The addressee is the person you are making the job offer to. His or her name and address should be spaced one line down from the date, flush left in alignment with the date.

③ Salutation
Although you have, most likely, become very familiar with the person to whom you are making the job offer, it is still very appropriate to open the letter as formally as possible.

④ Opening
The opening paragraph should be used to make the formal offer of employment. It should include pertinent job information such as job title and the start date for the position.

⑤ Compensation
The second paragraph of the letter should state the prospective new hire's salary in either monthly or weekly terms. Indicate when the candidate can expect to receive his or her first check, as well as any other important pay distribution information.

⑥ Salary Review
In the third paragraph indicate when the candidate can expect his or her first salary review. Make sure the new hire understands how pay increases are determined at your company.

⑦ Benefits
Close out the body of the letter by stating the terms of eligibility for benefits and listing those benefits the employee will be entitled to once he or she has successfully completed the initial employment period.

⑧ Agreement signatures
In conclusion, you need to request and provide a space for the candidate to sign his or her name to the letter indicating acceptance of the offer. A time period for signing and returning the letter should be given.

A company representative, yourself or perhaps the Human Resources director, should also sign the letter.

Hiring Success Story

Betsy Tomlinson, of *Tomlinson Associates*, has extensive experience recruiting, interviewing, and hiring people for various positions and businesses. She stresses the importance of hiring the right people and gives some tips on the interview process.

Every Hire Is Important

"I think in a small business every single hire that you make is critical. Even the receptionist is a key person—after all, he or she is the first person everyone who walks in the door needs to see. In terms of chemistry, personality, professionalism—in terms of the dynamics of the organization—every single person that you hire is going to be very important."

Ask Specific Questions

"I get very specific with people on the phone. The first thing I want to know is, 'Are you currently working?' If not, I want to know why he or she left his or her last employment."

Get References

"References are absolutely vital. The problem today is that most people are afraid to give references because they fear a lawsuit."

Streetwise Advice on Hiring

☞ Best candidate

Be careful to hire the best candidate for the job—not merely the most talented job seeker. In other words, just because somebody has a more polished-looking resume or is more articulate at the job interview doesn't mean that he or she is necessarily a better worker. Some people, for example, become very good at job hunting because they or their employers are never happy about their work!

☞ References

Be leery of putting too much weight on positive references. Virtually everyone has some positive references. Sometimes people even give positive references for people they have fired because they fear legal action, want to get them off unemployment because their company is indirectly paying for it, or just want to "help out" the job candidate.

☞ Second interviews

Conduct at least two interviews with a candidate before hiring him or her, especially if the position is very important. Candidates often relax and let their guard down somewhat during a second interview. This will give you a chance to "meet" the real person. It is entirely possible that you will get a different impression of a candidate during a second interview. Sometimes, a candidate will even respond differently to the same questions asked at the first interview!

☞ Two interviewers

Just when I think I've been doing pretty well at hiring people, I make a big hiring mistake that, in retrospect, I should have realized in advance. It happens to everyone. Hiring is not a perfect process. It is highly subjective and based on a good deal of soft information. So, whenever possible, have at least one other person carefully interview the final candidates for a position. You may to surprised with a fresh perspective.

☞ Set questions

Although it will take a time investment, you should have a strong list of questions ready before you begin interviewing a candidate. When interviewing multiple candidates for the same position, ask the same questions of each prospect in exactly the same manner. This will allow you to fairly compare candidate responses.

> "Be careful to hire the best candidate for the job—not merely the most talented job seeker."

Questions & Answers about Hiring

 Should I pay a significantly higher salary for a top candidate?

No. You should decide how much a position will pay prior to interviewing candidates and you should stick to this decision no matter what. Don't get mesmerized by an extremely talented candidate and offer more than you allocated. Examine extremely talented individuals carefully—are they actually overqualified for the position? Will they soon tire of your company and be on their way to a more appropriate position elsewhere?

When should I bring up salary?

For hourly and entry-level professional positions, put the salary or wage in the help-wanted ad. Even if the salary is stated in the ad, however, you need to be sure to review this information with each candidate before you invite him or her in for an interview. A lot of people either quickly respond to many help-wanted ads without considering wage issues, or they figure that the stated salary is only a starting point for negotiations.

Even for the most senior positions, open a salary discussion during the first phone call. Get the candidate to state his or her salary range expectations before you express your salary position. Too often a candidate will assent to a stated salary during the preliminary stages of the interviewing process, assuming he or she can negotiate upward if actually offered the position.

A lot of candidates will tell you that they will only discuss salary during face-to-face interviews. Tell these individuals that company policy requires that you know in advance of an actual interview what their expectations are. If they are still hesitant to discuss money, move on to another candidate.

Should I negotiate benefits?

It isn't wise to negotiate benefits. If a candidate is so strong that you want to offer something extra, despite earlier advice to the contrary, offer a better salary. One of the quickest ways to create animosity among your employees is to give a new hire a better benefit package.

What is the best way to tell if the candidate can handle the job?

There is nothing like the real thing! The best way is to hire the person first for a fixed period of time. This is one reason why larger companies hire students during vacation periods. But this option isn't realistic for most positions, or for smaller companies that need someone today!

Offer a candidate tests or scenarios that duplicate, as closely as possible, the actual job the person would perform. If the candidate will be doing data entry, consider testing on a data entry machine for an hour as part of the interviewing process. Give the candidate who will be doing editing a problematic passage to edit. Role-play with the candidate who will be selling. Ask those applying for a management position to offer decisions based on hypothetical situations that you pose.

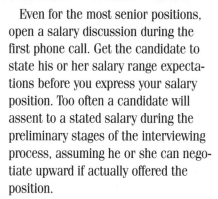

Questions & Answers about Hiring

Should I hire someone who has been fired?

First, ascertain why the person was fired and determine the likelihood of a similar situation occurring within your work environment. Keep in mind that companies are much quicker to fire people today, despite the legal risks, than they were years ago. Don't rule out a candidate simply because of firing.

On the other hand, if you have a choice between two candidates with roughly similar qualifications, and one has been fired from the last position but the other has not, chances are you should go with the one who has not been fired. It is often difficult to get to the truth of the matter in the case of firings. Previous managers are reluctant to divulge information about former employees, especially negative information. And often, even the job candidate doesn't fully comprehend exactly why he or she was fired. It is, after all, hard to admit that one's performance was unsatisfactory. Some people who are fired falsely attribute or explain to others that the firing was due to a personality conflict. These conflicts generally boil down to a difference in opinion regarding the employee's performance—the employee's opinion versus the supervisor's opinion.

How can I get references to talk freely?

If you call a reference and simply ask an open-ended question like "Tell me about their performance," you will probably get a short answer that won't reveal much. Instead, ask questions that zero in on specific concerns you have about the candidate. For example, "Joe seems to have good technical skills, but I am a little concerned about his lack of management experience. How well did he motivate the two people who reported to him at your firm?"

A more general question that is quite effective in getting references to open up is "If we were to hire Joe, what advice would you give us in order to help him succeed in his next position?"

Any special advice for hiring people long distance?

I have such confidence in phone interviews that I have successfully hired several key people long distance over the phone without even meeting them. I've saved a lot of money by not bringing candidates in for interviews at the company's expense, and feel that I've taken little additional risk in the process. In my business I'm less concerned about how a person looks and dresses and more concerned about how they are going to perform on the job.

What about using employment agencies or executive search firms?

If you have the time and are willing to learn a little you can become just as good at hiring as anyone in an employment agency. Employment agencies charge a lot of money and are, generally, more focused on making a placement than finding the absolute best "fit" between a candidate and a hiring firm.

One of the big advantages of using an executive search firm is that a good one will go after candidates who are not currently in the job market and are perhaps working for your competitor. This is something you might be uneasy doing yourself. And, some candidates not in the job market might be less resistant to overtures from a headhunter than from the manager of another firm.

At the same time, though, you may be able to act like a headhunter yourself. For example, in filling a key position at my firm I networked through third parties to locate the best possible candidate. While the candidate was not currently looking to make a move I was successful in wooing him. It took time and energy. The candidate actually refused my first offer and I had to approach the prospect again with fresh persuasion and a better deal. But you have to put a lot of weight in hiring the best people—they help run your business!

Performance reviews are typically approached with a lot of anxiety by both managers and employees. Managers tend to put off preparing for performance reviews because they can be an emotional issue. They also tend to rush through them to get them over with. This isn't fair to employees, and is bad for morale even if the overall performance is rated positively or above average. A quick, sloppy employment review sends a negative message. The person being reviewed will feel as though he or she is not important to you—that you really don't care about them.

Conducting a good performance review requires careful preparation in two different ways. You need to decide what you are going to say, and how you are going to say it.

Performance review criteria

Large companies generally have highly specific criteria for reviewing the performance of employees. Small companies often let individual managers determine how they will conduct their employee reviews. The problem with this haphazard approach is that employees will discuss their reviews with one another. Unless your firm has developed a consistent review process, some employees will feel that they have not gotten the same or as fair an appraisal as others.

A simple approach to performance review criteria would be to primarily review an employee's work based on quantity and quality relative to the job requirements. Secondary considerations might be attitude, willingness to help other personnel with their work when appropriate, and ability to get along with others.

Another approach would be to set a standard "laundry list" of factors that must be considered in reviews.

Whatever method you decide works best for your company and your employees, discuss it with your managers and make sure they are using the same performance criteria consistently.

Performance ratings

You should rate employee performance and do so in a consistent manner. Top performers like to hear affirmations from management regarding their exemplary efforts. Weak performers need to know that their performance requires improvement.

In addition, you may want to couple performance ratings with suggested annual pay increase ranges. Following is a sample rating system with suggested pay range increases.

Performance Reviews

This is a sample rating system with suggested pay range increases.

	Description	Suggested Raise
	Unsatisfactory Employee's performance is below minimum acceptable levels in major areas. Employee's performance must improve quickly and dramatically to allow for continued employment.	*0%*
★	**Below average** Employee's performance meets minimum requirements but is below the average expected performance for the position. Employee is expected to improve his or her performance.	*0–3%*
★★	**Satisfactory** Employee's performance is either generally satisfactory or at least meets minimum requirements in all areas, Any less than satisfactory performance in one area is offset by a greater than satisfactory performance in another area.	*4–5%*
★★★	**Good** Employee's performance is at least satisfactory in all major aspects of the position and measurably higher in some areas.	*6–7%*
★★★★	**Excellent** Employee's performance is measurably higher than satisfactory in all of the most important aspects of the position. In addition, the employee's performance was truly exceptional in one or more key areas.	*8–10%*
★★★★★	**Exceptional/Promotion** Employee's performance was excellent in all major dimensions of his or her position. In addition, the employee achieved a major accomplishment above the scope of their job description.	*+10%*

Performance Reviews

Because performance reviews can be highly emotional, especially for the employee, it is best to approach a review with a specific agenda in mind. Plan in advance what you are going to say during each part of the review. Be sure you can successfully deliver the message you intend regardless of the employee's response.

1 Greeting

Start the review with a warm greeting and perhaps some very brief small talk to help relax tensions and create a more conducive atmosphere for the review.

2 Summary

Be sure that the employee understands exactly how his or her overall performance ranks. Summarize the overall performance first, and then explain what the rating means. Don't announce any salary changes at this point. If you don't give the summary at the beginning of the review, the employee will spend the rest of the review trying to figure out what his or her overall performance is, based on your comments.

The employee may want to discuss the rating immediately after you offer it. Try to put this off until you have been able to thoroughly review the employee's strengths and weaknesses.

3 Strengths

Unless an employee's performance is unsatisfactory, compliment him or her on both major and minor strengths as they relate to their job. Avoid saying anything negative until you have reviewed his or her strengths. You can be either specific or general in describing strengths.

4 Weaknesses

Unless an employee's performance has been truly exceptional, you should provide feedback on areas of weakness, or at least suggest room for improvement. In reviewing weaknesses, be as specific as possible. For example, rather than saying "you have a poor attitude" cite a specific example of their behavior such as "you are often late for company meetings and several times throughout the year you complained incessantly about company policies."

5 Feedback

After you have discussed an employee's weaknesses, you should give him or her an opportunity to air their thoughts. Listen politely until the person is done. Avoid being argumentative, but do let the employee know that his or her feedback has not affected your review. For example, you may want to say "I understand that you don't agree with what I have said, but my perception of your overall performance remains as I have stated it."

6 Salary

Recap the employee's overall performance rating. Announce the new salary, if any, and the date on which the new salary will be effective.

7 Closing

Unless the employee's performance is substantially less than satisfactory, try to end the review on a positive note. You might say "The company and I very much appreciate your work, and we are glad to have you here!"

Performance Review Legal Issues

*T*he biggest job-related legal problems are often a direct result of unrealistic employment reviews. Managers often avoid conflict by failing to appraise a poor employee performance accurately and truthfully. Later, if the company fires the employee, it is easier for that employee to claim discrimination and offer his or her performance reviews as evidence of adequacy to carry out the job requirements.

First step

So, as a first step, you need to make sure that all managers give each member of their staff a realistic review. Additionally, all reviews should be issued in writing. The reviewed employee should receive a copy of his or her review.

Develop consistent review criteria

Another potential legal pitfall may be encountered when an employee claims that he or she has been discriminated against in the review. This is particularly likely to occur if the employee has been passed up for a promotion. To avoid this, you need to develop consistent review criteria and be absolutely sure that your managers adhere to the performance criteria. Reviews should also contain specific examples of negative and positive performance, not just generalizations.

Other steps

Other ways to avoid legal issues during reviews are as follows:

- Establish grievance procedures.
- Have more than one manager determine each employee's overall performance rating or at least provide input during the pre-appraisal process.
- Give employees feedback during the year, as appropriate, to avoid performance review surprises.
- Encourage managers to work with employees who are underachievers in an attempt to raise their performance to a satisfactory level.

> "You need to develop consistent review criteria and be absolutely sure that your managers adhere to the performance criteria."

A Sample Performance Review

Most performance reviews tend to go fairly smoothly if conducted properly. But some employees will become confrontational when their review is not as positive as they had expected. This can create a challenging situation for a manager. The following is a performance review dialogue centered around such a situation. Notice how the reviewer manages to stay calm, does not get sidetracked by the employee's interruptions, and persists in carefully outlining the pluses and minuses in the employee's performance.

 Manager
Hello, Kathy. Please have a seat. How are you today?

 Kathy
To be honest, I'm a little nervous.

 Manager
That's normal. I tense up before my reviews too. Overall, Kathy, your performance throughout the year has been satisfactory. Some aspects of your performance are strong and other aspects do need improvement . . .

 Kathy
Satisfactory? The customer surveys indicate that customers are very happy with our customer service!

 Manager
That's certainly correct! You deserve a lot of credit for the wonderful results on that survey! Not only does it reflect on your ability to provide high-quality service, but it also reflects very well on your ability to motivate the two people who report to you and . . .

A Sample Performance Review

 Kathy So why is my performance only satisfactory?

 Manager While the quality of customer service is very high, efficiency has fallen and your department is way over budget. We have discussed this throughout the year, and as you know, we have had to add temps during the busier periods to keep up with the calls.

 Kathy I know we are slightly over budget, but my job is to keep customers happy and there's no question about how happy they are . . .

 Manager Primarily because of the temps we've ended up a full 23 percent over budget. Our average number of calls handled per customer service person has fallen from twelve per hour last year to just under nine this year. That's a falloff of over 25 percent. You do need to work at improving the quantity of calls handled.

"Complaints do not necessarily come from just the people who get the really negative reviews. I find that people who get satisfactory reviews also complain about their ratings."

Streetwise Advice on Reviews

Salary

Never mention a change in pay until the end of the performance review. Most people will tend to tune out information during a review if they already know what their new pay rate is going to be.

Don't inflate reviews

Many supervisors give inflated reviews. This is particularly true if the employee's performance was lacking and the overall rating should have been negative. This can and does leave companies wide open to discrimination suits if the employee is terminated before his or her next review.

"Joe had a satisfactory review and then you fired him ninety days later for unsatisfactory work." This scenario won't play well for you before a jury!

Negative reviews

People tend to deny the reality of a negative review—or "invent" a false justification to save their pride. So if you have to deliver a negative performance review to an employee, don't mince words. Say exactly what you mean, without being insulting or demeaning.

Positive reviews

Even the very best workers will have a few shortcomings. Some managers find it easier to spend a review focusing on an employee's shortcomings rather than praising their strengths. Resist this temptation and keep the review in perspective. If the performance has been 75 percent terrific, then spend 75 percent of the review heaping on the praise. If you run out of specific examples of the employee's noteworthy efforts, repeat each strength or accomplishment a second time. Believe me, the employee won't mind the repetition!

Criticism

When you have to voice a criticism, be highly specific and cite actual examples of the employee's negative behavior patterns. Then offer suggestions on how the employee's shortcomings may be overcome.

"Never mention a change in pay until the end of the performance review. Most people will tend to tune out information during a review if they already know what their new pay rate is going to be."

Questions & Answers about Reviews

My top employee isn't satisfied with her salary review. What should I do?

Don't go back and redo a salary review unless you feel that your performance review preparation was sloppy. As soon as other employees hear that you are reconsidering review outcomes, you will become inundated with requests for reconsideration or will have sullen, resentful employees on your hands.

Self-test before giving a salary review. Ask yourself in advance, "If the employee complains about his or her salary increase, will I feel they are right and want to increase it?" If you would, pay the employee the money he or she deserves up front.

Give your top performers great increases, and give your laggards small increases, if any. Avoid the common tendency to make only modest differentials between the increase given to an excellent employee and the increase given to a poor employee.

Should reviews be in writing?

Absolutely. The most pressing reason for maintaining a written copy of a performance review is as a paper trail against a legal claim. And, be aware that in a discrimination action, you may need to provide the court with records on all employees, not just the one who has brought suit.

Written reviews also give you a means of tracking employees' progress over an extended period of time. You can use this documentation to assist them in improving their weaker points during the year. You can also use written reviews when considering which employees to promote or reassign.

What are the biggest mistakes managers make in reviews?

Inflating the review of an average or poor worker is the most common and most serious mistake managers make in giving performance reviews. You should always tell it like it is. Another common mistake is the tendency not to pay top performers what they really deserve.

Some managers focus on an employee's performance over the past couple of months, as opposed to over the entire year. Remember, employees are aware that their reviews are coming up and it is a natural tendency for them to pull out all the stops just before a salary review. To counter the effect of this, you should keep notes on each employee's performance throughout the year.

Managers usually have a good idea about who is likely to complain about a review—especially the salary increase component. There is a temptation to pay "whiners" more than they deserve to avoid an acrimonious review. Resist this. Salary increases should be rewards for performance and achievement, not bribes.

Plus, you need to keep total salary increases within target. If you overpay an underperformer to keep from hearing his or her complaints, an overachiever may have to suffer the consequences and receive less of an increase than he or she deserves.

Questions & Answers about Reviews

How do I present a really negative review?

More than anything else, don't sugar-coat a negative review. Remember, should you end up firing the employee, you greatly increase your chance of being hit with and losing a lawsuit if the fired employee's recent performance reviews have been positive. You can, however, search for some positives to show the employee you are being objective.

Repeat the overall performance summary twice to ensure that the employee gets the full impact of his or her review. Always state a few clear, specific examples of any shortcomings.

Don't get into a long-winded argument with employees. If they disagree with your appraisal, tell them that you understand that they are in disagreement with you. Tell them that, nonetheless, you stand firm in your beliefs regarding their performances. You may want to suggest continuing the discussion the next day so that an employee has a chance to cool off.

How can I keep employees from sharing their reviews and/or salary levels with one another?

The bottom line is that you can't. You can request review and salary confidentiality, but many people, especially younger employees, will share this information anyway. What you need is an equitable pay and review structure. That way, even if your employees know each other's salary level and review history, they will feel fairly treated.

My business is in a cash bind and can't afford raises. Should I skip or delay reviews?

No. Review employee performances even if you can't afford to offer increases right now. Be candid with your employees. Explain the situation realistically but portray the future in a positive light so that they will want to remain in your employ.

You have several alternatives for handling the issue of raises. You could tell your employees what their new rate of pay will be when the company can afford to implement the raise; you can inform employees that actual raise levels will be determined when the company's financial picture improves; or you can offer cash bonuses in lieu of raises if certain preset financial objectives are met within some specified period of time.

Should all employees be reviewed at the same time?

Yes. Try to to conduct all reviews at about the same time. An exception might be made for managers. You may want to review management staff a few days prior to reviewing support staff.

Even if you have policies to the contrary, many employees are going to share information regarding their reviews with coworkers. Some employees may expect better reviews than they receive if other employees have gotten great reviews in the recent past. And, with emotions running high at review time, work tends to slow. If you consolidate reviews to a specific period of time, you can minimize the effects of this and get on with business until next year!

Determining Compensation

Wage surveys

Wage surveys are available from many sources. These include the U.S. Department of Labor's Bureau of Labor Statistics, trade associations, consulting firms, and many trade publications that publish annual salary surveys.

While salary surveys make for interesting reading, most are of limited use in setting salary levels. Usually, a broad range of salaries are reported for identical positions. One reason for these discrepancies is that a job function at one firm may have a different title than the same function has at another firm. For example, the top financial executive at one $10 million dollar manufacturing firm may be called the controller, while the same function is served by the vice president of finance or the accounting manager at another firm of the same size. In any case, this makes dependence upon wage surveys for setting wage levels uncertain at best.

The most useful wage surveys show different salary ranges for different company sizes within the same business category. Some even further define wage earnings by separating the ranges by senior or junior levels of experience within particular job classifications.

Similar firms

One of the best ways to determine wage levels is to set them according to the salaries offered by highly similar firms located within your geographical region. If you develop a rapport with a key executive at another firm, see if you can share salary ranges for different job titles.

Job candidates

Another great way to expand your salary knowledge base is through interviewing job candidates. This is quite easy if you request salary information from prospective employees during your first phone interview with them.

However, don't make wage assumptions based on conversations with two or three job candidates. You need to gather wage information from a least a dozen job applicants before you can develop a reliable awareness of current marketplace salaries for a particular function in a particular industry and a particular region.

Salary history

One way to set a salary for a new employee is to match his or her previous pay or offer an additional 2 to 5 percent. One problem to this approach is, however, that you might wind up with a group of employees whose salaries are completely out of whack in comparison to each other. And, no matter how much you try and no matter how many policies you set regarding the confidentiality of salaries, this type of information will leak out sooner or later.

Factors to consider

Factors that you should consider when setting base pay levels are:

1. The skill or expertise required for the position
2. The amount of experience required for the position
3. Current shortage or abundance of appropriate candidates
4. What similar positions pay within your company
5. Special working conditions such as second- or third-shift hours, or extensive travel
6. Incentive pay
7. Fringe benefits offered

Finally, you might want to consider whether or not your firm wants to offer a premium over similar firms in order to attract and maintain the best people on a particular career path within a particular industry.

Incentive Pay Options

*T*here is nothing like a little extra carrot to motivate people to work at their best. Most people like to work hard if they are treated right. But the opportunity to earn a little extra cash makes work that much more inviting and fun. And if that little extra cash is part of a group or company-wide bonus, a sense of team pride is encouraged as well.

Years ago, the only employees offered incentive plans were sales personnel, piece workers, and top executives. Today, most large companies and many smaller firms offer an incentive package to all of their employees.

Commissions

Commissions are paid to salespeople. They are usually based on a percentage of actual sales made. Salespeople typically receive a base salary or draw that guarantees them a minimum income, which is especially important during periods when commissions might be below average. In years past, most salespeople were paid on commission. Now, most salespeople are compensated through some combination of salary and incentive bonus plan.

Bonus plans

Bonus plans follow many different models. There may be a company-wide bonus plan wherein each employee receives the same or differing bonuses if certain criteria, such as profitability or sales goals, are met during a specific period of time—typically on an annual or monthly basis. The bonus amount is usually based on a set percentage of each employee's base salary.

Most bonuses are awarded periodically unless an exceptional achievement has been accomplished. Some bonuses are awarded upon completion of preset goals.

Salary at-risk plans

Salary at-risk plans are widely used. They are primarily a way of shifting an existing work force or sales force to a more incentive-based remuneration plan. As an incentive, however, it doesn't necessarily work, and many participants in a salary at-risk plan aren't happy with their lot. Essentially, in a salary at-risk plan, a base salary is not guaranteed. To earn a base salary, an individual employee or the company as a whole must reach a set sales or profit goal, or come within a range that is typically set around 85 percent. If 100 percent of the goal is reached, participants receive a bonus above the base salary. Most salary at-risk plans offer higher bonus levels for achieving higher goals.

Profit sharing

Profit-sharing plans are generally applicable on a company-wide basis and are made available to all full-time employees who have been with the company for a preset amount of time. Usually the company will contribute a small percentage of its profitability to a pool, which is then divided among the eligible employees. Division is typically pro-rated according to the base salary of each participant. Profit sharing is generally, but not always, determined on an annual basis. Many companies will not make contributions to the pool unless profits reach a certain predetermined level.

Incentive Pay Options

Gainsharing

Gainsharing is more popular at manufacturing companies. With gainsharing programs decreases in costs caused by increases in efficiency are partially shared with employees. In some ways, gainsharing is similar to profit sharing.

Award programs

Cash or other awards for specific accomplishments can help direct employees toward specific goals. And the intangible results of these programs can be more important than the tangible ones. For example, by announcing a contest for cost-cutting ideas, the long-term benefit of having employees think more cost consciously is far more important than the typically short-term improvements that the program generates. Contests and award programs also help bolster the feeling that you care about your employees and that you really value their contributions. They also help make work more fun! The only drawback, really, is that ongoing award programs and contests can take a lot of management time and energy to administer.

Stock or stock options

Public companies may award stock or stock options to their employees or, at least, their most senior executives. If you have a small, privately held firm you should think twice about adopting this incentive plan. For starters, your firm must be a corporation in order to offer stock or stock options to employees. Then you will need to satisfy the regulatory agency requirements that accompany a broad distribution of stock. Finally, you need to remember that a minority interest in a small, privately held firm is less versatile than stock held in a public entity. It will be difficult, if not impossible, to sell your stock. An employee won't even be able to determine what his or her stock is worth. It probably wouldn't have any value in terms of collateral, even for a small personal loan.

Benefits

These statistics are based on results from a *1992 Bureau of Labor Statistics Survey* on employee benefits for small, private businesses.

	Benefit	Usually offered	Commonly offered	Rarely offered
1	Paid holidays	●		
2	Paid vacations	●		
3	Medical care	●		
4	Paid funeral leave		●	
5	Paid jury duty leave		●	
6	Paid sick leave		●	
7	Life insurance		●	
8	Retirement plan		●	
9	Educational assistance			●
10	Short-term disability			●
11	Long-term disability			●
12	Dental care			●
13	Support programs			●
14	Family benefits			●
15	Paid personal leave			●
16	Paid maternity leave			●

Benefits

1 *Paid holidays*

Paid holidays were available to 82 percent of full-time employees. Employees received, on average, nine holidays per year. For companies that offered paid holidays, 75 percent gave their employees a substitute holiday off when a holiday fell on a regularly scheduled day off.

2 *Paid vacation*

Eighty-eight percent of full-time employees received paid vacation time. The amount of vacation time a worker receives often depended on the length of time the employee had worked at a company. For one year of service, vacation time averaged around eight days per year. Vacation time rose to about fourteen days per year for ten years of service and to around fifteen days per year for twenty years of service.

3 *Medical care*

Medical care is one of the most common employee benefits offered by small businesses. Seventy-one percent of small business employees participated in a company-sponsored medical plan. One-third of the employees participating in these plans were covered by nontraditional medical care plans such as health maintenance organizations (HMOs) or preferred provider organizations (PPOs). All of the participants in medical care plans have coverage for hospital room and board, in-hospital physician visits, and surgery, x-ray, and laboratory services. Fifty-three percent of the employees were in individual-care plans that were paid for entirely by the employer and 27 percent had family-care plans that were paid for entirely by the employer.

4 *Paid funeral leave*

Paid funeral leave was available to 50 percent of full-time employees. Funeral leave averaged three days per occurrence.

5 *Paid jury duty*

Paid jury duty was available to 58 percent of full-time employees. The amount of paid time off depended upon the length of the jury duty service. It should be noted that some states mandate paid time off for jury duty.

6 *Paid sick leave*

About 50 percent of full-time employees had paid sick leave. Sick leave plans, on average, provided about nine days per year, with full pay for employees with over five years of service with the company.

7 *Life insurance*

Life insurance protection was available to 64 percent of full-time employees of small businesses. Typically, the cost of basic life insurance was paid for in its entirety by the employer. Nearly 40 percent of the life insurance plans offered were linked to the base salary of the participants.

8 *Retirement plans*

Forty-five percent of all full-time workers were covered by at least one retirement plan. Typically, retirement plans included defined contribution plans, such as 401(k), profit-sharing, and employee pension plans. These plans typically specified the level of employer and employee contributions to the plan. Individual accounts were set up for participants, and benefits were based on amounts credited to these accounts, plus investment earnings. Nearly one-fourth of the full-time employees were covered by a 401(k) plan, usually implemented through a salary reduction plan.

9 Educational assistance

Educational assistance programs provided full or partial reimbursement of employee expenses incurred for books, tuition, and fees associated with advancing or maintaining their level of education. Thirty-six percent of full-time employees were eligible for job-related educational assistance, and 5 percent were eligible for non-job-related educational assistance.

10 Short-term disability

Short-term disability was available to 26 percent of full-time employees and provided 50 percent of regular pay for a period of up to twenty-six weeks.

11 Long-term disability

Long-term disability insurance coverage was offered to 23 percent of all full-time workers. This coverage was three times more common for white-collar workers than it was for blue-collar workers. Long-term disability insurance typically offered 60 percent of regular pay, commencing three to six months post-disability.

12 Dental care

Dental care was available to 33 percent of full-time workers. Virtually all of the dental plans offered covered preventive care and restorative dental procedures.

13 Support programs

Support programs were available to 17 percent of all full-time employees and provided these employees with referral and counseling services for alcoholism, drug abuse, and emotional difficulties.

14 Family benefits

Family benefits include child care, elder care for parents or spouses, and adoption assistance. Only 3 percent of full-time workers were offered family benefits as employees of small businesses.

15 Paid personal leave

Paid personal leave was provided to 12 percent of full-time employees in small businesses.

16 Paid maternity leave

Two percent of full-time employees had paid maternity leave available to them.

Streetwise Advice on Compensation

☞ **Above average**

Pay your people well. For all positions you should pay at least a little more than is average. When employees feel that they are being treated well, they are going to be more motivated to perform well for you and your company.

☞ **Person, not position**

Pay the person, not the position. In small companies employees are often responsible for multiple tasks, or their performance is expected to make all the difference in the overall performance of the company. In this situation you should focus on an individual's contribution to the success of your company, not the job title. Some companies, for example, might even place a top salesperson on an incentive pay plan that allows him or her to potentially earn more than the president of the company. For example, at my grandfather's shoe manufacturing firm, the sales manager earned more in some years in total salary and bonuses than my grandfather did.

☞ **Annual reviews**

People expect to be reviewed every year. If you review their performances and salaries less often, they are bound to be disappointed. Some companies review people on the anniversaries of their hire dates. As much as possible, however, you should arrange to review all employees at the same time on the same date each year. Otherwise, as the company grows, you will always seem to be reviewing employees, and distract your other workers.

☞ **Compensation is a hot button**

Think compensation out carefully before you act. If you offer a candidate too much money or increase an employee's pay too much, the mistake will follow you as long as the employee is with the firm. Base pay and any change in base pay establishes a basis for future increases.

On the other hand, if you offer a candidate too little money or raise an employee's wages by too small an amount, you run the risk of losing a good candidate or a valued employee. Some employees will speak up and complain about an unsatisfactory increase. Others may just quietly start looking for another job.

☞ **Compensation is not just a retention issue**

I see many employers, especially small businesses, give their employees lousy increases because they assume that the employee will never leave the company. And they may be right, but they sure aren't going to get the full level of commitment from the employee that they would have gotten had they paid them what they really deserved!

I see paying people well or above average as a shrewd investment. And, believe me, it is one of the very few areas of running a business where I don't like to skimp. Time and time again, I have surprised top-performing employees with big, fat pay increases—much more than was necessary to retain them, but nonetheless well deserved. I love giving great pay raises—and I know that the money will come back many times over in stronger commitment and dedication to the business.

> *"When employees feel that they are being treated well, they are going to be more motivated to perform well for you and your company."*

Questions & Answers about Compensation

When should a new employee receive his or her first raise?

For entry-level positions paid on an hourly basis, a small increase should be put into effect ninety days after the employee has been hired, if he or she has performed to a satisfactory level. People in these types of positions tend to be transitory and are less likely to wait six to twelve months for their first review.

For professional positions, review salaries after twelve months of employment or during the next company-wide annual review period. However, if the company's annual review period is within three or fewer months from the employee's start date, review entry-level professionals six months from their start dates, and senior-level professionals during the succeeding review period, even if that is fifteen months away. Always inform a new employee when his or her first review will take place. If that review is scheduled for a time frame that exceeds one year, take that into consideration when determining a starting salary.

How do you weigh experience versus ability?

Take into consideration a person's current ability to do a job, your confidence in that person and his or her abilities, and how much, if any, additional experience will increase the person's ability to perform well. For example, if one person has one week of experience collecting change at a toll booth and another person has ten years of experience in the same position, it is doubtful that these different experience levels will significantly decrease or increase either individual's ability to perform satisfactorily. However, if one person has one week's worth of experience as a credit manager and another has ten year's experience, there will be a major difference in their ability to easily handle their jobs.

How do you weigh seniority versus ability?

This is a hot-potato issue. Some freshly minted MBAs may feel that raw ability is the only criteria that matters in determining wages. Many employees, however, feel that seniority should be rewarded.

Bloated labor costs can become a problem if you give wage increases based on an employee's increasing seniority. And some companies have gotten hit with discrimination suits when they have sought to cut labor costs by firing older employees with very high seniority-based wages.

But many employers underestimate how much seniority can affect ability. For example, new hires from the outside may have good "book"understanding of the sales techniques used in your industry but haven't developed a good sales style or learned the nuances of selling your particular product. They may have established customers, but those customers don't associate him or her with your product.

In a nutshell, pay on ability, not seniority. But do keep in mind that seniority can, in ways both subtle and not so subtle, positively affect ability.

Problem Employees

Virtually all people want to succeed at work. They want to offer their best and get along well with their managers, supervisors, and coworkers. When shortcomings or problems arise, they can usually be overcome with some additional instruction or coaching, or with a positive, but frank, discussion of the issues at hand. As much as possible, you want to leave people feeling that you are helping and supporting them, not reprimanding them. And, if you have anything at all negative to say to an employee, it needs to be done in private. Don't embarrass employees in front of other workers.

Sooner or later every employee, including the owner-operator, is going to have one or more significant difficulties in the workplace. If you take the "big stick" approach to every problem that arises, you will find yourself toiling away in a very lonely office or plant.

However, on occasion an employee simply cannot do the job or is too disruptive. More serious action is called for in this situation. You may need to reassign the problem employee's duties or deliver a written warning to the employee. In the end, you may even have to terminate the employee.

Lack of skills

First try to ascertain if the employee really lacks the skills necessary for the satisfactory performance of his or her duties, or if another issue is negatively affecting his or her ability to perform. Often, when a manager assumes that someone cannot do a job for lack of skill, the real problem is actually centered on sloppiness. And sloppiness is almost always correctable.

If the problem is skill-oriented, decide whether or not there is something you or the company can do to improve the employee's skills. Can a coworker help bring the employee up to speed? Would a professional seminar be worthwhile? Would studying a book or instructional software help?

You also need to evaluate how important the deficient skill actually is within the performance scope of the particular job. Consider how strong the employee might be in other aspects of job performance. A shop floor manager, for instance, may be not be great at giving performance reviews but absolutely terrific at scheduling and maintaining production runs and inventory management. Obviously, his or her strengths far outweigh the weaknesses in effectively carrying out the primary responsibilities of the job. It is often OK to have an employee with a serious weakness, as long as you are aware of the problem area and the employee compensates for one skill deficiency with a super skill strength.

If, despite all considerations, you feel that an employee should not remain in the current position, think about moving him or her to another area or level of responsibility within the company. There are two advantages to this strategy. First, since you already know where the employee's strengths and weaknesses lie, you have a good idea of what capacity he or she might satisfactorily perform in—much more so than you would for a new employee, for instance. Second, it is demoralizing for other employees to see a coworker fired, especially if that employee was trying hard at the job.

> *"Often, the real problem is sloppiness. And sloppiness is almost always correctable."*

Problem Employees

Slow pace

A slow work pace can be among the most difficult problems to resolve unless you have standards or goals against which to compare actual performance.

For most nonprofessional positions, you can create standards, or minimum quantitative measures of output. For example, warehouse workers may be expected to pack so many orders every day. Data entry people may be expected to process so many entries each day. Salespeople may be expected to make so many calls to new accounts, make so many face-to-face contacts, or close so many dollars in revenue each day.

The work of professional employees, on the other hand, generally does not lend itself to quantitative performance standards. However, you can usually set specific time goals for when you expect projects to be completed. For example, you may expect an accountant to accomplish month-end book closings within a three-day period at the end each month. You may expect a software engineer to write a particular program within two weeks. You may expect a graphic designer to design and lay out a specific small catalog within a three-week time frame.

If an employee doesn't measure up to a preset or measurable goal, the next step is a closed-door meeting with the employee. During this meeting, in an encouraging manner, present the facts in as simple a fashion as possible. For example you may say "You are packing ninety-three orders, per average day, whereas our standard is one hundred thirty-five. How do you think you can increase your output?" Or, "Together, we set a time frame of three days at month's end in which to close our monthly accounting books. It is typically taking four. Is there some way in which we can work towards the original goal?"

If you are pleasant and encouraging, the employee will probably say something like "Gee, I thought I was working at a pretty good pace, but I am confident that I can work at a little faster clip." In this case, say "This sounds great. I'm glad to hear it!" Then, follow up and be sure the employee knows exactly where he or she stands at the end of each day. Chances are, such employees will reach a higher performance level. If not, have them monitor themselves and record their progress every hour or day, as may seem applicable to the task. Consider having peers work with them and help them along. Or consider having the employee make progress reports to you at various intervals.

Sometimes an employee will tell you during your first meeting or during subsequent meetings that the standards or goals that have been set are not realistic, fair, or possible. In this case (assuming you don't agree with the assertion), promptly issue the employee a written warning and plan on terminating his or her employment unless the attitude and performance improves quickly.

> "A slow pace of work can be among the most difficult problems to resolve unless you have standards or goals against which to measure performance."

Sloppiness

Sloppiness is one of the most common workplace problems. Examples include missing errors when proofreading company literature, mispacking orders, entering shipping addresses incorrectly, and performing inaccurate accounting work. Sloppiness most quickly surfaces in clerical work, but it is also prevalent in the work of many professionals—although it is much more difficult to detect!

For the first incidence or two of minor sloppiness, you should simply kindly point the error out to the employee. Don't comment, but watch the person's work more carefully.

If the problem proves to be recurrent or is more serious in nature, you need to sit down with the employee outside of the earshot of his or her coworkers. Be positive. Remember that the employee probably has no idea that his or her work is sloppy. Most people take pride in their work. But be candid. Tell the employee that you are concerned about the work and cite specific examples of sloppiness. Relate the clearest or most serious infractions that you have evidence of. Don't discuss marginal problems or ones that you have little evidence of. This can lead to arguments and a feeling of unfair treatment. The point is to assist an employee in performing up to snuff, not to demoralize him or her.

Encourage feedback, but expect to hear something like, "These are isolated examples. Everyone makes errors and basically my work is fine." At this point, don't get into a long discussion about how serious or representative the cited problems are. Instead, shift to telling the employee how important his or her work is to the company. Let the person know how important it is to eliminate all errors and sloppy work, no matter how infrequently it may occur or how insignificant it may seem to be. Try to end the meeting on as positive a note as possible.

Keep observing the employee's work. If, after a few days, the work patterns are improving, be sure to compliment him or her. If the sloppiness continues, conduct another closed-door meeting. There is good chance that the employee is capable of better work and is simply refusing to recognize the existence of an ongoing problem. In this second meeting make a judgmental statement such as, "I am concerned about the overall errors or sloppiness in your work." Again, bring up the most clear or flagrant examples.

For a nonprofessional or entry-level employee, assign someone with good or exemplary work habits, especially in the problem employee's area of weakness, to work side-by-side with the problem employee for a small portion of each day. Have the "monitoring" employee suggest specific steps for achieving performance improvement. Have the monitor provide continuing feedback. Personally monitor the work of a professional employee. Discuss any progress, or lack of it, every few days.

As long as an employee has the basic skills necessary to effectively perform in the job, sloppiness can be overcome in almost every case. It only takes the efforts of a manager who is willing to invest time and tries, no matter how frustrating it may be, to adopt a coaching rather than a reprimanding approach.

Problem Employees

Difficult to manage

An employee who is difficult to manage can make your life absolutely miserable. They can be every bit as disruptive to the forward progress of your company as an employee who lacks the skills or initiative to do the job well.

The first thing you should do with a difficult employee is to bite your tongue and try to woo him or her. Go out to lunch and try to develop a positive rapport with the person. Often there is some issue that is causing the negative behavior he or she is exhibiting. Many times employees will be very reluctant to discuss these issues, whether they are professional or personal in nature. A casual, relaxed setting may put them at ease. They may open up and tell you what's really bugging them.

Often the underlying causes of employees' negative behavior patterns are quite simple. They may have the perception that they are not appreciated. They may feel they have not been complimented adequately for work well done. They may feel they deserve more attention. Remember, you should always be liberal with compliments. Key employees especially need attention from you. But this is advice that is easier to give than heed.

On the other hand, sometimes a difficult-to-manage employee's behavior is the result of personal problems—an ailing parent, a runaway child, a divorce, or financial difficulties. In this case, you want to show that you understand the predicament. If at all possible, offer the employee time off or an adjustment in work hours so that he or she can focus on resolving the personal dilemma.

However, if the problem is of an ongoing nature and is having a serious negative impact on your workplace, you need to let the person know that some sort of resolution is imperative.

If the problem persists, have a formal, closed-door meeting with the employee and address the most obvious examples of his or her inappropriate behavior in a forthright manner.

If an employee remains difficult despite all attempts at building rapport or providing help, you need to make a careful assessment. Be honest with yourself. Do you simply dislike the employee in question? Are the difficulties you are experiencing perhaps minor in character? If this is the case, drop the matter. But if the employee is truly exhibiting behavior problems that seriously disrupt the workplace, you need to take further action. Consider issuing a written warning that details the specific problems as clearly as possible.

If, after issuing such a warning, the employee's bad behavior persists, you may feel that the only solution is termination. Consult with an attorney before dismissing the employee. You need to know whether or not you have a strong enough case to withstand a potential lawsuit for wrongful firing. An employee who has been fired for issues relating to difficult behavior is much more likely to sue you than an employee fired due to poor work performance.

> *"Often, there is an issue behind negative employee behavior."*

Tardiness

Many good, hardworking people have a tendency to be habitually late.

Unless being precisely on time is crucially important, don't bring up the tardiness issue with an employee who is occasionally late. Such employees will appreciate your tacit understanding and they will take it as a sign of your trust in them. Of course, if the employee is a security guard and you are operating a nuclear power plant, any display of tardiness could be serious. Use your judgement!

On the other hand, an employee who is habitually late can have a demoralizing effect on other employees who arrive for work on time. Furthermore, habitual lateness is a infectious disease. Soon many employees may exhibit tardy behavior. Why do some otherwise great, hardworking employees have a problem being on time—well, who knows?

The key question is, where do you draw the line on tardiness? If a person is ten or more minutes late more than five times within a given month, it's time for a brief chat. Assuming that the employee's job performance is satisfactory in all other respects, say something like "Linda, overall I really enjoy having you on our team. I would really appreciate it, however, if you could cut back on your tardiness. I can understand being late on occasion for whatever or even no apparent reason. But enough is enough. Can I count on you for a little improvement in this area?"

Virtually all tardiness problems disappear after a gentle talk. Unless the problem is extremely severe, stick to a very light approach. But sooner or later you will encounter an employee who feels he or she shouldn't have to work on a schedule. One employee actually told me that she felt "professionals" should be able to come and go within the workplace whenever they pleased. She saw absolutely nothing wrong with arriving two hours late. Well, now she can still come and go whenever she pleases—she just can't do it at *our* workplace!

> "*Virtually all tardiness problems disappear with a gentle talk. Unless the problem is extremely severe, stick to a very light approach.*"

Firing Employees

*O*f all confrontations with an employee, the response you get from firing someone is the most difficult to predict. One employee may thank you for giving him or her the opportunity to work with you, while another may attempt to engage an immediate supervisor in a fist fight.

You need to prepare carefully before firing someone. You need to be ready to become fully engaged in what may become a very demanding encounter.

How you handle a firing will have a tremendous impact on how the employee feels about himself, you, and your company. This will, in turn, effect your chance of being sued. In addition, a poorly handled firing will have a negative impact on morale throughout your entire organization.

The decision to wait on a firing

How much time should you give an employee to improve his or her performance? There really aren't any specific guidelines. One thing to take into consideration, however, is the employee's length of service with your company. Loyalty does count. Give an employee who has served you for several years a few months to work out his or her performance deficits.

Remember too, that when you fire a long-term employee the negative effect on the morale of other employees will be far greater than, say, if you were to fire a recent hire. And when you work together with long-term employees in an effort to help them improve their job output, and ideally keep them gainfully employed, you create goodwill throughout the company.

On the other hand, if an employee shows poor work habits, has unsatisfactory skill levels, or displays attitude problems during the provisional ninety-day employment period, don't hesitate to fire him or her. (But beware of the legal risks—the courts do not recognize "provisional" employment periods.)

The decision to fire

While firing should definitely be a last-resort measure, many managers, especially newly minted ones, hesitate to terminate an employee until it is long overdue.

As demonstrated throughout the section on problem employees, by carefully working with an employee many performance shortcomings can be resolved. An employee's job achievement can be improved through care.

If these "gentle" tactics don't work, however, you must move on to a firm verbal warning that makes mandatory a work quality or attitude improvement and cites specific suggestions for effecting such an improvement. If that fails, issue a written warning. Some people just require the jolt of a firm warning to shift their work performance into high gear.

Of course, during the period when you are working with an employee in an attempt to improve their performance, you run the risk of having them decide to seek employment elsewhere. This risk increases if a written warning is handed down. If the employee quits or submits his or her resignation, that's OK. It is a lot easier to lose weak performers through their own proactive decisions.

How to fire an employee

After you have taken all of the preliminary steps, considered all of the potential ramifications, legal and otherwise, and have made the difficult decision to let someone go, stick to it. Don't torture yourself. Don't prolong the firing. It is, after all, inevitable.

Only the worker's direct supervisors, and any witnesses that will be present at the termination meeting, should be told about the termination decision in advance. An advance leak of a firing can only worsen the situation.

In the past, late Friday afternoon was considered the optimum time to let someone go. Today, earlier in the day or even the week is deemed appropriate. Some companies that take this approach offer the employee the option of either remaining for the rest of the day or week or leaving immediately with pay for the workday.

When you are ready to proceed with the termination, call the employee into the office. Approach him or her with "I have something to discuss with you."

After the employee and any other managerial personnel or witnesses have gathered in your office, get to the point quickly. Briefly explain to the employee that he or she is being fired. Summarize the main reasons for the firing, recap the warnings that have been issued, and the opportunities extended to improve his or her performance record. Give the person a check for monies due. If you are offering severance pay, detail the severance offer and present the employee with the forfeiture document to be signed if the severance is to be paid. Explain any continued work options. Offer to let the employee clean out his or her office or desk now, or have you mail any personal belongings to him or her later. If the employee elects to have you mail his or her belongings, have two people oversee the cleaning process to be sure that all of the employee's personal possessions are mailed.

Show appropriate sympathy for the employee, but not empathy. Do not waiver and change your mind. Do not overstate any aspect of the employee's performance.

Answer any question the terminated employee may have, even if he or she interrupts you. A termination is extremely emotional. Don't be surprised if the employee doesn't hear the basic message or doesn't understand the details of his or her firing. You may have to restate all or part of the termination.

As long as the employee doesn't lose control, extend him or her every reasonable courtesy. Certainly give the person an opportunity to say good bye to coworkers. He or she will only call these people up on the phone later anyway.

If the employee does lose control and becomes verbally abusive, ask him or her to vacate the building. Don't get upset. Remember, no matter what you think of the employee, that person is being terminated. He or she is leaving, not you.

Even if you or someone else in the office can overpower a suddenly violent discharged employee, the risk of a lawsuit is huge. The one time I did call the police, the employee fled the building before they arrived. But the (Boston) police told me its policy was not to refuse cancellations on this type of call because all too often the discharged employee returned with a weapon. In this case, the employee did return with his dog—but the dog was about the size of a miniature poodle, with about the same level of ferociousness.

The odds of you or another employee being endangered during a firing is slim, but you do need to be prepared for the unexpected.

"As long as the employee doesn't lose control, extend him or her every reasonable courtesy."

Firing Employees

Severance

First, by law, you need to immediately remunerate a terminated employee for any unused vacation or personal time, all regular and overtime hours worked, and previously unpaid, earned bonuses and any other earned pay.

When you fire an employee, even if he or she has only been with you for ninety days or less, for any just cause short of confiscating the queen's jewels, you should pay severance. It is decent, remaining employees expect you to have done it, and it makes you look better in the worst of situations. It also decreases your risk of a lawsuit.

Many firms that pay severance offer two weeks pay. Others pay two weeks plus one week for each year of service the employee has given to the company. Still others are considerably more generous, particularly to employees who held senior positions. In this case, six months' to a year's pay is not atypical and is predicated on the assumption that a senior-level employee will have a more difficult time obtaining a new and equal job than will an entry-level employee.

While it is nice to pay out a lot of money to departing employees, if you own a small business, you need to be concerned about staying in business and paying your remaining staff members. But whatever you decide to do regarding severance pay, in all termination situations, severance for similar positions with similar service time should be consistent. If you continually change your severance policies, you are only adding to your legal risks.

You should only pay severance, however, if the employee agrees to sign a document that forfeits their right to sue you for wrongful termination. Don't be cheap in this lion's pit of potential danger. Have a lawyer draw up the release document so that it is, as much as possible, bullet proof. You should give the employee twenty-four hours to review, sign, and return the document to you, otherwise it may not hold up in court should the employee decide to sue you anyway. If the employee is age forty or over you must, by law, grant the person twenty-one days to review such a document.

Legal risks

Thanks to your friends in the federal government, you need to carefully consider any potential termination from a legal perspective. If you aren't sure where you would stand legally should a terminated employee bring suit, consult an attorney before you take any action against that employee. To do otherwise would be "penny wise and pound foolish."

While there aren't any laws in the United States that take away the right of employers to fire employees for cause, including unsatisfactory quantity or quality of work, you still face a significant legal risk every time you fire someone.

Why? Once you fire an employee you have typically engaged the person's fury. This person seldom believes that his or her performance was as poor as you have claimed. Someone who decides to pursue "justice" through the courts will generally claim discrimination. Women, anyone over the age of forty, physically challenged persons, minorities, gays, and many other groups are protected by law from discrimination. Some form of legal discrimination protection blankets just about 80 percent of our national work force.

Courts, especially juries, tend to be highly sympathetic to fired employees. This sympathy is magnified if the fired employees remain unemployed or if they are older workers.

Avoiding a lawsuit

The first way to avoid getting sued is to be sure that you and all other supervisors understand discrimination law. Go one step further and be sure that all supervisors really believe in the importance of fighting discrimination—both on a practical and a subconscious level.

You need to remember that abiding by the law and being able to prove to a hostile jury that you have done so are two very different things. If you end up in court, you need to have a rock-solid case against any employee you fire. You should take whatever preventive steps you can to avoid the possibility of a suit altogether.

Create a paper trail long before termination is seriously considered. Write summaries regarding specific performance problems that were cited via direct verbal warnings to the employee and file a copy in his or her employment records. Be sure that you have issued the employee at least two written warnings.

If the employee knows and appreciates that you have tried to work with him or her towards improving such job performance, this can decrease the chance of a lawsuit.

How you handle a problem employee's performance reviews are critical. The recent reviews should not be positive. This is often a problem because employers, supervisors, and managers hesitate to write and present to an employee a negative review, even if such a review is warranted. If, during the review process, you give into the human temptation to say something like "your work really isn't all that bad" or "I know your work is improving," you are planting the seeds of a discrimination suit.

Another potential problem you should be aware of is how you handle reference calls for a former, and fired, employee. If you give out any information on such an employee, other than dates of employment and a salary confirmation, you risk a lawsuit. There was even an instance where a company lost a suit brought by a terminated employee because a good reference was supplied but the employee felt, and the jury agreed, that the reference wasn't good enough!

> "Create a paper trail long before a termination is seriously considered."

The following dialogue provides an excerpt from a firing that involves an employee who had sincerely tried to do his job but just hadn't been able to perform at a satisfactory level. Note how the manager shows patience and expresses sympathy but does not offer false praise or waiver in his decision.

In this excerpt one manager is handling the termination procedure. It is good practice, however, to have another manager present. Ideally, the second manager should not be someone the employee reported to either directly or indirectly. If the firing does not go smoothly, the second manager can be called upon as a witness should any legal action ensue at some later point.

Manager   Tom, please have a seat.

Tom   Thank you.

Manager   Tom, I know that you have tried hard to succeed at your job. Nonetheless, for some months now, your overall performance has not been satisfactory. There are too many instances of errors in the accounts payable reports and your attempts to carefully check over each report have slowed down the pace of your work considerably. We cannot retain you in this position and we must let you go.

Tom   You mean, I'm fired?

Manager   Yes, that is correct. I am very sorry that this did not work out.

Firing an Employee

Tom   I know I can do the job. Give me another chance. I really like working here.

Manager   Tom, we have given you at least two written warnings and several verbal warnings.

Tom   But my supervisor says the quality of my work is improving.

Manager   While the number of errors has decreased, the quality is still not satisfactory. And in working to decrease the amount of errors your work pace has become unsatisfactory. I know you have tried . . . but it's still not working out.

Tom   What about another position? I've never really liked payables. How about the entry-level position in accounts receivable? I'll really give it my all.

Manager   Tom, it's time to move on. We all like you here. This is a difficult decision for all of us. But the decision has been made. We truly wish you the best.

Streetwise Advice on Firings

☞ Don't take firing lightly

Usually, even a very weak job performance can be brought up to a satisfactory level. Firing, on the other hand, involves a significant legal risk. It also has a traumatic impact on other members of your staff, even if they understand and appreciate the reasons for the termination.

☞ Don't hesitate to consult with counsel

If you have any questions regarding a firing, consult with an expert employment attorney prior to the termination. You may save yourself the legal fees of a post-firing lawsuit.

☞ Plan what you are going to say

If you don't carefully plan out what you are going to say during a firing, and stick to it, chances are you will offer kind words regarding their work performance. This can lead to legal action. During a firing, you don't want to even hint at anything positive in the person's job performance.

☞ Be calm

Even if the employee you are firing irritates you, don't let on. If he or she lashes out verbally, don't get excited. Soon this person will be gone and will no longer be your problem.

☞ Be humane

Treat the employee you are firing as kindly as possible during the termination process. This is a very traumatic experience for them. Being kind, without conveying anything positive about their job performance, can assuage this trauma. And, of course, it can decrease the odds that someone will bring a wrongful firing suit against your company or place negative phone calls to your remaining staff.

☞ Avoid surprises

Give weak employees every opportunity to improve their work performance or attitude before opting to let them go. If you can prove that you have given them every possible chance, there will be less grounds for a lawsuit. Plus, other employees will feel less threatened by the implications of the firing.

Additionally, employees who have been aware for some time that their continued employment is on the line will find the actual firing less traumatic. It may well be that they will feel "clued," and will seek and find employment elsewhere before you can fire them.

At all costs, you want to avoid firing someone who has no idea that his or her job is in jeopardy.

☞ Have a strong paper trail

Good documentation of poor work performance or attitude is essential in defending against a wrongful firing suit. Make a record of any verbal warnings you have given to the employee and, if possible, issue written warnings to him or her well before the firing. Negative performance reviews are a must.

> "Usually even a very weak job performance can be brought up to a satisfactory level. Firing, on the other hand, involves a significant legal risk."

Should I consider rehiring a fired employee

Probably not. An employee who has been fired for cause is much more likely to have a poor attitude toward your firm than a fresh hire. Even if the problems that led to the firing have disappeared, don't rehire.

Any there any specific steps suggested to avoid an age discrimination suit?

In addition to the steps suggested throughout this section that should be observed prior to and during a firing, consider hiring an older individual to replace the fired employee. This isn't an ironclad guarantee of winning an age discrimination suit, but it sure won't help the plaintiff's case!

Is it better to fire several people at the same time?

If you have decided to fire more than one individual, it is best to fire them simultaneously. If you effect the firings piecemeal, remaining staff members will wonder, "Who's going to get the ax this week?"

Should I announce the reasons for a firing to others?

No. There's already enough risk involved in a firing. When customers or vendors call, instruct the receptionist or other personnel to simply say "John Doe is no longer with us. Sally Smith has taken over his duties. May I connect you with her?"

If the firee was a key manager, you may feel compelled to detail the reasons to other managers. This is OK, but don't reveal anything that you can't substantiate. Avoid negativity and insist that the topic remain confidential.

Should I fire someone who is leaving soon anyway?

Often, but not always, employees who have given notice slow down their work pace in the period before their actual departure. If you aren't happy with this, ask them, sincerely, if they would prefer to leave earlier.

If the employee would like to continue in your employ until the announced departure date, encourage him or her to keep up their work pace, but don't push the employee to leave earlier. The legal risk for the company and the trauma that may be caused to other members of your work force are good enough reasons to avoid a firing in this instance. Besides, the employee has done you the courtesy of giving you advance notice of departure.

What can I do to avoid a lawsuit after firing someone?

If you are seriously concerned about this possibility, contact an attorney that specializes in employment law. Depending on the situation, the steps the attorney recommends may include paying your standard severance pay package, offering extra severance pay in exchange for signing a legal release, carefully documenting the reasons for the termination, promptly processing unemployment claims, promptly sending the employee any personal belongings left behind, and paying the employee any past due wages at the same time as the separation as mandated by law.

Leadership

Leadership is being able to get others to want to follow you on your chosen path.

In order to effect leadership, you need a well-defined strategy. But even a well-defined strategy is not enough to ensure successful leadership. You must also communicate to the rest of your organization what the strategy is. You must explain why it is a good strategy. You must convince them that you can lead the organization successfully down the path you have chosen.

What does a good leader do?

A good leader gets out in front of his or her people. He or she shows them what direction the company is headed in and why it is headed in this direction. He or she demonstrates why the chosen direction will lead them toward success.

A good leader repeatedly reminds the organization what the strategy is. He or she sees that the organization's plans and activities remain in sync with that strategy. He or she also sees that everyone appreciates the qualities that distinguish their company from other firms.

People like to feel they are on the winning team. A good leader celebrates his or her company's triumphs. In good times as well as difficult times, he or she paints a clear picture of how the firm will succeed and prosper in future years.

Streetwise Advice on Leadership

☞ **Tell them, then tell them again, and then tell them what you told them**
You need to express the company's strategy and future direction to the work force in very simple terms. And you are going to need to repeat this message again and again, or people aren't going to remember it at all.

☞ **Be sure that people are really getting the message**
Ask people to be sure they are really getting the message that you are delivering. At group meetings, ask people what they see as the key components of the company's strategy. At individual meetings or in questionnaires, ask questions like, "Do you feel that the company has a clear, future direction?" or "Do you feel the company is successful?" or "Do you think the company will prosper in the future?"

If is turns out the people aren't comprehending the message, go out and give it again.

☞ **Regular group meetings build a feeling of direction**
Having regularly scheduled meetings—weekly or monthly—can help you lead the company ahead. Use these meetings to applaud the company's triumphs. Compliment exemplary personal or group performances. And keep reminding people about the direction you are leading them in. Remind them that they are on the winning team!

☞ **Extend leadership into all parts of the organization**
In large meetings or company-wide meetings, you can show leadership in a broad, visionary way. But you or your managers should have smaller meetings with people in each functional area. People want to feel that their department or function has a clearly defined role and direction within the overall plan.

☞ **Celebrate milestones**
Celebrating milestones is a good way to vividly remind people that they are on the winning team. If you just had your first million-dollar year, have a party! If you just completed a major project, have a party! If you just opened a branch office, have a party! And be sure everyone knows what is being celebrated.

"In large meetings or company-wide meetings, you can show leadership in a broad, visionary way."

Questions & Answers about Leadership

How is leadership different than management?

Management focuses on getting today's work done. Leadership focuses on the future. A good leader not only assures people that they will have jobs tomorrow, but assures them that they will have jobs with the winning team. A good leader inspires confidence that the company is going to succeed and prosper in the times ahead.

What is the best way to show people what direction the company is headed in?

Even in the high-tech era, there is no substitute for low-tech talk at a company-wide meetings. Just by getting people together, you create the feeling that everyone is moving forward in the same direction. It also gives you the opportunity to use emotion to convey your strategy and reveal your plan for the future.

How effective is electronic media or print literature for conveying leadership messages?

I created a colorful computer program to show everyone in our organization what we are about and where we are headed. I thought it would be a great and fun way to convey this sort of information. People really enjoyed using the program and I got a lot of compliments on it. But people used it once and forgot about it. Within a month virtually no one could even remember the most basic information regarding the company's strategy.

If multi-media won't convey the message adequately, the weaker print media won't either. You have to show your employees that you are personally leading the organization in a forward direction and, as experience has taught, the only way to do that is personally. There just isn't a substitute for a company meeting.

Should I be candid if the company is experiencing problems?

Yes. You need to be candid because the rumors might be worse and will certainly create worse problems. You need to take the bull by the horns and paint a clear picture regarding the major problems you face, and, at the same time, outline the direction you plan to take the company in order to get out of the difficulty.

Do hourly workers really care what direction the company is headed in?

Some lower-level employees may have little or no interest in what the company's future strategy is. But all employees will want to know that they are on a winning team. They want to be able tell their families and friends that they work for a great firm. If they feel they are working for a firm that is going to succeed and prosper, they are going to work harder and better, and be positive, upbeat employees.

Some people view company policies as a sign of encroaching bureaucracy and avoid issuing or observing them like the plague. There are even a few publicized cases of relatively large companies that have enjoyed tremendous success without benefit of company policies.

However, you will find that if you don't have some company policies, you will soon find yourself in a situation in which you wish you did. Policies can make it clear to employees what kind of behavior is expected in your workplace. They can set clear guidelines on what is and isn't appropriate. And policies can help you avoid, or at least defend against, lawsuits.

Employee handbooks

If you have more than a dozen employees, you should consider creating a company policy book, often referred to as an employee handbook. This type of book lays out in clear, simple language the patterns of behavior that are or are not acceptable within your workplace. These policies should be aimed at both managers and staff alike. A well-done handbook will go a long way toward protecting you against some employment-related legal claims.

If you do decide to create an employee handbook, have an attorney who specializes in employment issues review the document before you issue it to your employees.

Remember, too, that although you are the employer, you must follow the rules outlined in your employee handbook yourself and meet any requirements or responsibilities you have set within. Company policy books have been seen by the courts as legally binding contracts between employers and employees. Numerous employees have won lawsuits against companies because the employer has not honored the terms or conditions in their own handbooks.

Sexual harassment

Sexual harassment occurs in all types of workplaces, in all areas of the country, in all countries all over the world. You personally may not have witnessed it or been a victim of it, especially if you are a male, but believe me it exists!

Most women, and some men, have experienced sexual harassment during their careers. Many employees who do so become extremely upset by it. Even the perception of sexual harassment can have a very negative effect on employee—and, oftentimes, on everyone else in the workplace.

As an employer or manager, take the high road. Make it very clear to people that your firm is strongly against sexual harassment, not just because it is unlawful, but because it just isn't right. Most, if not all, of your employees will appreciate your position. If there are objections among members of your staff, they aren't the type of employee you want in your workplace anyway!

Sexual harassment is one of the most common grounds for employee-initiated lawsuits in our country. As an employer, you are responsible for your own actions, the actions of your supervisors. and your workplace atmosphere. If the environment you provide to your employees is or is deemed to be conducive to sexually negative behavior, such as sexually oriented joking, you are legally vulnerable. You need to state a clear policy against sexual harassment within your workplace. You need to take appropriate action against any employee who either condones sexual harassment or violates sexual harassment policies. And you need to assign an impartial party as the person with whom sexual harassment complaints can be registered. This allows employees to lodge complaints with someone other than their immediate supervisor, which could be a serious problem if the supervisor is the person the complaint is about.

Equal opportunity

In hiring and promoting personnel you need to be sure that you are an equal-opportunity employer—that women, minorities, people of all ages, people of all religions, etc. have an equal chance of employment or promotion at your firm. Under current U.S. law you also need to undertake some expenditures, if necessary and with the value being dependent upon the size of your company, to employ physically challenged people.

Take the high road. Make an effort to hire and promote people equally. It is the law, and it is the right thing to do.

You want to make sure that all supervisors are careful not to discriminate in their hiring and promoting practices. You also want to make sure that they are completely apprised of which questions are appropriate and legal to ask during interviews and which ones are not.

Being an equal-opportunity employer is not easy. Most people, yourself probably included, find it easiest to relate to those individuals who most closely mirror themselves. It is a natural human tendency to hire and promote those individuals whom you like. So if, for instance, an engineering department manager is a white male you would need to make sure he doesn't overtly or subconsciously overlook any qualified nonwhite or female candidates when he is interviewing for a new staff engineer.

Dress

Business dress is becoming increasingly casual. Many companies even designate a particular day, seasonally or year-round, as casual day. And some companies waste a significant amount of time defining what is and what is not appropriate as casual wear. It really isn't necessary, though, to spend too much time developing a dress code. Think simple.

If you don't greet customers or clients in your workplace, you may want to skip having a formal dress code. One exception might be offensive dress—skimpy outfits or T-shirts that carry profane messages or images. Of course, this liberal policy may result in sloppy dress on the part of some employees, but the rewards you reap by showing respect for your employees will be worth it.

If customers or clients frequent your workplace set a few basic standards for dress for those employees who interact with the public—shirts, not T-shirts; slacks, not jeans; shoes, not sneakers; and skirts, not shorts.

Hours

Set regular office or shift hours. You may want to offer certain employees reasonable flex-time schedules to accommodate special needs. For example, if an employee needs to arrive later and leave later to manage child care arrangements, you may allow him or her a working hour variance. But you should still insist that all employees observe a consistent schedule. By setting reasonable office hours, you will appear fair to all employees and will avoid having to memorize a myriad of different work schedules.

Even if an employee works overtime, you should require that he or she start each day at the designated starting time. Make no exceptions to standard or flex-time working hours unless the circumstances are extraordinary.

Phones

Avoid setting policies regarding personal phone usage, local or long-distance. The results of no policy may be reflected in your phone bills but the results of a specific policy will be reflected in employee attitude. You will be viewed as petty and, for this, employees will resent you.

Obviously, if a particular employee abuses your liberal phone policies action is called for. Sometimes a chat will do or you may have to make it difficult for the employee to access the phone altogether. Termination should not be an option if the employee performs satisfactorily otherwise.

Romance

There will always be dating in the workplace, whether you like it or not. This is especially true if you have young, single employees on staff. And, however unfortunate, it may even happen if you only happen to employ married people.

It certainly seems intrusive to regulate people's personal lives. Weigh the considerations and make your own decision. Things do get sticky in office romances—especially if the romance isn't between peers. If a supervisor dates a reporting staff member, the staff member may receive a glowing, but undeserved, performance review. Or, in the event of a breakup between someone in management and someone on staff, a recommendation that the staff member be dismissed for "unmanageable behavior" might result. Issues of sexual harassment might be raised if a staff employee declines to date someone in management. Because these types of situations breed tension and much worse, you may want to consider prohibiting management from dating anyone who reports to them directly.

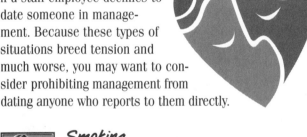

Smoking

More and more workplaces in more and more areas are being deemed smoke-free by law. Nonsmokers like and greatly appreciate smoke-free working environments, but this can be a tremendous source of tension for smokers.

You need to state a clear smoking policy. If one person smokes, you aren't working in a smoke-free environment.

You need to inform new hires of your smoking policy. If the new employee is a smoker, he or she might be shocked to find no one is allowed to puff away at his or her desk. Or nonsmokers may be greatly upset to find that their fellow workers can and do smoke in the office.

If someone is a smoker, and you have declared the office a smoke-free workplace, just what are the smokers supposed to do. Go outside? Well, typically that is the resolution. But it's cold in winter, and butts on the front sidewalk are unsightly. At our office, I found it unattractive to have people congregated in front of the building smoking, so we recently moved the smoking area to a remote side door. I know I can't make both smokers and nonsmokers happy, but, like most firms, I have a lot more people who don't smoke.

Employee loans

Most employees don't have strong financial educations and don't have the discipline to manage their finances. I suggest that you allow employees who have been with you for a few months to borrow modest amounts of money for short periods of time. And don't charge interest—it's just too petty. But do deduct the payback out of each payroll check and have the employee sign a simple demand note stating the amount loaned, the payment schedule, and a clause stipulating that the loan be immediately payable in full should the employee leave the company for any reason.

Set a limit on the amount you will agree to lend to any employee—and do this in advance of any requests. Sooner or later you will lose money when an employee leaves and you find that you cannot collect. But despite this drawback, remember, in the long run an employee loan policy will strengthen your firm.

I lost about $2,000 when one long-term employee was fired several years ago and I was unable to recover my loan. But I have loaned money to hundreds of other employees over a period of years without incident.

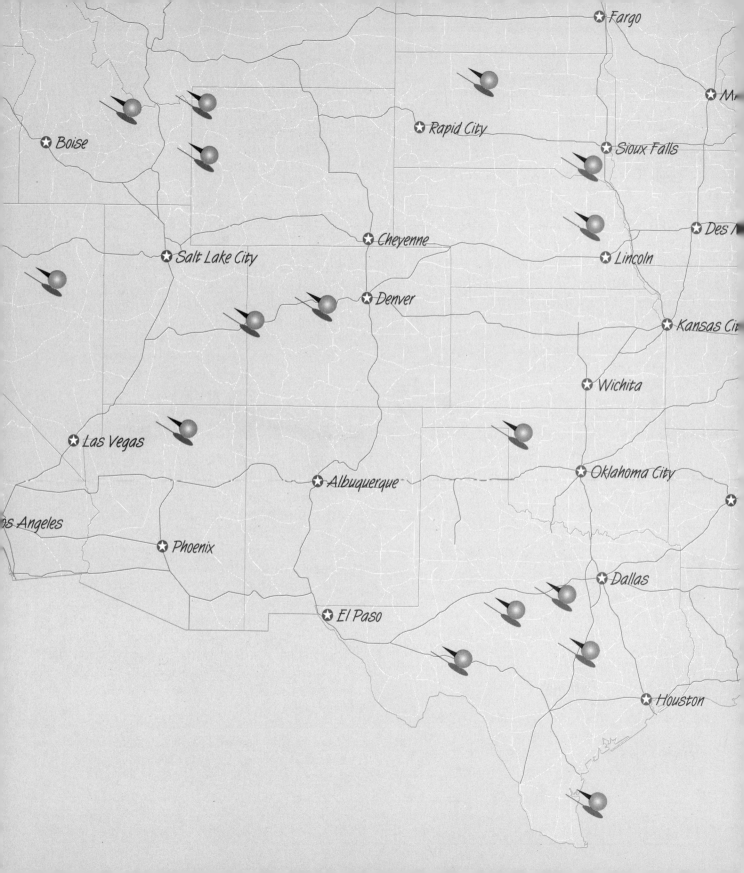

M · O · N · E · Y

6

Basic Accounting .... ▶ 269

Pro Forma .... ▶ 281

Credit .... ▶ 292

Purchasing .... ▶ 300

Taxes .... ▶ 305

Getting Money! .... ▶ 310

Cash Is King! .... ▶ 317

Money Problems .... ▶ 322

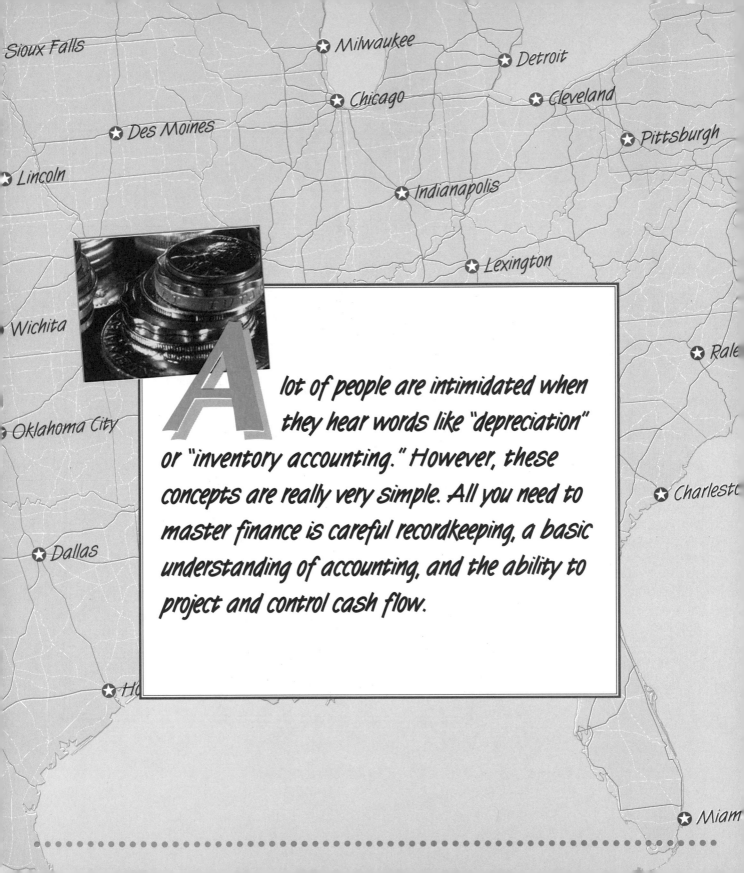

A lot of people are intimidated when they hear words like "depreciation" or "inventory accounting." However, these concepts are really very simple. All you need to master finance is careful recordkeeping, a basic understanding of accounting, and the ability to project and control cash flow.

Basic Accounting: Income Statements

An income statement, otherwise known as a profit and loss statement, is a summary of a company's profit or loss during any one given period of time, such as a month, three months, or one year. The income statement records all revenues for a business during this given period, as well as the operating expenses for the business.

What are income statements used for?

You use an income statement to track revenues and expenses so that you can determine the operating performance of your business over a period of time. Small business owners use these statements to find out what areas of their business are over budget or under budget. Specific items that are causing unexpected expenditures can be pinpointed, such as phone, fax, mail, or supply expenses. Income statements can also track dramatic increases in product returns or cost of goods sold as a percentage of sales. They also can be used to determine income tax liability.

It is very important to format an income statement so that it is appropriate to the business being conducted.

Income statements, along with balance sheets, are the most basic elements required by potential lenders, such as banks, investors, and vendors. They will use the financial reporting contained therein to determine credit limits.

1 Sales

The sales figure represents the amount of revenue generated by the business. The amount recorded here is the total sales, less any product returns or sales discounts.

2 Cost of goods sold

This number represents the costs directly associated with making or acquiring your products. Costs include materials purchased from outside suppliers used in the manufacture of your product, as well as any internal expenses directly expended in the manufacturing process.

Gross profit

Gross profit is derived by subtracting the cost of goods sold from net sales. It does not include any operating expenses or income taxes.

3 Operating expenses

These are the daily expenses incurred in the operation of your business. In this sample, they are divided into two categories: selling, and general and administrative expenses.

Sales salaries

These are the salaries plus bonuses and commissions paid to your sales staff.

Collateral and promotions

Collateral fees are expenses incurred in the creation or purchase of printed sales materials used by your sales staff in marketing and selling your product. Promotion fees include any product samples and giveaways used to promote or sell your product.

Advertising

These represent all costs involved in creating and placing print or multi-media advertising.

Other sales costs

These include any other costs associated with selling your product. They may include travel, client meals, sales meetings, equipment rental for presentations, copying, or miscellaneous printing costs.

Office salaries
These are the salaries of full- and part-time office personnel.

Rent
These are the fees incurred to rent or lease office or industrial space.

Utilities
These include costs for heating, air conditioning, electricity, phone equipment rental, and phone usage used in connection with your business.

Depreciation
Depreciation is an annual expense that takes into account the loss in value of equipment used in your business. Examples of equipment that may be subject to depreciation includes copiers, computers, printers, and fax machines.

Other overhead costs
Expense items that do not fall into other categories or cannot be clearly associated with a particular product or function are considered to be other overhead costs. These types of expenses may include insurance, office supplies, or cleaning services.

4 Total expenses
This is a tabulation of all expenses incurred in running your business, exclusive of taxes or interest expense on interest income, if any.

5 Net income before taxes
This number represents the amount of income earned by a business prior to paying income taxes. This figure is arrived at by subtracting total operating expenses from gross profit.

6 Taxes
This is the amount of income taxes you owe to the federal government and, if applicable, state and local government taxes.

7 Net income
This is the amount of money the business has earned after paying income taxes.

INCOME STATEMENT • DECEMBER 31, 1995

for

JUNIPER TOYS, INC.

1	**SALES**		**$1,000,000**
2	**COST OF GOODS SOLD**		**$500,000**
	Gross profit		$500,000
3	**OPERATING EXPENSES**		
	Sales force salaries	$150,000	
	Collateral and promotions	$25,000	
	Advertising	$30,000	
	Other sales costs	$8,000	
	Total Selling Expenses	**$213,000**	
	Office salaries	$100,000	
	Rent	$21,000	
	Utilities	$25,000	
	Depreciation on office equipment	$1,500	
	Other expenses	$50,000	
	Total General Expenses	**$197,000**	
4	**TOTAL EXPENSES**		**$410,000**
5	**NET INCOME BEFORE TAXES**		$89,500
6	**TAXES**	$17,900	
7	**NET INCOME**		**$71,600**

Basic Accounting: Balance Sheets

A balance sheet is a snapshot of a business' financial condition at a specific moment in time, usually at the close of an accounting period. A balance sheet comprises assets, liabilities, and owners' or stockholders' equity. Assets and liabilities are divided into short- and long-term obligations including cash accounts such as checking, money market, or government securities. At any given time, assets must equal liabilities plus owners' equity. An asset is anything the business owns that has monetary value. Liabilities are the claims of creditors against the assets of the business.

What is a balance sheet used for?

A balance sheet helps a small business owner quickly get a handle on the financial strength and capabilities of the business. Is the business in a position to expand? Can the business easily handle the normal financial ebbs and flows of revenues and expenses? Or should the business take immediate steps to bolster cash reserves?

Balance sheets can identify and analyze trends, particularly in the area of receivables and payables. Is the receivables cycle lengthening? Can receivables be collected more aggressively? Is some debt uncollectable? Has the business been slowing down payables to forestall an inevitable cash shortage?

Balance sheets, along with income statements, are the most basic elements in providing financial reporting to potential lenders such as banks, investors, and vendors who are considering how much credit to grant the firm.

1 Assets

Assets are subdivided into current and long-term assets to reflect the ease of liquidating each asset. Cash, for obvious reasons, is considered the most liquid of all assets. Long-term assets, such as real estate or machinery, are less likely to sell overnight or have the capability of being quickly converted into a current asset such as cash.

2 Current assets

Current assets are any assets that can be easily converted into cash within one calendar year. Examples of current assets would be checking or money market accounts, accounts receivable, and notes receivable that are due within one year's time.

- **Cash**
  Money available immediately, such as in checking accounts, is the most liquid of all short-term assets.

- **Accounts receivables**
  This is money owed to the business for purchases made by customers, suppliers, and other vendors.

- **Notes receivables**
  Notes receivables that are due within one year are current assets. Notes that cannot be collected on within one year should be considered long-term assets.

3 Fixed assets

Fixed assets include land, buildings, machinery, and vehicles that are used in connection with the business.

- **Land**
  Land is considered a fixed asset but, unlike other fixed assets, is not depreciated, because land is considered an asset that never wears out.

Basic Accounting: Balance Sheets

Buildings

Buildings are categorized as fixed assets and are depreciated over time.

Office equipment

This includes office equipment such as copiers, fax machines, printers, and computers used in your business.

Machinery

This figure represents machines and equipment used in your plant to produce your product. Examples of machinery might include lathes, conveyor belts, or a printing press.

Vehicles

This would include any vehicles used in your business.

Total fixed assets

This is the total dollar value of all fixed assets in your business, less any accumulated depreciation.

4 Total assets

This figure represents the total dollar value of both the short-term and long-term assets of your business.

5 Liabilities and owners' equity

This includes all debts and obligations owed by the business to outside creditors, vendors, or banks that are payable within one year, plus the owners' equity. Often, this side of the balance sheet is simply referred to as "Liabilities."

Accounts payable

This is comprised of all short-term obligations owed by your business to creditors, suppliers, and other vendors. Accounts payable can include supplies and materials acquired on credit.

Notes payable

This represents money owed on a short-term collection cycle of one year or less. It may include bank notes, mortgage obligations, or vehicle payments.

Accrued payroll and withholding

This includes any earned wages or withholdings that are owed to or for employees but have not yet been paid.

Total current liabilities

This is the sum total of all current liabilities owed to creditors that must be paid within a one-year time frame.

Long-term liabilities

These are any debts or obligations owed by the business that are due more than one year out from the current date.

Mortgage note payable

This is the balance of a mortgage that extends out beyond the current year. For example, you may have paid off three years of a fifteen-year mortgage note, of which the remaining eleven years, not counting the current year, are considered long-term.

Owners' equity

Sometimes this is referred to as stockholders' equity. Owners' equity is made up of the initial investment in the business as well as any retained earnings that are reinvested in the business.

Common stock

This is stock issued as part of the initial or later-stage investment in the business.

Retained earnings

These are earnings reinvested in the business after the deduction of any distributions to shareholders, such as dividend payments.

6 Total liabilities and owners' equity

This comprises all debts and monies that are owed to outside creditors, vendors, or banks and the remaining monies that are owed to shareholders, including retained earnings reinvested in the business.

Balance Sheet

BALANCE SHEET • DECEMBER 31, 1995
for
ZYZ TRANSPORT, INC.

① ASSETS

② CURRENT ASSETS		
Cash		$35,000
Accounts receivables		$45,000
Note receivables		$15,000
	Total Current Assets	**$95,000**

③ FIXED ASSETS		
Land	$50,000	
Building	$350,000	
Office equipment	$12,000	
Machinery	$125,000	
Vehicles	$37,000	
Less: Accumulated depreciation	($135,000)	
	Total Fixed Assets	**$439,000**
	▶	**$534,000**

④ TOTAL ASSETS

⑤ LIABILITIES AND OWNERS' EQUITY

Current Liabilities		
Accounts payable		$38,000
Notes payable (less than one year due)		$23,000
Accrued payroll and withholdings		$75,000
	Total Current Liabilities	**$136,000**

Long-Term Liabilities		
Mortgage note payable (beyond one year due)		$125,000
	Total Liabilities	**$261,000**

Owners' Equity		
Common stock	$31,400	
Retained earnings	$241,600	
	Total Owners' Equity	**$273,000**
	▶	**$534,000**

⑥ TOTAL LIABILITY AND OWNERS' EQUITY

Basic Accounting: Depreciation

*T*he concept of depreciation is really pretty simple. For example, let's say you purchase a truck for your business. The truck loses value the minute you drive it out of the dealership. The truck is considered an operational asset in running your business. Each year that you own the truck, it loses some value, until the truck finally stops running and has no value to the business. Measuring the loss in value of an asset is known as depreciation.

Depreciation is considered an expense and is listed in an income statement under expenses. In addition to vehicles that may be used in your business, you can depreciate office furniture, office equipment, any buildings you own, and machinery you use to manufacture products.

Land is not considered an expense, nor can it be depreciated. Land does not wear out like vehicles or equipment.

To find the annual depreciation cost for your assets, you need to know the initial cost of the assets. You also need to determine how many years you think the assets will retain some value for your business. In the case of the truck, it may only have a useful life of ten years before it wears out and loses all value.

Straight-line depreciation

Straight-line depreciation is considered to be the most common method of depreciating assets. To compute the amount of annual depreciation expense using the straight-line method requires two numbers: the initial cost of the asset and its estimated useful life. For example, you purchase a truck for $20,000 and expect it to have use in your business for ten years. Using the straight-line method for determining depreciation, you would divide the initial cost of the truck by its useful life.

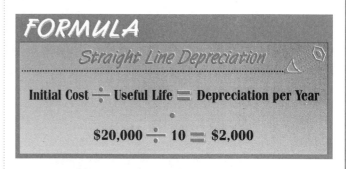

FORMULA

Straight Line Depreciation

Initial Cost ÷ Useful Life = Depreciation per Year

$20,000 ÷ 10 = $2,000

The $20,000 becomes a depreciation expense that is reported on your income statement under operation expenses at the end of each year.

For tax purposes, some accountants prefer to use other methods of accelerating depreciation in order to record larger amounts of depreciation in the early years of the asset to reduce tax bills as soon as possible.

You need, additionally, to check the regulations published by the federal Internal Revenue Service and various state revenue authorities for any specific rules regarding depreciation and methods of calculating depreciation for various types of assets.

Basic Accounting: Depreciation

Book value

Depreciation is also reflected on your balance sheet as the difference between the "book" or "carrying" value and the initial price of an asset. You determine this by adding up the accumulated depreciation expense and subtracting it from the initial cost of the equipment. For example, you purchase a truck for $20,000 in 1992. It has an estimated useful life of ten years. The annual depreciation expense is $2,000. It is now December 31, 1994, and you want to show the book value on your balance sheet. Your entry on your balance sheet would have the following line items:

At the end of the tenth year, the book value of the truck will be zero because the truck will have no value.

Cost of truck acquired on January 1, 1992	$20,000
Accumulated depreciation expense	
January 1, 1992 to December 31, 1994	
$2,000 per year x 3 years	$6,000
Book Value = amount of truck cost not allocated to depreciation expense ✓	$14,000

Basic Accounting: Amortization

*I*n the course of doing business, you will likely acquire what are known as intangible assets. These assets can contribute to the revenue growth of your business and, as such, they can be expensed against these future revenues. An example of an intangible asset is when you buy a patent for an invention.

Calculating amortization

The formula for calculating the amortization on an intangible asset is similar to the one used for calculating straight-line depreciation. You divide the initial cost of the intangible asset by the estimated useful life of the intangible asset. For example, if it costs $10,000 to acquire a patent and it has an estimated useful life of ten years, the amortized amount per year equals $1,000. The amount of amortization accumulated since the asset was acquired appears on the balance sheet as a deduction under the amortized asset.

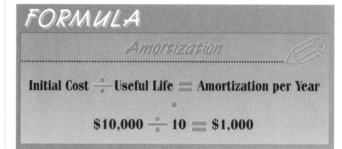

FORMULA

Amortization

Initial Cost ÷ Useful Life = Amortization per Year

$10,000 ÷ 10 = $1,000

Basic Accounting: Inventory Accounting

*I*nventory accounting may sound like a huge undertaking but in reality, it is quite straightforward and easy to understand. You start with the inventory you have on hand. No matter when you sell product, the value of your inventory will remain constant based on accepted and rational methods of inventory accounting. Those methods include weighted average, first in/first out, and last in/first out.

Weighted average

Weighted average measures the total cost of items in inventory that are available for sale divided by the total number of units available for sale. Typically this average is computed at the end of an accounting period.

Suppose you purchase five widgets at $10 apiece and five widgets at $20 apiece. You sell five units of product. The weighted average method is calculated as follows:

First in/First out

First in, first out means exactly what it says. The first widgets you bring into inventory will be the first ones sold as product. First in, first out, or FIFO as it is commonly referred to, is based on the principle that most businesses tend to sell the first goods that come into inventory.

Suppose you buy five widgets at $10 apiece on January 3 and purchase another five widgets at $20 apiece on January 7. You then sell five widgets on January 30. Using first in, first out, the five widgets you purchased at $10 would be sold first. This would leave you with the five widgets that you purchased at $20, which would leave the value of your inventory at $100.

Last in/first out

This method, commonly referred to as LIFO, is based on the assumption that the most recent units purchased will be the first units sold. A "widget" is an imaginary item that could be just about any product. The advantage of last in, first out accounting, or LIFO, is that typically the last widgets purchased were purchased at the highest price and that by considering the highest priced items to be sold first, a business is able to reduce its short-term profit, and hence, taxes.

Suppose you purchase five widgets at $10 apiece on January 4 and five more widgets at $20 apiece on February 2. You then sell five widgets on February 20. The value of your inventory, using LIFO, would be $50, since the most recent widgets purchased, at a total value of $100 on February 2, were sold. You were left with the five widgets valued at $10 each.

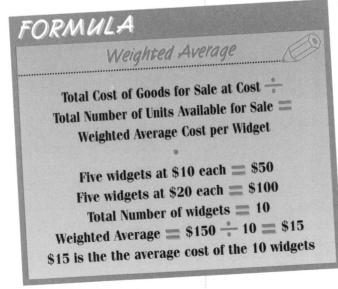

FORMULA
Weighted Average

Total Cost of Goods for Sale at Cost ÷
Total Number of Units Available for Sale =
Weighted Average Cost per Widget

•

Five widgets at $10 each = $50
Five widgets at $20 each = $100
Total Number of widgets = 10
Weighted Average = $150 ÷ 10 = $15
$15 is the the average cost of the 10 widgets

☞ Not just a measuring unit

Accounting is not just a yardstick to figure out how much money you made last year or what your tax liability is. Used properly, accounting also helps you identify trends in sales and expenditures. The ability to track and identify trends allows you to make decisions that can quickly boost your profitability or enable you to avoid cash shortages.

☞ Do it monthly

Every month, you should calculate the profitability of your business by putting together an income statement. Ideally, you should also examine your balance sheet. By looking at your financial statements every month, you can quickly adjust expenditures and sales efforts to keep your business within budget. Otherwise, at the end of the year, you will probably find that your expenses have crept upward, leaving your profit margin below your initial projection.

☞ Meticulous records

No matter how strong or weak your understanding of accounting is, you need to keep very careful, well-organized records.

One reason to keep good records is for tax purposes. If you ever get audited, the tax people are going to want to see some receipts, not just cancelled checks. If you can't produce the receipts requested during an audit, the IRS isn't going to be understanding about it!

There are lots of other reasons to be organized. For example, it is not uncommon for large, as well as small, companies to pay the same bill twice—sometimes overpaying by thousands of dollars. And it isn't uncommon for vendors to claim that you never paid a particular bill despite the fact that you have.

One year a state revenue division came after me for taxes they claimed were unpaid. I had organized records and could prove payment. Despite this, claims regarding the same issue were made again. Finally, I was forced to complain to the tax commissioner. But at least I had proof of payment!

☞ Basic principles

Don't be awed by accounting or its fancy terminology. The basic concepts are very simple. Even if you decide to use an outside accountant on a regular basis, you need to invest some time in understanding the basic principles yourself.

> " The ability to track and identify trends allows you to make decisions that can quickly boost your profitability or enable you to avoid cash shortages."

How can accounting help me make money?

Quite simply, accounting tells you if you are making money. If you create a profit and loss statement each month, you can ascertain your position quickly. If you arc losing money, you can make changes in your operations, such as increasing prices or reducing expenses, to correct the situation long before the year's end and ensure that your overall year will still be profitable.

Can't I just write checks, make deposits, and file taxes?

If you don't do any accounting, then that's probably all you're doing—making deposits, writing checks, and paying taxes, but not making any profit! Even in a very small business you need to be in control of your expenses. This doesn't just mean having the money, it means knowing what portion of your revenue gets spent for what purposes. What percentage of revenue do you spend on marketing each month? What about labor? What about supplies? If you don't track and control these expenditures, you are not managing your business—you are just  blindly hoping there might someday be a profit.

Can't I hire a bookkeeper to do the accounting for me?

A good bookkeeper or even a good accounting software program can help you organize your accounting quickly. But you still need to understand the basic principles of accounting. This will allow you to use the information supplied by the bookkeeper or software program intelligently, enabling you to make the changes in your business that will keep it on track toward success and profitability.

What's more important, income statements or balance sheets?

At the risk of sending all accountants into apoplexy, I feel that the income statement is the more important document. The income statement tells you if you are making money and delineates your costs and expenses.

How can a balance sheet help me?

A balance sheet shows you how your assets are being used. For instance, from a balance sheet you should be able to tell whether or not your inventories are too large, whether your receivables are growing, or whether your ratio of debt to equity is getting too high.

Do I really have to understand the different depreciation formulas?

Not at all. Let your accountant figure these out, precisely, at the end of the year. Just plug "ballpark" numbers into your monthly profit and loss statements if you like.

Do I really need to create a balance sheet each month?

If your business is really small, you can manage it fine without creating a balance sheet each month. But any size business, including a part-time one, needs to create a good profit and loss statement each month. And, if inventories or accounts receivables are important in your business, balance sheets will clearly point out any significant fluctuations that you should be aware of.

Pro Forma Income Statements

A pro forma income statement is similar to a historical income statement, except it projects the future rather than tracks the past. Pro forma income statements are an important tool for planning future business operations. If the projections predict a downturn in profitability, you can make operational changes such as increasing prices or decreasing costs before these projections become reality.

Pro forma income statements provide an important benchmark or budget for operating a business throughout the year. They can determine whether expenses can be expected to run higher in the first quarter of the year than in the second. They can determine whether or not sales can be expected to be run above average in June. The can determine whether or not your marketing campaigns need an extra boost during the fall months. All in all, they provide you with invaluable information—the sort of information you need in order to make right choices for your business.

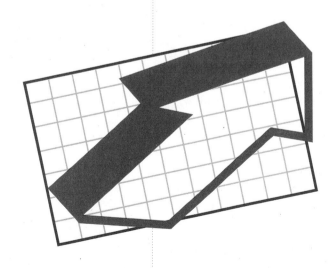

Pro Forma Income Statements

How do I create a pro forma income statement?

Sit down with an income statement from the current year. Consider how each item on that statement can or will be changed during the coming year. This should, ideally, be done before year's end. You will need to estimate final sales and expenses for the current year to prepare a pro forma income statement for the coming year.

1 Pro forma gross profit

Let's assume that you expect sales to increase by 10 percent next year. You multiply this year's sales of $1,000,000 by 110 percent to get $1,100,000. Then, in this case, you assume there will be no increase in the cost of each item you are selling, but you will need 10 percent more items to sell in order to achieve your sales goals. So, you multiply this year's cost of goods sold (let's assume a figure of $500,000), by 110 percent to get $550,000.

To figure your pro forma gross profit for next year, subtract the pro forma cost of goods sold from the pro forma sales. $1,100,000 minus $550,000 equals your gross profit, or $550,000.

2 Pro forma total expenses

Let's assume salaries and other expenses will increase by 5 percent. So, you multiply your historical salaries of $200,000 and your historical expenses of $100,000 by 105 percent each. Your pro forma salaries for next year will be $210,000 and your pro forma expenses will be $105,000.

You then figure your pro forma total expenses by adding pro forma salaries and pro forma other expenses together. In our sample case your pro forma total expenses will be $315,000.

3 Pro forma profit before taxes

Pro forma profit before taxes is figured by subtracting the pro forma expenses from the pro forma gross profit, or $315,000 from $550,000 for a pro forma profit before taxes of $235,000.

4 Pro forma taxes

Pro forma taxes are figured by taking your estimated tax rate, in this case 30 percent, and multiplying it by the pro forma profit before taxes of $235,000. This produces a pro forma tax bill of $70,500.

5 Pro forma profit after taxes

Pro forma profit after taxes is figured by subtracting the pro forma tax bill of $70,500 from the pro forma profit before taxes of $235,000. Your pro forma profit after taxes, in this case, would be projected at $164,300.

Remember that pro formas are essentially best guesses. You should continually update your projections by recalculating your pro formas using any new and actual financial information you have as a base. Doing this on a monthly or quarterly basis will help to assure that your projections are as close to being accurate as possible.

Pro Forma Income Statement

PRO FORMA INCOME STATEMENT FOR 1996
for
THE BIG BOX COMPANY

		1995 Historical	Projected Increase	1996 Pro forma
	Sales	$1,000,000	× 110% =	$1,110,000
	Cost of goods sold	$500,000	× 110% =	$550,000
1	**GROSS PROFIT**	**$500,000**		**$550,000**
	Salaries	$200,000	× 105% =	$210,000
	Other expenses	$100,000	× 105% =	$105,000
2	**TOTAL EXPENSES**	**$300,000**		**$315,000**
3	**PROFIT BEFORE TAXES**	**$200,000**		**$235,000**
4	**TAXES**	**$60,000**		**$70,500**
5	**PROFIT AFTER TAXES**	**$140,000**		**$164,500**

Pro Forma Balance Sheets

A pro forma balance sheet is similar to a historical balance sheet, but it represents a future projection. Pro forma balance sheets are used to project how the business will be managing its assets in the future. For example, a pro forma balance sheet can quickly show the projected relative amount of money tied up in receivables, inventory, and equipment. It can also be used to project the overall financial soundness of the company. For example, a pro forma balance sheet can help quickly pinpoint a high debt-to-equity ratio.

1 Pro forma current assets

Cash

To obtain your company's estimated cash position, you need to do a careful cash flow projection. Cash flow projections are covered later in this chapter. Let's assume that the projected cash flow for a company called Bright Lawn, or the anticipated funds in Bright Lawn's checking account on December 31, 1996, will be $50,000.

Pro forma accounts receivable

To estimate the accounts receivable on December 31, you need to take into consideration the average collection time of receivables and the sales projections for prior periods. For example, let's assume that Bright Lawn receives payment thirty days after services are performed.

So, in this case, we need to look at the projected sales for December, which are $70,000. Because it takes thirty days to collect payment, we would expect to have all of December's billings outstanding on December 31. Bright Lawn's account receivables would be estimated at $70,000.

Pro forma total current assets

Pro forma total current assets are determined by adding projected cash and projected accounts receivable.

2 Pro forma fixed assets

Pro forma land

Land is the easiest of pro forma asset values to calculate. Because land does not depreciate, it will always have the same value. Just enter the value of the land at its original purchase price. Bright Lawn's land holdings are valued at $30,000.

Pro forma buildings

Buildings do depreciate. Let's assume we are depreciating the building over thirty years. Bright Lawn bought its building for $300,000. Each year the building will depreciate by $10,000. By December 31, 1996, the building will be three years old, so the total depreciation will be $30,000. This will be reflected later in the accumulated depreciation total. Under the building heading we show the original value of the asset or $300,000.

Pro forma vehicles

Vehicles also depreciate. They depreciate over a much shorter period of time than do buildings. Let's assume we are depreciating Bright Lawn's truck over a seven-year period. The truck was purchased for $73,500 on January 1, 1996. So, each year the truck will depreciate by $10,500. On December 31, 1996, after one year of depreciation, the truck will have an accumulated depreciation of $10,500.

Pro Forma Balance Sheets

- **Pro forma total assets**
Pro forma total assets are determined by adding up the pro forma total current assets and pro forma total fixed assets.

3 Pro forma current liabilities

- **Pro forma accounts payable**
Pro forma accounts payable are determined by figuring out how much you will spend on supplies during the last months of 1995 and how long it takes you to pay your bills. Because Bright Lawn pays its bills in thirty days, it should only have outstanding bills for the supplies it anticipates purchasing in December as of December 31, 1996. Since Bright Lawn estimates a supply expenditure of $30,000 in December, it will have a pro forma accounts payable of $30,000.

- **Pro forma accrued payroll**
It should be easy to determine a pro forma accrued payroll. Just check your payroll calendar to find out what employee pay periods will remain unpaid by the beginning of the pro forma balance sheet period. Bright Lawn's weekly payroll is $10,000. Since it pays employees on a weekly basis, the pro forma accrued payroll will be 10,000 on December 31.

- **Pro forma notes payable**
Pro forma notes payable include all notes or portions of notes that are payable within one year. Bright Lawn will include in its pro forma notes payable the portion of its outstanding mortgage that will fall due during 1997 on its year-end 1996 balance sheet. The amount is calculated to be $15,000.

- **Pro forma total current liabilities**
To obtain pro forma total current liabilities, you add up pro forma accounts payable, accrued payroll, and notes, or portions thereof, payable, within one year. Bright Lawn's total current liabilities are projected to be $55,000.

4 Pro forma long-term liabilities

- **Pro forma mortgage note payable**
The size of a pro forma mortgage note payable is calculated by taking the mortgage note payable at the end of the current year and subtracting the principal, not interest, payments that will be made during the upcoming year. To obtain that portion of the mortgage that will be classified as a long-term liability, you need to subtract what is classified as current liability. In Bright Lawn's case, $15,000 is subtracted from the current remaining principal payments of $200,000. Therefore, the long-term portion of Bright Lawn's pro forma mortgage note payable is $185,000.

- **Pro forma total liabilities**
Pro forma total liabilities are determined by adding up current and long-term liabilities. Bright Lawn's pro forma total liabilities are $240,000.

5 Pro forma owners' equity

- **Pro forma common stock**
The common stock portion of the owners' equity will not change from year to year unless new stock is issued.

- **Pro forma retained earnings**
Pro forma retained earnings can be tricky to determine. They are the last item to be calculated on a pro forma balance sheet.

Total assets must balance the total liabilities and owners' equity. In Bright Lawn's case, we already know that the total pro forma liabilities must total $483,000.

Also, total liabilities added to total owners' equity must equal total liabilities and owners' equity. So, you can determine total owners' equity by subtracting total liabilities from total liabilities and owners' equity.

Common stock added to retained earnings must equal total owners' equity. So, by subtracting common stock from total owners' equity, retained earnings can be determined.

This completes a pro forma balance sheet.

PRO FORMA BALANCE SHEET FOR 1996
for
BRIGHT LAWN COMPANY

ASSETS

1 **Current assets**
Cash $50,000
Accounts receivables $70,000
                                        Total Current Assets   **$120,000**

2 **Fixed assets**
Land $30,000
Buildings $300,000
Vehicles $73,500
Less: Accumulated depreciation   ($40,500)
                                        Total Fixed Assets   **$363,000**
                                                           ▶ $483,000

Total Assets

LIABILITIES AND OWNERS' EQUITY

3 **Current liabilities**
Accounts payable $30,000
Accrued payroll $10,000
Notes payable (less than one year due) $15,000
                                        Total Current Liabilities   **$55,000**

4 **Long-term liabilities** $185,000
Mortgage note payable (beyond one year due)
                                        Total Liabilities   **$240,000**

5 **Owners' equity**
Common stock $40,000
Retained earnings $203,600
                                        Total Owners' Equity   **$243,000**
                                                           ▶ $483,000

Total liabilities and owners' equity

Pro Forma Cash Flows

A pro forma cash flow is created to predict inflow and outflow of cash to your business. It is particularly valuable in predicting when your business may experience a cash shortage. This allows you to determine in advance whether or not you will need to cover your cash shortage by borrowing money, selling more stock in the business, or taking other steps, such as cutting expenses, to improve your cash position.

Pro Forma Cash Flows

① Starting cash

To create a pro forma cash flow, you need to know your current cash position. To demonstrate the steps of building a pro forma cash flow, let's use a hypothetical company, West Coast Shoe Wholesaler's, Inc. West Coast Shoe is beginning 1997 with $90,000 in its checking account.

② Cash sources

• Receivables (sales)

West Coast Shoe sells to retailers on a credit basis. Retailers pay their accounts to West Coast Shoe thirty days after they are shipped their shoe orders. This means that in January 1997, West Coast Shoe will not receive cash from sales made in January, but will be collecting on sales made in December 1996. Those sales totaled $30,000, so that amount is entered in the January sales column of the cash flow.

• Total cash sources

This is a totaling of all cash received from all sources. Receivables from sales to retailers constitute the only source of cash for West Coast Shoe. Your cash sources may be more involved.

③ Cash uses

• Cost of goods

West Coast Shoe purchases the same dollar value of shoes from manufacturers each month—$15,000. And West Coast Shoe pays immediately for receipt of these purchases. $15,000 is entered as the cost of goods. Your company may try to balance its receipt of goods to match anticipated sales. This will result in a vacillating cost of goods figure each month. Most firms buy goods on credit and delay paying for those goods as long as they can to improve their cash flow. These factors need to be taken into consideration when creating a pro forma cash flow. Small, new firms, however, often have to prepay for goods until credit is established.

• Operating expenses

The operating expenses for West Coast Shoe are $10,000 per month.

• Income taxes

Income taxes for most businesses fluctuate from month to month because both state and federal taxes are paid as estimates on a quarterly, not monthly, basis. West Coast Shoe paid its estimated tax installments in December and doesn't have any tax payments due in January.

• Total cash uses

This is a totaling of all cash expenditures. In the case of West Coast Shoe, in the month of January, this amounts to $25,000 derived from cost of goods and operating expenses.

④ Net change in cash position

This figure is derived by subtracting the estimated cash uses from the estimated cash sources. For West Coast Shoe there is a net change in cash position of +$5,000.

By adding the net change figure to the starting cash figure, you will have the starting cash figure for the next month or time period for which you are calculating a cash flow. In this case, West Coast Shoe will begin February with $95,000.

1996 PRO FORMA CASH FLOW
for
WEST COAST SHOE WHOLESALERS, INC.

		January	February
1 STARTING CASH		**$90,000**	**$95,000**
2 CASH SOURCES			
Receivables		$30,000	
Total cash sources		**$30,000**	
3 CASH USES			
Cost of goods		$15,000	
Operating expenses		$10,000	
Taxes		0	
	Total cash uses	**$25,000**	
4 NET CHANGE IN CASH		**$5,000**	
ENDING CASH		**$95,000**	

Streetwise Advice on Pro Formas

👉 Multiple scenarios

Some people suggest that you make several sets of pro formas—most likely, best, and worst case scenarios.

I recommend that you carefully assemble one set of pro forma forecasts based on the most likely case. Developing pro formas is a tedious process. In creating one set of forecasts, you will probably remain more sensitive to your assumptions and their validity regarding sales forecasts, receivable collections, bad debt allowances, and delivery schedules. Also, in creating several sets of pro formas, each based on a different set of assumptions, you are increasing the risk of significant calculation errors.

Most banks will be very happy to see one well-done set of forecasts. But for larger, highly leveraged businesses, banks may expect more. For example, after one of my friends graduated from business school he sought financing to buy a group of major market radio stations. The lenders told him that three scenarios were absolutely insufficient and he needed to show at least seven.

👉 Sales forecasts

Accurately predicting sales is one of the most important factors in making projections. However, making sales assumptions carries a high risk of inaccuracy.

Use last year's sales as your starting point for sales projections. If you are a start-up business, use your break even sales point for sales projections.

Unless you are selling low-ticket items, last year's total sales results should not be the only factor considered. A more detailed breakdown is required. Estimate sales product line by product line and customer base by customer base. Estimate the impact of price increases, marketing plans, competitors, and any other major factor that could possibly have an effect on your sales potential.

Get your first sales projection from your sales manager. Remember, though, when you are reviewing his or her projections that salespeople tend to be optimists. Conduct a second review with your other managers. If you don't have a sales manager or other key personnel who can provide input into the sales forecast, seek the advice of someone else you can trust—your accountant, perhaps.

👉 Break-even forecast

Especially when starting a new business, people tend to underestimate how long it will take to build sales. For a new business (unless it's an established franchise) it's very difficult for anyone to estimate sales. So what I suggest is that you estimate what sales level you need to break even. Then, if you are not hitting this break-even level, you can immediately take steps to put the business back on track (such as cutting expenditures), before you get into trouble (such as running out of cash).

👉 Tools, not prophecies

First, think of pro formas as tools for running your business, and only second as predictions of the future.

The true strength of pro formas lies in your ability to make changes in them before their scenarios occur. If profitability looks too low (and it usually does in your first pass through your pro formas), take steps to improve it. Are prices too low? Is there any expense that can be cut? Is there a product or service that is not profitable that could be eliminated?

Questions & Answers on Pro Formas

How often should I create pro formas?

If your business is growing, start from scratch once each year. Additionally, the cash flow pro forma should be updated on a monthly basis. The cash flow is the most critical pro forma statement. If you run out of cash, you effectively are out of business!

If major changes are anticipated during the year, you may want to update your profit and loss pro formas at that time. Balance sheets really need to be updated only yearly if you are concerned about violating any bank loan agreements you have made that references your balance sheet.

Is it really worth the time to create pro formas?

Yes! To do it right will take a lot of time. But it is certainly time well spent. Pro forma profit and loss statements will allow you to see whether or not all of your hard work will, in all probability, lead to profits. Pro forma balance sheets tell you whether you will be depositing money in the bank or using it to keep your business running. Pro forma cash flows provide an early warning for cash flow problems.

Which pro forma is the most important?

Cash flow! It's nice to project a profit, and knowing you have a solid balance sheet can make you feel good—but if you run out of cash, your business will be dead in the water!

Just about all small businesses will feel a cash crunch sooner or later, and for most businesses it will happen sooner, later, and fairly regularly. But if you keep your cash flow projection up to date, you can take steps to avoid cash shortages before the problem becomes acute. Otherwise, you will go merrily along your way until one day you may find you have no money in the bank, your bank credit is exhausted, your payroll is due, your key vendors are howling for payment, the IRS is calling, and customers are still paying their bills slowly. Remember, cash crunches happen all the time in successful, profitable, growing businesses too!

Any tricks for quickly updating a cash flow pro forma?

Since any pro forma takes quite a while to carefully update, there may be times when you need a shortcut to get a ballpark estimate. I would first revise sales estimates and changes in collection cycle (the amount of time it takes you to get paid from customers who buy on credit) and any costs that directly change with sales, such as costs of goods sold in a product business, or the costs of labor and major supplies in a service business.

You're going to find that the process of extending credit is one of the most onerous aspects of running a business. If you can get away with being paid up front, or on delivery, by all means do it!

You will generally be able to get away with requiring immediate payment if you provide products or services to consumers. Accepting credit cards will help, and many of your customers will perceive this as a convenience. Credit card fees may run as high as 5 percent, but accepting them will speed your cash flow and save the time and effort involved in billing and collection procedures. It also cuts down on bad debt.

In almost all types of business-to-business transactions you will be expected to extend credit in order to close the sale. In some industries it is standard to require a percentage of the sale up front—especially if the client is new or the business is a start-up.

Budding entrepreneurs have a remarkable tendency to overlook the importance of carefully extending credit and aggressively collecting on overdue accounts receivable. Collections activities begin in earnest only when cash flow is negative. Don't overlook this important aspect of running a business. Get good people and sound policies in place as soon as possible!

Credit

You need to establish credit policies before orders start coming in. You need to inform customers up front if orders exceed their limits so that they can prepay the credit overage before shipment or scale their orders back.

The percentage of fraudulent orders (orders placed with no plans to pay for the goods received) placed in business are statistically insignificant. But many businesses of all sizes are constantly running into cash flow binds and are forced to pay their own bills weeks and months after they are actually due. If you are a new, small supplier you will probably be the last in line to get paid.

As soon as you open an account or get an order, you need to run a credit check on the customer. When accepting orders from large companies, request confirmation in writing via a purchase order. One of the best ways to get paid on old invoices is to insist that an account be brought up to date before new orders are processed or shipped.

The best indicator of a client's intentions of and ability to pay a new debt can be found by reviewing past payment patterns. However, if you are a new or smaller supplier, you may not have a recent payment history for some or even any of your clients. In this case, you should make reference checks before extending credit terms. Ideally you should develop credit contacts with credit departments at similar-sized firms in your industry. You can exchange credit information with these contacts.

You cannot unilaterally deny credit to a client on the basis of your credit contacts, as this could put you at risk for legal action, but you can share factual information. As a second choice you can request credit references from the client or as a third choice you can purchase credit reports from commercial credit reporting services.

There are other more sophisticated methods for analyzing credit. Generally, however, current payment patterns provide the best and easiest indicator.

Invoicing

Be sure to follow invoicing instructions to the letter of the customer's instructions, even if they are cumbersome or if payment might be significantly delayed.

Typically, you will need to cite their purchase order number and mail the invoice separately from the shipment. Often the purchase order number will need to be included on the shipping label or in documentation accompanying the order. If the purchase order is missing, some firms may refuse to accept delivery of the order. And many large firms have instituted draconian penalties for not following shipping instructions precisely.

Statements

In addition to sending an invoice at the time of the order, you should send each customer a statement each month that summarizes account activity. Statements should include outstanding invoices, payments received during the month, and any other credits or charges. If you are a very small firm dealing with other relatively small businesses, an alternative to mailing statements may be to send copies of any outstanding invoices marked "reminder" or "second notice."

CLAIRE'S CLEVER CANDLES

INVOICE
786755

14 Baxter Street • Bangor • ME 04401 • 207 555 5555

SOLD TO: Ms. Alice Beecher
Beecher's Gift Emporium
110 South Main Street
Milford, MA 01757

CUSTOMER PURCHASE ORDER NO.: 12345678

DATE: April 23, 1996

QTY	ITEM #	DESCRIPTION	UNIT PRICE	TOTAL PRICE
1	2345	Vanilla Scent Birthday Surprise Candle	$25.95	$29.95

Collection letters

If an invoice becomes overdue, you should send out a polite letter or reminder to the customer. Your letter might say: "Thank you for your recent order. Our records indicate that payment for our invoice number 786755, your purchase order number 12345678 for $29.95, has now become due and we have no record of your payment. If you have not done so already, kindly send payment now.

Thank you again for choosing to do business with us."

If this first letter doesn't produce a result, you should either make a phone call or send out increasingly strong letters. Be careful to avoid being unduly negative, especially if you hope to continue doing business with the client in the future.

Your second reminder letter might read: "If you have not already done so, please send payment at this time for our invoice number 786755, your purchase order number 12345678 for $29.95. This invoice is now seriously overdue. Thank you for taking care of this matter."

Collection calls

Unfortunately, paying bills late has become a standard way of doing business for many firms of all sizes. When you place early calls on overdue bills, you want to be upbeat and positive. In most situations, being pleasant is the fastest route to getting paid as soon as possible.

If you lose your cool and get excited on the phone, the person on the receiving end will probably tune out your message. In all likelihood the firm won't do business with you in the future again, either, and almost certainly will refuse subsequent collection or sales calls.

You do need to try to get a commitment regarding payment. Ask the person with whom you are speaking to send the payment today. If a firm indicates that it does not have the money, push it to send at least a partial payment that day.

Once you obtain a payment commitment, stay with it. If the payment doesn't show up as promised, place a follow-up call. Mention that you have not received payment and ask for another commitment.

Remember that the person with whom you are speaking may not be the person who decides whether or not to actually pay you that day, next month, or ever. He or she may just be fielding "overdue payment" phone calls and reciting a pat message to appease you temporarily.

Court

You really want to avoid going to court to get paid. This is particularly true if your sales are confined to one industry. You can quickly get a negative reputation for taking customers to court.

Proceeding with a formal court claim can cost thousands of dollars in legal expenses and take years to settle. And you just can't be sure that you will get the favorable judgement you think you deserve. The defense attorney may claim that your product was defective. He or she may try to have the case thrown out of court on an obscure legal technicality.

Furthermore, the cost to you in terms of time—time that could have been spent on big-profit projects—can be an enormous hidden loss in financial terms as well. Finally, even if you do win a judgement, you still might not get paid. If a company simply doesn't have the funds to pay you or if there are bank or tax claims on the company's cash assets, chances are you won't see your payment no matter what the court order may be.

Small claims court is a possible alternative for relatively modest claims. But small claims court is not an easy solution. A clever defendant will be able to forestall his or her court appearance for the first couple of dates. You, however, need to appear for each date or else your claim will be automatically dismissed.

Small claims court procedures are not very formal. Judges tend to listen most carefully to the consumer's arguments. And even if you do win the judgement, several more court appearances may be necessary to enforce such a judgement.

CLAIRE'S CLEVER CANDLES
14 Baxter Street • Bangor • ME 04401
207 555 5555

June 7, 1996

Ms. Alice Beecher
Beecher's Gift Emporium
110 South Main Street
Milford, MA 01757

Dear Ms. Beecher,

Thank you for your recent order. Our records indicate that payment for our invoice number 786755, your purchase order number 12345678, for $29.95, has now become due and we have no record of your payment. If you have not done so already, kindly send payment now.

Thank you again for choosing to do business with us.

Sincerely,

Claire Fielding

Claire Fielding

CLAIRE'S CLEVER CANDLES
14 Baxter Street • Bangor • ME 04401
207 555 5555

June 7, 1996

Ms. Alice Beecher
Beecher's Gift Emporium
110 South Main Street
Milford, MA 01757

Dear Ms. Beecher,

If you have not already done so, please send payment at this time for our invoice number 786755, your purchase order number 12345678 for $29.95. This invoice is now seriously overdue.

Thank you for taking care of this matter.

Sincerely,

Claire Fielding

Claire Fielding

A Collection Call

When you place a call to collect on an overdue invoice, remember that being as pleasant as possible is the fastest route to getting paid as soon as possible. The receptionist has just connected you to the Accounts Payable Manager...

 Tom Tom Smith here.

 Sally Tom, this is Sally Cotton calling from Innovative Software. How are you today?

 Tom Fine, thank you.

 Sally Tom, are you the person responsible for paying bills?

 Tom Yes, I am.

 Sally Great! I bet you can help me out. We have an invoice outstanding that is almost a month overdue. I wonder if you can tell me when it will be paid?

 Tom Oh yes, I'm familiar with that invoice and I can assure you that we will pay it as soon as we can.

 Sally Well, Tom, I really need to get paid now because that invoice is a month overdue. How about sending a check today?

 Tom Well, I'd like to send a check today, Sally. But we are in the middle of a cash flow crunch. Don't worry, though, I'll pay it as soon as we can.

 Sally Tom, I certainly appreciate the fact that you are being candid with me. But I do need something. How about sending a partial payment— half today and half within a couple of weeks?

 Tom Okay, I'll tell you what, I will send half today and the remainder of the payment by the end of the month.

 Sally That would be great, Tom. I really appreciate it. Thanks, and have a nice day.

☞ Don't offer it

If it is possible, run your business without extending credit. Ask for advance payments or give prepayment discounts. If you can't get full payment up front, request partial prepayments.

If you are running a service business and are not receiving prepayments, don't be shy about asking a business or consumer for payment in full upon completion of the service. Include the proviso "payment due upon completion" on your bid sheet. Or get your customers to agree in advance to staged payments with the final payment due upon completion.

Having outstanding receivables means the customer has your money and you don't. Most businesses and many consumers tend to pay bills after the stated terms. Many won't pay bills at all unless you send reminder letters or place collection calls. And there will be a certain percentage of your client base that won't pay their bills at all—they either can't, or have a complaint about your product or service.

☞ Have policies

Even if you have a full-time experienced credit manager on staff, you need to set policies for extending credit and making collections. You might want to request that all new clients prepay their first orders. You might want to give fifteen days grace on outstanding invoices before placing a collection call.

Another issue to consider is the demeanor of your credit manager. Even with collections experience from another industry, he or she may have some trouble adjusting to the "etiquette" observed in your industry. He or she may be too aggressive or not aggressive enough. Work with your credit manager to have the right tone and make the right effort behind collection activity.

> "Even if you have a full-time credit manager on staff, you need to set policies for extending credit and making collections."

☞ Keep it legal

You need to be sure that anyone making credit decisions on your company's behalf understands the legal issues involved. For example, when determining credit eligibility, you need to be sure that factors such as race, sex, or ethnic origin are not considered.

If you are extending credit, especially to consumers, you may be required to give certain disclaimers or comply with limitations on interest rates or other agreement terms.

If you are extending credit to businesses, you need to be sure not to make a decision in concert with any other company that would limit credit to a particular firm.

In making collection calls, you need to check on and observe certain federal, state, or local legal regulations. Generally, you can't make collection calls late at night, you can't threaten legal action unless you intend to pursue it, you can't continue to call people if they request that you discontinue your calls, and you can't verbally abuse people in any way.

Streetwise Advice on Credit

☞ Use the phone

When monies owed you are overdue and the amount is in excess of a few dollars, your best bet for collection activity is via the phone. Phone calls are simply much more effective than letters.

☞ Keep it positive

Always keep a positive, upbeat attitude when you are pursuing collections, whether through written correspondence or over the phone. Maintaining a positive, but firm, rapport with people who owe you money is the most effective means toward possible payment. Even if the customer becomes emotional with you, keep your cool and politely keep asking for your money.

☞ Size is no guarantee

Just because a customer is large doesn't mean it can pay its bills. Many large firms have gone bankrupt. In fact, as I am writing these comments, two of the three discount department stores in my area are in bankruptcy proceedings. So, especially if you are considering extending credit to a large company, run a credit check first.

☞ Timing can be important when considering extending credit to a firm that has recently emerged from bankruptcy

My experience has been that in the few months after a firm emerges from bankruptcy it is usually in pretty good financial condition and, usually, you won't be taking an excessive risk when you extend credit at this time. But you should still do a credit check.

However, when a company has been out of bankruptcy for two or three years, you should be a bit more wary. At this point, the weak management or tough market conditions that placed the company in trouble the first time might have retaken the company. Any financial strength it gained by writing off its debts could have ebbed away, and the company may once again have difficulty paying its bills.

☞ Tier credit decisions

For small credit requests, set up criteria so that a lower-level clerk can quickly make a decision. For large credit requests, have a credit manager or accounting manager make the decision. For very large credit requests, have your top financial person make the decision. And for the largest requests, you, the owner of the business, should become involved. Don't hesitate to bump complex credit requests up the decision-making heirarchy. One big credit mistake could be disastrous!

☞ Keep salespeople away from credit decisions

Salespeople are invariably too loose with credit. Pay very little attention to their credit recommendations, no matter how much seniority or experience they have. Let the accounting or credit departments handle credit decisions.

Questions & Answers about Credit

Should I check credit for every business customer?

If the cost of checking credit will take a whopping chunk out of your profit margin, don't bother. For example, I don't check credit on businesses placing orders under $50 net. But be sure to have firm credit extension policies, otherwise your credit department won't check anyone's credit!

Should I have different credit policies for established customers?

This depends on how aggressive you want to be. When first offering credit, you may want to be conservative with terms and limits, even if the applicant has excellent credit. Once a good payment record has been established, you might extend your credit limits or terms. Many businesses, especially service businesses, require partial prepayments for new customers, progress payments, and/or final payments due immediately upon completion.

If you want to be more aggressive, consider how long a customer has been doing business with you and whether or not its credit references and financial condition are solid.

A small retailer owes us $500, but it can't pay it. What should I do?

Get on the phone and push, as nicely as possible, for payment today. If the retailer refuses to make a commitment to pay immediately, go for a commitment to partial payments. Suggest $50 or $100 per week until the account is settled.

A homeowner owes us $1,200 for landscaping, but I haven't seen a dime. What should I do?

First, make phone calls or send letters, as per your collections policy, requesting payment. If you still don't get paid, go to the home and nicely ask for the payment in person. If all else fails, take the homeowner to small claims court.

How much money can I expect from a bankrupt business customer?

Typically, even if the customer is filing Chapter 11 bankruptcy and reorganizing to continue the business, you can expect only pennies on the dollar. This is often ten cents or less on every dollar owed to a very small business. And even this minimal amount might take years to collect. Remember, lawyers get paid first, then secured lenders, then tax authorities, then unsecured lenders and then, and then only maybe, general creditors, such as yourself.

*P*urchasing may not be quite as razzle-dazzle as creating exciting marketing campaigns, but it can be just as crucial to your bottom line. If your business has a profit margin of 10 percent on sales and you cut expenses by just over 5 percent, your profit will soar by 50 percent! Without changing the profit margin, sales would have to increase by 50 percent to achieve the same result!

Spec sheets

Before making purchases, you need to create exact specification sheets for the items you want to buy. For items such as office supplies, developing spec sheets won't be very time-consuming, especially if you purchase some items on a regular basis.

What should a spec sheet include? Let's assume that you want to purchase a computer. You may not want to specify a particular brand and model. You may, instead, want to specify a price ceiling or price range. You will need to list any special computer features or options that are necessary. And you may want to list features and options that you would like if price criteria can still be maintained.

Spec sheets should also specify delivery times, warranty or service requirements, and payment terms such as COD, net thirty, or credit card use.

Vendors

For some products and most services you will want to prequalify vendors by getting testimonials from satisfied customers, reading product reviews, visiting vendor plants, meeting with key personnel, or perhaps sampling the product or service.

Quotes

CLAIRE'S CLEVER CANDLES

14 Baxter Street • Bangor • ME 04401 • 207 555 5555

QUOTATION

Quotation No.: 643

QUOTE TO: Ms. Alice Beecher
110 South Main Street
Milford, MA 01757

DATE: April 23, 1996

VALID UNTIL: May 23, 1996

QTY	DESCRIPTION UNIT PRICE	UNIT PRICE	TOTAL PRICE
100	4" Cube Beeswax Candles; royal blue base with	$35.00	$3500.00
	multi-color "Hanson" family crest applied to front. Quote		
	includes hand creation of crest for each candle.		

TERMS AND CONDITIONS: Family crest art with colors indicated must be supplied at time of order. Lead-time of

Once you have developed your spec sheets and made a list of eligible vendors, you are ready to go out for quotes. For almost any purchase of $100 or more, it is recommended that you get at least two quotes. If the item or service being purchased costs considerably over $100, three quotes are recommended. When requesting quotes, ask the vendor when you might expect to receive its quotation.

Never just send out a written request for a quotation or the vendor will be unlikely to give your request serious attention. Always talk to a salesperson. If it is a significant quote, meet with the salesperson face to face.

Never hesitate to ask a salesperson to come and visit you. Often a salesperson can influence the price and other terms attendant to your order. If the work involves developing a quote, the sales representative can usually push the estimator to work within a tighter margin. Even if the company offers standard pricing, a sales representative may be able to extend higher volume pricing to you if you establish a good rapport. Especially if yours is a new business, a good word from the salesperson to the credit manager may mean the difference between cash in advance and thirty-day terms.

Purchase orders

Once you have decided on a vendor and are ready to proceed with a purchase, it is always a good idea to use written purchase orders. If you don't use purchase orders you are going to find yourself receiving goods and services that are the wrong style, type, or color than those you ordered. You may be charged a higher price or sent the wrong quantity.

The purchase order should specify the name of the item or service being purchased, and any details specified in your spec sheet. You need to state the quantity being

BEA'S BETTER BOOKS

110 Dutcher Street • Hopedale • MA 01747 • 508 555 5555

PURCHASE ORDER

786755

ORDER TO: Willow Press
Attn.: Ms. Hanson
17A Cascade Road
Ashland, OR 97520

SHIP TO: Bea's Better Books
Attn: Mr. Roger Roy
110 Dutcher Street
Hopedale, MA 01747

DATE: April 23, 1995

QTY	ITEM #	DESCRIPTION	UNIT PRICE	S&H	TOTAL PRICE
12	2345	Holiday Edibles and Other Confections By Alexandra Appleton	15.95	31.50	222.90

Delivery Date: Required before October 15, 1996
Shipping: Ship via UPS Ground
Packing: 1 box or carton.
Delivery: Shipping and Receiving Department at rear of 110 Dutcher Street building.
Billing: Bea's Better Books. Credit terms established.
Terms: Net 30

THANK YOU.

purchased, delivery date, delivery address, shipping method and payment, and packing and receiving requirements.

You should detail each cost you are incurring and also state the total cost of the items or services ordered to avoid misunderstanding.

It is also a good idea to use purchase orders printed with your company name. If you don't, you are more likely to be asked for a prepayment or deposit on goods or services ordered.

Acceptance

When the product is delivered, be sure that whoever signs for the package also inspects the order. When you sign for delivery from a trucking company or other shipper you are generally agreeing that the quantity is correct and that the shipment bears no obvious damage. Have your shipping and receiving department or other personnel count the quantity or number of cartons delivered. Receiving should also check for any visible damage to the outside of the shipping containers. Receiving needs to get a copy of the receipt for delivery that has been signed. This will serve as your receiving slip.

As soon as possible, the shipment should be opened and inspected. Quantity, quality, and adherence to purchase order specs should be checked. If there is any problem, you are in a much stronger position if you call the vendor and point out discrepancies immediately.

Don't hesitate to complain about problems or seek improvements. Call the salesperson you have been dealing with. Most vendors want to build long-term relationships with their customers!

Invoices

Eventually you will receive an invoice for the merchandise or service you have purchased. Compare your purchase order and receiving slip against the invoice. Don't be surprised if the invoiced payment due is higher than the purchase order total.

Many businesses are very good at adding extra charges. They may state price increases or cite some "minor" charge that they neglected to inform you about up front. Call them. Say, "Too bad!" Your purchase order specifies exactly what you intended to pay for the merchandise or service and you are not obligated to pay for any additional charges. Be firm, but be polite. You can always say that you will be happy to pay the hidden charges next time—that is, if you use the vendor next time!

> "Don't be surprised if the invoiced payment due is higher than the purchase order total. Many businesses are very good at adding extra charges."

☞ Proportionate effort

A slight variation in the overall costs of running your business can have a huge effect on profitability. But you and your key managers cannot spend all of your time dealing with all purchasing-related issues. So focus on those purchases that are crucial. Expensive repeat items are the types of merchandise or services that demand your extra attention.

In key areas you should watch your costs carefully. Search out alternative sources. Work closely with vendors and continually seek innovative solutions.

For less expensive items, such as office supplies or one-time purchases, buy frugally, but don't involve yourself or key personnel in the process.

☞ Bid everything

Even for relatively small purchases—excluding buys such as a dozen pencils—get multiple quotes. Get your quotes in writing, purchase by issuing purchase orders, and hold vendors to their quotes and the purchase order when you are invoiced.

☞ Clear authority

Clearly delineate who may buy what and how much he or she can spend. If someone in your business acts and looks he or she has the authority to make a purchase, the business will be held responsible for those purchases.

Assign authority for specific categories of goods to specific people. Set spending limits on these authorities. If their intended purchases exceed their limits, assign sign-off authority to a superior. Requiring the use of purchase orders will make your employees think twice as to who has the authority to make a purchase.

☞ By budget

Make sure that whoever is making purchasing decisions is working from a budget and understands the impact his or her purchase will have on the budget—and your company's profitability!

Remember, owner-operators tend to be the biggest culprits when it comes to forgetting about budgets. Curb that tendency to get excited about new, discretionary purchases.

"Clearly delineate who may buy what and how much he or she can buy. If someone in your business acts and looks like he or she has the authority to make a purchase, the business will be held responsible for those purchases."

Questions & Answers about Purchasing

How much detail does a purchase order need?

The most important detail on any purchase order is the price. You also need to clearly specify the items being purchased, the quantity being ordered, and any aspect of the goods being ordered that need clarification such as size, color, or model type. Other issues that you may want to specify are payment terms, freight method, applicable discounts, and delivery dates. If you don't specify payment terms, the vendor may demand payment with delivery. Be careful with freight charges. Generally they cost extra, so make note on the purchase order if they are included in the purchase price.

Don't be tempted to verbally specify details to a sales representative. The benefit of a written purchase order is that it will get forwarded to the people responsible for filling orders and the chances of confusion will be lessened.

Should I arrange for freight?

For smaller, bulk items you will typically be better off leaving the shipping up to the vendor. The vendor probably does

volume shipping and is eligible for discounts. Be aware, however, that more and more firms are sending merchandise via the fastest, and generally most expensive, way possible. Ask if the vendor intends to use an overnight air courier. If you don't need this service, request a less expensive delivery.

If you are ordering large, bulk items, particularly full tractor trailer loads, you can usually get a better price through your own negotiations with trucking companies or independent tractor trailer operators.

What kind of scams should I be on the look out for?

You should be leery of buying from any firm that pitches you over the phone but refuses to send you a brochure or catalog. Also be leery of firms that don't accept credit cards and insist on check or cash prepayments. And don't fall for offers to advertise your products on national TV for a fee—never pay for publicity!

Do I have to pay for an overage?

In some industries, it is customary to consider a small variance in a delivery quantity as acceptable. This is particularly true of custom items—such as printed material—because it may be difficult to halt the manufacturing process at a precise count. In industries where variances are

allowed the acceptable variance is usually plus or minus 10 percent of the ordered quantity. Specify acceptable variances in your purchase order and check quotes from vendors for variance stipulations.

What do I do if the goods appear damaged in transit?

If the container in which your goods are delivered is damaged, make note of this when you sign for the delivery. Otherwise you are basically testifying to an undamaged delivery. Contact the vendor immediately if goods are damaged. While goods damaged in transit are generally the responsibility of the transit company, it is worth trying to get the vendor to arrange for reimbursement—it will save you both time and effort.

What standard determines unacceptable quality?

If a dispute finds itself in a courtroom, a judge will examine the purchase order and the vendor's quote for quality instructions. Catalog or advertising claims might also be considered. And the quality of any prior deliveries from the same vendor will also likely be taken into account. Beyond this, acceptable industry standards and expert testimony from witnesses for either the defendant or the plaintiff will be reviewed. But don't go to court! Try to settle this out of court.

Taxes

Why can paying taxes be fun? Because they are more fun than going through an audit! And audits can be more fun than having your assets seized for failure to pay taxes! Besides, Bill Bruns, one of my favorite Harvard Business School professors, says, "I want to pay more taxes"—meaning you should look at an exorbitant tax bill as a measure of your success.

Unfortunately, as Bill is well aware, while income taxes will be the largest burden by far on a profitable firm, there are plenty of other taxes that need to be paid even if you aren't making any money at all.

Employment taxes

Whether you have one employee or a hundred, you will be way ahead of the game if you get an outside firm to handle your filings and payroll taxes. So, before you do anything else, get yourself a payroll service to take all of the time, hassle, anxiety, and risk out of the payroll process.

Employment tax rules are extremely complex. If you try to handle them yourself, you are bound to make a costly mistake—and you'll pay interest and penalties. If a payroll service makes the mistake, typically, it will pay.

As an employer you have a tremendous fiduciary responsibility to collect and withhold taxes from employees on virtually every paycheck you issue. Throughout the United States, you must withhold an appropriate amount for federal income and other earnings-related taxes. Many states and some municipalities also require the payment of an income or other tax on earnings.

Your employees must fill out a federal W-4 form and a Form I-9 from the Immigration and Naturalization Service. States that do not use the same income basis for determining tax liability as does the federal government may require that employees fill out state filing forms.

You, or your payroll service, must determine the appropriate amount to be withheld for each individual. If you withhold too little from your employee's incomes, you will be penalized by the governments involved. The federal government also requires that you withhold your employees' share of federal Social Security and Medicare taxes.

Tables for calculating federal withholding taxes are available from the Internal Revenue Service at

1-800-TAX-FORM

State withholding tables may be obtained from your state income tax department.

Budgeting for your share of the payroll taxes

The employer is also responsible for a share of their employee's unemployment, Social Security, and Medicare taxes. The amount that you pay will depend on many factors—salaries, your firm's balance, if any, in your state's unemployment insurance account, dates of hire, and a host of other considerations. As a quick and dirty rule of thumb, allowing 13 percent on top of your gross payroll should cover your share of the payroll taxes.

Timing of employment tax payments

If you are a growing company, paying employment taxes yourself can be very frustrating. Employment tax rules change as the size of the company increases—both your liability and the time frame in which the taxes must be paid. Following are two general guidelines:

- New employers pay federal withholding taxes on a monthly basis. As the business grows, the frequency increases to semi-weekly. For the largest businesses, taxes are due within twenty-four hours of each payroll.

- Each state has its own rules for frequency of payment. Generally, payments are not required more frequently than are federal taxes. But be sure to check with your state tax office.

Collecting sales taxes

In most states and in many cities, you must collect sales taxes on applicable sales. Generally, sales taxes apply on the sale of just about anything to just about anyone.

Exceptions are sales to resellers, such as wholesalers or retailers, who have valid state resale certificates. Ask to see the resale certificate of any wholesaler or retailer with whom you conduct business. Another exception is sales made to tax-exempt institutions, such as public schools and libraries. In some states, sales taxes apply only to products, while in other states, sales taxes apply to services as well.

A particularly gray, frustrating, and rapidly changing area is the collection of sales tax by firms that sell products or taxable services in states where they do not maintain a clear physical presence. Physical presence is clear if you have an address, store inventory, or maintain an employee, such as a sales representative, within a state. But individual states have taken out-of-state companies to court for the collection of sales tax based on the presence of mail-order catalogs within their state. Results on these suits have been mixed. But, the definitions of physical presence are changing and bear watching.

If you are making taxable sales in other states, you should check with your accountant or legal advisor for an up-to-date opinion on your particular situation. The safest route, of course, is to simply collect sales tax in every state where you sell products or services.

Use taxes

Use taxes basically mean that a business that buys items from out-of-state vendors, which are not collecting sales taxes, must pay the tax themselves to the taxing authority. Some states are particularly aggressive about collecting such taxes and won't hesitate to take an entire industry to court or push gray areas of the law in an effort to collect every last red cent they can.

For example, for some time at Adams we published a help-wanted newspaper and some of our distribution was through newspaper racks. The printing of newspapers and the purchase of newsstand racks for newspapers is clearly exempt from sales and use tax in the state in which we operate. Nonetheless, a tax collector argued that, since we had little editorial content, our newspaper really wasn't a newspaper. He demanded the instant payment of tens of thousands of dollars in taxes for every printing of the "non-newspaper" since its founding several years previous. He also demanded taxes on the newspaper racks that had been purchased out of state and, of course, wanted penalties and back interest as well. A challenge could have been launched through the state courts, but it would have cost a lot of money and victory might have gone to the state in any case. We paid.

Income taxes

In the United States your business, if incorporated, must file and pay federal income taxes, state income taxes in most states, and local income taxes in some areas.

If your business is incorporated, you may elect to become an "S" corporation (formerly known as Sub-Chapter S) for federal income tax purposes. As an S corporation, your company will not pay direct taxes in most cases. Instead, income and losses are passed on to stockholders. Therefore, the individual stockholders pay the income tax.

Some states treat S corporations in the same manner as does the federal government, and taxes the stockholders. Other states do not recognize S corporation status, and tax the corporation directly.

Remember that the federal corporation tax returns (regardless of S corporation election) are due one month earlier than individuals'—on the fifteenth day of the third month after the end of the company's year. For example, if your fiscal year ends on December 31, your filing date is March 15. The payment for a corporation with an S election is still part of the individual return due on April 15. Be sure to check the section on estimated taxes to know when estimated tax payments are due.

If your business is a sole proprietorship or a partnership, the income is taxed directly to the owner or partners for federal income tax purposes. Most states follow the same rule. However, a few jurisdictions tax the business entity directly. Check with your tax consultant for the rules and regulations that apply to your business.

Remember, you need to file tax returns, and pay a minimum tax in some areas, even if your business has yet to earn a profit.

Estimated income taxes

At the beginning of your second year in business, you may be in for a little surprise. Not only do federal, and in some localities state and local, tax authorities require payment of income taxes on the first year's earnings, but they want you to start paying taxes on next year's earnings. Yes, before the year has ended!

Estimated federal corporation taxes are due when the annual tax is expected to be at least $500. Payments of 25 percent each are due on the fifteenth day of the fourth, sixth, ninth, and twelfth months of your fiscal year. If you are on a calendar fiscal year, for instance, estimated payments are due on April 15, June 15, September 15, and December 15. Each state has its own minimums and payment schedules, often varying from the federal ones.

If you are self-employed or in a partnership, you also will have to pay income tax estimates. They need to be figured into the total estimated tax the individual owes.

Property taxes

Of course, you will have to pay real estate taxes on any real estate that you or your business owns. Also, many commer-

cial and industrial leases are written so that the lessee, not the lessor, is responsible for taxes. Sometimes the lessor will pay what is referred to as the "base-year taxes." This means the lessor pays tax equal to the taxes of the base year—often the year before the lease was signed—set as the base year; then the lessee pays any increase.

For most localities, the tax rate on commercial and industrial property is significantly higher than the rate applied to residential property. Furthermore, many communities assess the value of businesses, particularly those with nonlocal owners, at ridiculously high levels to minimize the tax burden on local voting citizens. This practice is so widespread that there is a whole group of attorneys who specialize in suing towns and cities in an attempt to receive fair tax treatment for their business clients. These clients are often national chains.

If you feel that your tax assessment is too high but the amount owed is not huge, file a request for a new assessment before hiring expensive, specialized legal help.

Personal property taxes

In addition to taxing real estate, localities impose personal property taxes on just about everything else a business owns, including inventory, equipment, and furniture. The percentage of the estimated value is usually quite small, but total dollar amount can add up if you own a lot of property.

Inventory and tangible property taxes

Many states place a tax, based on a small percentage of actual value, on tangible property held within their state, including inventory housed on a certain annual date. This date is usually the last day of the year.

Other taxes

Your business may be subject to additional taxes. Some of these types of taxes are applicable only within certain industries. For example, most localities levy specific taxes on lodging establishments, some on amusement facilities, and others on restaurants.

☞ **Not your bank**

Too many small businesses view their tax bills like trade debts and delay paying taxes during cash crunches. Invariably, they regret this decision. You can usually delay vendor payments, pay up later, and have all forgotten. When you don't pay the tax authorities, they seek penalties and interest. These penalties were designed to be severe enough to discourage you from treating the government like a financing company. Furthermore, it is a lot easier for the tax authorities to seize your assets for tax delinquency than it is for a trade vendor to do so!

☞ **Work with the IRS**

While it true that tax collectors are bound by many rules and regulations, they are often quite flexible to deal with. If you have made an honest tax mistake, have really run out of money, or haven't filled out the proper form, you might be able to avoid penalty or even interest payments. You just need to find the proper way to channel your request.

For example, in making the giant mistake of handling my own payroll taxes, I neglected to change to a faster payment schedule when the company employee count increased in size. The IRS allows a single occurrence of this oversight without penalty. Unfortunately, I made this mistake more than once and was hit with a several-thousand-dollar, and perfectly legal, penalty. I paid the penalty but also decided to write to the IRS and plead for a rescindment. Ten months later the IRS refunded my penalty with interest! Naturally, however, the interest was subject to taxes.

☞ **Decisions and taxes**

While taxes are a heavy burden on any successful business, you are generally better off if you avoid making business decisions based on their tax implications. Avoiding taxes can mean avoiding profits!

☞ **Tax preparation**

Have an outside accountant do your taxes. Even though you might have a great conceptual understanding of tax regulations and filing procedures, someone who files hundreds of tax returns a year will simply be able to do yours more effi-

ciently than you can. And they should be up on the very latest in rules and allowances—many of which you may not be aware of. It will save you time, if not money, in the long run.

☞ **Don't underreport income**

No matter how determined you are to be aggressive with your tax return, don't underreport your income. The IRS is increasingly suspicious of taxpayers, especially small business owners, who seem to have lifestyles that cannot possibly be supported by the incomes they report. You could find yourself the subject of a "lifestyle audit."

☞ **Consider a new fiscal year election**

If your business experiences its strongest profitability toward the end of the year, you might be better off ending your fiscal year mid-year. This would delay your income tax payments on year-end profits, as well as your higher estimated income taxes toward the next year's tax bill.

Questions & Answers about Taxes

Can I deduct the cost of my home office?

The rules on home office deductibility seem to change constantly. The U.S. Internal Revenue Service is very careful about the proper deduction of home office expenses. By deducting your home office, even legitimately, you increase your audit chances.

To deduct a home office, the office must be used exclusively as the principal place for operating your business. The U.S. Supreme Court has ruled that more than 50 percent of the total time spent operating your business must be spent in the home office. This is a problem for consultants who spend a significant amount of time at client locations, or for salespersons, who are typically on the road.

How should I prepare for a tax audit?

The best time to prepare for a tax audit is now. It is much easier to keep good records today than to try to recreate them two or three years later.

Usually a tax audit will specify the year being audited. Be sure to have all your records for the specified year organized and accessible prior to the audit.

An auditor will expect you to instantly support any questioned items. Try to determine, in advance, which items the auditor intends to question, and have ready answers. Remember, the auditor's questions will stem from information you supplied on your tax return. Are your office supply expenses extremely high? The auditor may want you to substantiate these expenses with invoices and/or cancelled checks.

I suggest that you have your outside accountant present during the audit. Ask him or her for advice relevant to your situation. If you are nervous, consider having the accountant be your representative and don't attend the audit in person.

Can I recover previous years' taxes if I have a loss?

A corporation will be able to carry-back a loss for up to three years in order to recover federal taxes previously paid. And the IRS will actually pay you in cash! If there is more loss than can be carried back, it can be carried forward for up to fifteen years. Most states do not permit loss carrybacks, but do allow loss carryforwards to the extent of any federal carryforward.

Similar federal rules apply to individuals who have substantial business losses. Most states, however, do not permit individuals to adjust for business losses.

Can I delay filing my tax return?

Any corporation, S corporation, partnership, or individual can get an automatic extension of time to file a tax return by simply filing the appropriate federal and/or state form. Any tax due, however, must be included with the extension on the orginal date due. All taxes paid after the original date due are subject to interest charges. Inadequate payment with the extension request can also lead to additional penalties.

Although a tax return has been extended, all estimated tax payments remain payable as per the regular schedule.

What if my estimated tax payments appear to be too low at a later date?

If you find during the year that your income tax liability is going to be greater than the estimated taxes you have paid will cover, you should revise any remaining payments to account for the increase. It is best to make any catch-up payments with the next payment due.

Getting Money!

Banks

Banks are the primary financing vehicle, other than owner's savings, for small businesses.

Banks like to use hard assets such as buildings, motor vehicles, or equipment as collateral against loans. They will loan against receivables and inventory, but, especially in the case of smaller businesses, tend to heavily discount the protection these assets offer. They are afraid the inventory and receivables will be converted to cash in order to cover operating losses if the business experiences any financial difficulties.

While banks like the ultimate protection of hard assets, they also want to feel that there is little chance that the business, or the bank, will have to call upon these assets to pay off the loan. Banks don't care whether or not your business has sky-high profit potential. They are only interested in the business' ability to cover the principal and interest payments.

In making a proposal for a loan, the bank will want to see all of your recent tax returns, financial statements, and cash flow projections. They will also want to know how much you would like to borrow. And, if yours is a small business, it will expect you to conduct all of your business banking activities through its institution.

Banks are reluctant to loan to businesses that cannot show at least two years of profitable operation. They want to see that the owner of the business is heavily invested in the enterprise. And, typically, they won't make loans in amounts that exceed 50 percent of the firm's capitalization.

Many bankers feel they are extending a loan not only to the small business, but to the owner-operator as well. They will feel more comfortable loaning business funds to someone with community ties, who has experience related to the business he or she is conducting, and who has made a complete and total commitment to that business.

Small business loan criteria vary greatly from one bank to another. It can even vary from one loan officer to another. If you have been turned down by nine out of ten banks in your region—go ahead and try the tenth. While all banks and loan officers consider the same factors when weighing a loan request, they will place different emphasis on those factors. Some bankers place great store in hard asset collateral, some in the profitability or continuity of the business, and yet others will go with their impression of the owner as the deciding factor.

Personal loans

Personal loans are a great back-door alternative when seeking financing for a small business venture.

One of the most common means for attaining funds for use in operating a small business is through a home equity loan. If you have been paying your mortgage for a few years, you have probably built up some sizable equity in your property. Banks loans taken against a person's primary residence are low-risk—no matter what the funds are going to be used for. You can take the proceeds garnered from a home equity loan and use them to operate your business. Then, technically, you are financing your business, not the bank.

If you use the proceeds from a personal loan to finance your business you do, however, need to make this clear on your loan application. If you lie on a loan application you have committed fraud—a serious criminal offense.

Friends and relatives

You, like most of us, are probably reluctant to ask friends and relatives for money. But a lot of people do, at one stage or another, when they are running their own businesses. If you are really serious about starting and/or staying in business, swallow your pride and go beg for those funds.

If your friends and family express an interest in assisting you with your business financing, pitch them professionally. Make a sound, cohesive loan request presentation—just as you would to a bank or other lending source. Don't be embarrassed to show financial statements, tax returns, or whatever else they want to see. Do anything to get that money!

You will want to prepare a written agreement about any loans. If you don't, bitter arguments are bound to sour the relationship eventually. Even some minor detail, such as the timing of interest payments, can cause great friction if arrangements aren't backed up in writing.

Don't be surprised when your friends and relatives suddenly turn into business tycoons once they have agreed to lend you funding. They may insist on terms that are more stringent than those you might get through a commercial bank!

Lease financing

Leasing is a super financing alternative if you are seeking funding to obtain business equipment. Finance companies, banks, and many firms that sell high-priced equipment will lease to you.

When you lease an item, the lessor retains ownership of it. You use the equipment by virtue of the monthly payments you will be required to make. You can often purchase the equipment at the end of the lease term for its market value or less.

A great advantage to leasing is that it may be allowed to be "off the balance sheet." This means that leases can be disclosed as balance sheet footnotes. They do not appear as debt even though they represent an ongoing company liability. This may sound like financial doublespeak, but it's not. Let's say a supplier is considering whether or not to extend credit to you, or a bank is weighing a loan proposal you have submitted. The lease commitment will play a relatively minor role in evaluating your debt burden.

Banks also tend to consider their total exposure when lending to small businesses. If you have obtained lease financing through a third party, they are more likely to lend you funds than if all of your borrowing needs have been met through them. This is very important if you have a relatively small business, because most banks expect you to use them exclusively for traditional lending but may not care if you use a nonbank source for lease financing. In any case, though, do keep your bank informed regarding any significant lease commitments you are considering prior to actually signing any agreements.

Factoring

Factoring refers to a practice whereby you sell your receivables for a discount before they are due. Historically, factoring has been heavily used in some industries, such as the garment industry, and less in others. Today, however, entrepreneurial factoring companies are willing to buy creditworthy receivables from just about any industry.

Factoring is a relatively expensive means of obtaining financing. You are paying for the cost of the capital, the extra risk including bad debt, and the paperwork factoring requires. If you can finance your business through other sources, particularly the more traditional ones, you will certainly save money.

However, factoring can be a cash bonanza to a growing business, especially one that cannot obtain the necessary capital through traditional borrowing.

SBA loans

In the United States, the Small Business Administration (SBA) will consider loan requests from businesses that have already been rejected by several banks. What the SBA does is guarantee loans from commercial banks and will, on occasion, loan money directly. Of course, how much money the SBA has available for loans or loan guarantees is subject to appropriations from Congress.

If you can't get money from another source, the SBA is a solid option. There are drawbacks, though. First, the

Getting Money!

paperwork can be cumbersome. Second, it may take longer to get approval than a commercial source would. And third, the SBA, as you might expect from any government agency, is less flexible about loan agreement terms than commercial lenders typically are.

Venture capital

Despite all of the attention venture capital firms get in the business press, they actually finance very few businesses. The better venture capital firms are deluged with proposals from budding entrepreneurs. But most of these entrepreneurial proposals are inappropriate to the goals of venture capitalists.

Most venture capitalists concentrate their financing efforts on later-stage business funding. Some venture capital firms will, however, consider financing a start-up. What they want to see from any entrepreneur seeking funding is a history of start-up successes under the applicant's belt. They are best known for financing high-tech firms, but they do finance other types of businesses—over 50 percent non-high-tech businesses for some venture capitalists.

Venture capital firms prefer to cut deals that provide an exit path within five years. They view the probability, or not, that a firm will be successful enough to go public or be purchased by a larger company. They also expect very high returns for their investment risk that only the fast pace of highly profitable growth will bring. They want to see a management team in place that can handle rapid growth. And they want that management team to be well balanced with all types of experience and skill represented —creative, engineering, financial, marketing, and management.

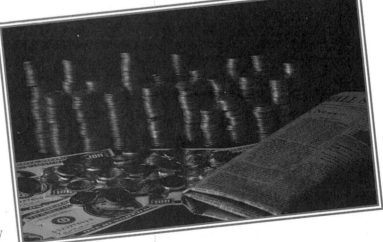

Going public

Going public, that is, selling stock or debt to the general public, is an extremely complex and massive undertaking. You should not consider going public unless your business is earning well over a million dollars in after-tax profits, has steady profitability, excellent growth prospects, and a tremendous thirst for funding that other sources can not provide.

Entrepreneurs who have taken their firms public are generally shocked by the amount of energy and anxiety that goes into the initial public offering. And, later, they are frustrated by the added demands placed on them as a CEO of a public as opposed to a private firm.

Advice on Seeking Bank Financing

from the business owner's persepctive

Howard Davis is the president of Datel Communications. As a business owner he has had many opportunities to interface with banks and request loans. Here, he offers his perceptions on what makes for a great relationship between a bank, the banker, and the small business owner being financed.

Communication

"When I chose my bank I made sure that I would be able to communicate with my banker on a one-on-one basis. The bank allowed me to borrow money from it, but I could still run my business the way I wanted to."

Time for a Change

"The bank outgrew me, I guess. It started to want to know more about my business—why payroll was a certain amount, why expenses were a certain amount. Around that time, I started to realize that it was time for a new bank."

The definition of your role

"Your job as the client is to give the bank as much information as you feel comfortable with, without allowing it to move into your company and become an 'owner of your company.'"

Avoid the overbearing

"Banks now advertise that they want to know your business and get involved in your business. That's the kind of bank to avoid. You want your bank to lend you money and let you run your business the way you see fit."

from the bank loan officer's persepctive

Levin Waters, V, is a commercial loan officer. He offers advice on how to be a smart loan applicant.

Have no fear

"I don't think that a small business owner should feel badly at all about going in and asking for a loan. That's what banks are for. That's how banks make their money."

Clarify your needs and responsibilities

"I think the most important aspect of a business plan is a very clear description of what the loan proceeds are going to be used for and a very clear description of how the small business borrower intends to pay the loan back."

Shop around

"It's worthwhile for the small business owner to shop around a little bit. Ask for references. Talk to friends and other small business owners who have received loans and find out where these people have had good and bad experiences."

Streetwise Advice on Getting Money

☞ **Simple presentation**

In raising money for a smaller business, you need to make a quick, simple presentation. You need to show why the business is sound, how much money you need, when the money will be paid back, and what collateral you can offer.

☞ **Bring numbers**

If your business is up and running, bring your latest annual and/or monthly income statements and balance sheets. If your business is a sole proprietorship, a partnership, or a small corporation, you may have to personally guarantee any loan. In this case, bring a statement showing your personal net worth. Also, you should provide a cash flow projection that shows when borrowings will be repaid.

☞ **Play the part**

The financier's opinion of your capability and trustworthiness will be a major factor in the bank's loan decision. So dress conservatively. Appear relaxed and confident about your business prospects. If you are seeking funding for a relatively new business, include a resume of your previous accomplishments in your presentation package.

☞ **Tailor your presentation**

Appeal to the needs of the person you are approaching for money. If you are seeking debt financing, emphasize the certainty of your ability to repay the loan—don't emphasize prospects for sky-high profits. Remember, debt financiers do not share in profits. Big talk about profits will make a debt financier view you only as a risk taker or unrealistic dreamer.

On the other hand, if you are making presentations to equity investors, you certainly want to emphasize your upside profit potential.

☞ **Avoid personal guarantees**

Many small corporations' borrowings will have to be backed by personal guarantees by one or more shareholders. Avoid this, if you can.

We all assume our businesses will succeed. But it is conceivable that they won't. Many personal guarantees will never be called. But wouldn't it be more reassuring to know that your personal assets are protected from business creditors?

Some years ago, the bank that financed my grandfather's shoe business changed ownership. The new bank suddenly demanded that he personally guarantee the company debt. He refused and immediately took the firm's banking business across town to a bank that offered him financing without requiring a personal guarantee.

" The financier's opinion of your capability and trustworthiness will be a major factor in the bank's loan decision."

Questions & Answers about Getting Money

Why can't I get a loan for 100 percent of my receivables?

Once a business gets into trouble, particularly with operating losses, receivables have a tendency to disappear as the entrepreneur struggles to keep the business alive. Liquid assets are usually burnt up in the process. It also becomes much more difficult for a bank to collect the receivables of a business in trouble.

Some years ago, when my current bank cut off my borrowing, I visited at least a dozen banks offering my recievables as collateral. Only one would loan me money, and even that bank discounted the value of my receivables to one-third of their actual worth!

Should I go to a big or a small bank?

Generally you are better off at a smaller bank. Larger banks will assign your account to a junior lending officer who is bound to be moving up eventually. You need to think in terms of establishing a good relationship with a banker, not just a bank. The banker you deal with should be relatively stable in

his or her job position and interested in you and your business.

The first bank I chose to approach for a business was the bank that I kept my significant checking and savings account with. I was very disappointed to note that the banker I was referred to had no interest in my business, let alone in lending me money. I eventually arranged borrowing through a branch of one of the largest banks in my area. A few years later, my account was reassigned to a new hire—the first banker I had seen at my personal bank. Would you believe that the bank refused to lend me additional funds shortly thereafter?

I next went to a smaller bank with a reputation for lending to smaller businesses. During the ten years that I was with that bank, I had only two bankers, and each was extremely attentive and willing to understand the financial demands of my business.

Should I shop for the lowest loan rate?

No. I may have harangued about frugality and conservation in other sections of this book, but in terms of borrowing you need to view interest rates with perspective. For a growing business, you generally need to be a lot more concerned about the availablity of money than the cost of that money. If a bank offers you a very low interest rate but only half the money you require, what good is the low

interest rate? Furthermore, interest rates will be in the same ballpark from one bank to the next.

Interest rates do not constitute the only cost of borrowing money. Some banks will require you to keep some offsetting balance when you take out a loan. This means that your effective interest rate is higher than the actual interest rate, because you can't use all of the money you have been lent. Other banks will require that you pay a small percentage fee to keep a line of credit open even if you aren't accessing that credit. And, since most banks will require a small business to do all of its banking there in order to finalize the loan, you need to take into consideration the entire cost of the banking relationship.

At my bank, I know that I am not getting the lowest interest rate in town. But I do know that money is always available to me, even if my business is experiencing a temporary downturn. Plus, I won't have to go through a lot of red tape when arranging for funding.

What interest rate should I expect to pay?

Typical interest rates for small business loans are from 2 percent to 4 percent over the prime rate. The prime rate is supposedly the rate that the largest banks charge their biggest and most secure customers. But in reality, the largest corporations often pay even less than the prime rate when they borrow money. Just as the prime rate fluctuates, so does the interest rate on small business loans.

Do I have to dress up to visit the bank?

Absolutely! Even if you are running a ditch-digging service, you need to put on professional business attire to visit a loan officer. There is an old saying that bankers prefer to lend money only to people who look like they don't need it! Heed this advice.

Will a banker want to visit my business?

If you are borrowing a relatively small amount of money, few bankers will want to actually visit your business. They will be more interested in you. They will observe how you present yourself, how committed you are to your business, and what your previous experience is. And, of course, they will be very interested in paper confirmation of your business' past and potential profitability—the information contained in your financial statements and tax returns.

How concerned should I be if it looks like I'll be 30 days late for a loan payment?

Don't be concerned at all. But tell your banker if you are sure you are going to be late. Explain why and indicate when you expect to pay. Be short with your explanation and don't sound like you are in a panic.

Cash Is King!

*B*efore you start a business your thoughts about finance may focus on how much money you can make and how long it may take for you to become profitable. As soon as you have started your business, however, your financial focus will quickly shift to cash flow. Even if your business is highly profitable, you are probably going to have less cash available than you might ideally like. How well you manage cash is going to have a major impact on the success, and often even the very survival, of your business.

What is cash flow?

Cash flow is simply the money that flows in and out of your business. It is not the same thing as profit.

For example, let's say a boat dealership sells a yacht outright, without supplying financing, for $100,000. The boat dealership had previously bought the boat from the manufacturer for $70,000. So, the boat dealership has realized a profit of $30,000. However, the dealership has realized a positive cash flow of $100,000 because it now has $100,000 more in its bank account today than it did yesterday. (See the illustration on the following page.) If the dealership buys a similar boat from the manufacturer to maintain its selection of boats, then the positive cash flow realized from the sale will be depleted by the purchase of the replacement yacht. Assuming that the second yacht costs $70,000, too; then the total net cash flow realized will be $30,000. The cash flow equals the profit.

On the other hand, if the boat dealership had sold the boat on credit without any down payment, it wouldn't realize any positive cash flow until the first loan installment was paid. On paper, however, the firm would have realized a $30,000 profit.

Let's say the same boat dealer decided to install a huge crane to lift boats in and out of the water. The dealership pays $50,000 in cash for the crane. Since a crane only loses value over a long period of time, the depreciation will occur over a number of years. So, the first day that the crane is purchased, the profitability of the business remains unaffected. The dealership will have $50,000 less in cash, though. But it will have $50,000 in assets.

As you can see from these examples, how you manage inventory, credit, and receivables and how you finance major capital expenditures can have a very strong impact, at least in the short term, on the cash flow and profitability of your business.

Cash Is King!

$ $ $ Cash Flow Scenarios $ $ $

Cash Sale Scenario

• **Cost of Purchasing Item from Manufacturer**	**$70,000**
• **Cash Merchandise Sale**	**$100,000**
• **Profit**	**$30,000**
• Positive Cash Flow without Inventory Replacement	+ $100,000
• Positive Cash Flow with Inventory Replacement	+ $30,000

Credit Sale Scenario

• **Cost of Purchasing Item from Manufacturer**	**$70,000**
• **Credit Merchandise Sale**	**$100,000**
• **Profit**	**$30,000**
• No Change in Cash Flow without Inventory Replacement)	$0
• Negative Cash Flow with Inventory Replacement	– $70,000

Asset Acquisition Scenario

• **Asset Value (Price Paid in Cash for Asset)**	**$50,000**
• **Business Profit**	**$0**
• Negative Cash Flow	– $50,000
• No Change in Value of Business	$0

Cash Is King!

Cash eaters

Many one-time start-up expenses are going to cost more than you anticipated. No matter how carefully you plan, it is impossible to forecast all the expense items you will encounter or have to cover. Maybe the building you are moving into will require more work than you had planned on. Maybe help-wanted advertising will prove to be more expensive than you budgeted for. Maybe a brochure will have typographical errors and have to be reprinted.

• Early losses

Even businesses that become highly successful almost always rack up some significant losses in the first year, or even during the first several years. Depending upon the type of business you are running, you will need to allocate some cash for start-up losses. Precisely how long start-up losses will be a factor with an impact on your operating budget—well, who can say? You just won't know until you have some operation time under your belt and can forecast sales trends with reasonable accuracy.

• Inventory and receivables

Unless your inventory and receivables are 100 percent financed, they will burn up cash. As your business grows, your inventory and receivables will grow. More cash will be required to finance them.

• Growth dangers

Ironically, if your business is highly successful and growing very quickly, the cash needed to finance your business, particularly inventory and receivables if applicable, will almost certainly outstrip your cash flow from operations. This will create a larger and larger cash crunch. In fact, it is not impossible for a highly profitable and fast-growing small company to run out of cash and be forced into bankruptcy.

This is why all businesses, but particularly growing firms with inventory and receivables, need to carefully project and continually adjust their cash flow demands.

Cash savers

• Suppliers

Get your suppliers to extend payments on your purchases. If you are a retailer or wholesaler, don't be afraid to ask for consignment terms, in which you pay only when and if the goods are sold. And buy from firms that offer longer payment terms than other firms are offering.

• Inventory turnover

The faster you turn over your inventory, the less money you will have tied up. If you currently have, for example, $200,000 tied up in inventory, you could free up $100,000 in cash if you doubled the pace of your inventory turnover.

Especially if you are a smaller or fast-growing firm, don't get lured into deeper discounts for larger-quantity purchases that you don't need immediately. Instead, focus on keeping adequately stocked and maintaining some of your cash.

• Tighten receivables

Be sure you are getting paid as fast as you can without alienating your customers. Stay on top of overdue situations and offer incentives for prepayment.

• Frugality

The best way to save cash is to cut expenses. When you make cuts you are directly increasing profitability and making your business more competitive, too!

Sit down with a printout of your most recent financial statement. If you don't get monthly financial statements, sit down with a list of every single item that was bought—office supplies, phone usage, heat usage, water usage, furniture, coffee, etc. Determine whether or not all purchases were necessary. Trim accordingly.

Not doing it "right"

Don't let anyone tell you that you are not doing it right by skimping here and there and everywhere (except on safety!) to save money. The only thing the best equipment, the most spectacular office furnishings, and the greatest four-color literature in the business will do for you, a business start-up, is deplete your cash. You will be broke before your grand opening is over!

Instead, decide what you need, what you can afford to spend, and what you can buy for that amount. Check out used furnishings and equipment if possible. Go to auctions, used office furniture firms, and liquidators.

Do everything you can to hold off completely on purchases that you won't be using immediately. In a new business, cash flow can change quickly—and change negatively. Be sure you can weather unexpected surprises. Keep as much cash as you can to stay as financially strong as you can be.

Cash Flow Crisis Management

John Adams has helped many entrepreneurs find success in running small businesses as a bank loan officer, and later in his career as a business broker. Mr. Adams talks about the number-one business obligation during difficult periods, and the importance of monitoring a business's cash flow during these times.

Payroll Has to Have Priority

66 Payroll is obviously number one. If an employee is not paid on time, he or she won't be back. 99

Know Your Cash Situation

66 You've got to be on top of your cash flow all the time. You should know every day what your cash position is. If someone doesn't pay and promises to pay you, you want to call that person up and say, 'I've got to a payroll to meet. I have to have some money in.' And get a fixed date for the payment—not when it's going to be put it in the mail, but the date you're going to receive it. You've got to keep the cash flowing. If the cash doesn't come in, the lifeblood of the business dries up. 99

Money Problems

If you are starting out undercapitalized, like most small businesses do, and if you have big growth plans, you are sooner or later going to run out of money. How severe a cash shortfall you have will be dependent on how early you realize that you have a problem, and on how rapidly and aggressively you work to correct it. Other sections of this chapter have focused on projecting cash flow and minimizing cash flow under normal operation conditions. This section focuses on the most effective steps that you can take during a severe cash crunch.

Basic strategies

Speeding inflow

The first area that can be adjusted during a cash crunch is cash inflow. Look at all of the receivables owed to you. Determine whether or not there is some means by which you can receive payments earlier than anticipated.

Get on the phone. Use your most upbeat tone, and try a little honest begging—"We're a little tight on cash right now, and I would greatly appreciate it if you could pay us now." If necessary, offer small discounts for faster payments or larger discounts for prepayments.

If you are working on custom projects for businesses or consumers, don't hesitate to ask for progress payments, even if they weren't part of your initial terms.

Slowing outflow

Decide how serious your situation is. Then decide which bills you must pay. Remember, very few businesses of any size pay their bills within the stated terms.

If you owe a particularly large amount of money to one key supplier, be cautious. If you intend to pay some of the bills significantly late, advise it of this in advance. If you are fairly certain as to when, specifically, you will be sending payment, consider offering this information as a promise in exchange for continued credit on new purchases.

Crucial creditors

Make sure that *you* decide who gets paid and when, not your creditors. Don't be pressured by phone collectors, or by the firms that complain the loudest. Pay those creditors that are most important to the continuation of your normal business operations first.

Some creditors may threaten, "We'll be taking further action," or "We'll be turning your account over to a collection agency," or "We'll see you in court." Don't panic. If your account is turned over to a collection agency, this will be the least of your worries. If a creditor does take you to court, the hearing date will be months down the road.

If you don't know when you will be able to pay a bill, don't let a creditor push you into making a payment promise. If you renege on a payment promise, the creditor will only become more aggressive. Instead, tell creditors that you have placed them on your payment list. Assure them that you haven't forgotten about them. Let them know they will be paid as soon as possible, but you just can't say when exactly that will be.

Noncrucial creditors

Don't forget about noncrucial suppliers, but pay these vendors only when you have the extra funds. Again, as you did with crucial creditors, prioritize and pay those suppliers whose continued services or goods are most important to the maintenance of your business.

When Money Is Tight

When your cash crunch is looking particularly severe and you can't pay all of your creditors, decide which ones to pay first. While every situation will be different, the following provides a good base strategy for prioritizing payment importance.

1 Payroll and sales taxes

Unlike income taxes, you collect your employees' shares of payroll taxes and sales taxes as an agent for the appropriate taxing authority. You are merely holding this money in trust until you turn it over to the government. If you can't pay these taxes, it is not the same as not paying an ordinary bill. It is the same as having used the government's money for your own purposes, and the government will enforce severe penalties for failure to make payment. Even if your corporation goes bankrupt, the IRS may still seek payment from former officers or shareholders.

2 Income and other taxes

While it is usually possible to do some negotiating with the tax authorities regarding income taxes, particularly in arranging installment or delayed payments, the penalties and interest can be stiff. Also, once the IRS or other tax authority is determined to collect money from you, it will be much quicker than any other creditor to place liens against your bank account or completely freeze your assets.

3 Utilities

If you are approaching a cutoff date for utility payments, remember that few utility companies will allow business customers to continue service use without paying bills in full. If you need electricity, water, heat or phones, you'd better not fall too far behind in your payments.

4 Wages

If you miss even one payroll, your best people, if not everyone, will begin looking elsewhere for employment. Suppliers may soon forget, or at least forgive, a late payment, but your employees never will.

Technically, if a company goes bankrupt, you will not be responsible for its debts, including payroll debt. But most companies in this situation find some way to pay their employees in full for work already completed. You should too!

5 Key suppliers

Pay your key suppliers enough money to continue delivery of those goods, materials, and/or services that are absolutely essential to the operation of your business.

6 Debtors

If you think your business may go under and you have personally borrowed money or personally guaranteed business loans to finance your company, consider paying these types of debtors before paying your key suppliers. No matter what happens to your company, including bankruptcy, funds borrowed from friends or relatives, funds used from home equity loans, any personal loans garnered for business use, and/or any business loans with personal guarantees will still be due and payable in full—by you.

How Far You Can Push Your Cash

As long as you have been with a bank for a couple of years and have given the bank some advance warning regarding a few upcoming late payments, it will probably still want to keep your business. If you can present a good case for your company's future, with accompanying numbers, it may even extend your credit limit in order to assist you during your cash crunch.

However, if you are going to be missing a lot of payments and can't predict when you be able to catch up, the bank will be much more interested in recovering its capital than retaining your patronage. In this case, the bank will not be interested in extending your credit limit, no matter how much you may need the cash.

On the other hand, if a bank feels it has a reasonable chance of recouping all or a significant portion of its loan at some point in the future, it probably won't attempt to foreclose on your assets.

Even though a bank may have carefully considered the existence of solid collateral such as real estate or equipment in lending you money, very few banks are eager to press a customer into foreclosure to offset loan losses. Banks seldom realize market value when they auction off foreclosed property or equipment. Foreclosure proceedings cost time, money, and community goodwill.

Always keep your bank apprised of any major financial changes in your company—even when they are negative. And, in this case, offer it a realistic plan detailing its eventual payment in full.

Alternative Financing When Money Is Tight

Asset-backed financing

While you are unlikely to obtain new or additional unsecured bank lending if you are facing a cash crunch, you may be able to obtain asset-backed financing. Try approaching nonbank sources such as commercial financing companies. Unlike most bank lending, true asset-backed lending focuses primarily on the value of the asset used for security, rather than the ongoing cash from the business.

You do need to keep in mind, however, that such lenders, unlike banks, will seldom hesitate to seize your assets after even a few missed payments. And you may also have to pay a stiff premium over traditional commercial bank loan rates.

If you are already borrowing from a bank, you need to be sure that borrowing from another source does not violate your loan agreement. And, even if it doesn't, do keep your bankers apprised of any other borrowing you undertake. If you do look creditworthy to another lending institution, even if it is nonbank, your banker will probably look more favorably upon your account.

Factoring

If you have a good amount of solid receivables, factoring may enable you to raise a lot of cash in a hurry. Factoring firms are private, nonbank lenders that buy, outright, your creditworthy receivables and collect them at their own risk. Even discounting the element of risk that factoring companies assume, they will typically seek a higher premium than bank lenders offer. This is especially true if your business is facing difficulties.

Lease-back

Look around your office. The furniture, computers, fax machines, phones, and any other equipment you may own have a cash value. You can realize the value of your assets in instant cash and still retain the equipment for use in your business! You just need to find a leasing firm willing to buy the items from you and lease them back to you.

Leasing is similar to asset-backed lending. First, the financing is based on the value of the asset. Second, you will probably pay a significant premium over that of a bank loan. One major difference, though, is that the leasing firm will actually own everything you lease. Since all the equipment belongs to it, it won't hesitate to take physical possession if you fall behind in your payments.

A big advantage to leasing is that, even though it must be disclosed as a footnote in your financial statements, it doesn't actually appear as debt on your balance sheet. It isn't considered to be as onerous as debt by debtors and other lenders or suppliers.

Extreme Solutions to Money Problems

Individual settlement

You may pick and choose among your creditors the ones you need to pay by arranging individual settlements. Many suppliers will consider foregoing all claims on overdue accounts if you agree to promptly pay a portion of their claims. Some of them may even continue conducting business with you.

It is difficult to predict which suppliers might be willing to consider an individual settlement and which will not. The only way to find out is to ask. Before proceeding, however, make absolutely sure that you want to pursue this course of action. It is possible that such a tactic could place a risk on the size and availability of your future credit lines. If you do proceed and the size of the debt to be forgiven is significant, get an agreement in writing before you meet the payment.

General settlement

A general settlement for all creditors is a much more serious step than pursuing individual settlements with selected creditors. General settlements are often made when companies are one step away from bankruptcy. They can sharply limit your ability to obtain future trade credit and debt financing.

However, seeking a general settlement for creditors is almost always a better solution than filing for bankruptcy. Be aware, though, that creditors don't always agree to general settlements.

Often, a settlement for creditors is arranged after a business has decided to close its doors. But it is sometimes pursued by businesses that plan to stay open—although they frequently emerge as scaled-down enterprises.

If you are seriously considering this option, whether yours is a large or small business, consult with an experienced attorney.

Bankruptcy

Bankruptcy is an option of last resort. Even if you are flat out of money and have no intention of continuing with your business, it isn't necessarily the best course of action. Often, informal individual settlements or formal general settlements offer the best solution.

A voluntary bankruptcy, however, may allow you to pre-empt the legal actions of unsympathetic creditors. It may allow you to hold off payments to creditors while you come up with a new business plan. But it is important to consult with a lawyer before taking this option.

Sometimes creditors will try to force a business into an involuntary bankruptcy. They will pursue such action if they feel that the company will not make a rapid turnaround and that there will be little chance of realizing payment otherwise.

Any type of bankruptcy involves tremendous legal and accounting costs. And, before any creditors realize payment on their debts, the lawyers and accountants get paid first. A bankruptcy will also require a great deal of management effort and energy over an extended period of time. And, of course, it may scare away some of your vendors, customers, and employees.

Cutting costs

While you should always try to cut costs, you need to step up this strategy when a cash crunch is at hand or looming. Remember, for any business to grow and be profitable over the long term it must, first and foremost, survive.

Cutting expenses is difficult. Come up with a bottom line goal—set a total companywide spending figure. Review each of your functional areas and determine where you can make cuts without doing long-term or irreputable harm to your product quality or sales efforts. Do this with the input and guidance of your key personnel.

Extreme Solutions to Money Problems

Employee participation

Never try to hide a serious cash crunch from your employees. Inform them of the problem. They are probably aware that it exists anyway. If you aren't honest, the rumors may fly, and people may assume a scenario worse than the reality!

Ask employees to pitch in. Encourage your staff to make savings suggestions. Even in the midst of a cash crunch, it's a good idea to offer financial incentives for great suggestions if at all feasible. Or organize a contest. Creating an awareness of the problem and offering each employee the opportunity to be part of the solution boosts morale and breeds loyalty even in the worst of times. If employees participate in suggesting cost-cutting measures, they are more likely to be cost conscious every day as well.

Layoffs

Everyone wants to avoid layoffs. But it is better to lay off a few people at once rather than let everyone go because you are shutting your doors. Employee attitudes can be volatile during a downturn in business. You need to be very careful in your handling of employment issues during this period.

If you can avoid a layoff by freezing hiring and assigning idle workers to vacant positions in other job functions, do so. Or consider having everyone pitch in a little to cover an open position.

Avoid cutting salaries if possible. If you must make cuts, start with your own. Key executives should be next in line for pay cuts. Cut only the salaries of your rank-and-file employees as a last resort. But definitely cut pay before cutting benefits. Employees are generally more attached to their benefits than to the specific amount of their wages.

Another step you should consider before laying off staff is instituting a four-day work week. You may want to discuss this option with your employees and get their feedback first.

If you must proceed with a layoff, don't do it incrementally. Do it once, and then reassure the remaining staff that their jobs are secure. Be sure that the cuts you have made are sufficient enough to forestall a reoccurrence for some time to come.

> "Organize a cost-cutting contest. If employees participate in suggesting cost-cutting measures, they are more likely to be cost conscious every day as well."

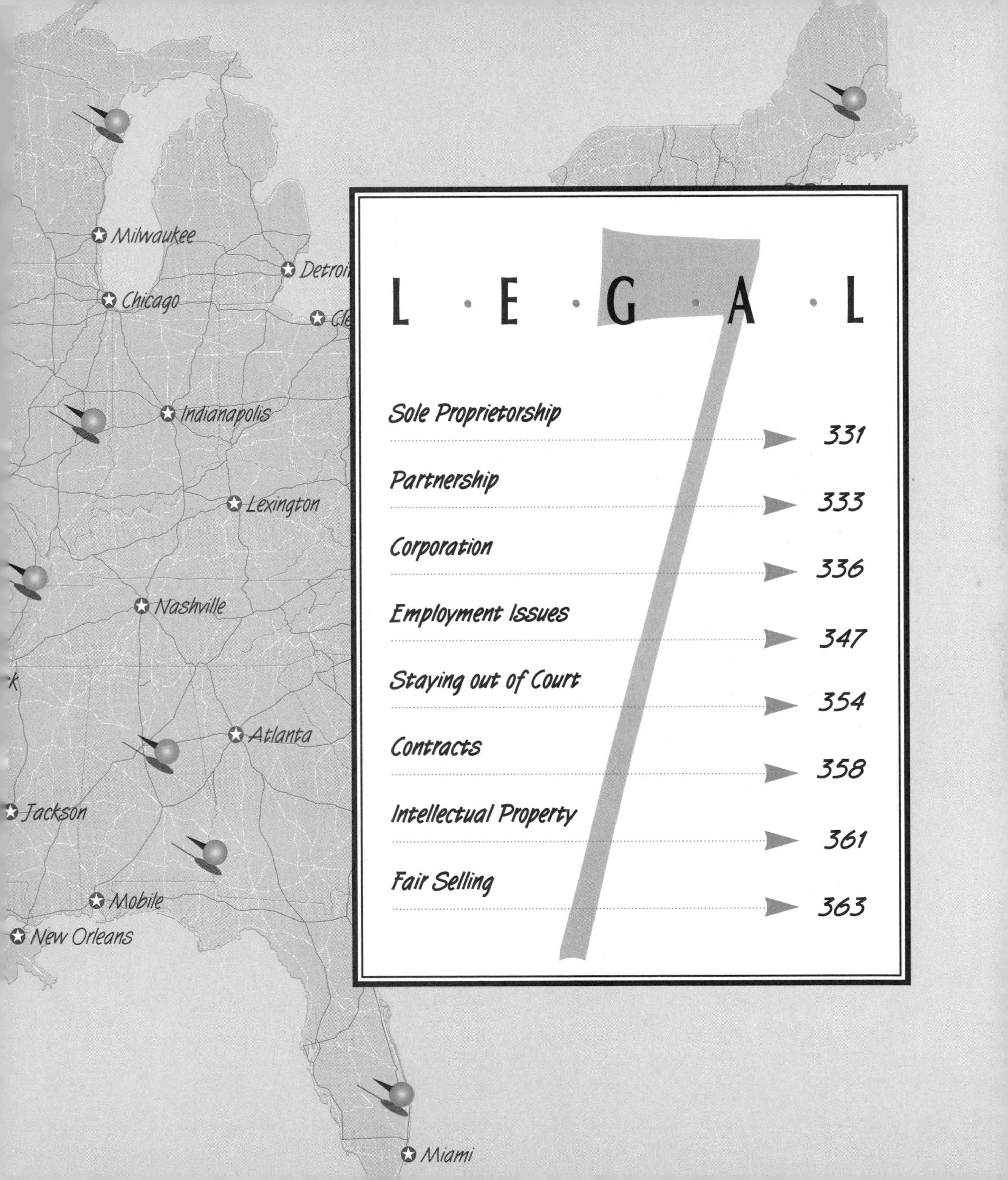
Milwaukee
Detroit
Chicago
Indianapolis
Lexington
Nashville
Atlanta
Jackson
Mobile
New Orleans
Miami

7 L · E · G · A · L

Sole Proprietorship 331
Partnership 333
Corporation 336
Employment Issues 347
Staying out of Court 354
Contracts 358
Intellectual Property 361
Fair Selling 363

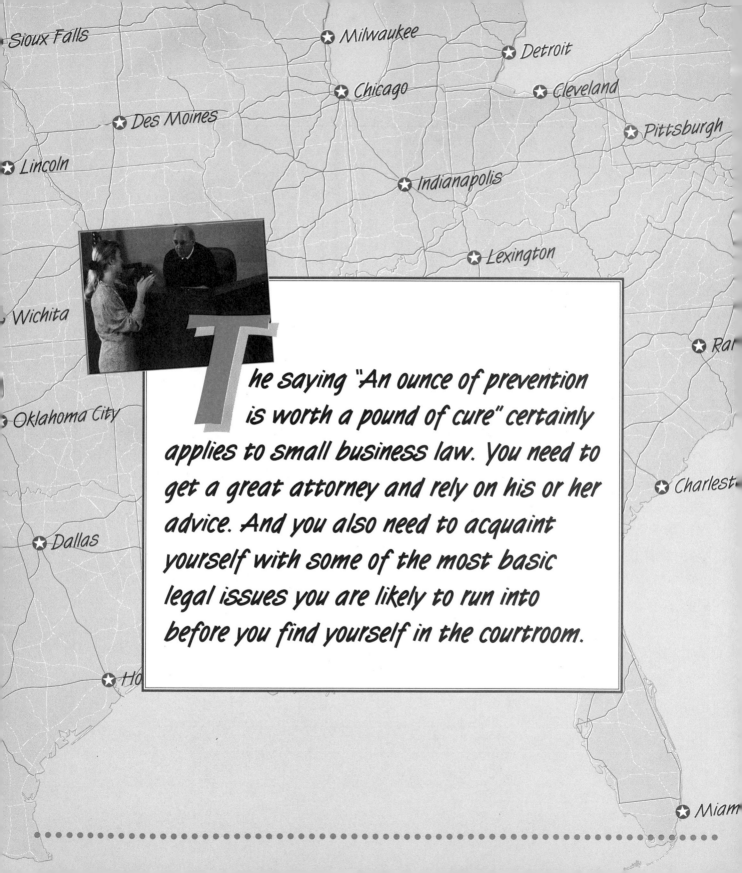

The saying "An ounce of prevention is worth a pound of cure" certainly applies to small business law. You need to get a great attorney and rely on his or her advice. And you also need to acquaint yourself with some of the most basic legal issues you are likely to run into before you find yourself in the courtroom.

Sole Proprietorship

This form of business is the easiest to start because you need obtain only whatever licenses that are required in order to begin business operation. The sole proprietorship gives you absolute control over your business, more so than other business structures such as partnerships or corporations. Very often, a small business owner will choose to start with a proprietorship. As the business grows, he or she might explore the possibility of forming a partnership or a corporation.

You will need to contact your local county or city clerk's office to determine what is required in order to operate a business in your area. If your business involves the sale of a product or service in other states, you may need to obtain a federal license or permit.

The Department of Commerce in Washington, D.C., can give the necessary information for obtaining a license for interstate commerce.

The sole proprietor's income from the business is treated as personal income. You can declare this income as part of Schedule C, Profit and Loss from a Business or Profession, with a standard 1040 Federal Individual Income tax return. You will also need Form 1040ES, Declaration of Estimated Tax for Individuals. The IRS will supply you with vouchers for submission of quarterly estimated tax payments. These payments are made in January, April, June, and September.

Sole Proprietorship

dvantages

➕ **You are in business**

➕ **Easy to form**
There are hardly any restrictions and very few forms to fill out. You need only file with your local city or county clerk's office.

➕ **Control of profits**
As a sole proprietor, you control all of the money made by the business.

➕ **Control of decision making**
You make all business operation calls.

➕ **Flexibility**
You are management and, thus, can respond more quickly to day-to-day changes and decisions.

➕ **Freedom from bureaucracy**
You experience less government control and taxation.

➕ **Simpler Taxes**
You don't have to do a separate tax return for the business and, particularly, you don't have to prepare a balance sheet for the business.

Disadvantages

➖ **Unlimited liability**
As a sole proprietor, you are responsible for 100 percent of all business debts and obligations. This liability covers all of the proprietor's assets, including his or her house and car. Additional insurance coverage may be needed to cover personal injury or physical loss that may hamper the continuity of the business.

➖ **Fragile business existence**
The death, physical impairment, or mental incapacitation of the owner can result in the termination of the business.

➖ **Difficulty raising capital and financing**
It is typically more difficult for sole proprietors to raise operating cash or arrange long-term financing because they have fewer assets.

➖ **One view, one way of doing business**
All the decision-making power rests with one individual.

➖ **Less professional appearance**
A sole proprietorship appears less professional than a partnership, and certainly less so than a corporation.

Partnership

The Uniform Partnership Act defines a partnership as "an association of two or more persons to carry on as co-owners of a business for profit." Although not required by law, you may have to submit written Articles of Partnership. This would apply, for instance, if you wanted to open a company bank account. These article would define the contributions made by the partners to the business—financial, managerial, material, or other. They would also define the roles of each partner in the business relationship. All articles should be filed with your secretary of state.

A partnership differs from a corporation in terms of the limited life of the partnership, the unlimited liability of at least one of the partners, the co-ownership of the assets, mutual agency, share of management, and share in partnership profits.

Partnership

 dvantages

 isadvantages

 Easy to form
Set-up expenses are kept to a minimum, and the legal documentation required to form a partnership is more straightforward and less complicated than that needed for incorporation.

 Direct rewards
Partners have more motivation, as they directly share in the profits.

 Improved growth possibilities
It is generally easier to attract capital for financing a business operating under a partnership than it is for a sole proprietorship.

 Flexibility
It is easier to execute decisions than it would be in a corporation, but it is more difficult than it would be in a sole proprietorship.

 Freedom from bureaucracy
This arrangement will give you more freedom from federal regulations and taxation.

 Unlimited liability of at least one partner
One or more partners must assume the business risks and purchase considerable insurance to protect the business.

Instability
If any one partner decides to quit or passes on, the partnership is dissolved. The business can still operate based on the right of survivorship and the creation of a new partnership. Partnership insurance should be considered.

Difficulty in obtaining large sums of capital
Long-term capital may be difficult to find. Using partnership assets as collateral makes it somewhat easier than in the case of a sole proprietorship.

Firm is tied to the acts and judgement of one partner as agent
All partners can be held liable for partnership business activities and the commitments of any partner.

Severing partnership ties
Buying out a partner can be a difficult process, unless an agreement is reached at the beginning of the partnership.

Partnership

What types of articles might be found in a partnership agreement?

- Name
- Purpose
- Domicile
- Duration of agreement
- Character of partners: general, limited, active, or silent
- Contributions by partners: at inception, at a later date
- Business expenses
- Authority
- Separate debts
- Books, records, and method of accounting
- Division of profits and losses
- Draws or salaries
- Rights of continuing partner
- Death of a partner; dissolution and winding up
- Employee management
- Release of debts
- Sale of partnership interest
- Arbitration
- Modifications of partnership agreement
- Settlements of disputes
- Required and prohibited acts
- Absence and disability

Are there specific types of partnerships?

Yes. This is especially true if the partners are unequal in some way. Examples are:

- *Ostensible partner*
  Active and known as a partner
- *Active partner*
  May or may not be ostensible as well
- *Secret partner*
  Active, but not known or held out as a partner
- *Dormant partner*
  Inactive and not known or held out as a partner
- *Silent partner*
  Inactive, but may be known as a partner
- *Nominal partner*
  Not a true partner, but can be represented in name or by some other representation
- *Subpartner*
  Not a member of the partnership, but contracts with a partner to participate in the interest of such partner in the firm's business and profits
- *Limited partner*
  Assuming compliance with the statutory formalities, the limited partner risks only his or her agreed investment in the business

Corporations

Since the corporation is considered a distinct legal entity with no ties to the individuals who own it as a legal structure, it is a very attractive option for small business owners. Incorporating is, however, a complicated undertaking. It gives you the opportunity to present your firm to the public as a bigger company than it actually is. It also gives you a better shot at obtaining long-term financing. Since you are not held personally responsible for the corporation, your personal assets, including your personal bank accounts, may remain untouched if the business fails. There are, however, more regulations and government filings to deal with than there are in sole proprietorships and partnerships.

Before you decide to incorporate, ask yourself

- How much risk are you willing to absorb?
- If something happened to the principal(s), how long would the company be able to function?
- What legal structure would offer the greatest flexibility in terms of administration?
- How will the laws of the incorporating state influence your decision on method of incorporation?
- What are your prospects for attracting capital?
- What is the goal of your enterprise?
- Are you willing to share control of the business with outsiders?
- Is there a tax advantage or incentive for you to incorporate?

Corporations

 dvantages

 isadvantages

 Limited liability
If the company is sued, the individual members of the company are protected under the corporate shield. In other words, they cannot be held liable unless the company is successfully sued for an outrageous act.

 Activities limited by charter and various laws
Depending upon which state you incorporate in, you may have flexibility or you may have no options whatsoever.

 Going concern
If a principal of the firm passes on or becomes incapacitated for any length of time, the business will continue to exist as a legal entity.

 Extensive government regulations
Filing reports for federal, state, and local governments can be tedious and time-consuming. Filings can include financial statements, such as a balance sheet.

 Selling stock in the corporation
It is easier to sell small amounts of stock to raise capital.

 Double taxation
You must pay corporate income tax on corporate earnings. If the earnings are distributed to shareholders as dividends, you must also pay personal income tax on those same earnings.

 Lower tax rate
In some cases, the tax rate for corporations may be less than it would be for other forms of business structures.

 Professionalism
Incorporating makes your firm look bigger and more important in the eyes of customers, suppliers, and the financial community.

Filing for Incorporation

Although incorporation is considered the most complex of legal business structures, it is possible for a small business owner to incorporate without legal counsel. To minimize legal fees, consider obtaining and filling out all forms for incorporation yourself. Forms and guidelines are available from your state secretary of state's office.

However, prior to filing with the state, you should have your attorney advise you as to whether or not incorporation is the right step for your business. If so, have him or her review your incorporation documentation to ensure that you have included all required information.

A corporation is formed with the authority of a state government. Incorporation allows capital stock to be issued while the principals create an organization. Approval for incorporation must be obtained from the secretary of state's office after filing articles of organization. The secretary of state in the filing state will issue a charter for the corporation stating the powers and limitations of the corporation. Officers of the corporation can be employees of the corporation while owning stock in the corporation. As such, they can be held liable for such items as withholding tax, unemployment tax, Workers' Compensation, and Social Security.

Filing for Incorporation

Incorporation forms require the following:

1 Company name

You begin the process of incorporating very simply, by selecting a name for your corporation. The name must have the words "Corporation," "Inc.," "Limited," or "Ltd." contained within to indicate that the liability of the shareholders is limited.

You need to reserve that name with the secretary of state's Corporate Division office. If you have an out-of-state company, check to see whether or not you can use your company name in that state. In some states you will have to pay a reservation fee, typically around $20, to reserve the name for a 120-day waiting period. Once your name has been accepted by the state, your corporation can officially use that name; however, this does not protect you from being sued for trademark infringement.

2 Mailing address

You must have a mailing address for your company. In some states a P.O. box is not acceptable unless your business is located in a rural area with no formal street address.

3 Period of duration

Corporations are usually considered to be perpetual, ongoing entities unless otherwise stated. It is highly unusual to specify a date in the future when the corporation will no longer be in existence.

4 Lawful reason or a specific purpose for the business

Some states may require that you define your specific purpose in terms of what the company will do to make a profit. A statement such as "and all other legal acts permitted for general and business corporations" may be included as part of this section. Educational or not-for-profit organizations may have to submit additional documentation to support their organizational purpose.

Number of shares to be issued and a statement of par value, if applicable

5 If the corporation decides to issue more than one class of shares, or if a class of shares has two or more series, then you must include a statement that outlines various condition. Those conditions may be total number of shares of each class authorized for issue, total number of shares issued for a series, or a fixed number authorized by the board of directors. In addition, a designation of each series or class of shares and the rights, preferences, privileges, and restrictions granted to or imposed on the respective classes must be included in the statement. If the board of directors authorizes a fixed number of shares, the articles of incorporation may also authorize the board to increase or decrease shares without going below the number of shares outstanding.

Number of directors constituting the initial board of directors and their names and addresses

6 Typically, in most states, only one director is required. If you are the only director, you will most likely be named president and secretary as well. Individuals can serve dual roles as officers and board members.

Name and address of the incorporator

7 The incorporator is the individual who is the founder of the corporation. If there is more than one individual involved, only one should volunteer to provide his or her name and address as the incorporator

Date when corporation existence will begin

8 Choose a starting date. This should coincide with the date you expect to formally operate your business as a corporation.

Notarize documents

9 Some states require the signature of a notary public on all incorporation forms.

Name and address of registered agent

10 The registered agent of the company is the individual who is incorporating the business and who received all the formal information about incorporating the business from the secretary of state's office.

Starting a Corporation

 ## Hold an organization meeting to elect directors and officers

In some corporations, the officers will consist of one or two individuals—the president and a treasurer.

 ## Adopt bylaws

The corporate bylaws should spell out, in detail, the methods by which your company will operate. They should specify the time and place of the annual shareholders' meeting, shareholder voting rights, the titles and authority of the officers of the company, and the specific powers granted to the president and the board of directors. Bylaws are not filed with the state and are not accessible to the general public.

 ## Issue shares of stock

As part of the incorporating process, a certain number of shares of stock, generally 1,000, need to be issued at a predetermined value. This value is usually $1 per share.

 ## Adopt banking resolutions

Banks use a special form that you must fill out to establish a formal banking relationship and open a corporate account. The form will include special instructions for depositing and withdrawing funds, signatures that will be required on checks or withdrawal forms, borrowing privileges, letters of credit, how the company will repay the bank for any loans that are due, and what assets of the corporation the bank can seize as part of that repayment.

 ## Fix a fiscal year

Some companies use a calendar year beginning January 1 and running through to December 31; others use from July 1 to June 30 of the following year.

 ## Obtain your tax I.D. numbers from the Internal Revenue Service

Tax I.D. numbers are used for employee withholding on federal and state tax forms. These forms must be filed with the Internal Revenue Service and will be used for filing income tax forms. Tax I.D. numbers can be obtained from the Internal Revenue Service office in your state.

 ## Obtain a corporate seal

The corporate seal is typically a round emblem that has the words "Corporate Seal" included in the design. The name of the corporation and the state in which the company does business should also be a part of the seal. Corporate seals are available from your secretary of state's office.

 ## Contact county and local agencies regarding area business requirements and restrictions

Some county or local government agencies will have restrictions such as zoning laws, requirements for building modifications, and/or regulations regarding fire exists and sprinkler systems. Check with your local governments—some of these regulations will likely apply to your business.

Hold shareholders' and board of directors' meetings on a regular basis

There should be annual shareholders' and board of directors' meetings.

Take minutes at board meetings and make them available to shareholders

Minutes are very important. They are proof that your firm is acting as a corporation. They provide protection against individuals who may try to "dent" the corporate shield in a legal dispute with the corporation.

Advise shareholders of board of director elections, including ballots and candidate profiles

All shareholders should be notified of impending elections, including the number of openings, a description of potential candidates for the board, and a sealed ballot to vote for candidates.

Advise shareholders of changes in stock disbursements

As your company grows, the potential for stock swaps with other companies, mergers, takeovers, and stock splits become a matter for shareholder vote. The corporate by-laws may require a special meeting in the event of a takeover or merger or other stock disbursement.

File taxes

Corporations are required to file income taxes as well as quarterly estimated tax payments with the Internal Revenue Service and state and local tax authorities, when applicable.

Special Types of Corporations

S Corporations

In some cases, to alleviate a tax burden, individuals may choose to form an S Corporation (formerly known as a Subchapter S Corporation). An S Corporation is a corporation for which an election has been made with the Internal Revenue Service for the income to pass through and be taxed directly to the stockholders on a pro-rata basis. This allows the small business owner to avoid dealing with the double taxation of profits and dividends. Also, shareholders may be able to offset business losses by the corporation against their personal income, subject to certain restrictions.

Some provisions for forming an S Corporation are

- The corporation mush have thirty-five or fewer shareholders who are either individuals, estates, or certain qualifying trusts
- The corporation may have only one class of stock
- Nonresident alien shareholders are ineligible
- All shareholders must consent to an election
- The corporation may not own 80 percent or more of another corporation
- At least 75 percent of the company's receipts must be derived from the business rather than outside investments or passive income
- Former S Corporations that have revoked or had their S status terminated must wait five years before making a new election

Limited liability companies

The limited liability company (LLC) is a relatively new business structure that is valid in almost every state. It is a cross between a corporation and a partnership. Essentially, a LLC carries the limited liability advantages of a corporation but operates with the flexibility and tax obligations of a partnership. In terms of taxes, it is less restrictive and less expensive than an S Corporation.

LLC Corporations, at the time of this book's printing, are allowed in all states except Hawaii, and Vermont. Both of these states have the legalization of the LLC structure under consideration.

The LLC is becoming a very popular form of organization for new, small businesses.

☞ Go corporate

If after reading the pros and cons on incorporating a business, you are still unsure as to whether or not you should incorporate, just do it. Unless your business is going to stay extremely small and relatively risk free, you would be "penny wise and pound foolish" not to incorporate.

☞ Keep control

If you are setting up a partnership or investing with others in a corporation, do everything you possibly can to maintain control. Fifty-one percent of a two-person corporation is worth infinitely more than 50 percent. A minority share in a closely held corporation can be worth very little. The majority shareholder may set salaries, determine expenditures, or sell control—do just about anything he or she pleases unless the corporate by-laws state otherwise. Similarly, a partnership agreement that gives one partner decision-making power, rendering the other partner powerless, is worth less financially.

☞ Death, taxes, disagreements

Don't kid yourself! No matter how harmoniously your relationships with other major investors in a corporation or partnership begin there will inevitably be disagreements. There might, and probably will, be major disagreements. You need to clearly figure out what will happen when, not if, a major disagreement occurs.

☞ Think it through before you start

I've seen plenty of small business owners not give enough thought to structuring their business before plunging into it. I saw one women give a 50 percent partnership to another woman who was essentially going to be her secretary. The value of your share of your business, and your business as a whole, can be dramatically affected by the decisions you make during the formative stages. So weigh the issues carefully.

☞ Consider your needs for "cashing out"

One important factor to consider in setting up a business structure is how and when you hope to take large amounts of money out of the company. It might seem like a dream now, but suppose your plans all work out. When do you want to cash out and how?

If you plan on cashing out by selling the firm to a large corporation in five years, for example, a traditional C corporation may suit your purposes fine. If you never plan to sell the business, and don't plan to have many employees or assets, but still want the protection of a corporate "shell" then an S corporation or a limited liability company would serve your needs better.

"If you are setting up a partnership or investing with others in a corporation, do everything you possibly can to maintain control."

Is it possible to change the type of organization my business is?

Yes, it certainly is. For example, my book publishing business started out as a sole proprietorship. Later, I transferred the assets to a corporation. Initially the corporation was an S Corporation; it is now a traditional corporation.

There may be significant tax liabilities incurred in changing the structure of your firm. But a knowledgeable CPA or tax lawyer should be able to help you either avoid or minimize that liability.

If you switch to a corporate structure to avoid a legal action, you are unlikely to protect yourself from the ramifications of any incidents that ccurred prior to your incorporation.

Can my corporation buy stock in other corporations?

A corporation can buy stock in other companies. It can borrow money from banks or conduct any type of financial transaction permitted an individual. Note, however, that an S corporation may not own more than 80 percent of another corporation.

Can I loan money to a corporation that I own?

Yes. One of the advantages of formally loaning money to a corporation that you wholly own is that you will have a greater chance of recouping your money as a debtor than as a shareholder, should the company experience difficulties.

Another advantage is that you can pay yourself interest that is tax deductible for the corporation. Remember, though, that you have to pay taxes on the interest. The interest you charge should be at market rate at the time of the loan.

If your loan balance is too high and your equity investment is too low, the IRS can reclassify part of the loan as equity, and your interest payments will become nondeductible dividends.You can pay yourself a salary as well. Make sure that it is within reason. If the tax authorities consider it to be excessive, they will restate the "excess" salary as a dividend and tax it as both corporate and personal income.

If you think that either your loan to or salary from your company is tipping the scales, check with a qualified tax advisor.

Can I buy assets in my own name and then lease them to my corporation?

Yes. This is usually done for two reasons. One is for tax purposes. If you own assets such as machinery, buildings, or vehicles, they may be depreciated. Depreciation, under most circumstances, allows you to reduce your tax bill. Check with your accountant to see if your current salary and nonsalaried income levels allow you to qualify for income offsetting depreciation under the latest tax laws.

Another reason to personally own assets is to protect them from seizure should the corporation get into trouble. Also, if the personally owned asset is real estate, for instance, you will personally realize the profits from any appreciation in value. Remember, though, if you own the assets, you are in a personally liable position.

Leasing assets to your own corporation is one way to get money, other than salary, out of the corporation. There are special tax rules, however, that prevent you from using leasing as a method to avoid the "passive loss rules" in the tax code.

Is it easier to dissolve a partnership or a corporation?

Legally, it is easier to dissolve a partnership. Remember, a partnership is merely an agreement between two or more people. A corporation, however, is a distinct legal entity. Dissolving it will take a fair amount of time and expense.

The biggest hurdle in dissolving a partnership is arriving at an agreement with the other partner or partners regarding distribution of assets and liabilities and who, if anyone, will continue to run the business.

If you see your business as having a limited life with low risk you should run it as a sole proprietorship. If you are short on funds, try borrowing from friends before forming a partnership.

Employment Issues

Minimum wage

In most developed and developing countries there is a minimum wage law. In the United States the minimum wage is currently $4.25 per hour.

There are exceptions to this law. One is the tip credit, which allows an employer to claim a credit of up to 50 percent of the minimum wage for employees who earn tips.

States, in some cases, may impose higher minimum wages. In these cases the state prevails, and employers must pay the state mandated rate to minimum wage earners.

A training wage of 85 percent of the minimum wage may be paid to certain employees under the age of 20 for a limited period of time. The regulations attending to this exception are complex. If you want to avail yourself of this exception, contact the nearest office of the Department of Labor, Employment Standards Division.

Exempt/non-exempt

An exempt employee is basically one who is exempt from minimum wage and overtime requirements. There are tests to be met in order to determine this employee status but, basically, the employees' work should be professional, administrative, or managerial. They should be paid a salary significantly higher than the minimum wage.

Overtime pay

In the United States overtime pay is mandated at a minimum of one and one-half times regular pay for all hours worked beyond forty in a single week. This rule applies only to nonexempt employees.

Posters

Even if you only employ one person, you need to place certain posters in a highly visible area regularly accessible to your employees—at the entrance to the work area or in a break room, for instance. These posters include U.S. Department of Labor disseminated materials that make public information on the minimum wage, overtime pay, equal pay, child labor, age discrimination, equal opportunity, handicapped workers, employee polygraph protection, and family and medical leave laws. OSHA distributes information regarding worker health and safely that is required posting as well. Some states also issue mandated signage.

Poster requirements change from time to time. As a starting point, contact your nearest Wage of Hour Department of the U.S. Department of Labor for currently applicable posters.

Independent contractors

An independent contractor is someone who performs a service for your business, but is not considered to be an employee by federal or state tax authorities.

When you use the services of an independent contractor you do not have to pay employer taxes, process payroll checks, and withhold employee tax shares on behalf of the contractor. You may also have less potential legal liability when these services are no longer required.

In the United States, however, the IRS and state revenue departments are vigorously trying to minimize lost revenue by carefully examining the status of "independent contractors" at many firms. If your "independent contractors" are deemed employees by the tax authorities, you could be forced to pay back taxes, employee benefits, interest, and penalties.

Employment Issues

There is no hard and fast rule regarding who does or doesn't qualify as an independent contractor. The IRS examines each situation individually. Here are some of the standard considerations they use as guides:

Guidelines to determining independent contractor status

- Does the hiring firm or the independent contractor determine when, where, and how work is performed?
- Is the hiring firm providing the independent contractor with training?
- How do the independent contractor's services integrate into the business?
- Are the services rendered by the independent contractor performed personally by him or her?
- How does the company hire, supervise, and pay independent contractors?
- What is the continuing relationship between the independent contractor and the firm that has hired him or her?
- Does the hiring firm set the working hours for the independent contractor?
- Does the hiring firm require the independent contractor to work full-time?
- Does the independent contractor work on the hiring firm's premises?
- Is the work order or sequence of work performed set by the hiring firm?
- Does the hiring firm require written or oral work progress reports from the independent contractor?
- Does the hiring firm pay the independent contractor by the hour, week, or month?
- Does the hiring firm pay travel and other business expenses on behalf of the independent contractor?
- Does the hiring firm supply the tools and equipment necessary to the performance of the task?
- Does the independent contractor have a significant investment interest in the hiring firm?
- Does the independent contractor realize profits and losses from the hiring firm?
- Does the independent contractor work for more than one firm at a time?
- Does the independent contractor make his or her services available to the general public?
- Does the hiring firm have the right to discharge the independent contractor?
- Can the independent contractor terminate his or her arrangement with the hiring firm without liability?

General rule of thumb: If you are using the services of independent contractors as a means to avoid employment taxes, you are probably headed for trouble. If you have doubts about your use of independent contractors, don't "hire" their services under the independent contractor status. The potential for financial risk is draconian should that status be deemed inappropriate by the tax authorities.

Employment Issues

Family and medical leave

The United States Family and Medical Leave Act of 1993 requires employers covered by this law to provide up to twelve weeks of unpaid leave per year for "eligible" workers. In addition, these workers must be guaranteed their original job, or an equivalent position with equivalent pay, benefits, and other employment terms, upon their return to work.

- **Eligibility requirements**
  - Birth and care of a newborn child
  - Placement of a child for adoption or foster care
  - The care of a spouse, child, or parent with a serious health condition
  - The inability of an employee to perform his or her normal work duties due to a serious health condition
  - Eligible employees must have worked for a covered employer for one year and at least 1,250 hours in the last twelve months.

- **Employer requisites**

  Employers must continue coverage under a group health plan during the leave. Use of the leave may not result in loss or reduction of any benefits previously accrued.

  The United States Family and Medical Leave Act of 1993 applies, at the time of this book's printing, to firms that employ fifty or more persons, including part-timers.

  Even if your firm is not technically covered by this act, you should consider honoring it. It is just a great way to do business. You'll look like a Scrooge if you don't, and many of your employees won't understand why the law doesn't apply to them.

Equal opportunity

Employers are prohibited from discriminating in the hiring, promotion, discharge, pay, fringe benefits, and any other aspect of employment on the basis of race, color, sex, national origin, age, or disability.

Remember, your business is responsible for any discriminatory actions taken by managers or supervisors. You need to be sure that everyone on your management team understands discrimination law and abides by it.

In addition to being bad for business, violation of this law subjects you to potential government action. The greatest risk you face, however, is from an employee or job applicant filing a civil suit.

And don't just quietly abide by the law. Make it obvious to the world that you are an equal opportunity employer. Certainly hire and definitely make an effort to promote women, racial minorities, people over forty, and the physically challenged. This will create a public image of your company as a progressive, forward-looking employer. It will demonstrate to those in protected groups that they can be hired by and get ahead within your firm. This reputation will also enable your company to defend itself against "false" discrimination suits brought by bitter or disgruntled employees or job applicants.

Sexual harassment

While many men don't understand or realize it, sexual harassment is widespread within the workplace. Many women, and yes, a few men, will experience sexual harassment during their work careers. While some victims can get beyond the negative impact of sexual harassment, others suffer severe emotional stress.

You, as an employer, need to be particularly aware of sexual harassment issues. No matter how small a business you run, no matter how much you dislike formal workplace rules—you absolutely must have a solid, enforced policy on sexual harassment.

- **The definition**

  Sexual harassment is a form of sex discrimination that violates Title VII of the Civil Rights Act of 1964.

  Unwelcome sexual advances, requests for sexual favors, and other verbal or physical conduct of a sexual nature constitute sexual harassment when submission to or rejection of this conduct explicitly or implicitly affects an individual's work performance or creates an intimidating, hostile, or offensive work environment.

Some states further refine this definition, and those state laws must be adhered to in addition to the federal laws.

The law

Even if you have one employee and he or she seems perfectly happy in the position, you need to consider sexual harassment and have a basic understanding of the laws that attain to it.

Sexual harassment is prohibited by federal law in all U.S. workplaces with over fifteen employees. Many state laws further reduce the size of companies that must adhere to sexual harassment regulations. Suits for damages resulted from sexual harassment may, and often are, brought against employers. While your company is liable only for the managerial behavior regarding discrimination practice, in the case of sexual harassment you are responsible for the actions of all employees.

Sexual harassment suits can generally be classified into one of two categories: "quid pro quo" and hostile environment.

A "quid pro quo" lawsuit

"Quid pro quo" harassment occurs when a coworker or supervisor pressures another employee into an unwelcome sexual activity by either promising a positive award such as a promotion, or threatening negative consequences such as dismissal. It is possible to lose a sexual harassment lawsuit even if the suggestion of sexual activity and the threat are only implicit. For example, a supervisor who repeatedly asks a subordinate for a date despite his or her repeated refusal may be deemed to be implicitly seeking sexual favors and, because of the nature of the reporting relationship, to be implicitly offering "quid pro quo."

Even if the firm has a policy against sexual harassment, if the single "quid pro quo" situation occurs with only one supervisor, and senior management has not been informed regarding the situation, the company may be held liable for sexual harassment.

A hostile environment lawsuit

The courts are beginning to define a hostile environment using what is referred to as "a reasonable woman standard." This is because most, but not all, sexual harassment affects women. The courts will hold an environment to be sexually hostile if the behavior is severe and/or pervasive enough for a reasonable woman to feel it is interfering with her work performance or creating an intimidating, hostile, or offensive working environment. Unfortunately, there is a lot of room for interpretation here, and the ruling of one court may differ significantly from that of another.

Because there are activities that one person may find offensive while another does not, the safest route to developing a nonhostile sexual environment within your workplace is to eliminate all activities that may cause offense. Ban sexual jokes, the posting of female calendars in men's rooms, or even comments on dress or appearance that may pose offense to some.

And, because the courts have interpreted a hostile environment as defined by "a reasonable woman," you need to pay quick and sharp attention to any feedback from people who feel offended within your workplace.

Policies

You should have a written policy on sexual harassment no matter how small a company yours may be. Offices that provide employment for two people, with no third party present, can create a sense of tension in some employees from the outset, and can cause the implications of comments, real or not, to be magnified. Small commercial or home office environments might more conducive to sexual harassment than would be true of a big, bustling office employing hundreds.

Your policy should specifically prohibit sexual harassment. You may wish to cite examples of what would be considered sexually harassing behavior. You should implement a grievance procedure that allows complainants to bring their complaints to someone other than their supervisor. Employees should have the option of placing grievances before either a male or a female. If you don't have enough personnel to effectively set up a grievance committee within your organization, appoint an outsider—perhaps your attorney.

Your written policy on sexual harassment should be posted in a highly visible location and/or distributed to all employees, including new hires. You should go over your policy, verbally, in a company-wide meeting and record any such meetings.

• Taking action

If a sexual harassment claim is made, it should be carefully investigated regardless of how trivial it may seen. Remember, each person has a different personal code for what he or she deems to be offensive behavior.

It is important that appropriate steps be taken against any employee whose behavior has been found to be sexually offensive. Depending upon the nature of the offense and its duration, the disciplinary action may only be a quiet closed-door chat, or it may be as extreme as termination of employment.

You absolutely must take appropriate action in sexual harassment matters, but you need to be careful that you don't trample on the rights and respect due the alleged offender. Determining appropriate disciplinary action won't be easy, especially if the offender denies the behavior. You should always consult with an attorney when you are facing the ramifications of a sexual harassment charge, especially if the nature of the charge is different than those you may have dealt with previously. Remember, you could end up being sued by both the victim and the alleged offender, and it isn't beyond the realm of possibility that both claimants could win their legal suits!

Employment references

While giving truthful employment references is not legally actionable, references, by nature, tend to be highly judge-mental. The employer's view of the truth may be different than the employee's view of the truth. This is particularly true in the case of under-performing employees.

In the case of employment that has been involuntarily terminated, it is a fair assumption that the employee will typically feel some ill will towards his or her former employer and may just be looking for an excuse to file a legal suit. Often employees who leave the service of a company voluntarily have done so because they were unhappy in the company or in their positions. In any case, references given for former employees can create an opening for legal action if the employee does not feel he or she has been fairly represented by the former employer.

Some small business owners feel they can be less cautious when giving verbal references than they would be in the case of supplying a written one. Not true! Any type of reference can be legally actionable.

While many courts are sympathetic to the need of employers to give references, others are not. Courts have been known to judge for an employee because a reference given, while good, was not good enough!

It is a safe policy to offer no references at all beyond confirming dates of employment, position held, and rate of pay earned. This may not seem right, but your responsibility is to keep your business running smoothly and out of court so that your current employees can enjoy a healthy working environment.

Workers' compensation

It is mandatory to provide a minimum level of workers' compensation insurance to all employees. Even if you are having trouble meeting bills, don't let your workers' compensation insurance payments lapse. You do owe it to your employees, and it is the law. Not paying it constitutes a serious offense, and courts have gone directly into the pockets of shareholders and corporate officers to make good on employee compensation claims that should have been covered.

Biggest concerns

There is an incredible variety of legal issues involving employees that you need to be concerned about.

There are two in particular that you really need to focus on. Be careful if you are firing any employee over forty. And be careful in your handling of sexual harassment issues. These two issues seem to bring more and more companies into the courtroom. Age discrimination and sexual harassment suits are notoriously difficult for companies to win, and juries often award plaintiffs very large judgements.

Proactive policies

Just being fair to your employees is not a wise policy for avoiding legal trouble. You must implement proactive measures before trouble brews. You need to institute formal policies on issues such as discrimination and sexual harassment that will assist, inasmuch as possible, in heading off trouble, and lay a foundation for any legal defense you may need to launch should suit be brought.

Employment laws were written to help re-elect politicians, not to assist small business owners. And disgruntled employees don't always have a high regard for the truth. This combination, in court, may spell disaster for you. Plan ahead—be proactive with solid, written policies.

Legal help

Don't skimp on legal counsel before firing an employee or changing personnel policies. Some statistics suggest that over one-half of all fired employees consult with attorneys and consider taking legal action against former employers.

When considering firing someone, consult with your lawyer. Remember that in a courtroom it is your word against that of the employee, and juries are, typically, composed of employees, not employers. And whether or not a claim ever sees the inside of a courtroom, it is going to cost you substantially in both time and money. Spend a few bucks on advance advice, to avoid spending huge sums to mount a legal defense.

Weak lawyers

Your regular lawyer may be a really nice person. He or she may be quite astute regarding business issues. But when you are dealing with employment issues, seek an expert in employment law.

Employment law is continually and rapidly evolving. Decisions in employment-related suits change the legal face of employer-employee relationships every day. Advice that was sound last year may be useless this year. You need to consult with an attorney who makes employment issues his or her one and only specialty whenever you are dealing with sticky employment-related situations.

"Just being fair to your employees is not a wise policy for avoiding legal trouble. You must implement proactive measures before trouble brews."

Questions & Answers about Employment Issues

Do employees fabricate claims of discrimination?

There is no question that many employees who file suits or claims of discrimination don't really believe they were discriminated against. They are angry about a firing or a missed promotion, or just want extra money. But even though you may know that a claim is pure fabrication doesn't mean you shouldn't treat it seriously.

How can I be sure my supervisors don't discriminate?

Sit down with them as a group or individually and go over the laws against discrimination. It can even be a great idea to divide the issues into several topics and conduct a series of meetings, each devoted to a segment of discriminatory practice. People tend to have better recall when they digest information in smaller chunks.

Another way to help ensure against discrimination is to always have at least two people involved in any hiring situation. This offers a double-check system during the hiring process itself and gives you two witnesses should any legal action result.

Consider sending your managers and supervisors to workshops that deal with discrimination law and its implications. Or have them read books and articles on the subject.

And, if you have a manager who has a sizable department bereft, or relatively bereft, of females or ethnic minorities—be suspect.

Be absolutely sure your management team, including supervisors, understands the laws against discrimination and what your company policy on discrimination is, and that discrimination in your workplace won't be tolerated.

Do I have to pay wages during pregnancy leaves?

No. The Family Medical Leave Act guarantees an employee's right to take time off for pregnancy and guarantees that employee's right to the same or an equal job upon her return. It does not require that the employee continue to receive wages or salary during her absence. Regular benefits, however, must continue to be given.

Is it discriminatory to not hire smokers?

It is not currently considered discriminatory to deny employment to smokers. But while many firms ban smoking within their buildings, few employers prohibit the hiring of people who smoke.

Are there any issues in moving an employee to contractor status?

Yes. The IRS frowns on this move. They are more likely to challenge the reclassification of an employee to independent contractor than they would the status of anyone originally hired as an independent contractor.

Should I refer to a new hire's first ninety days of work as a temporary period?

Many firms consider new hires temporary employees for the first ninety days of their employment. The problem with classifying an employee as temporary for any period of time is that a court may consider anyone retained after the ninety-day "temporary" period as a permanent employee—permanent, as in an employee for life!

To avoid any possibility of a semantic misinterpretation of your intent, you may wish to refer to the first ninety days of a new hire's employment as an initial work period.

Along the same line of reasoning, don't refer to an employee's salary as a rate of pay per year. This may be interpreted to mean that you are offering someone a job for a period of at least one year. Refer to wages as dollars per week.

Finally, courts do not recognize "initial" employment periods, and you could be liable for a discriminatory discharge suit by an employee.

Staying out of Court

In all but the most extreme cases, you want to avoid going to court either as a plaintiff or a defendant. Think about it. Do you really want to shell out the huge legal fees you are likely to incur? Or have your time tied up for months or even years? Do you want, after all the expense and time, to lose your case? Courts offer uncertain outcomes. Even if you are right and see the situation as clear-cut, you can still lose your case.

You might not be drawing a big salary, but your time and the time of your key managers is valuable. Time spent in court or thinking about a court case is time spent away from growing your business.

The outcome of going to court is extremely uncertain, and a loss could significantly change the way you do business. And, win or lose, a court case will have the same effect on your cash flow—flowing out.

The uncertainty of the outcome can be exacerbated by the timing of the outcome. It is difficult to predict how long a court case will last. While a small claims hearing might not take years, the possibility of any other type of case lasting that long is quite real.

If you suspect that you might eventually be forced to pay out a settlement, you might get lulled into delaying the end of a court case. But remember that you need to disclose outstanding suits in your financial statements, and such disclosures may affect your ability to borrow or raise cash. Also, settlements can be subject to interest.

Staying out of Court

Avoidance

The best way to stay out of court is to avoid problems before they occur. Run your business within the law. Run your business with humanity—make your workplace a fun place to be. Develop good, solid employment policies, especially in the critical areas of hiring, promoting, firing, and sexual harassment.

Use contracts whenever appropriate, with all the key details spelled out clearly in writing. And include in your contracts, whenever possible, a proviso that directs all disputes into binding arbitration, not court.

Finally, don't be shy about consulting an attorney whenever you have questions about employment or business decisions that may portend a legal risk for you. Spending a few bucks for a half of hour advice here and there is certainly worth saving the major expense of a court battle.

Early response

In many potentially litigious situations, an early response may avert a legal suit. Often legal claims arise out of misunderstandings, which good communication can alleviate.

For example, if you have decided not to pay the full bill invoiced by a supplier because the quality of the goods delivered was not satisfactory, call the supplier with your complaint immediately. Back up your verbal communication with a letter to that same supplier. You need to get the vendor to see the quality issue from your point of view and instill empathy for your situation. Just not paying the bill, without apprising the vendor of the problem, is begging for a court appearance.

Similarly, if a customer is not happy with goods supplied by you, handle the situation as soon as possible. By listening to that person's complaint, trying to understand the problem from his or her perspective, and showing empathy for the situation, you have gone a long way towards avoiding a legal suit. And, you may have retained the customer!

If an employee complains about sexually hostile behavior in your workplace, promptly take action to eliminate the behavior. This may satisfy the victim and keep you out of court altogether. But even if the case does end up in court, your attempts to correct or alleviate the problem will count in your favor.

Generally, in any negative business situation, respond quickly and maintain dialogue and rapport with the other party. This policy never hurts!

Settlement meetings

A face-to-face settlement meeting with the opposing party can help avoid the courtroom. Any such meeting should be conducted on a peer-to-peer basis. This means company president to company president, for example. Of course, if you are the sole proprietor of a company and the other party is IBM, don't expect the president of IBM to meet with you. But do insist on meeting with someone in as similar a position to yours as possible. For example, if you are trying to resolve a problem with a large supplier, try to speak with a product manager or regional sales manager—not your regular sale representative or the purchasing agent for your account.

If you encounter problems in attempting a settlement with another party through informal meetings, try a more formal approach. Try meeting in a neutral location with attorneys for both parties in attendance.

The presence of attorneys signals confidence. It sends the message that both you and the disputing party are willing to pursue the matter through the courts if necessary. Through such a meeting you will be able to ascertain the strength of the opposing party's claim or defense, and hear his or her arguments much as you would should the case go to court. Of course, the opposing side will be able to size up your case or defense as well.

Arbitration

If you can't resolve an issue with calls or meetings, consider binding arbitration. In this case, both parties agree on an arbitrator (often a retired judge arranged for through an arbitration organization) and agree that the results of the arbitration will be binding and may be entered into the prevailing court. Be sure to get the agreement to arbitrate in writing.

In court

There are exceptions to avoiding or delaying an appearance in court. Sometimes you will want to get there as quickly as possible. If your rights as a small business owner are being wantonly trampled on by a large corporation, think about going for it. Corporate giants typically figure that a small entrepreneur will back down because he or she hasn't got the funds to do legal battle or will jump at the first pathetic settlement offered.

But do be absolutely sure that you want to pursue your claim through to resolution before you file with the courts. Have your attorney advise you. Find out what the costs might be, what the time element might be, and what the various outcomes, good and bad, might be.

Avoiding Court Success Story

Bob Adams, president of Adams Media and author of this book, speaks from personal experience.

How Settlement Meetings Can Help You Stay Out of Court

" We refused to pay a full bill because a vendor had not even come close to meeting an agreed-upon delivery schedule. My purchasing people and I had numerous meetings and calls with representatives of the other firm at all levels, from sales rep to president. I was sure we would not be able to get anywhere without going to court.

My attorney convinced me to have a formal meeting, with each of us bringing our attorney and our expert. To my surprise, we were not only able to settle the case for much less than I thought we would, but in listening to the other side, I was surprised to see how valid many of its arguments were. I would have even settled for a lot less. "

Contracts

Like most people, small business owners tend to shy away from signing anything. They avoid contracts like the plague. But this is a risky way to do business.

When you are making a major product or service sale or purchase, you need to get the details of the transaction in writing. If you don't, you will inevitably find yourself in the middle of a heated discussion over specific terms. Does the purchase include freight costs? Can sanctions be imposed if delivery isn't met? What if the services rendered are considered unsatisfactory? In many cases a purchase order and/or a written estimate will provide the answers to these types of questions and serve, in effect, as a contract.

For small, routine purchases and sales, you may wish to have an attorney review the basic purchase order or sales documents that you will be using. For larger or unusual transactions, you may wish to have your attorney review the contract you intend to use, if not draft it. After you have been in business for a while and have learned a thing or two from your attorney, you will gain the ability and confidence to write many of your own contracts.

For more important contracts, retain the original copy containing the original signatures from all parties. True, in many situations a photocopy or even an agreement without signatures offers adequate proof of a purchase or sale agreement, but nothing can beat an original copy as legal protection.

Any substantive changes to a contract should be noted in writing. If they are in the body of the contract, then each change should be initialed by all parties involved. If it is in the form of an addendum, it should be signed by all parties involved. A contract should specify that it represents the entire agreement between the parties and that any changes must be in writing.

To avoid court and the legal costs associated with lawsuits, contracts should, generally, have a clause specifying that disputes will be arbitrated. The method of arbitration should be stated and the results of the arbitration should be held binding.

Streetwise Advice on Contracts

☞ Yours vs. theirs

Whenever possible, provide the contract yourself. Don't use someone else's. You may save the cost of creating a contract, but you will lose that important control over content advantage a contract gives you.

☞ Understand it

Understanding "legalese" may seem like an overwhelming task, if not an impossibility. But if you intend to build a growing business you need to become comfortable with contracts, their language, and their meaning. You should have your lawyer review every contract you don't fully understand. And you should have him or her carefully and clearly explain any terms or passages you don't completely understand.

As a business person you must understand that every business transaction has implications for your company. Don't sign anything blindly. Get past the legal jargon so that you can fully understand the contracts you are signing and be able to protect the best interests of your business.

☞ Standardize

If your business involves a lot of contracts, negotiate hard-to-get customers and vendors to adhere as closely as possible to your standard contract. Changing a long contract takes a lot of hard and time-consuming work. Any change in contractual wording requires that the entire contract be reviewed and proofed again. A change in one area can create misleading implications in another area of the contract. And a simple retyping can result in a serious typographical errors or omissions.

Any substantive change needs to be viewed suspiciously. Are there hidden implications that the other party has insisted upon?

Standardization can save you time, money, and headaches.

☞ Safekeeping

It is so easy to misplace contracts—even crucial ones. Keep copies of your contracts in your bank safe deposit box. If the contract is particularly important, have your lawyer keep a copy on file as well. Have one or more office copies available for easy reference. Don't use the original as your reference copy!

> "Understanding "legalese" may seem like an overwhelming task, if not an impossibility. But, if you intend to build a growing business you need to become comfortable with contracts, their language, and their meaning."

Questions & Answers about Contracts

Do big corporations alter standard contracts for smaller firms?

Yes, it happens frequently. But more often the smaller firm just signs the standard agreement that it is given. Depending upon how much another corporation wants your service or product and how agreeable the particular people involved are, you may or may not be able to negotiate deviations from the standard contract.

How can I determine what points are negotiable?

Perhaps you can find someone else in your industry who has previously negotiated with the firm in question. If not, you have two basic options. One is to make a formal proposal or counterproposal. The other is to have a more casual discussion. For example, you could say, "I'm used to having the the customer pay the freight," or "For two-year service we add an additional fee," and listen carefully to what the initial response is.

How can I avoid going to court if a contract is broken?

The best way to avoid a court battle over a broken contract is to have specific remedies for specific, potential problems written right into the original contract. A cover for a potential delivery problem, for instance, might be, "The payment will be reduced by a certain amount for every day the delivery is late." On another level, you can stipulate within the contract that the entire contract go into binding arbitration, not court, in the event of a dispute.

Do I need to have my attorney read every contract?

After you have been in business for a period of time, you will begin to feel more confident in your ability to read contracts. Until then, however, I would have an attorney review every major contract and explain any passages or clauses in minor contracts that cause you difficulty.

What should I watch out for in contracts?

Watch out for any items that are inserted into your contracts by any other parties involved. These items may significantly alter the meaning of the contract. This is not an isolated occurrence—it happens all the time. Often, but not always, it is done innocently. Nonetheless, you need to be on constant guard against this problem. Don't sign anything that isn't exactly what you thought you were agreeing to.

Intellectual Property

Copyrights

Items protected by copyright law include books, magazines, software, advertising copy, newspapers, music, movies, audio recordings, and artwork.

Items not protected by copyrights include concepts or ideas, titles, names, and brands. For example, our publishing company once considered publishing a book entitled *Who Am I?* First we did a little research to see if anyone else had previously used this title. We found not one, but nine books bearing this title. They were all distinct works by different authors. While not protected by copyrights, names and brands are subject to other protection, particularly trademark protection.

In the United States, copyright protection automatically extends to any appropriate material. This is the case whether you file for a copyright notice or not.

However, if it is at all practical, you should spend the small fee (currently $20 in the United States) to formally register your copyright if the material is of significant value to you. This will increase both the legal protection of your work and the value of any rewards you might recover in an infringement of copyright lawsuit.

You should put a copyright notice on all copyrighted materials. This will decrease the likelihood of infringement. The copyright notice should be in a highly visible place on the property and should include the word copyright or the copyright symbol, the first year the work was issued to the public and the formal name of the holder of the copyright.

© *1996 Adams Media Corporation*

To obtain U.S. copyright forms or for more information contact the Copyright Office, Library of Congress, Washington, D.C. 20559.

Most other countries offer copyright protection that is roughly similar to that offered in the United States. And U.S. copyrighted material will usually be protected in other countries. While a few countries, particularly in Southeast Asia, have long ignored or not enforced copyright protection, the trend has been toward enforcing a strong uniform protection of copyrights worldwide.

Trademarks

Unlike copyrights and patents, trademarks affect all businesses. When you use the name of your business publicly, you are using it as a trademark. When you sell products using a brand name, you are using that brand name as a trademark. The brand name of any service you provide is a service mark or, essentially, a trademark for services. A trademark or service mark may consist of letters, words, graphics, or any combination of these elements.

You automatically have some protection for your trademark if you were the first person to use that trademark in commerce, even if you did not register your trademark.

However, many small businesses get into trouble by doing an inadequate trademark search. They often, although inadvertently, use a name already employed by another firm. You should hire an attorney to do a trademark search for you, especially if you intend to do business on a national basis. There are also commercial firms that provide trademark search services and/or offer access to their electronic trademark databases.

Trademarks do not necessarily offer protection across the nation, let alone internationally. Typically, they cover those geographic regions in which the trademark is being used. They also generally don't cover multiple classes of goods, but only the class of goods the trademark is being used in. For example, if you operate a local retail business called Big Balloons in the state of New York, it would not necessarily be in conflict with a retail store operating in California under the same name. Similarly, if a Big Balloon Flying School were to open in New York, it would not be in conflict with the Big Balloon store because the type of product being offered is noncompetitive.

If you are going to use your trademark nationally, you should register it with the U.S. federal government. Contact the U.S. Patent and Trademark Office, Washington, D.C. 20231. You can also seek protection for your trademark in individual states, but it is much weaker than federal registration. You will have to seek separate protection from every foreign country you want trademark protection in.

If you obtain federal registration in the United States, you should use the registered trademark symbol at the end of the mark. But you may not use this symbol until and unless the federal registration has been issued.

Mr. Cheaps®

You cannot using someone else's trademark. Additionally, you need to make sure your trademark doesn't bear any resemblance to another firm's trademark in order to avoid confusion.

In order for trademarks to offer protection the copy cannot be merely descriptive of your function or product. For example, "Bicycle Store" would not offer trademark protection, but "The Merry Cycle Place" probably would.

The validity of a trademark is subject to many variables. One examiner at the federal trademark office may have one opinion regarding the validity of a trademark application, and another examiner an entirely different opinion. So if your trademark registration or creation is important to you, consider hiring a specialized attorney.

Patents

Many people think of patents in connection with inventions. But patents are granted for a wide range of creations. You can be granted a design patent that will protect the "look" of a product or even a plant patent to protect a particular hybrid plant.

For a patent to be effective in the United States, you need to apply for the patent within one year of the first commercial use of the product. But it is recommended that you apply for the patent before the product is placed on the market.

The authority of a patent is limited to the country in which you have applied for that patent. You need to apply for a patent in each country you intend to market your product in. In most countries, application for the patent must be made prior to placing the product on the market.

Most U.S. patents have a life span of twenty years, commencing with the date of application. Patents cannot be renewed. Design patents offer protection for fourteen years.

To be awarded a patent, an invention must be considered novel and nonobvious. And, even though the federal government may award a patent, it may later be revoked if it is found to infringe on another patent.

A patent gives you the right to litigate against another party whom you believe is infringing upon your patent. You must take your case to the court—there is nothing automatic in patent protection. If the alleged infringer is a major corporation, be prepared for rapidly mounting legal expenses. You also need to consider the very real possibility that another individual or company may take legal action against you for infringing on their patent, even though you hold a valid patent for your product, design, or invention.

A basic patent application fee can be several hundred dollars, depending upon the size of your business. The process is quite complex, though, and you would be well advised to spend the several thousand dollars necessary to have the filing done by a patent attorney. If you are awarded the patent, you will need to pay additional fees to the patent office over the course of the patent life in order to keep the patent active throughout its term.

Fair Selling

If you are selling products to the retail or wholesale trade, you need to sell on equal terms to outlets that may be deemed to be competing with each other, unless you can economically justify different terms. You cannot sell one hundred green pencils to stationery store A for $30 and sell an identical batch of one hundred green pencils to a competing stationery store for $35 without clear economic justification.

A clear economic justification may be that one store pays cash in advance for your product, while another store retains the right to return unsold goods to you after a period of time. One store may require that your product be individually boxed.

High volume can be a basis for a deeper discount if it can be economically justified. You must be able to show that the higher volume actually lowers your cost of doing business.

Not only must pricing be nondiscriminatory, but other terms of the sale must be equal as well. Those terms may include payment method, advertising allowances, and freight allowances, among others.

The main concern of the courts is that larger retailers and wholesalers may be demanding and getting better terms than their smaller rivals without any cost justification.

O·F·F·I·C·E

8

Home Office ➤ 367

Commercial Office ➤ 373

Equipment ➤ 378

Getting Organized ➤ 383

Successful Time Management ➤ 386

Conducting Meetings ➤ 389

Customer Service ➤ 392

Tips on Negotiating ➤ 393

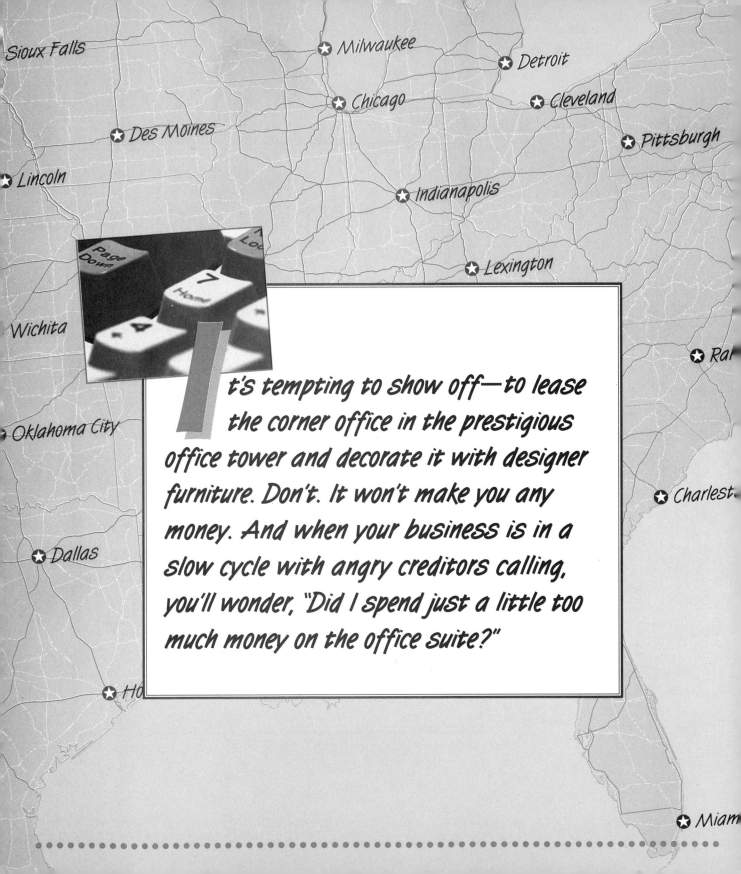

It's tempting to show off—to lease the corner office in the prestigious office tower and decorate it with designer furniture. Don't. It won't make you any money. And when your business is in a slow cycle with angry creditors calling, you'll wonder, "Did I spend just a little too much money on the office suite?"

Setting up a Home Office

If you are debating whether to set up an office in your home or lease commercial space, think quite seriously about keeping the office in your home if you can.

Unless you are operating a retail store or expect clients to regularly visit your office, your face to the world will be your products, your services, your literature, and your marketing. Spend money in areas that your customers will really appreciate.

The cost of setting up a commercial office is more expensive than just the cost of a lease. Even if you are not remodeling you will, undoubtedly, undertake a few leasehold improvements. You might install additional electrical outlets, put in new carpeting or, at the very least, paint the place. If you haven't previously leased commercial space, you will have to place deposits with the phone, electric, and maybe even the heating fuel company. And your fixtures and furnishings expenditures for a commercial space will probably be more than they would be for a home office.

Setting up a Home Office

Location

Your home office should offer privacy and enough elbow room to hold the equipment and furniture you will require to effectively conduct your business. If you plan on holding client meetings in your home office, look for a room or rooms that are removed from your family surroundings. Maintain as much of a professional atmosphere as possible.

Budget

Run numbers. Determine how much you can comfortably afford to spend outfitting your home office with equipment and furniture. Don't forget to budget for additional phone lines, electrical wiring, carpentry, and supplies for the office. Before you go and spend a nickel, look around your home. Do you own items such as pens, paper, scissors, extra phones, tables, chairs, and desks that you can use in your home office?

Building permits

You will need an occupancy permit if you intend to run a business from your home in a residential area that is not zoned for business. Your local building and zoning department, typically located in your town or city hall, should be able to provide you with the necessary permits and advise you on all local zoning restrictions.

Insurance

Homeowners' insurance usually provides a rider that can be attached to cover computers and office equipment including copiers, fax machines, scanners, and printers. Check out the latest pricing on the equipment you own and select coverage limits that will protect your investment. You may also need insurance for vehicles used in your business and liability coverage for accidents related to the use of your product or service.

Answering options

Decide whether or not you want an answering machine, voice mail, or an outside service to field calls during your absence or unavailability. If it is important in your business to have a responsive human being answer customer calls, go for the service. Voice mail systems can either be software-based systems that are installed on your personal computer, or purchased through an outside service provider, such as a telephone company, that offers voice mail boxes.

If you can afford it, have someone other than yourself answer your phones. Hire a receptionist, even a part-time one, or enlist the assistance of a family member or friend to help out two or three times week. You'll be surprised at what a great, professional impression this makes on outsiders. You'll appear to be very well established!

Create an image

Look professional. Create a logo. Use it on letterhead stationary, business cards, matching envelopes, four-color brochures, and sales collateral materials. Be consistent in your design. Carry the logo and color schemes throughout all of your business printing. Use good paper for printing.

And here's a great attention-getter—sponsoring a community event where your company name and logo will be prominently displayed.

Discipline

Focus on running your business. Eliminate distractions such as children, neighbors, and friends. Let your friends and family know that you are serious about your work—tell them that they just can't pop into your office whenever they feel like it.

Don't wander into your kitchen for coffee. Don't answer your personal phone. Don't check on the dog. These diversions will hamper your effectiveness in managing and growing your business. Remember, you are at work—and not really at home!

Setting up a Home Office

Zoning Laws

Many localities do not permit any businesses to be operated in residential neighborhoods without a specific variance, which many zoning boards are very reluctant to grant except under extenuating circumstances. Often, variances are only given after an extensive public hearing including invitations for presentation of objections by all nearby residents.

Just because there are already some businesses operating in your neighborhood does not mean that your neighborhood is zoned commercially or that you will easily obtain a variance. Many businesses currently operating in residential neighborhood were "grandfathered in," meaning that they were in operation before the zoning laws took effect and were therefore almost automatically granted variances.

There are literally millions of businesses operated in the U.S. out of homes in violation of local zoning ordinances. If all of these zoning laws were strictly enforced, all of these businesses would be forced to shut down and the entire U.S. economy would be dealt a significant blow.

Local government officials do not inspect homes to see if you have a small business office tucked away in a small corner of your home. However, if a neighbor complains, then the building inspector is obliged to enforce the zoning ordinances. Furthermore, hanging out even a small sign, having commercial vehicles on the property, putting in additional parking spaces, or having a lot of client or employee traffic is likely to trigger a complaint even if you have friendly neighbors.

If your business is going to involve heavy truck or car traffic you also need to consider the safety of your neighbors. I remember one business property I considered buying in a residential neighborhood in South Boston had a commercial variance, but the variance prohibited any truck traffic after 2 p.m. in the afternoon because of the potential hazard to children attending a nearby school.

Home Business Owner Success Story

Cheryl McKeary operates a desktop publishing and computer training firm out of her home in a family room that she converted to an office. She relates how it feels to share her home with *McKeary Desktop Designs*.

It's Tempting to Work All the Time

66 My housecleaning has probably suffered because of the office. Even on weekends, I'll go into the office and think, 'Oh, I'll just do this one little thing.' Well that one little thing can take two hours to do. So I'm more distracted when I'm in the house—I have to fight not to go into the office—than I am in the office. 99

A Business Phone Is Important

66 I got a separate phone line for the office. I felt that was very important. I have a Yellow Pages listing too. 99

Admit It!

66 People ask me, 'Do you work out of your home?' It took me a while to comfortably say, 'Yes, I do work out of my home,' but I'm very comfortable with it now. 99

Working out of an apartment

For several years I ran my growing book publishing company out of two different basement apartments in residential neighborhoods in the Brighton section of Boston. In each case, dozens of neighbors were aware of my business, and no one ever complained.

At each address we had daily UPS deliveries. Once a week or so tractor trailer trucks pulled up to make deliveries. My employees described some of these trucks as being as big as aircraft carriers. In fact, at one location I had to ask several neighbors to move their parked cars for these deliveries—the trucks had to back into an alley and unload through my kitchen window! But they were happy to help us out!

Problems on Cape Cod

Not all home business stories are happy ones. I ran into a bit of trouble running one of my entrepreneurial ventures out of my parents' summer home on Cape Cod.

The road the house was located on was "Corporation Road," and half a dozen commercial businesses were located on this street. The road was residentially zoned, however.

On one of my summer vacations I bought and sold used boats from my parent's home. The boats were concealed in the back and side yards and I wasn't displaying any business signage on the property. My immediate neighbors thought my work ethic was great and told me so.

Apparently, though, a distant neighbor—half a mile or so down the road—wasn't quite as impressed. He complained to the building inspector.

My parents received a certified letter from the town demanding that all business activity on the premises cease and desist within seven days. If my business continued to operate beyond this date, the property would be seized and sold at auction.

What an opportunity this presented! I moved all of the boats into the front yard and placed huge placards and advertisements announcing the forced closing of my business. Those boats went fast!

I was amused, however, to note how happy people were as they cashed in on my "misfortune" and snapped up my boats cheap.

I still didn't give up, though. I began storing boats down at the town boat dock in the local harbor. Unfortunately, several days later the town issued a new ordinance limiting the number of boats any one person could leave at the dock at once.

Building permits

Get proper building permits before beginning any construction work on a residential home. If your property is in a neighborhood that is zoned residential, try to avoid doing any work that might require a building permit if you think your chances of getting a variance are slim.

There have been instances, in some localities, where construction was ordered dismantled because the proper permits were not obtained.

Also, obtain any appropriate electrical, plumbing, or similar permits. And if you are doing electrical work, use a licensed electrician, or at least get the work inspected and signed off by one. The downside liability risk, not to mention safety risk, of shoddy electrical work is enormous.

Questions & Answers about Home Offices

What really makes a home office appear professional?

The key is separating it from the house as much as possible. Ideally you should have a separate entrance. And living areas should not be visible from the office.

At the very least, remove all non-business-related furnishings from the room you are using as an office. Another good idea is to erect internal doors to separate this room from the rest of the house. And, if there are any rooms or hallways that connect from the house to the office, always make sure they are neat and kept as professional-looking as possible.

What should I give my first effort to?

Chances are, like most small businesses, that you are going to do most of your business over the phone. So, one of your first concerns should be how your office "sounds." Answer your business phone with the name of your business. Have calls forwarded to an answering service if you are not going to be in your office. And try to block

out any background noise that may sound like you are in a home environment.

There are some people who try to change their voice to create the impression of a larger office. This is a transparent ploy. Don't do it.

Are there inherent problems in having employees working in my home office?

The first obstacle may be in attracting people who want to work in a home office. Many people object to this sort of environment. But it is certainly possible to attract very talented, hardworking people who will work with you in your home.

If you intend to employ people within your home, check your insurance coverage and determine whether or not you need additional liability coverage. You must also get workers' compensation coverage, as this is mandated by law. You need to make sure your premises are safe in every way. And you should be aware that you increase your chances of zoning problems with every employee you bring into your home office.

Do I need to notify the post office of my business name?

If you tell your regular mail carrier verbally that you are going to be receiving mail addressed to your business name, problems will arise each time your neighborhood is served by a substitute. So, yes, inform the post office or put the name of your business on the mailbox. Place it in very small letters, though, so as not to alarm your neighbors.

Do I need a separate business phone line?

If you live by yourself, you may want to skip the expense of another line. Remember, though, this means you need to answer the phone every time it rings as though it were a business phone.

You could install a second residential line, which is generally not as expensive as business service. The phone company may call after a couple of weeks, however, to see if you are using the second line for business purposes. I've been through this. I once fielded a phone call from a phone representative on a newly installed residential line by answering with my business name. An interesting discussion ensued, but I did manage to convince the phone company not to bill me at the business rate.

Considering Commercial Space

Moving into a commercial office space can be an exciting time for a small business owner. It signals a coming of age for a business that has outlived the usefulness of a home office. More space is needed to house new employees and more equipment, and to conduct meetings, conferences, and product demonstrations. A commercial office gives a small business owner the feeling of taking the business to its next level of growth—with continued growth expected and eagerly anticipated.

Space

When considering how much commercial space to lease, add some extra space for growth to the total square footage of the space you are currently occupying. Determine how many employees you expect to be housing by the end of the next year. Determine what furnishings and office equipment you will need in order to accommodate them.

Decide whether or not you will need a reception area. Decide on the image you want to project through the layout and design of your space. Determine your need for conference and/or demonstration rooms.

Try to project two or three years out from the start of the lease—will the new space accommodate your anticipated growth?

Location

Where you locate your business is very important. If you locate in an upscale suburban neighborhood or a fashionable area of downtown, you may attract consumers with plenty of disposable cash. But you will also face high rents or leasing costs, and that puts you at risk for business failure. Less upscale areas may offer tax incentives or spaces with attractive lease options. However, these areas may have high crime or vandalism rates. And how about the commute? How far is it from your home to your new office space? All of these considerations need to be carefully examined when deciding where to locate your business.

Parking

You should determine what both your employee and customer parking needs will be. Does the space you are considering offer enough parking for your needs and the needs of surrounding businesses? Is the parking underground or on-street metered parking? Is handicapped parking available?

Tenants

Check out the other tenants in the building or office complex you will be leasing in. Find out how long they have occupied the building. Ask if they are on good terms with the landlord. Find out if their experiences as tenants have been largely satisfactory. Inquire about insurance premiums, building security, and cleaning services for the building.

Handicap access

Check to see if the building you are considering leasing in meets with handicap access regulations, including appropriate bathroom facilities. Make sure your office space has been designed so that physically challenged employees can easily move around and are afforded an opportunity to be fully productive.

Public transport

If on-street or off-street parking is limited or unavailable, locating your business in close proximity to public transportation takes on added significance. Public transportation accessibility can even be used as an advertising tool to attract customers.

Expansion

If you are attracted to a particular office space but envision remodeling that space to suit your needs—building partitions for work cubicles or removing walls to open up a reception area—make sure the landlord has no objections. Get permission in writing. And see if you can negotiate a reduction in the lease payments in exchange for doing the remodeling work yourself.

Utilities

Find out what the typical costs are for heating, electricity, and air conditioning in an office space similar to the one you are considering within the same building. Ask either the landlord or other building occupants for copies of the last six month's utility bills. Inquire about required new account deposits from each of the utility companies you will be using. If you have a prior billing history with any of the utility companies, you may not need to submit a deposit.

Commercial Office Space Plans

You have three basic choices in office floor plans: division by partition, open office, or individual, closed rooms. A combination of any of these floor plans is also a possibility.

Partitions

Open offices divided by partitions were in vogue at many large corporations in the 1960s and 1970s. The advantage to this space design configuration is that its flexible nature offers the chance for change while, at the same time, affords a moderate level of visual and aural privacy. No one is looking directly at another employee and conversations can be conducted without fear of being overheard.

There are a wide range of partition systems available. They can be extremely elaborate and complex or inexpensive and simple.

Open floor plan

Another approach to organizing space is the open design. It isn't extremely common, but many newspaper offices and banks have embraced the open office concept and have their employees working openly side by side.

This design creates a strong feeling of community among workers, but suffers the drawbacks of noise and visual confusion.

Closed rooms

Closed rooms can be a very expensive office design option. This option doesn't offer the flexibility of either the partitioned or open space plans. It does offer the ultimate in privacy, however.

If you go for this plan, be sure to get the landlord's permission to complete any construction work required to meet your needs.

Combination

Some combination of the partitioned, open, and closed room floor plans is another approach. You might have, for example, completely open areas for secretarial or support staff, partitioned cubicles for mid-level employees, and closed areas for senior staff.

Office Design Considerations

Functionality

Functionality is an important consideration when considering office design. The first functional aspect that you need to address is noise reduction. Your employees need to be able to hear clearly in order to effectively conduct phone conversations. You need to place fax machines, copiers, and other loud equipment out of the way and out of earshot.

You also need to create nice passageways that allow employees ease of movement from one area of the office to another. These pathways should also provide efficient traffic patterns.

Don't forget to group people together according to their functional need to interface with each other.

Customer perspective

A customer's impression of your office space as he or she first walks in the door is critical. The same holds true for employees, and especially for new hires.

Consider creating a waiting area at your entranceway. It can be very simple, yet still welcoming, comfortable, and professional. All you really need is a couple of nice chairs and a table.

A meeting room may also be important in your business. This room should be as impressive as possible even if you can't afford to go all out designing and furnishing other areas of your office space. Set up a nice room near the reception area with a conference table and nice chairs. This will give any customer a good feeling about your organization.

Assigning space

Assigning space to personnel can be an incredible political football, even among employees who don't typically get riled. Seasoned employees have been known to fight tooth and nail for that window spot or the biggest office space. This is an issue of prestige, of course, and many employees link space allotment to the direction of their career paths.

The best approach is to make the assignments and have that be the end of the story. Make it clear that you have given the assignments careful thought, and this is simply the plan you have devised and will be sticking to. Do try to give each person adequate space in which to carry out his or her job. And anticipate the objections any given individual may have. Cut complainers off at the pass. If you don't assign space decisively, people are going to grab whatever space they can or they are going to whine and complain. Either way, it will be a headache for you.

Also, decide in advance to what extent employees will be allowed to decorate their space, paint the walls, or hang photographs or posters. In short, set guidelines for personalizing office space. You don't want to find yourself in the uncomfortable position of requesting the removal of any decorative elements because they clash with the office design concept.

Creating the design

Start by making a quick, rough sketch of your office design layout and concept with pencil and paper. Then you might want to flesh your scheme out by using space layout software or creating a more detailed sketch.

Use a scale for the sketch—x inches equals x square feet—or do your layout on a gridded chart. Before you move in and start knocking down walls or dragging desks about, take out the tape measure and mark walls, corridors, partitions, and desks in with masking tape. Bring your employees in to discuss the layout. This creates a feeling of community, and the group's approval on a final layout alleviates the possibility of major space wars on move-in day.

☞ Cheap space is good space

Every entrepreneur who looks at office space for the first time is tempted to spend more money than anticipated or budgeted. Resist! You will need that extra cash to get you through start-up or growing pains.

Lease space as cheaply as you can. It may not be all you've ever dreamed of, but you're more likely to get to your dream space and stay there if you play it conservatively now.

☞ Leave some extra space

If you envision growth for your company, especially in terms of employee count, leave some space open to accommodate new hires comfortably.

☞ Try for one floor layouts

Like lots of other business people, I've learned from experience that having all of your office space—especially warehouse, manufacturing, or engineering space—all on one floor is much more efficient for interacting with everyone and getting work done. Discount the effectiveness of commercial space that you look at that requires additional floors.

Of course, multiple floors is a lot better than multiple buildings—a situation that I am in right now. Our warehouse is a mile down the street and is really inconvenient for a couple of dozen people—and a much bigger drag on productivity than I thought it would be when I leased the facility.

☞ First appearances count!

Even if you won't receive many customers in your office, put a little extra effort into the entrance of your office. Set up a couple of decent chairs for guests and for job candidates.

Don't spend tons of money, even on your "front" office. But a little energy expended on creating a pleasant atmosphere in your front office will definitely be worthwhile. Employees and visitors alike will appreciate it.

☞ Create an office that people want to work in

If you can create an office environment that people really want to work in, you'll be a lot better off. You don't want your employees to be scared off or unhappy. Great locations and pleasant interior surroundings aren't the most important assets either. More important is how you run your business, and how much fun it is to work at your company.

Nevertheless, how you set up your office will have some impact on employee morale. Set aside a small space as an employee lounge area for use at break time, lunch, or even for a late-night rest when work gets demanding. Supply soda and candy—the little touches that keep people going.

> "Every entrepreneur who looks at office space for the first time is tempted to spend more money than anticipated or budgeted. Resist!"

Equipment

It is easy to get caught up in the latest and greatest equipment for your office. You want it to look fabulous and make a statement about your success. But don't lose sight of your budget. Your cash flow could wind up looking like the national debt.

Don't despair! It really is a breeze to make good decisions about purchasing equipment and furniture, have a good-looking office, and make your business run smoothly and efficiently.

New vs. used

Some people think that they have to have the latest equipment to hit the market. Cost doesn't matter. This kind of thinking can lead one to buy equipment with superfluous features, or furniture that goes out of style next week.

Before you equip your office, think about your real needs—what you need to make a fair impression, work efficiently, and be able to maintain a good and continuing cash flow situation. Check into used furniture and equipment. A good bargain may just be the ticket to really fulfilling your needs!

Phones

Do you really need all of the bells and whistles available in certain phone equipment today? Is voice mail necessary or will an answering machine suffice? Don't get caught up in the hype—think about your business and what you need to handle your day-to-day communication needs. Make a list of the types of phone equipment that you absolutely must have to run your type of business professionally. Then shop for prices at least three different outlets.

Software

Just about every business today has a computer that handles a variety of tasks, from accounting to human resource management. No matter what computer platform you are using, there are a host of programs available that will cut down on the time and expense of accounting, billing, creating financial projections, letter writing, creating graphics and drawings, and even managing your day for you! Again, determine what you need in order to adequately fulfill a function and shop for the software package that will best meet your needs and your budget.

Furniture

You are projecting an image with the type of furniture that you choose to outfit your office with. Buying it used can certainly help offset costs, and comes as a recommended solution for keeping costs in check, but make sure that it is in tip-top shape. New or used, your furniture should be professional in appearance. Try for a coordinated look and a simple color scheme carried throughout your office. Good, simple, tasteful design is paramount if you intend to have clients visit your office on a regular basis. Also, look for furniture that is comfortable and suited to working around for at least eight hours a day. If you use desktop computers, make sure your desks and chairs are ergonomically designed to minimize physical stress.

Equipment

E-mail

E-mail can be the bane of the business professional's existence. The decision to purchase e-mail will hinge a great deal on the culture of your company and how open you are about allowing your employees to freely communicate company information, both internally and externally.

Copiers

If you lease a copier, make sure you have a strong service commitment from the copier or leasing company. You need to know how quickly you can get a replacement machine delivered should your leased equipment fail. Get everything regarding the leasing terms and the service offerings in writing. And keep good records of service visits and the type of work performed.

Fax machines

It is nearly impossible to find a business that does not use some form of fax machine. Some business use standalones while others fax via software and modems that are a part of their personal computer. Some companies tie their networked computers into one fax machine. Whatever method you choose, you really should have some fax capability. You will quickly find a need to both send and receive information via fax, and it can also be used as a highly successful marketing tool.

Equipment List

SAMPLE

Draw up a list of what you think you need for your office, and shop around for the best deal or price.

Item	Price	Item	Price
IMPROVEMENTS		✔ Phone equipment	TBD
✔ Additional electrical outlets	TBD	✔ Copiers	TBD
✔ Building permits	TBD	✔ Fax machines	TBD
✔ Architect	TBD	✔ Software	TBD
✔ Walls	TBD		
✔ ~~Ceilings~~ *Don't need!*	~~TBD~~	**OFFICE SUPPLIES**	
✔ Heating or AC work	TBD	✔ Printer cartridges	TBD
✔ Loading ramp work	TBD	✔ Fax paper	TBD
✔ Painting	TBD	✔ Stationery	TBD
✔ Carpeting	TBD	✔ Computer disks	TBD
✔ Cleaning	TBD	✔ Pens, pencils, and markers	TBD
✔ Signage	TBD	✔ Note and message pads	TBD
		✔ Staplers, scissors, glue	TBD
FURNITURE		✔ Paper clips	TBD
✔ Chairs	TBD	✔ Phone equipment	TBD
✔ Desks	TBD	✔ Copiers	TBD
✔ Files	TBD	✔ Fax machines	TBD
✔ Wastebaskets	TBD	✔ Software	TBD
✔ Tables	TBD		
✔ Storage cabinets	TBD	**GENERAL SUPPLIES**	
✔ Safe	TBD	✔ Coat racks *Check attic at home*	TBD
✔ Bookcases	TBD	✔ Bathroom and cleaning supplies	TBD
✔ Desk lamps	TBD	✔ Artwork	TBD
		✔ Plants	TBD
EQUIPMENT		✔ Whiteboards	TBD
✔ Computers	TBD	✔ Corkboards	TBD
✔ Printers	TBD	✔ Coffeemaker and coffee	TBD

☞ Simple is OK

You don't need lavish furniture or the latest equipment to run a successful business. In fact, all too many people start a business with the attitude that they are going to "do it right." They rush out and purchase the best of everything they need—and don't need. I can't emphasize it enough—this is a big mistake! You are much better off doing everything "wrong." Buy the cheapest of everything, and conserve your cash for running your business.

When I was in my teens I visited my grandfather's shoe company, Crest Shoe, in Lewiston, Maine. I was expecting to find a smaller version of a TV-set Fortune 500 company. Instead, I found an old, dirty, and dilapidated building. The furnishings and general appearance of the interior were depressing. My father pointed out that a fancy office wasn't necessary to conducting a successful business. The fact is, Crest Shoe remained a profitable business for decades after just about all the other shoe companies in Lewiston had gone under.

☞ Auctions

Bankruptcy auctions offer a terrific opportunity to acquire furniture, fixtures, and equipment. You can often pick up desks, computers, and chairs for a fraction of what they might cost at a secondhand dealer.

Some of my office furnishings were culled at an auction for a Boston consultant that operated from a spectacular office suite in a prestigious suburban office park. I'm sure the decor impressed the consultant's clientele. But so what? It was going out of business, and these high expenditures may have played a part in that.

The day after the auction, while I was filling up a truck with my finds, I noticed the bankrupt company's stationery on a desk. The chairman had been one of my Harvard Business School professors.

Remember, it is better to have cash in the till than designer desks and chairs filling the office.

☞ Liquidators

When large corporations dispose of their furnishings, which happens when the old colors don't mesh with the new CEO's color palette, office liquidators negotiate to buy the entire lot of furnishings. They then sell it off, in smaller lots, to other businesses. Prices are higher than at auction, but the selection is usually broader and delivery and merchandise guarantees are often included.

When I was first starting out in business, I purchased some beautiful wood desks from a hotel liquidator. These desks were in like-new condition, cost 10 percent of their replacement value, and came with a bonus. They were formerly housed at the Boston Sheraton Hotel. I was blessed also with complimentary bibles!

☞ Leasing

Leasing is a great way to pay for equipment that is more difficult to locate secondhand than basic office furniture. Even a new business with no credit history can obtain equipment through leasing. Even if you have to pay leasing rates that are higher than you might like, you will still have cash left with which to keep your business running.

Questions & Answers about Equipment

Will household furniture work in an office?

A lot of household furniture will not hold up to the heavy usage office furniture gets. If you move household furniture into the office, you may be surprised to find out how soon legs break on chairs, drawers fall apart, and desks become wobbly.

Why are some file cabinets so cheap and others so expensive?

Much of the furniture designed for home offices is junk. File cabinets are an excellent example. The cheaper file cabinets feature drawers that jam even before you leave the store. I am surprised the warrantees don't promise breakage before you even get home!

A good filing cabinet that really holds up can be quite expensive. So, it is better to buy a better-quality used item than a cheap new one.

Should I rent furniture?

The rates that furniture rental companies charge are usually exorbitant. It is better to buy.

Whom can I arrange to lease equipment from?

Consider the leasing options available from the manufacturer first. Then check the options available from a leasing firm. Banks also offer leasing, but this may affect your borrowing limits in the future.

You can also approach any friends or relatives who have helped you finance your business—and even those who refused. They may be willing to purchase your furniture and lease its use to you while retaining title. It may be viewed as less risky than actually lending money.

I once had my attorney buy an inexpensive typesetting machine and lease it back to me. As we sat over breakfast, after ironing out the details, he only had one complaint. We had just eaten all of his profit!

What about buying through the mail?

You can usually negotiate a better price with a local dealer than you can get through a mail order house. But check it out. Mail order may be your best route, especially if you don't live in an major metropolitan area where furniture pricing can be highly competitive.

While I certainly have purchased furniture and equipment through the mail, I offer one caution. One prominent cut-rate electronics mail-order dealer I once used went bankrupt. You should know that if you prepay for merchandise and the company goes belly-up after you have sent your check but before they have shipped your merchandise, then you are a general creditor. In other words, you have no special claim on the item you ordered and the check you sent is no longer yours. You are merely one of many on a long list of creditors and you would be extremely lucky to get a full settlement on your claim. To avoid this situation, ask to be billed or pay with a credit card.

Getting Organized

Start with your computer

The computer is the focal point of an organized office. Used properly, a computer can be a miracle worker for bringing organization to even a chaotic workplace. Make an effort to do and save your work on a computer whenever possible. Even when you are just brainstorming, for example, jot your thoughts into your computer so that your thoughts won't be lost, the way they might if you used a notepad or piece of paper.

To get truly organized, divide your computer files into related groups and store them in different directories and subdirectories. As a rule of thumb, for quick location and easy access to any given item, you should maintain no more than seven files in any given directory. Use easily recognized names for directories, subdirectories, and individual file names. Don't be stingy about creating new directories when existing ones aren't appropriate.

Paper items

When you can't store items on your computer, use files, as opposed to stacking papers and documents in desk drawers or in cabinets. Get color-coded files so that related items can be easily filed and retrieved. Clearly label all of your files.

How clutter multiplies

To get organized, you need to ruthlessly eliminate any clutter that begins to accumulate in your office—especially on your desk. Once clutter starts to mount, the common tendency is to think "It would take too long to even try to organize this mess—why bother? I'll just keep throwing things on top of the heap." Soon you won't be able to find anything and you'll need a shovel to even find your desk.

Make organization a habit

Unless you train yourself to keep constantly organized, you are going to be wasting a lot of time looking for things you can't find. All too often, people finally clean up their clutter after they have wasted ten minutes trying to find a misplaced pen or document. If you spend ten minutes a day looking for lost items, you will be wasting over forty hours a year! This doesn't even count the time you spend driving out to the office-supply store at the mall to replace that red marker.

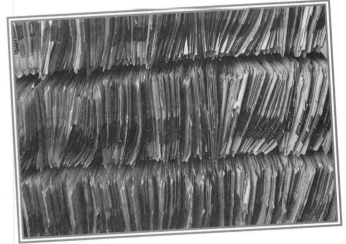

☞ Back up without fail

Always, always, back up your computer files. And be sure everyone else in your organization does too!

My organization once lost three person months of work because one department neglected to back up its work for several weeks. Consider installing a tape back-up so that you don't have to back up your files individually on disks.

☞ Assume the worst

Suppose you got to your office one day and find it surrounded by firetrucks—the building ablaze. How secure would your computer files be? If this seems farfetched, think again. It happened to me when my company shared a multi-tenant old manufacturing building in South Boston. So be sure that any files you really need to save are not only backed up, but that you store a second set off-site.

☞ The round file is the best file

Throw out anything that you are sure you don't need. And do it as soon as possible. Remember one of the golden rules—"If in doubt, throw it out!"

☞ Prune your workspace regularly

Every few months or so, go through your desk, file cabinets, and every other nook and cranny in your office. Throw away anything you find that you don't need.

Go through your computer files as well. Delete any files you haven't used in the last twelve months. But do save your "discarded" files on disk just in case.

☞ Organization can be contagious

If you keep your desk and files well organized, other people will tend to do the same. If you don't, others won't. Set a good example!

> "Every few months or so, go through your desk, file cabinets, and every other nook and cranny in your office. Throw away anything you find that you don't need."

Questions & Answers about Getting Organized

Is a larger desk easier to keep organized?

The larger the desk, the greater area to accumulate clutter. The real problem, of course, isn't the desk but the person who sits behind it.

Is there a less expensive alternative to file cabinets?

In my years in business I used a lot of plastic stacking trays. They don't cost much and sure helped to keep me organized.

Should I try to save computer work to disk only and keep my hard drive free?

Whenever possible, use your hard drive as the primary file storage location. You are much less likely to misplace your hard drive than you are a diskette.

Do I really need to back up my hard drive?

Absolutely. Several computer "experts" over the years have told me there is no need to back up a hard drive. After all, they fail so infrequently. But my experience says otherwise!

And never believe the technician promises to leave your files intact when he or she takes your computer to the shop for repair. Again, experience has proven otherwise.

What shouldn't I throw out when cleaning my office?

Among the items you should save is any paperwork you might need to substantiate tax returns, product deliveries, or service performances for which you have yet to be paid, personnel records, information needed to substantiate any current or potential claims, and original software manuals.

Successful Time Management

Daily and weekly planning

1

You can't be an effective manager if you can't plan your time wisely. Map out the details of each day as carefully as possible. And, for each week, list the most important tasks you are going to tackle.

What's urgent vs. what's important

2

In order to productively allocate your time, you need to make a clear distinction between which tasks are most urgent or time-sensitive and those tasks that will have the most impact on the overall success of the company.

Some tasks may be both urgent and important. For example, a proposal that needs to be written by tomorrow and that may land a new customer is both urgent and important. But more often than not, the urgent tasks are not the most important tasks.

Many small business owners tend to begin each work day by diving into the day-to-day issues they face. They never seem to get around to less pressing but more important work, such as a reevaluation of a product line, the development of a new marketing angle, or annual planning.

To really drive your business ahead, you need to set aside plenty of time for important work. Do this even if it is at the expense, temporarily, of more urgent work.

Working flexibility into your schedule

3

Business owners always face unexpected demands on their time. They can't plan out entire days in advance without losing control of their schedule. A better approach is to allot a chunk of time—maybe a couple of hours after lunch—for dealing with or examining those unplanned issues or tasks that arise every day.

Streetwise Advice on Time Management

☞ **Have your time management methods support the company's strategy and plan**

Be sure the tasks that you assign priority to are in sync with the company's strategy and its annual plan. The only exception should be when your firm is facing a crisis that threatens its very survival.

☞ **Plan out your time the day before**

Most people benefit from their greatest energy level first thing in the morning. So you want to begin your workday by delving right in the tasks at hand, not determining what those tasks should be.

Planning your daily schedule is a good task for lower-energy times—the end of the previous workday or at home the night before. You want to arrive at work with a firm direction for the day's work already set in your mind.

☞ **Try focusing on one important goal each day**

Each day you may have to deal with several on-the-spot developments and emergency matters. Despite this, try to focus as much time each day on one task. Don't jump from one issue to the next without realizing resolution of or progress on anything.

☞ **Delegate**

It's hard to do, but in order to make your business grow, you need to learn the art of delegation. Every day, scan the list of tasks to be completed and determine who in your organization may be able to help you out. Delegate the task, or a portion of it, to that person.

☞ **Use lunchtime productively**

Lunchtime meetings can be ideal for discussing certain types of issues with other employees. Try brainstorming, weighing the pros and cons of upcoming decisions, or getting a progress report from a department head over a deli sandwich or Chinese buffet. But don't use the lunch hour to discuss highly emotional issues such as performance reviews.

☞ **Coach others on planning their time effectively**

Sit down with others and help them plan their time. Emphasize the goals you have set for them and for their function. But do give people some latitude. Let them develop their own time planning method. Some people have a favorite calendar program on their computers, while others prefer printed daily planner books.

> *"Be sure the tasks that you assign priority to are in sync with the company's strategy and its annual plan."*

Questions & Answers about Time Management

Should I keep my schedule on a computer or in a printed desk diary?

Use whatever works best for you. I use both. At my desk I use my computer. I tried carrying a laptop around the building and off-site, but it got to be a bit cumbersome. Instead, I now carry a printout of my schedule and a notepad. Even though I can access my computer from home, I prefer to sit in an easy chair late at night and scribble thoughts about the next day's schedule on paper.

How can I avoid having people constantly interrupt me?

I have instituted a company-wide quiet time from 8:00 to 11:30 a.m. every day. It's quite successful. During this period of time people may not interrupt others except for dire emergencies. This works out exceptionally well for key management people who tend to fall prey to a constant barrage of questions and interruptions.

Should I rank each task by how important or critical it is?

Don't spend a lot of time prioritizing the tasks on your schedule. Instead, divide tasks into three groups—what absolutely must get done, what you would like to complete, and what would be nice to complete on any given day.

Won't eliminating meetings save a lot of time?

While meetings can chew up huge blocks of time, they can also be important. They instill team spirit in the participants. They allow people to share viewpoints. They improve communication. And they help cut down on the amount of unscheduled interruptions, because people have been kept apprised of tasks at hand and directives. You can keep meetings short and infrequent, but don't eliminate them.

Can e-mail save time?

Yes and no. If you use e-mail sparingly for delivering information that would otherwise have to be delivered via memo or phone or in person, then yes, time will be saved. But many firms find that e-mail wastes time because too many people send trivial messages. Also, face-to-face discussions are best in any situation that may involve an exchange of ideas or a disagreement. E-mail is best used for conveying brief, factual material.

Conducting Meetings

These are several basic keys to running effective meetings.

If people expect your meetings to ramble on or lack focus, they aren't going bring a lot of attention, energy, or enthusiasm into the meeting room. If, on the other hand, your meetings are quick, snappy, and interesting, people will look forward to them. They will leave feeling recharged, not drained.

Not so simple

This sounds so simple. If only it was! No matter what people tell you in advance, everyone brings their own agenda into a meeting. So, when people start to get off track, you have to remind them what the appropriate topics are. You have to act as moderator.

Some people are more long-winded than others. And some long-winded people don't take kindly to being cut off. It only takes one long-winded person to derail a meeting. Don't hesitate to cut people off, no matter what the objections may be, in order to keep a meeting moving along.

Get people in on time.

Keep the meeting focused.

Keep the meeting brief.

Get people out quickly.

☞ **Good meetings can pull a company together**

Good meetings make people feel like they are part of a team—like they are all rowing together in the same direction. While meetings do take time, time spent in brief, focused meetings is time well spent.

☞ **Keep the first part of the meeting structured**

If a meeting stops going forward or strays from the topic you intended to discuss, it will be very difficult to get back on course. This is especially true if it occurs at the outset of a meeting. If other people have issues they feel "must" be discussed, ask them to hold them for later in the meeting.

☞ **Don't let people get into endless disagreements**

People, whether from different or similar functional areas, can get into unresolvable disagreements. Recognize the disagreement with a statement like "We all realize how Sally feels and how Joe feels," and then just move the discussion onward.

☞ **Ask quiet people for their opinions**

Just because someone is quiet doesn't mean that he or she doens't have something intelligent to add to the discussion at hand. Ask quiet people for their viewpoints—especially when there is vocal disagreement on the issue.

☞ **Avoid phone calls and other interruptions**

Disconnect the phone if you have to. Phone calls during meetings are annoying.

☞ **Try to make decisions**

Everyone at a meeting won't necessarily agree on the same course of action. In this situation, it is tempting to put off making a decision until a consensus can be reached or more information is gathered. Don't do this! Try to make decisions as soon as possible. If you wait for unanimity, you'll never get your business into high gear!

> "Good meetings make people feel like they are part of a team—like they are rowing together in the same direction."

Questions & Answers about Conducting Meetings

Are there basic meeting types?

There are four basic meeting types. Presentation meetings are used to convey information to people. Coordination meetings verify schedules and determine whether or not a project is on track with all team members working in sync. Decision-making meetings offer a forum for discussing issues and finalizing directions. Brainstorming meetings allow people to create new ideas.

What types of meeting should a small business have?

This will vary from one business to the next. Generally, however, all small businesses should have a company-wide presentation meeting at least once a month, if not weekly. During this meeting management can update everyone on key developments and announce any new directions the company plans on pursuing. A decision-making meeting should also be held monthly or weekly. This can be very important, even for small companies. The value of coordination or brainstorming meetings will vary, depending upon the type of business being run.

How long should meetings take?

Presentation meetings that don't involve participant interaction should take twenty minutes or less. During nonparticipatory meetings you will find that people's concentration flags even after ten minutes. Decision-making meetings should take fifty minutes. If they need to run for a longer period of time, take a break every hour.

What is the best time of day for conducting meetings?

That depends on the type of meeting. If the meeting is going to cover complex topics or involve difficult discussions, hold it early in the morning. If the meeting is a simple, straightforward presentation meeting, it could be held later in the day.

How can I keep one person from talking too much during a meeting?

First, try asking everyone to keep their comments brief. Then, if that doesn't work, cut the offender off in an upbeat way by saying "Thank you, Tom. We see where your thoughts are going on this. Anyone else have a comment?" As a final measure, if the meeting is a regularly scheduled meeting, disband the group and organize a new group that eliminates the chatterbox.

Customer Service

Customer service guidelines

- **Create a policy and stick to it**
  Clearly articulate your policies to both your company personnel and your customers.

- **Simplify all paperwork**
  Simplify all paperwork so that complaints can be resolved quickly and easily.

- **Provide a way for the customers to give feedback**
  Encourage your customers to let you know how you can best serve them. Send out letters or reply cards asking for customer feedback. Be sure to let customers know if you decide to use their suggestions.

- **One service message**
  Summarize your service into one simple message. "Satisfaction guaranteed or your money back," is a slogan your company and your customers can understand. You should realize, however, that when you use a slogan that guarantees something for the customer, you are creating an implicit contract with that customer. Honor your word!

Return policies and refunds

- **Set a maximum return time**
  If you sell a returnable product, set a maximum return time. Your policy might state that a customer can return a product within sixty days of the purchase date. Print your policy on the receipt or the invoice. If you have a catalog, you should print the return policy there as well.

- **Give credit, as opposed to cash**
  Offer credit for returned merchandise, as opposed to cash, whenever possible.

- **Set a batch return policy**
  If you offer cash returns, it is easier to write all of the return checks at the same time. It is time-consuming and paper-intensive to write a check each time merchandise is returned.

- **Protect yourself with a tracking system**
  Design a tracking system that can enable you to check sales even if a receipt is not given. A tracking system will help protect you from people who might try to take advantage of your company. Do not offer cash for returns without a receipt.

- **Watch out for fraudulent returns**
  Inspect all returns for possible damage caused by fraud before exchanging merchandise or giving a customer cash.

Tips on Negotiating

In order to succeed at negotiating, you need to develop a strategy and make your key decisions in advance of the negotiating process. If you walk into a negotiation meeting cold, without a specific game plan, sooner or later you are bound to make a costly mistake.

You absolutely need to decide what your final position is going to be before you start negotiating. Don't be forced into making a decision during the heat and excitement of a negotiation. And don't waiver from your decision unless you are presented with new, substantive information.

You should also decide, in advance, which parts of a negotiation are most important to you. And be prepared with some good arguments for your position.

Win/lose negotiating

Many people view negotiating as a win/lose proposition. This outlook is detrimental and can jeopardize any negotiation. It can kill deals even after they have been verbally agreed to. It can damage business relationships. And, most importantly, it can drastically limit your ability to succeed at negotiating.

If you appear to be too aggressive and come off with that "out to beat the other guy" attitude, your counternegotiator will be uneasy or even suspicious of you. Even if you do negotiate the deal you want, beating up the other party could hurt the possibility of any future relationships and may result in a cancellation of the deal some time down the road.

Be pleasant. Try to view issues from the other side's point of view, even if you are negotiating a dispute that is already in the courtroom.

Win/win negotiating

Always search for the win/win solution. Seek a resolution that works out well for all parties.

For example, in arguing for a price reduction on book prices with our Canadian importer, I discovered that he was being charged more money by his Canadian bank to convert payments into U.S. currency than our U.S. bank would charge. We agreed to accept his payments in Canadian currency, and he was able to reduce the price of our products without narrowing his profit margin.

It is unusual to find a true win/win solution. But you might find something in between. Most business negotiations involve a lot of different negotiating points. Determine which points are most important to each party and use these as a basis for a compromise that is favorable to all parties. For example, in negotiating with our Canadian distributor, I found that his primary concern was currency fluctuation. By agreeing to accept exchange responsibility, I took on the fluctuation risk.

A Negotiation

The following conversation was taken from a conversation in which Bob Adams was negotiating for a reduced card rate for spot announcing a new book via radio advertising with a radio station advertising manager. The book was *Mr. Cheap's Boston.* Initially Bob shows no hesitation in offering a very low price for the ads. He uses the tactic of suggesting an intention to go with another radio station. But Bob is pleasant and gracious despite his hard-ball tactics. Finally, he switches to a win/win proposal.

 Bob
Thank you for taking the time to meet with me today.

 Steve
The pleasure is mine. Bob, I know your book is going to sell great on our station. Our demographics are perfect. And, I'm pleased to offer you 10 percent off the rate card.

 Bob
I appreciate your offer, Steve. And, I appreciate how strong your radio station is. I am ready to sign today for a run of sixty drive-time ad spots.

But I need a rate that is 60 percent off the rate card.

 Steve
I can't go that low.

 Bob
I appreciate your feelings, but the profits on books are a lot less than on cars or probably just about anything else you usually advertise. I have spoken to competing stations and they are showing a little more flexibility . . . .

 Steve
Well, if you commit to the sixty spots today . . . I will give you 40 percent off. But that's the absolute best I can do. That's the rate that I give to our largest customers.

 Bob
Okay. I'll go along with that if we can pay for half the cost in cash and the other half in books. I'll even value the books at their wholesale price and you can use them for giveaways or even as favors for your richer advertisers.

 Steve
Well, that might be interesting . . .

☞ Be ready to walk away

Don't get emotionally committed to a deal before the negotiation is complete. Always be ready to walk away if your terms can't be met.

☞ Don't compromise

Once you set your bottom line, stick to it. All too often, inexperienced negotiators compromise a little and come to regret it later.

☞ Don't show your hand early

Most people want to feel that they have negotiated you downward from your opening position. If you state your bottom line position early on in the negotiations, they will either feel like they aren't pushing hard enough or you aren't compromising enough.

☞ You set the price, I'll set the terms

This saying emphasizes the extreme importance of terms. A million-dollar price tag doesn't mean much if the terms are payments of $1 per year. Most people negotiate price a lot harder than terms. Take advantage of this and push hard for favorable terms.

☞ Build rapport first

A difficult negotiation will go a lot more smoothly if you develop a good rapport with the other parties before the proceedings begin. Even if you know the other players involved quite well, engage in some small talk immediately before the negotiations begin. This creates a positive atmosphere.

☞ Don't accept changes

Once a deal has been verbally agreed to, don't accept any changes. Insist that the other parties stick to the exact terms of the deal.

"*Don't get emotionally committed to a deal before the negotiation is complete. Always be ready to walk away if your terms can't be met.*"

Questions & Answers about Negotiations

Should an agreement be put in writing before people leave the negotiating table?

No! It just isn't practical to get an agreement written up immediately. More importantly, it creates an unprofessional air of mistrust to attempt to get people to wait while the written agreement is created. Instead, create it the next day and send it overnight to the other parties.

Should attorneys be present?

If either party is likely to feel a need to consult with an attorney during negotiations, having attorneys present could keep negotiations from stalling.

What should I do if negotiations stall on a major issue?

Keep the negotiations moving by shifting focus to another point. If you can come to an agreement or even come close to an agreement on other points, even minor ones, it will help create an optimistic environment. It may also become easier to break deadlocks.

When should I pull out of negotiations?

If new information is discovered that makes you uncomfortable about your bottom-line position, don't hesitate to postpone or adjourn negotiations to another day.

If you are negotiating on a deal that involves working closely with the other party and you become so uncomfortable with that party that you feel working with them may be extremely problematic, walk away.

Should I begin discussions?

Let the other party state their position first. You may be surprised to find out where they stand on particular issues.

Should I try to cut long-winded discussions short?

No. Remember, this isn't a company meeting. Let the other parties air everything they want to. Try to refrain from interrupting or cutting off anyone at the negotiating table.

Common and costly mistakes of small business owners

1 Not developing and following a clear strategy for their business

2 Not reevaluating their entire way of doing business from time to time

3 Not using monthly profit and loss statements as a basis for decisions to boost profitability in future months

4 Not forecasting cash flow adequately

5 Not focusing enough on nonadvertising marketing avenues, such as publicity and promotions

6 Not carefully tracking the results of all marketing efforts

7 Focusing more on sales than on profits

8 Underpricing products or services (except for independent retailers, who tend to overprice versus their larger competitors)

9 Not motivating employees with results-based bonus or profit-sharing programs

10 Running tremendous legal risks by not understanding the laws and failing to have established policies for sexual harassment, hiring, firing, and performance reviews

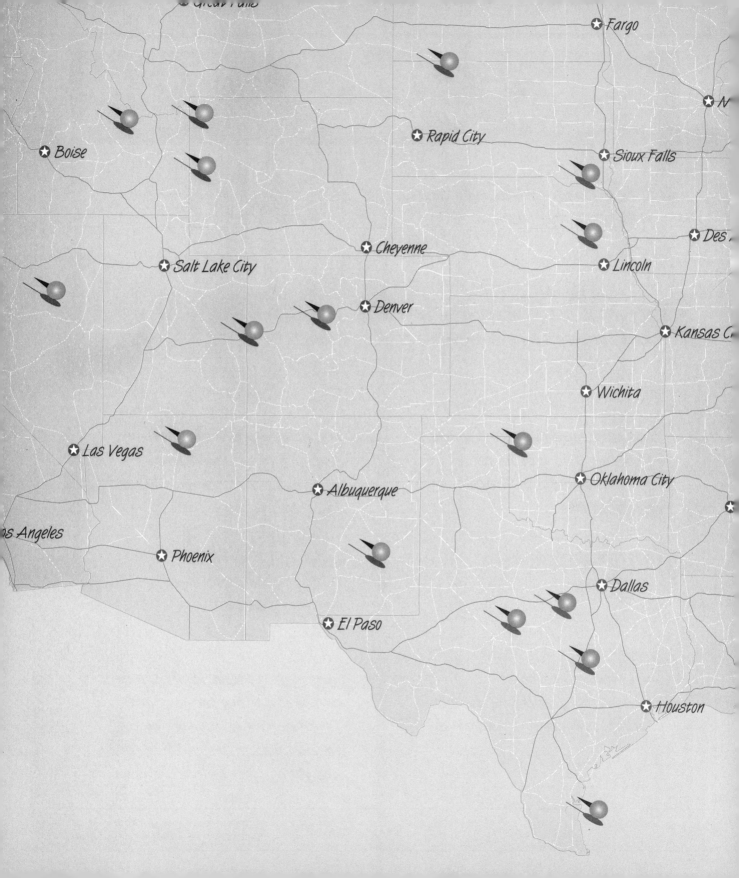

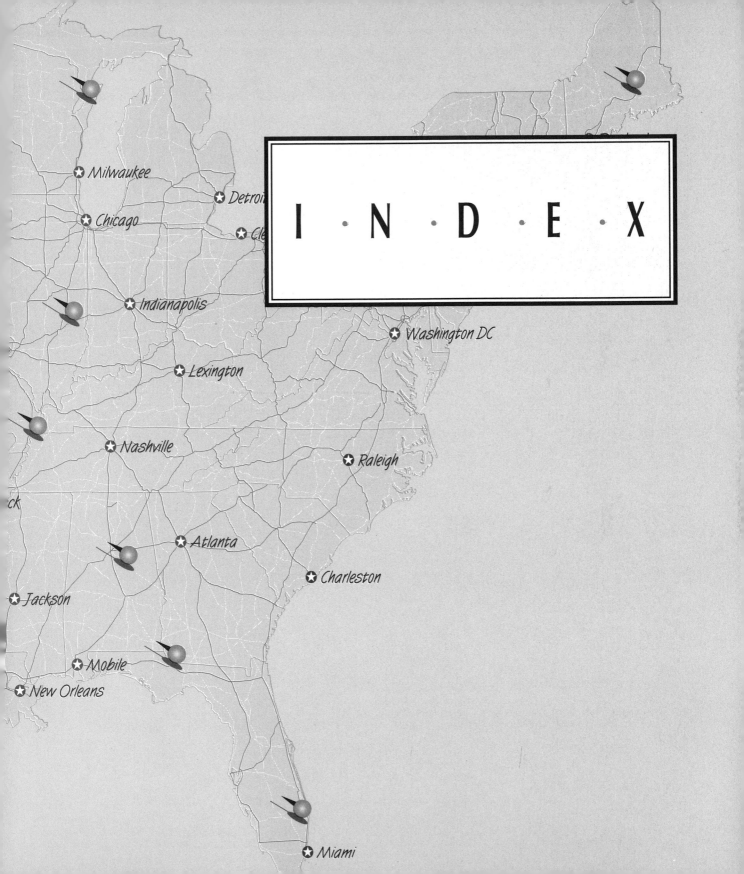

I·N·D·E·X

Milwaukee

Detroi[t]

Chicago

Cle[veland]

Indianapolis

Washington DC

Lexington

Nashville

Raleigh

[Litt]le [Ro]ck

Atlanta

Charleston

Jackson

Mobile

New Orleans

Miami

A

accounting
amortization, 277
balance sheets, 272-74, 279, 280, 284-86
cash flow, 287-89
depreciation, 270, 275-76, 280
income statements, 269-71, 279, 280, 281-83
inventory, 278
keeping records, 279
pro formas, 281-91
purpose, 279, 280
Adams JobBank Online, 216
advertising, 4
agencies, 166
businesses for sale, 62
in business plans, 33
business-to-business, 162
by franchises, 16
choosing medium, 157-63
common mistakes, 207
compared to publicity, 99
costs, 86
direct mail, 159, 160, 161, 162, 163, 167-75
direct response, 163
frequency, 164-65
help-wanted, 52, 215, 216-17, 220
image, 160, 186, 201
local service, 161
magazine, 158, 159, 160, 162, 163, 181-86
mail-order catalogs, 184
in marketing plans, 75-76
newspaper, 158, 159, 160, 161, 162, 163, 176-80
outdoor and transit, 158, 159, 160, 203-6
price, 159
radio, 158, 159, 160, 161, 162, 193-98
starting businesses in, 8
television, 158, 159, 160, 161, 163, 199-202
trade show publications, 110
unique selling propositions (USPs), 70
using publicity quotes, 99
by wholesalers, 146
writing copy, 166

Yellow Pages, 161, 162, 187-92
Africa, exporting to, 151
age discrimination, 258, 352
alliances, with other companies, 117
amortization, 277
annual plans, 49, 50
distinction from business plan, 30
involving employees, 47, 50
measuring performance against, 47
process, 48, 50
purpose, 28-29
qualitative aspects, 47
strategies and, 20
updating, 50, 53
using in day-to-day management, 387
answering machines, 368
answering services, 192, 372
arbitration, 356
Articles of Partnership, 333, 335
asset-backed financing, 325
assets, 272-73
book value, 276
current, 272, 284
depreciation, 270, 275-76, 280
fixed, 272-73, 284
intangible, 277
pro forma, 284
attorneys. See legal advice
Australia, exporting to, 151
award programs, 239

B

balance sheets, 272-74, 279, 280
pro forma, 284-86
banking resolutions, 341
bankruptcy
of customers, 298, 299
voluntary, 326
banks
credit lines, 54
dealing with in cash crisis, 324
loans, 310
relationship with, 313, 315, 316, 324
selecting, 55, 313, 315
benefits, 240-42
cutting, 327
during family and medical leaves, 353
negotiating, 226
billboards. See outdoor and transit advertising
boards of directors, 34, 340, 341, 342

bonuses, 238
broadcast faxing, 148
brokers, business, 15, 57, 62
budgets. See annual plans
building permits, 368, 371
business brokers, 15, 57, 62
business cards, in press kits, 92
business plans, 29-47, 49
elements of, 30-34
financial statements, 34, 48
involving employees, 47
purpose, 29, 31
sample, 35-46
See also annual plans
business structure, 331-37, 343-46
business-to-business selling, 122, 134, 135, 162
buying existing businesses, 10-11, 12-15
brokers, 15
legal advice, 13
non-compete agreements, 14, 15
recent startups, 15
valuation, 13

C

calendars, 387-88
Canada, exporting to, 150
cash flow, 317-18
in franchises, 18
improving, 319-20
monitoring, 3, 53, 321
problems, 319, 321-24, 326-27
pro forma, 287-89, 291
sources, 288
uses, 288, 319
celebrations, 212, 260
China, exporting to, 151
Civil Rights Act of 1964, 349
collections, 292, 299
calls, 294, 296, 297, 298
letters, 293-94, 295
commissions
independent sales representatives, 136, 141
salespeople, 238
common stock. See stock
compensation
benefits, 226, 240-42, 327
in cash crises, 323
cutting, 327

incentive pay, 238-39
increases with performance reviews, 229, 234, 235, 236
minimum wage, 347
new employees, 226, 237
overtime, 347
owner's salary, 345
reviews, 243, 244
salespeople, 126, 238
setting, 237, 243, 244
surveys, 237
competitive advantage, 9, 32
competitors
    assessing, 9, 22
    in business plans, 32
    of existing businesses, 12
    of franchises, 16
    large, 9, 111-17
    reactions, 76
    at trade shows, 107
    working with, 116-17
computers
    backups, 384, 385
    e-mail, 379, 388
    software, 378
    storing information on, 383, 385
consignment selling, 147
consultancies, 7
consumer analysis, 32, 74
contests, 86
contracts, 358-60
copiers, 379
copyrights, 361
copywriters, 172
corporate seals, 341
corporations, 336-37
    bylaws, 341
    control, 344
    directors, 34, 340, 341, 342
    leases, 345
    lending to, 345
    names, 339
    officers, 338
    registered agents, 340
    regulations, 341
    shareholders, 342
    starting, 338-41, 344
    stock owned by, 345
    Subchapter S, 306, 307, 342
    taxes, 337, 342
    tax I.D. numbers, 341
    See also stock
counter displays, 102

coupons, 86, 174
court. See lawsuits
credit
    checks, 292-93, 298, 299
    customer statements, 293
    invoicing, 293
    legal issues, 297
    manager, 297
    obtaining, 54
    policies, 292-93, 297, 298, 299
    See also collections; financing
credit cards, accepting, 175, 292
creditors, 322, 323, 326
customers
    analyzing needs, 21
    bankrupt, 298, 299
    complaints, 355, 392
    direct mail to, 174
    of existing businesses, 12, 14
    new, 88
    as potential buyers of business, 61
    promotions, 86-88
    service policies, 392
    statements, 293
    surveys, 25, 114
    at trade shows, 105, 107
    treatment of, 4
    voice mail of, 126
    See also credit

D

debt. See financing; liabilities
delegating, 387
depreciation, 270, 275-76
desks, 385
direct mail, 167-75
    best uses, 159, 160, 161, 162, 163
    break-even point, 172, 174
    bulk rate mailing, 175
    costs, 158, 167
    impact, 158
    letters, 169, 170-71
    mail houses, 172
    mailing lists, 168, 172, 174
    materials, 168, 169, 173
    producing, 172
    response mechanisms, 175
    testing, 174
directors. See boards of directors
direct response advertising, 163

discrimination claims
    age, 258, 352
    by fired employees, 253-54
    fabricated, 353
    preventing, 264, 349, 352, 353
distributors, 146, 147, 149
    finding, 106-7, 149
    foreign, 106, 149
dress policies, 264
dumps, 102

E

Eastern Europe, exporting to, 150
e-mail, 379, 388
employees
    benefits, 226, 240-42, 327
    communicating problems to, 327
    communicating strategy to, 25
    exempt/non-exempt, 347
    of existing businesses, 12, 14
    family and medical leave, 349, 353
    fun, 211-12
    handbooks, 263
    high-quality, 52
    in home offices, 372
    independent contractor issue, 347-48, 353
    informing of potential sale, 59
    layoffs, 327
    loans to, 265
    managing, 211, 248, 387
    office space, 376
    performance reviews, 228-36
    performance standards, 247, 248
    policies, 262-65
    problems, 245-50
    regulations relating to, 347-51
    retirement plans, 241
    salespeople, 126, 141, 238, 298
    selling business to, 59
    skills, 246
    tardiness, 250
    time management, 387-88
    at trade shows, 105, 109
    treatment of, 4, 211, 212
    workers' compensation, 351
    See also compensation; firing; hiring
employment agencies, 215, 227
employment law, 352
employment taxes, 305-6, 323
equal opportunity, 264, 349

equipment, 378-82
  copiers, 379
  depreciation, 270, 275-76, 280
  fax machines, 379
  leases, 311, 379, 381, 382
  software, 378
  used, 378
  See also telephones
equity, owners', 273
estimated income taxes, 307, 309, 331
Europe, exporting to, 150
executive search firms, 216, 227
expansion. *See* growth
expenses
  associated with growth, 52
  comparative data, 50
  cutting, 117, 319-20, 326
  monitoring, 49, 50
  office, 367, 368
  operating, 269-70
  overhead, 270
  prioritizing, 323
  pro forma, 282
  start-up, 319, 320
  trade shows, 108, 109
  See also purchasing
exporting, 149-52

F

face-to-face selling, 122, 123-27
facilities
  commercial space, 373-77
  of existing businesses, 12
  home offices, 309, 367-72
  impact of growth, 53
factoring, 311, 325
fair selling, 363
family, financing from, 310-11
family and medical leave, 349, 353
fax-back services, 148
fax machines, 379
fax marketing, 148
files, 383
  cabinets, 382, 385
  computer, 384, 385
  saving, 385
financial statements
  balance sheets, 272-74, 279, 280, 284-86
  in business plans, 34, 48
  of existing businesses, 12, 14

income statements, 269-71, 279, 280, 281-83
pro-forma, 34, 281-91
for selling businesses, 57
See also accounting
financing
  asset-backed, 325
  bank loans, 310, 313
  business plans, 29, 31
  expansion, 31
  factoring, 311, 325
  friends and relatives, 310-11
  going public, 312
  leases, 311, 325
  Small Business Administration (SBA), 311-12
  sources, 310-12
  start-up, 31
  venture capital, 48, 312
  work-out, 31
firing employees, 251-58
  documentation, 231, 257
  legal issues, 253-54, 257, 258
  problem employees, 245-50
  rehiring, 258
  severance pay, 252, 253
fiscal years, 308, 341
floor displays, 102
forms of business, legal, 331-37, 343-46
franchises, 16-19
frequent-buyer programs, 87, 113
friends, financing from, 310-11
fun, 211-12
furniture, 378, 381, 382, 385

G

gainsharing, 239
gifts, promotional, 87
goals. *See* annual plans
graphic designers, 103, 172
growth, 51-55
  financial implications, 52-53, 54
  financing, 31, 54, 55
  slowing, 54, 55
  sustaining, 51, 55
  See also hiring

H

handicap access to offices, 373
hiring
  advertising, 52, 215, 216-17, 220
  agencies, 215, 227
  finding candidates, 215-16
  former employees, 227
  importance of, 224
  initial work periods, 353
  interviewing, 52, 214, 218-19, 220, 225
  job offers, 222-23
  keeping records, 220
  legal issues, 220-21, 353
  phone interviews, 213-14, 224, 227
  process, 51-52, 54, 213-16
  references, 224, 225, 227, 351
  tests, 226
hobbies, 9
home equity loans, 310
home offices, 367-72
  costs, 368
  employees in, 372
  insurance, 368, 372
  tax deduction, 309
  telephones, 368, 372
  zoning, 368, 369, 371
home pages (World Wide Web), 142-43
Hong Kong, exporting to, 151
hostile environment lawsuits, 350

I

illustrators, 172
image advertising, 160, 186, 201
importers, 145
incentive pay, 238-39
income
  net, 270
  underreporting, 308
income statements, 269-70, 280
  frequency, 279
  pro forma, 281-83
  sample, 271
income taxes, 306-7
  audits, 309
  corporate, 337, 342
  estimated, 307, 309, 331
  filing extensions, 309
  home office deduction, 309
  loss carrybacks, 309

preparing, 308
sole proprietorships, 331
incorporating, 336, 338-40, 344
independent contractors, 347-48, 353
independent sales representatives, 136-41
    commissions, 136, 141
    finding, 106, 136, 139-40
    firms, 136
India, exporting to, 151
insurance
    home offices, 368, 372
    workers' compensation, 351, 372
intellectual property, 361-62
interest rates, 315-16
Internal Revenue Service (IRS)
    800 number, 305
    estimated tax payments, 307, 309,
        331
    independent contractor issue, 347-48,
        353
    penalties, 308
    tax I.D. numbers, 341
    withholding tables, 305
Internet
    help-wanted advertising, 216
    marketing, 142-43
interviews, job, 213-14, 225
    involving others, 52, 214
    legal issues, 220, 221
    questions, 218-19, 221, 224, 225
    telephone, 213-14, 224, 227
    tests, 226
interviews, publicity, 90
    newspaper, 101
    radio or television, 100-101
inventions, 362
inventories, 278
    of existing businesses, 12
    taxes, 307
    turnover, 319
investors
    equity, 29, 48
    importance of key people to, 47, 48
    information needed, 34
    lenders, 29, 54
    See also financing
invoices
    customer, 293
    vendor, 302
IRS. See Internal Revenue Service

J

Japan, exporting to, 151
jobbers. See wholesalers
job offer letters, 222-23
journalists. See media contacts

K

Kuala Lumpur, 151

L

Latin America, exporting to, 150
lawsuits
    against large competitors, 116
    avoiding, 354-57
    collecting from customers, 294
    disclosing in financial statements,
        354
    discrimination, 253-54, 258, 349,
        352, 353
    employment references, 351
    pursuing, 356
    settlement meetings, 355, 357
    sexual harassment, 263, 350, 352
    small claims court, 294
lawyers. See legal advice
layoffs, 327
leadership, 259-61
leases, 311, 381, 382
    -back agreements, 325
    commercial space, 377
    copiers, 379
    of existing businesses, 12
    to own corporation, 345
legal advice
    buying existing businesses, 13
    contracts, 358-60
    employment policies, 352
    firing employees, 257, 258, 352
    in negotiations, 396
    patents, 362
    selling businesses, 56, 59
    settling lawsuits, 355, 357
    specialized, 352
    trademarks, 361, 362

letters
    collection, 293-94, 295
    direct mail, 169, 170-71
    job offer, 222-23
liabilities, 272, 273, 285
Library of Congress, Copyright Office,
    361
licenses, business, 331
limited liability companies (LLCs), 343
literature, marketing, 103
loans
    to employees, 265
    home equity, 310
    interest rates, 315-16
    to own corporation, 345
    payments, 316
    personal, 310
    personal guarantees, 314, 323
    small business, 310
    using receivables as collateral, 315
    See also financing
local service advertising, 161
logos, 103, 368
loss leaders, 112

M

magazine advertising, 181-86
    best uses, 158, 159, 160, 162, 163,
        184
    color in, 182, 186
    costs, 181, 186
    design, 185, 186
    frequency, 186
    local, 184
    product samples, 181
    readers' service cards, 185
    specialty magazines, 184
    trade magazines, 184, 186
    writing, 182, 185
mailing lists, 168, 174
    brokers, 172
mail order
    equipment, 382
    placing products in catalogs, 184
Malaysia, exporting to, 151
management agreements, for sold
    businesses, 58
managers
    dealing with change, 52
    leadership, 259-61
    problem employees, 245-50

manufacturer's representatives. *See* independent sales representatives

marketing
   competing with large companies, 111-17
   competitive advantage, 9
   by fax, 148
   on Internet, 142-43
   literature, 103
   point-of-sale displays, 102
   tactics, 86-88
   trade shows, 104-10
   unique selling propositions (USPs), 67, 68, 70-72

marketing plans, 33, 73-85
   benefits, 84
   developing, 74-76, 83
   distinction from annual plans, 84
   elements, 73, 74-76
   financial projections, 76
   responsibility for, 83, 85
   updating, 85

markets
   niche, 23, 112
   positioning products in, 32-33, 67
   research, 9, 21, 74
   segmentation, 31-32, 74
   target, 31-33

master distributors, 145
maternity leave, 242, 349, 353
media. *See* advertising; publicity
media contacts, 90, 97, 100-101
Medicare taxes, 305

meetings
   boards of directors, 342
   conducting, 389-91
   purposes, 260, 261, 388
   sales, 141
   settlement, 355, 357

Mexico, exporting to, 150
Middle East, exporting to, 150
minimum wage, 347

mistakes
   advertising, 207
   common, 397
   performance reviews, 235
   sales, 153
   strategic, 63

N

negotiating
   advertising rates, 179, 197, 202

buying existing businesses, 13, 14
   tips, 393-96
net income, 270
new business ideas, 5-11

newspaper advertising, 176-80
   best uses, 158, 159, 160, 161, 162, 163
   costs, 176
   design, 180
   help-wanted, 215, 217, 220
   pitfalls, 178
   rates, 179
   writing, 177

newspaper interviews, 101
New Zealand, exporting to, 151
niche markets, 23, 112
Nigeria, exporting to, 151
non-compete agreements, 14, 15

O

officers, corporate, 338

offices
   commercial space, 373-77
   costs, 367, 377
   furniture, 378
   handicap access, 373
   locations, 374
   space planning, 375-76, 377
   See also home offices

Ogilvy, David, 186
operating expenses, 269-70
organization, 383-86
OSHA (Occupational Safety and Health Administration), 347

outdoor and transit advertising, 203-6
   best uses of, 158, 159, 160, 203, 206
   producing, 206
   writing, 204

owners' equity, 273

P

partnerships, 333-35
   articles, 333, 335
   dissolving, 346
   income taxes, 307
   types, 335

patents, 362
pay. *See* compensation
payroll services, 305
payroll taxes, 305-6, 323

performance reviews, 228-36
   legal issues, 231, 234, 235
   ratings, 228-29
   salary increases, 229, 234, 235, 236
   timing, 236

personal property taxes, 307
pitch letters, 92, 96
planning, time management, 386-88
plans. *See* annual plans
point-of-sale displays, 102

policies, 262-65, 352
   credit, 292-93, 297, 298, 299
   customer service, 392
   dating, 265
   dress, 264
   employee handbooks, 263
   employee loans, 265
   equal opportunity, 264
   hours, 264
   sexual harassment, 263, 350-51
   smoking, 265, 353
   telephone, 264

positioning products, 32-33, 67-72
   differentiation, 68
   unique selling propositions (USPs), 67, 68, 70-72

posters, 102, 347
post office, guidelines, 172
press kits, 89, 90, 92-93
press releases, 92, 94-95
price advertising, 159

prices
   of businesses, 61
   fair, 363
   product, 76, 85
   strategies, 25

prime rate, 316
printers, 172

products
   differentiation, 68
   information in press kits, 92
   launching at trade shows, 105-6
   point-of-sale displays, 102
   positioning, 32-33, 67
   setting prices, 76, 85
   strategies for, 23
   See also marketing plans

profit margins, 3, 53, 83
profits, gross, 269

promotions (sales), 75-76, 86-88
   contests, 86
   coupons, 86, 174
   cross-, 88

exclusive offerings, 87
frequent-buyer programs, 87, 113
gifts, 87
giveaways, 88
new customer offers, 88
special events, 87
trades, 88
by wholesalers, 146
property taxes, 307
publicity, 89-100
interviews, 90, 100-101
media contacts, 90, 97
pitch letters, 92, 96
press kits, 89, 90, 92-93
press releases, 92, 94-95
trade publications, 106
public relations specialists, 90, 91
purchasing, 300-304
contracts, 358-60
invoices, 302
monitoring costs, 303
purchase orders, 301-2, 304
quotes, 300-301, 303
receiving deliveries, 302, 304
scams, 304
selecting vendors, 300
shipping, 304

R

radio advertising, 193-98
best uses, 158, 159, 160, 161, 162
costs, 193, 197
live or recorded, 198
monitoring, 196
roadblocks, 196-97
writing copy, 193, 198
radio interviews, 100-101
readers' service cards, 185
real estate taxes, 307
receivables
as collateral, 315
of existing businesses, 12
factoring, 311, 325
monitoring, 319, 322
See also collections
references
former employees, 254, 351
prospective employees, 224, 225,
227, 351
refunds, 392
registered agents, 340
relocating, 11

rental businesses, 7
reporters. See media contacts
resale certificates, 306
research and development, 33
restaurants, 6
retail
fair selling, 363
new business ideas, 5
sales taxes, 306, 323
retained earnings, 273, 285
retirement plans, 241
return policies, 392
roadblocks, 196-97
Russia, exporting to, 150

S

salary. See compensation
salary at-risk plans, 238
sales
business-to-business, 122, 134, 135
calls, 127
channels, 75, 121-22
common mistakes, 153
competitive advantage, 9
contracts, 358-60
face-to-face, 122, 123-27
forecasts, 50, 76, 290
independent representatives, 136-41
Internet marketing, 142-43
meetings, 141
strategy, 33
telemarketing, 122, 128-35
salespeople
commissions, 238
credit decisions and, 298
hiring, 126, 141
motivating, 126
paying, 126, 238
Yellow Pages, 190
sales taxes, 306, 323
SBA. See Small Business
Administration
scenarios
in business plans, 34
in marketing plans, 83
S corporations, 306, 307, 342
See also corporations
secondhand stores, 5
selling businesses, 56-62
advertising, 62
brokers, 15, 62
disclosing potential competition, 116

financial information needed, 57
informing employees, 59
to large corporations, 58
legal advice, 56, 59
management agreements, 58
partial sales, 57
potential buyers, 61
prices, 61
qualifying buyers, 59-60
seller financing, 60, 62
startups, 61
valuation, 58
service, 23, 113
service businesses, 6, 10, 25, 26, 73
service marks, 361-62
settlements
with creditors, 326
lawsuits, 355, 357
sexual harassment, 349-51
acting on claims, 351, 352, 355
claims, 263, 265, 350
hostile environment, 350
policies, 263, 350-51
quid pro quo, 350
shareholders, 342
majority, 344
of S corporations, 343
See also stock
shelf talkers, 102
shipping and receiving departments,
302
Singapore, exporting to, 151
Small Business Administration (SBA)
loans, 311-12
small claims court, 294
smoking policies, 265, 353
Social Security taxes, 305
software, 378
sole proprietorships, 307, 331-32
South Africa, exporting to, 151
South America, exporting to, 150
spec sheets, 300
stock
on balance sheet, 273
incentive programs, 239
offerings, 312, 340, 341
options, 239
owned by another corporation, 345
shareholders, 342, 343, 344
strategies, 20-27
in business plan, 30
changing, 25, 63
common mistakes, 63

communicating, 25, 27, 260, 261
compared to unique selling
　propositions, 71-72
competing with large companies, 111-
　17
consistent, 115
elements of, 21-23
importance, 3, 20, 26, 115
service businesses, 25, 26
using in day-to-day management, 387
Subchapter S corporations. *See* S
　corporations
success, rules for, 3-4
suppliers. *See* vendors
supplies. *See* purchasing
systems and procedures, 54

Taiwan, 151
taxes
　corporate income, 337, 342
　decisions based on, 308
　delaying payment, 308
　employment, 305-6, 323
　estimated, 307, 309, 331
　fiscal years, 308, 341
　in growing businesses, 53
　home office deduction, 309
　income, 306-7, 308, 309, 337, 342
　inventory, 307
　Medicare, 305
　personal property, 307
　preparing, 308
　property, 307
　sales, 306, 323
　Social Security, 305
　state, 305
　unemployment, 305
　use, 306
　withholding, 305-6
tax I.D. numbers, 341
telemarketing, 122, 128-35
　business-to-business, 134, 135
　calls, 128-30, 133
　costs, 128
　inbound, 128
　introductory letters, 134
　outbound, 128
　prospect lists, 134
　scripts, 133
telephones
　additional lines, 192, 372

answering machines, 368
answering services, 192, 372
collection calls, 294, 296, 297, 298
job interviews, 213-14, 224, 227
policies, 264
preventing neck pain, 134
selecting, 378
toll-free numbers, 175
voice mail, 368
television advertising, 199-202
　best uses, 158, 159, 160, 161, 163,
　　201
　costs, 199, 201, 202
　producing, 199
television interviews, 100-101
testimonials, 92, 171
time management, 386-88, 389-91
trademarks, 361-62
trade publications, 106, 184, 186
trade shows, 104-10
　benefits, 104, 110
　costs, 108, 109
　dealing with unions, 110
　demonstrations, 107
　displays, 106, 108
　employees at, 105, 109
　publications, 110
　setting objectives, 104-7
transit advertising. *See* outdoor and
　transit advertising

unemployment taxes, 305
Uniform Partnership Act, 333
union labor, at trade shows, 110
unique selling propositions (USPs), 67,
　68, 70-72
United States
　Department of Labor, 347
　exporting to, 150
　Family and Medical Leave Act of
　　1993, 349, 353
　Patent and Trademark Office, 361
　See also Internal Revenue Service
use taxes, 306
utilities, 323

V

valuation of businesses, 13, 58
vendors
　complaining to, 302, 355

credit from, 54
paying, 319, 322, 323
as potential buyers of business, 61
salespeople, 4, 301
selecting, 300
venture capital, 48, 312
　See also financing
Vietnam, 151
voice mail, 126, 368

wages. *See* compensation
Western Europe, exporting to, 150
wholesalers, 144-47
　collaborating with, 117
　fair selling, 363
　new business ideas, 8
　promotions, 146
　sales tax exemption, 306
　working with, 146, 147
withholding taxes, 305-6
workers' compensation, 351
World Wide Web, 142-43

Y

Yellow Pages, 187-92
　best uses, 161, 162
　costs, 187, 190
　salespeople, 190
　testing, 190, 191
　writing copy, 188, 190, 191

Z

zoning regulations, 368, 369, 371

Notes

Adams Streetwise Small Business Start-Up is also available as a software product!

Microsoft Windows 95 · **CD-ROM** · **3.5" DISK** · **Mac OS**

Designed for Windows®3.1, Windows®95, and Macintosh®

"This multimedia extravaganza provides case studies, how-tos, forms and templates for every aspect of running a business. . . . It's slick, it's savvy, and it's tax deductible."
—*Windows Sources* magazine

▶ Over 30 hours of video and audio clips

▶ Over 200 multimedia workshops and interactive charts

▶ Over 100 planning, financial, legal, and business operations templates to fill in and edit to fit your situation, from a complete business plan to a balance sheet, from a press release to collection letter.

▶ Advice from the trenches: listen and watch as a dozen small business owners explain on video what's worked for them and what hasn't.

Also available at software retailers nationwide:

500 BUSINESSES YOU CAN START · DO-IT-YOURSELF **ADVERTISING** · **HIRING** TOP PERFORMERS · **MANAGING** PEOPLE

Visit our exciting job and career site at http://www.careercity.com

Bob Adams...

Streetwise ENTREPRENEUR

Bob Adams has started and operated many small businesses—some successful and some ***not so successful.*** These include a house painting business, a job fair business, an employment agency, a dinghy manufacturing business, a bicycle rental business, a boat brokerage firm, a tourist map business, a phone directory business, a college newspaper, a classified advertising newspaper, a book publishing business, a magazine publishing business, an online information service, and a software publishing business. A number of these ventures have become profitable and ongoing enterprises, while others Adams had to shut down. In the long run, he has lost thousands, but made millions.

Bob Adams started his current business, Adams Media Corporation, 16 years ago in a small basement apartment in Boston. While still in school, he made an initial $2,000 investment to publish the *Boston JobBank*—a job search reference guide for Boston's thousands of students. The company is now a $10 million a year enterprise.

Adams is a 1980 graduate of the Harvard Business School, where he received first year honors. He earned his B.A. from Carleton College and his streetwise training in the real world of small business and "the school of hard knocks."